# SWIMMING & diving

StayWell

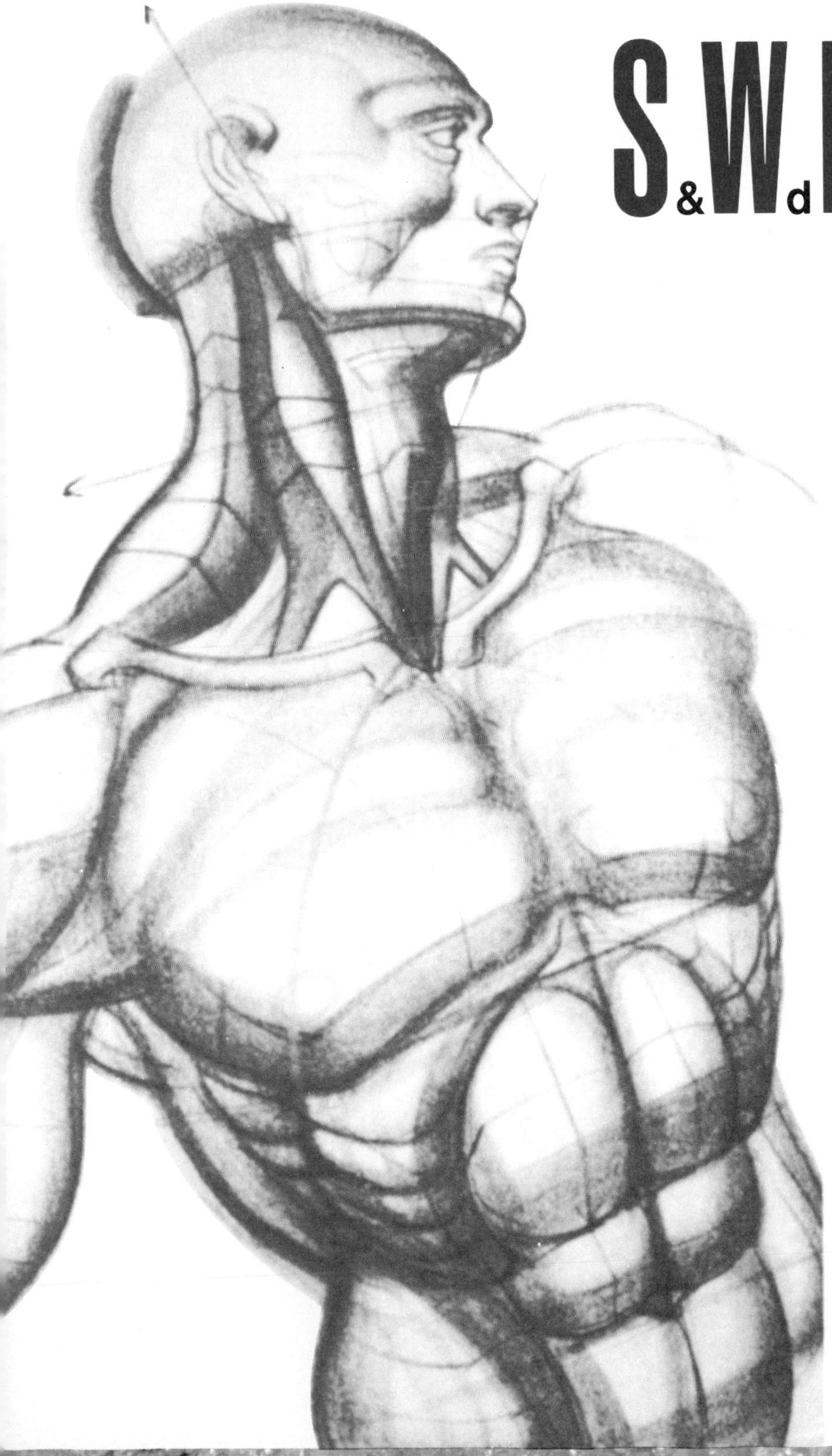

# SWIMMING & diving

StayWell



Printed in the United States of America

StayWell
263 Summer Street
Boston, MA 02210

**Library of Congress Cataloging in Publication Data**

Swimming & diving/American Red Cross
p. cm.
Includes bibliographical references (p. ) and index.
Summary: Discusses the history and techniques of swimming and diving, safety guidelines and rescue techniques, and skills for a variety of aquatic activities.
ISBN 0-8151-0595-9
1. Swimming—Juvenile literature. 2. Diving—Juvenile literature. 3. Aquatic sports—Safety measures—Juvenile literature. [1. Swimming. 2. Diving.] I. American Red Cross. II. Title: Swimming and diving.
GV837.6.S96 1992
797.2'1—dc20 92-4568
CIP
AC

02 03 04 05 B 15 14 13 12

# ACKNOWLEDGEMENTS

This book was developed and produced through a joint effort of the American Red Cross and the Mosby–Year Book Publishing company. Many individuals shared in the overall process in many supportive, technical, and creative ways. This book could not have been developed without the dedication of both paid and volunteer staff. Their commitment to excellence made this book possible.

The Health and Safety Program Development team at American Red Cross national headquarter responsible for designing and writing this book included: Earl Harbert, Manager, Aquatics Project; Thomas J.S. Edwards, Ph.D., Kathy D. Scruggs, M.A., and Trudi Van Dyke, M.S., Associates; Terry Cooper, Treecee Engler-Polgar, and Susan Stimpfle, M.Ed., Analysts. Administrative support was provided by Debra E. Clemons and Gloria Harris.

The following American Red Cross national headquarters Health and Safety paid and volunteer staff provided guidance and review: Frank Carroll, Manager, Rhonda Starr, Senior Associate, Bruce Carney, M.A.Ed., Israel M. Zuniga, Associate, and Stephen Silverman, Ed.D., National Volunteer Consultant, Program Development; Karen White, Marketing Specialist, External Relations; Kathleen Cole Oberlin, Senior Associate, Operations; and Michael C. Giles, Jr., Analyst.

The Mosby–Year Book Editorial and Production team included: Virgil Mette, Executive Vice President; David T. Culverwell, Vice President and Publisher; Richard A. Weimer, Executive Editor; Rina Steinhauer, Developmental Editor; Carol S. Wiseman, Project Manager; Dave S. Brown, Production Editor; Kay Kramer, Director of Design; Jerry A. Wood, Director of Manufacturing; Patricia Stinecipher, Special Product Manager; and Theresa Fuchs, Manufacturing Supervisor.

Special thanks go to Tom Lochhaas, Ed.D., Developmental Editor; Joseph Matthews, Elizabeth Roll, and Daniel Cima, Photographers; Patricia A. Terrell, Photographic Specialist; Joe Chovan, Art Director; Michael Cooley, Jan Warren, and Carl R. Jones, Illustrators; Gijsbertus H.G. Vander Mark, Designer; and Chris Handley, Desktop Designer.

Cover photo: Swimmer courtesy of Chimene Lassere, KORN, Paris. Landscape courtesy of Gary Braasch, "Image of pond at dusk," © 1991 Gary Braasch.

Illustrations appearing on the following pages are reproduced from *Dynamic Figure Drawing,* 1970, Watson-Guptill, New York, with the permission of the artist, Burne Hogarth: p. 3, 25, 91, 151, 173, 207, 246, 267, 285.

Illustrations appearing on the following pages are reproduced from *Dynamic Anatomy,* 1958, Watson-Guptill, New York, with the permission of the artist, Burne Hogarth: p. 71, 96, 110, 111, 125, 148, 164, 165, 183, 206.

Guidance, writing, and review were also provided by members of the American Red Cross Swimming Advisory Committee.

**Stephen Langendorfer,** Ph.D.
Committee Chair
and
Associate Professor of Motor Development/ Developmental Aquatics
School of Physical Education, Recreation, and Dance
Kent State University
Kent, Ohio

**Elaine Bird,** M. Ed.
Committee Vice Chair
and
Associate Director and
Aquatic Director
Division of Leisure Sports
Louisiana State University
Baton Rouge, Louisiana
and
Field Service Chairman
American Red Cross
Region 3, Territory 11
Baton Rouge, Louisiana

**Chrys Baird**
Health Specialist
American Red Cross
Montgomery County Chapter
Silver Spring, Maryland

**Bruce Carney,** M.A.Ed.
Deputy Director of Safety and Health
American Red Cross in Greater New York
New York, New York

**Paul Crutchfield**
Assistant Director of Parks and Recreation
Spokane Parks and Recreation Department
Spokane, Washington
and
Member, Board of Directors
American Red Cross
Inland Empire Chapter
Spokane, Washington

**Gerald DeMers,** Ph.D.
Assistant Professor and Director, Aquatic Program
Physical Education and Recreation Administration Department
California Polytechnic State University
and
Health and Safety Volunteer Specialist
American Red Cross
San Luis Obispo Chapter
San Luis Obispo, California

**Terri Elder,** M.Ed.
Aquatic Coordinator
The Heskett Center
Wichita State University
Witchita, Kansas
and
Volunteer Safety Specialist in Water Safety
American Red Cross
Region 3, Territory 2
Wichita, Kansas

**Susan Grosse,** M.S.
Physical Education Instructor
Milwaukee High School of the Arts
Milwaukee, Wisconsin
and
Volunteer Instructor Trainer
American Red Cross
Greater Milwaukee Chapter
Milwaukee, Wisconsin

**Mark Hokkanen,** M.S.T.
Director
Aquatic and Wellness Center
Oklahoma City Community College
Oklahoma City, Oklahoma
and
Volunteer Instructor Trainer
American Red Cross
Oklahoma County Chapter
Oklahoma City, Oklahoma

**Neill Miller,** M.S.
Associate Professor of Physical Education
Department of Sport and Recreational Sciences
Barry University
Miami Shores, Florida
and
Member, Health and Safety Committee, and
Volunteer Instructor Trainer
American Red Cross
Greater Miami Chapter
Miami, Florida

**Ed Morford,** M.Ed.
Director of Aquatics
State University of New York
Delhi, New York
and
Volunteer Instructor Trainer
American Red Cross
Delaware County Chapter
Delhi, New York

**Fontaine Piper,** Ph.D.
Director and Associate Professor Biomechanics/Motor Learning Laboratory
Division of Health and Exercise Science
Northeast Missouri State University
Kirksville, Missouri
and
Adjunct Associate Professor of Anatomy
Department of Anatomy
Kirksville College of Osteopathic Medicine
Kirksville, Missouri
and
Volunteer Instructor Trainer
American Red Cross
Adair County Chapter
Kirksville, Missouri

**Craig Ritz,** M.Ed.
Aquatics Coordinator
Office of Recreational Services
Rutgers University
New Brunswick, New Jersey
and
Past Chair
American Alliance for Health, Physical Education, Recreation & Dance—Aquatics Council
Reston, Virginia
and
Volunteer Aquatics Coordinator
Health and Safety Committee
American Red Cross
Central New Jersey Chapter
New Brunswick, New Jersey

External review was provided by the following organizations and individuals:

**Dot Shields**
Past Chair
American Alliance for Health, Physical Education, Recreation & Dance—Aquatics Council
Reston, Virginia
and
Academic/Recreational Aquatic Director
University of Florida
Gainesville, Florida

**Albert E. Cahill**
Member, National Health and Safety Committee
National Council
Boy Scouts of America
Irving, Texas

**Louise Priest**
Executive Director
Council for National Cooperation in Aquatics
Indianapolis, Indiana

**Donna L. Nye**
Senior Program Specialist
Girl Scouts of the USA
New York, New York

**Samuel J. Freas,** Ed.D.
President and CEO
International Swimming Hall of Fame, Inc.
Fort Lauderdale, Florida

**Nancy Weiman,** M.A. Ed.
Enterprise Coordinator
Maryland National Capital Park and Planning Commission
Riverdale, Maryland

**Lester Kowalsky,** M.M.E., M.B.A.
Chairman of the Board of Directors
National Swimming Pool Foundation
San Antonio, Texas

**Carvin DiGiovanni**
Technical Director
National Spa and Pool Institute
Alexandria, Virginia

**Selden Fritschner**
Director of Aquatics
Special Olympics International
Washington, D.C.

**Janet L. Gabriel,** M.A.
Director of Education, Safety and Development
United States Diving
Indianapolis, Indiana

**Rose Milo**
Age Group Coordinator
United States Swimming
Colorado Springs, Colorado

**R. Ann Hood Weiser,** M.S., M.F.A.
Coordinator of Aquatics Instruction
University of North Carolina
Greensboro, North Carolina

**Orv Kersten,** M.A.
Assistant Professor of Physical Education
Northern Illinois University
De Kalb, Illinois

**Dennis A. Munroe,** M.S.
Director of Aquatics
University of Oregon
Eugene, Oregon

**Tom Griffiths,** Ed.D.
Director of Aquatics
The Pennsylvania State University
University Park, Pennsylvania

**Virginia Reister,** M.Ed.
Aquatics and Rehabilitation Management Consultant
Johnson City, Tennessee

**Jim Comstock-Galagan**
Executive Director
Advocacy, Incorporated
Austin, Texas

**Judith Sokolow**
Manager, Program Services
Advocacy, Incorporated
Austin, Texas

## Photo Credits

The American Red Cross would like to thank the following individuals and facilities who provided talent and locations for much of the photography in this book.

- Atlantis, The Water Kingdom, Hollywood, Florida
- Central Park Pool, Plantation, Florida
- Jillian Cicione, Allandale, Florida
- Joya Cox, McLean, Virginia
- District of Columbia Department of Recreation and Parks, Washington, D.C.
- Fairfax County Park Authority
  George Washington Recreation Center
  Oak Mar Recreation Center
  Providence Recreation Center
  Spring Hill Recreation Center
- Fort Lauderdale Swim Team, Fort Lauderdale, Florida
  Jack Nelson, Coach
- George Washington University, Department of Human Kinetics and Leisure Studies, Washington, D.C.
- George Washington University Hospital, Department of Cardiology, Washington, D.C.
- Erik Hansen, Colorado Springs, Colorado
- Lori Heisick, Colorado Springs, Colorado
- International Swimming Hall of Fame Aquatic Complex, Fort Lauderdale, Florida
- Lake Anna, Virginia State Park, Spotsylvania, Virginia
- Tyler Page, Littleton, Colorado
- Jean Skinner, Fairfax County Park Authority, Fairfax, Virginia
- Southport Fitness Center, Alexandria, Virginia
- Spotsylvania County Rescue Squad, Spotsylvania, Virginia
- Timberlake, Oakton, Virginia
- Phil Trinidad, Colorado Springs, Colorado
- Waterful Aerobics, Waterful, Inc., Coral Springs, Florida

Animated or kinematic motion measurement graphics provided courtesy of Peak Performance Technologies, Inc., Englewood, Colorado.

# Preface

AMERICANS—as many as 103 million a year, according to a recent survey—have made aquatic activities the number-one recreational pursuit in the country. This can be traced, in part, to an increase in leisure time and the expanding availability of aquatic facilities and to the interest generated by the feats of world-class athletes. It is also a result of the growing variety of aquatic activities and the differing purposes—fitness, play, socializing—that are met in the water. Finally, it happens because entire groups of people, such as senior citizens, preschoolers, and individuals with disabilities, have learned that they can perform well in the water.

THIS BOOK PROVIDES THE BEST INFORMATION available on a wide spectrum of aquatic activities. The six most widely used swimming strokes are explained in detail and reflect the latest research. A discussion of hydrodynamic principles (Chapter 4) and an application of them to each stroke (Chapter 6) will help you learn to swim or improve your skills. Other chapters cover topics such as the history of swimming and diving, safety guidelines and rescue techniques, diving, starts and turns, and skills for all types of aquatic activities. If you are interested in fitness, Chapter 10 provides information to help you attain your personal goals. Training and competitive activities ranging from swimming to triathlons are covered, and a list of organizations is provided to support your interests. Regardless of your skill level, from novice to advanced swimmer, this text can expand your knowledge, improve your skills, and serve as a reference guide if you teach or plan to teach aquatic skills.

THE GOAL OF THIS TEXT is to integrate all of these interests with the common theme of safety in, on, and around the water and to provide you with the information and resources to make participation in aquatic activities a lifetime pursuit.

# Contents

American Red Cross

# SWIMMING & diving

CHAPTER 1

# HISTORY OF swimming AND DIVING

## KEY TERMS

**FREESTYLE:** A competitive event in which any stroke is allowed. The term is frequently used for the front crawl, since that is the stroke most often used in this event.

**HYDRODYNAMICS:** The science that studies the motion of fluids and forces on solid bodies in fluids.

**INDIVIDUAL MEDLEY:** An event in which the competitor swims one quarter of the total distance using a different competitive stroke in a prescribed order (butterfly, backstroke, breaststroke, freestyle).

**RECOVERY:** The stage of a stroke when the arms and/or legs relax and return to the starting position.

**STROKE MECHANICS:** The analysis of the hydrodynamic principles that affect how swimmers move in the water and can improve propulsion.

**SYNCHRONIZED SWIMMING:** Rhythmical water activity of one or more people performed in a pattern synchronized to music.

**UNDULATE:** To move in a wavy, sinuous, or flowing manner.

# Objectives

***After reading this chapter, you should be able to—***

1. Describe the beginnings of swimming.
2. Describe how swimming strokes evolved.
3. Describe the development of diving.
4. List aquatic sports and activities that have developed from interest in swimming.

5. Describe how swimming evolved as a competitive event.
6. Define the key terms at left.

*Courtesy of United States Water Polo*

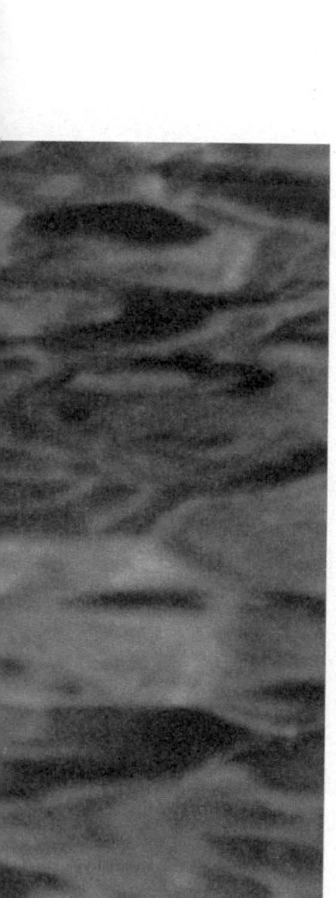

SOME PEOPLE LIVE TO SWIM. You'll find them at pools and beaches all summer or in competition year 'round. Others quietly swim their laps and mark their distance in personal notebooks or on public charts. Still others join teams for water polo, diving, or synchronized swimming.

OTHER PEOPLE SWIM TO LIVE. The lives, not just the livelihoods, of sailors and commercial fishermen depend on their ability to function in, on, and near the water. Most of us fall between these two extremes. Some of us want to know how to swim well enough to be safe around the pool. Others might be curious about the new ways to do the strokes we learned long ago. Still others have discovered the fitness advantages of doing aerobic exercise in the water.

THREE FOURTHS OF THE EARTH'S SURFACE is covered with water, so it is not surprising that evidence of swimming appears throughout history. However, most of the developments in stroke mechanics occurred in the last two centuries, with the most intensive research in the last two decades. This chapter reviews these developments, discusses the current status of aquatics, and points to some expectations for developments yet to come.

LEARN TO SWIM
ORIGIN
A
C
D
LEISURE, FITNESS, COMPETITION

## The Past: Swimming in History

Swimming research pioneer Benjamin Franklin.

### Beginnings

Ancient civilizations left ample evidence of their swimming abilities. Bas-relief artwork in an Egyptian tomb from around 2,000 B.C. shows an overarm stroke like the front crawl. (For detailed descriptions of swimming strokes, see Chapter 6.) The Assyrians showed an early breaststroke in their stone carvings. The Hittites, the Minoans, and other early civilizations left drawings of swimming and diving skills. Even the Bible refers to movement through the water—in Ezekiel 47:5, Acts 27:42, and Isaiah 25:11. Competitive swimming is at least as old as 36 B.C., when the Japanese held the first known swimming races.

The earliest published work on swimming was written in 1538 by Nicolas Wynman, a German professor of languages. In 1696, *The Art of Swimming* by the French author Thevenot first described a type of breaststroke done with the face out of the water and an underwater arm ***recovery*** (the stage of a stroke when the arms and/or legs relax and return to the starting position). This stroke gives the swimmer good stability, even in rough water. After the English translation of Thevenot's work became the standard swimming reference, the breaststroke was the most common stroke for centuries.

**An Early Researcher**

*In the 1700s, Benjamin Franklin researched buoyancy, back floating, and gliding, using his kite for propulsion and devising an early form of hand paddles and fins.*

*As he wrote, "When I was a boy I made two oval palettes, each about ten inches long and broad, with a hole for the thumb, in order to retain it fast in the palm of my hand. They much resembled a painter's palettes. In swimming I pushed the edges of these forward, and I struck the water with their flat surfaces as I drew them back. I remember I swam faster by means of these palettes, but they fatigued my wrists. I also fitted to the soles of my feet a kind of sandals; but I was not satisfied with them. . . ."*

*Armbruster believed that the "fins" failed because Benjamin Franklin was using a breaststroke kick.*

### The Rise of Competitive Swimming

The English are considered the first modern society to develop swimming as a sport. By 1837, when modern competitive swimming began in London, several indoor pools already existed. The National Swimming Society regulated competition. The breaststroke and the recently developed sidestroke were used. In 1844, Native Americans swam in a London meet. Flying Gull swam 130 feet in 30 seconds to defeat Tobacco and win a medal. Their stroke was described as thrashing the water with their arms in a motion "like a windmill" and kicking in an up-and-down motion. This early form of the front crawl was successful in that race, but the English continued to prefer the breaststroke for competition.

The English also liked to compete against nature. In 1875, Captain Matthew Webb first swam the English Channel (Fig. 1-1). With the breaststroke, he swam the 21.26 miles in 21 hours and 45 minutes. The first woman to swim the channel was Gertrude Ederle in 1926. Marcus Hooper, the youngest person to complete the swim, swam the channel in 1979 at age 12. In 1983, Ashby Harper swam the channel just a few days before his 66th birthday, making him the oldest. Penny Dean has held the world record for the channel swim since 1978. This challenge continues to attract distance swimmers as the ultimate feat in this sport.

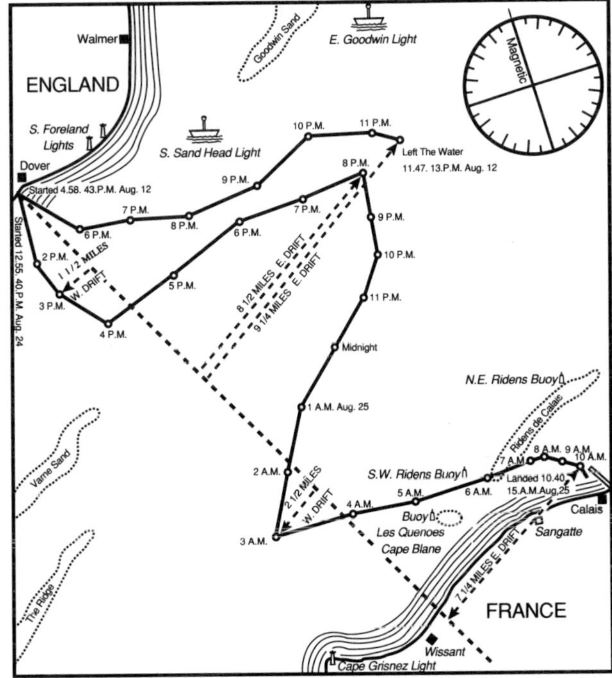

Fig. 1-1 Map showing the routes of Captain Matthew Webb's English Channel swims in August 1875. His first attempt was abandoned after 6:48:30 because he drifted $9^1/_2$ miles off course. His second attempt was completed in 21:44:35.

## Early Interest in Stroke Development

Throughout the 1800s, a series of swimming strokes evolved. The sidestroke, in which the swimmer lies on one side, was soon modified to become the overarm sidestroke. One arm was recovered above the water for increased arm speed. The legs were squeezed together in an uncoordinated action. In 1895, J. H. Thayers of England, using the overarm sidestroke, swam a record 1:02.50 for 100 yards. (*Note:* Swimming times are expressed in minutes, seconds, and hundredths of seconds. So this record means the 100 yards were swum in 1 minute, 2 and 50/100 seconds. A time of less than a minute would be designated as 48.25—48 and 25/100 seconds. Times that last longer than an hour—as for a triathlon or a marathon—would be expressed 3:22:15.30, for 3 hours, 22 minutes, 15 and 30/100 seconds.)

John Trudgen developed the hand-over-hand stroke, then named the trudgen. He copied the stroke from South American Indians and introduced it in England in 1873. Each arm recovered out of the water as the body rolled from side to side. The swimmer did a scissors kick with every two arm strokes. This stroke was the forerunner of the front crawl. Kick variations included different multiples of scissors kicks or alternating scissors and flutter kicks. F. V. C. Lane showed the speed of the trudgen in 1901 by swimming 100 yards in 1:00.0.

## Modern Times: Swimming in the Twentieth Century

### Leisure Swimming

Swimming for leisure has become tremendously popular since late in the last century. The first municipal pool in the United States was built in Brookline, Massachusetts, in 1887. Soon after that, New York City built public facilities, then called "baths." In the 1920s, the first boom for swimming pools occurred, with several thousand pools built in this country. At the same time there was a great rise in "estate pools," as residential pools were then called. Construction of swimming pools has not slowed since and shows no sign of ending. The National Spa and Pool Institute, a trade association representing the pool and spa industry, reports that there are now about $6^1/_2$ million pools in the United States.

Today, pools are almost everywhere. Many hotels and motels, private associations, apartment buildings and condominiums, commercial operations, schools and universities, and municipalities have pools. Water theme parks with rides, slides, and artificial waves attract large numbers of thrill-seekers. As in the past, swimming in oceans, lakes, rivers, canals, and quarries continues to be popular, even though most swimmers use pools.

Just as the number of places for swimming has increased, so have the kinds of activities people enjoy in and on the water. Boating and water skiing, snorkeling and SCUBA diving, surfing and sailboarding, fishing, and an unlimited number of games—from tag to water polo—are all increasingly popular. The variety of relaxing water pastimes, such as hot tubs, saunas, and whirlpools often located at or near swimming facilities, also are growing in popularity.

Leisure swimming also has great social value. Family and neighborhood ties are strengthened by weekends at the beach, vacations by mountain lakes, pool parties, and just "having the neighbor kids over to use the pool" (Fig. 1-2).

FIG. 1-2

**The Red Cross and Water Safety**

*The Red Cross became involved in swimming and water safety largely because of one person, Commodore Wilbert E. Longfellow. At the turn of the century, the Commodore was one of the first to become concerned with the number of drownings in the United States. He saw that the increasing death toll would assume the proportions of a national tragedy, unless drownings were curbed. He saw the need for a nationwide program of swimming and lifesaving instruction. His vision, plus his aquatics skills, teaching abilities, showmanship, and enthusiasm, made him the natural leader of this enterprise.*

*Eager to do what he could to prevent loss of life, Longfellow carefully studied the literature on aquatics trends, activities, and safety procedures. He wrote features on water safety, waterfront rescues, and steps taken to safeguard swimmers. He became proficient in various swimming styles and lifesaving skills. He also offered his spare-time services to the U.S. Volunteer Life Saving Corps, a young organization in New York City, and began sharing his aquatics knowledge and skills with other swimmers. Soon he was organizing his better pupils into volunteer crews for safeguarding the lives of swimmers. Under his direction, this lifeguarding gradually spread to nearby towns and cities.*

*In 1905, in recognition of his already noteworthy achievements, Longfellow was awarded the title of "Commodore" by the Life Saving Corps. In 1910, the Corps appointed him to the salaried post of Commodore in Chief. In recognition of his abilities and achievements, he was designated general superintendent of the organization.*

*Based on his successes in water safety and lifesaving education, the Commodore began planning his most ambitious program yet, "the waterproofing of America." However, the Life Saving Corps decided it could not afford a nationwide expansion of its activities because of the large amount of additional funds required.*

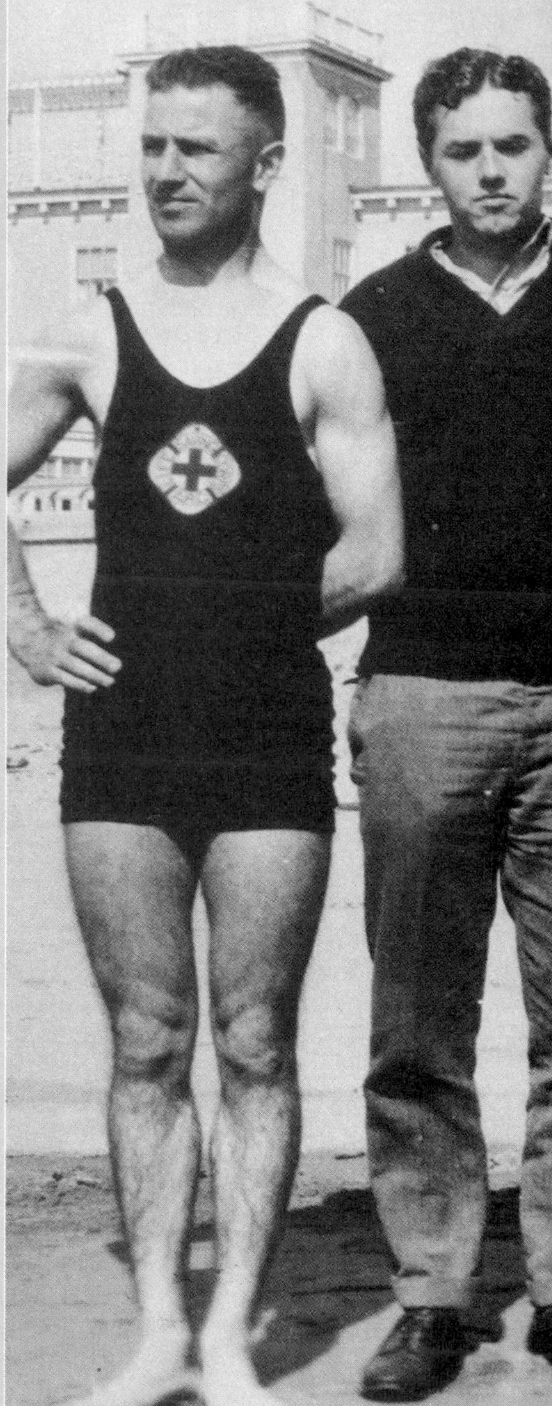

*Looking for a way to accomplish his great purpose, Longfellow presented his plan to the American Red Cross in 1912.*

Seaside, Oregon, June 1925. Seaside Institute Faculty (*left to right*) Paul Huedepohl, Ed H. Carroll, Commodore Wilbert E. Longfellow, Millie Sebloth, and L. E. Palmer.

*A committee representing several national organizations prepared a plan, which the Red Cross adopted for a nationwide program in January 1914. The following month the Red Cross Life Saving Corps, forerunner of the present-day Red Cross water safety courses, came into being. Longfellow was appointed to organize the lifesaving program. He was awarded Red Cross Lifesaving Certificate Number One and the lifesaving emblem that has since been earned and proudly worn by millions.*

*Soon the big fellow with the Red Cross emblem on his swimsuit began to appear at beaches and swimming pools all over the country. Everywhere he was recognized as an expert in aquatic arts and lifesaving skills.*

*The Commodore put the lifesaving plan into operation in a simple way. In each community, he gathered good swimmers, trained them in lifesaving and resuscitation, organized them into a volunteer corps, and asked them to supervise swimming activities in the community. He then persuaded owners and operators of swimming facilities to staff their beaches and pools with these trained lifeguards.*

Commodore Longfellow demonstrates rescue techniques.

September 1939, Hampton Beach, Massachusetts. Commodore Longfellow presents the one-millionth lifesaving certificate.

*The next step, which was more difficult and perhaps more important, was to provide sound, large-scale swimming instruction in the communities. Longfellow selected outstanding swimmers from each corps that he organized, gave them additional training, and authorized them to teach swimming. In this way, sound swimming instruction multiplied many times over.*

*Finally, it was necessary to consolidate public interest and support, which the Commodore did with amazing success. He gave talks and demonstrations, wrote for newspapers and periodicals, created and produced water pageants, and, with the advent of radio in the 1920s, put his message on the air. The water pageants illustrate very well the Commodore's philosophy of teaching, which was to "entertain the public hugely while educating them gently." Under Longfellow's guidance, a pleasurable activity for participants and spectators alike became a solid educational experience.*

*He was always the cheerful crusader, the self-styled "amiable whale," the man whose mission was to lure Americans to the water, to teach them how to be at home in it, how to have fun in it, and how not to drown.*

*"Water is a good friend or a deadly enemy," the Commodore often told his pupils. "After you have been properly introduced to it, keep on good terms with it. Don't slap it; try hugging it—an armful at a time!"*

*From 1914 until his retirement and then death 3 months later on March 18, 1947, Longfellow worked with devotion and enthusiasm in the nationwide water safety program of the Red Cross. The results of his efforts were astonishing. The Commodore saw the nation's drowning rate cut in half—from 10.4 people per 100,000 in 1914 to 5.2 in 1947. He also*

## *Fitness and Aerobics*

The restorative power of water has long been recognized. Ancient cultures such as Greece and Rome had their "baths." The Romans wrote that "health comes from water" on the walls of their public facilities.

In our own time, the importance of aerobic exercise and the advantages of exercising in water are well known. Water exercise leads to less stress and fewer injuries to tendons and joints (Fig. 1-3). From 1961, the Red Cross Swim and Stay Fit program has encouraged fitness by keeping track of one's swimming distance. Research on conditioning and aerobics in the 1960s revolutionized the world of water and most other sports. The emphasis changed to cardiovascular conditioning rather than simply developing muscles. Physical fitness now focuses on heart rate, progressive resistance, overload, metabolism, and other aspects of fitness. Chapter 10 discusses fitness swimming and aquatic exercise in detail.

FIG. 1-3

*witnessed a tremendous upsurge in the popularity of swimming, boating, and other water activities. It reached the point where an estimated 80 million Americans were participating in some form of aquatic recreation. Thanks to the dedication and untiring efforts of those who followed his example and continued his work, by 1990, the drowning rate dropped further, to 1.9 per 100,000.*

*The Commodore's efforts, enthusiasm, and foresight are carried forward now by his successors, who face the never-ending challenge of preventing serious injuries and loss of life by promoting aquatic safety.*

# THE DEVELOPMENT OF MODERN STROKES

Although people have swum since ancient times, swimming strokes have been greatly refined in the past 100 years. Competitive swimming—notably the modern Olympic Games, begun in Athens, Greece, in 1896—increased interest in strokes. Scientific stroke analysis has helped produce more varied strokes, greater speeds, and a better understanding of propulsion through the water.

## *Front Crawl*

The inefficiency of the trudgen kick led Australian Richard Cavill to try new methods. He used a stroke he observed natives of the Solomon Islands using, which combined an up-and-down kick with an alternating overarm stroke. He used the new stroke in 1902 at the International Championships and set a new world record (100 yards in 58.4 seconds). This stroke became known as the Australian crawl.

Olympic swimming great Duke Kahanamoku and Commodore Longfellow (*second and third from right*) are shown when the Commodore introduced Red Cross lifesaving methods to the Hawaiian Islands in 1920.

The Australian men's swimming team introduced a front crawl stroke with more body roll at the 1956 Olympic Games in Melbourne. This roll decreased the water resistance and thus increased speed.

### *Backstroke*

In the early 1900s, swimming on the back was not done in competition. Since the breaststroke was still the stroke of choice, the backstroke was done like an upside-down breaststroke. As the front crawl became popular, however, swimmers tried the alternating overarm style on the back. Combined with a flutter kick, this made a faster stroke than the breaststroke. In 1912, the backstroke became a competitive event. The continued effort to gain greater speed, along with studying and experimenting with the stroke, led to the back crawl as we know it today.

**Early Champions**

*The front crawl was further changed by "Duke" Kahanamoku, a Hawaiian, who learned the stroke by watching old Hawaiian swimmers. His stroke was characterized by a truly vertical six-beat flutter kick. The Duke was an Olympic record holder and an Olympic gold medal winner for the 100-yard front crawl in both the 1912 and the 1920 games.*

*Johnny Weissmuller* (shown as Tarzan at right) *also influenced the stroke. He dominated sprint swimming in the period including the 1924 and 1928 Olympic Games. In 1927, Weissmuller swam 100 yards in 51 seconds flat in a 25-yard course, setting the record for almost two decades. His style featured a deep kick, which allowed the chest and shoulders to ride higher; a rotating of the head for inhalation that was independent of the action of the arms; and an underwater arm action in which the elbow was bent slightly for greater positive action.*

*The popularity of Duke Kahanamoku, Johnny Weissmuller, and Buster Crabbe, an Olympic swimming champion in 1932 who succeeded Weissmuller as Tarzan in the movies, contributed greatly to the development of the front crawl. Their popularity also led to this becoming the stroke used to teach beginners.*

Archive Photo

Johnny Weissmuller and teammate Buster Crabbe at the 1932 Olympics.

Courtesy of International Swimming Hall of Fame

## *Breaststroke and Butterfly*

Swimming research has helped the breaststroke evolve. Other strokes are faster, but the breaststroke is still a competitive event. Until the 1950s, the breaststroke was the only stroke with a required style. The underwater recovery of both arms and legs in the breaststroke is a natural barrier to speed.

In 1934, however, David Armbruster, coach at the University of Iowa, devised a double overarm recovery out of the water. This "butterfly" arm action gave more speed but required greater training and conditioning. Then in 1935, Jack Sieg, a University of Iowa swimmer, developed the skill of swimming on his side and beating his legs in unison like a fish's tail. He then developed the leg action face down. Armbruster and Sieg combined the butterfly arm action with this leg action and learned to coordinate the two efficiently. With two kicks to each butterfly arm action, Sieg swam 100 yards in 1:00.2. This kick was named the *dolphin fishtail kick* (Fig. 1-4).

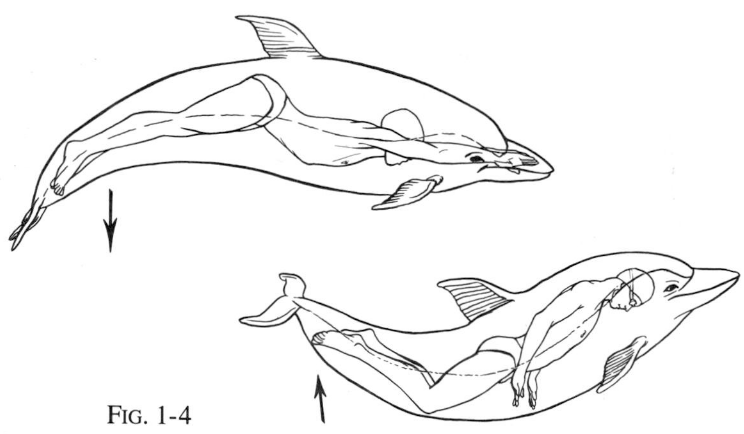

FIG. 1-4

Even though the butterfly breastroke, as it was called, was faster than the breastroke, the dolphin fishtail kick was declared a violation of competitive rules. For the next 20 years, champion breaststrokers used an out-of-water arm recovery (butterfly) with a shortened breaststroke kick. In the late 1950s, the butterfly stroke with the dolphin kick was legalized as a separate stroke for competition. Many swimmers say the "wiggle" is the key to the stroke and that a swimmer who can ***undulate*** through the water naturally can more easily learn the butterfly.

### COMPETITIVE SWIMMING

As swimmers refine strokes or make changes, the best way to see if the new stroke is an improvement is to use it in competition. This is why so much attention is paid to speed and endurance records.

## *Swimmers Setting Records*

Alfred Hajos of Hungary won the first Olympic men's swimming gold medal in the Olympic Games in Athens in 1896. He had a time of 1:22.20 for the 100-meter ***freestyle,*** a competitive event in which any stroke is allowed. Since then, new swimming records have been set regularly. At this writing, the world record for that event is 48.42, set by Matt Biondi in the 1988 Olympics.

While names have come and gone from the record books, several U.S. swimmers have left their mark on the swimming world. Johnny Weissmuller won 5 Olympic medals and 36 national championships and never lost a race in his 10-year career. His record of 51 seconds for the 100-yard freestyle stood for over 17 years. Tracy Caulkins set world records in the 200-meter butterfly and the 400-meter ***individual medley*** (an event in which the competitor swims one quarter of the total distance using a different competitive stroke in a prescribed order: butterfly, backstroke, breaststroke, freestyle). She broke her own world record in the 200-meter individual medley three times. Besides winning three Olympic medals, she is the only swimmer ever to hold all of the U.S. records at the same time. Mark Spitz won seven gold medals in the 1972 Olympics in Munich, more than any other swimmer in the history of Olympic competition (Fig. 1-5).

Terry O'Neil/Stern/Black Star Publishing

FIG. 1-5 Mark Spitz, winner of seven gold medals at the 1972 Olympics.

FIG. 1-6 Red Cross Women's Lifesaving Corps, Jacksonville, Florida, 1920.

VARIETY OF EVENTS. The first modern Olympic Games had only four swimming events, three of them freestyle. The second Olympics in Paris in 1900 included three unusual swimming events. One used an obstacle course; another was a test of underwater swimming endurance; the third was a 4,000-meter event, the longest competitive swimming event ever. None of the three was ever used in the Olympics again.

For a variety of reasons, women were excluded from swimming in the first several Olympic Games. In 1896 and again in 1906, women could not participate because the developer of the modern games, Pierre de Coubertin, held firmly to the assumption, common in the Victorian era, that women were too frail to engage in competitive sports. In 1900, the committee organizing the Paris games allowed women to participate in golf and tennis, since these were popular sports in Europe. (Until the International Olympic Committee was formed, events at Olympic Games were chosen by the host committee.)

The 1904 games in St. Louis were dominated by the President of the Amateur Athletic Union (AAU), James E. Sullivan, who allowed women to participate only in archery, a demonstration sport. Sullivan's control not only of the Olympics but of the AAU is attested by the fact that one month after his death in 1914, women's events were allowed by the AAU. In 1908, women were allowed to compete in archery, and women's gymnastics was a demonstration event.

Women's swimming made its debut in the 1912 games at the prompting of the group that later became the International Olympic Committee. As early as 1914 in this country, the Women's Swimming Association of New York, another outgrowth of the U.S. Volunteer Life Saving Corps (Fig. 1-6), provided the first opportunity for women to train for national and international competition.

From the humble beginning with four swimming events, the Olympics have developed to 32 swimming races, 16 for men and 16 for women.

COMPETITION FOR PEOPLE WITH DISABILITIES. Swimming competition for people with disabilities also has a long history. In 1924, the Comite International des Sports des Sourds (CISS—the International Committee for Sports for the Deaf) held the first Summer World Games for men and women who were deaf. Athletes with cognitive disabilities first joined in international swimming competition in 1968, with the International Summer Special Olympics. The most recent Special Olympics had 22 events for men and 22 for women. Other organizations also provide aquatic competitions for people with disabilities. (See Appendix A.)

## Research and Training Techniques

Unlike walking and other motions, swimming is not a natural activity for the human body. A standing position on land does not translate easily to a horizontal swimming position. Therefore, people throughout history have experimented with different ways to swim better. Our ability to use a variety of swimming techniques is due to the ball and socket joints of our shoulders and hips.

Early swimmers experimented by trial and error and watched others. In 1928, however, David Armbruster first filmed swimmers under water to study strokes (Fig. 1-7). The Japanese also photographed and studied world-class athletes, using their research to produce a swim team that dominated the 1932 Olympic Games. This marked the beginning of research into ***stroke mechanics.***

At the same time, others advanced the role of conditioning. The 1956 Olympic Games in Melbourne, Australia, showed the clear value of conditioning. The host team for those games had fantastic success, which was due to their training program, not their stroke technique. American swimming coaches began adopting training methods like those used by track coaches to help runners break the 4-minute mile.

Current research focuses on the forces that act on a body moving through the water. The main points of this science, ***hydrodynamics,*** are presented in Chapter 4. Dr. James Counsilman, Charles Silvia, and Dr. Ernest Maglischo have revolutionized stroke mechanics with their pioneering and painstaking work.

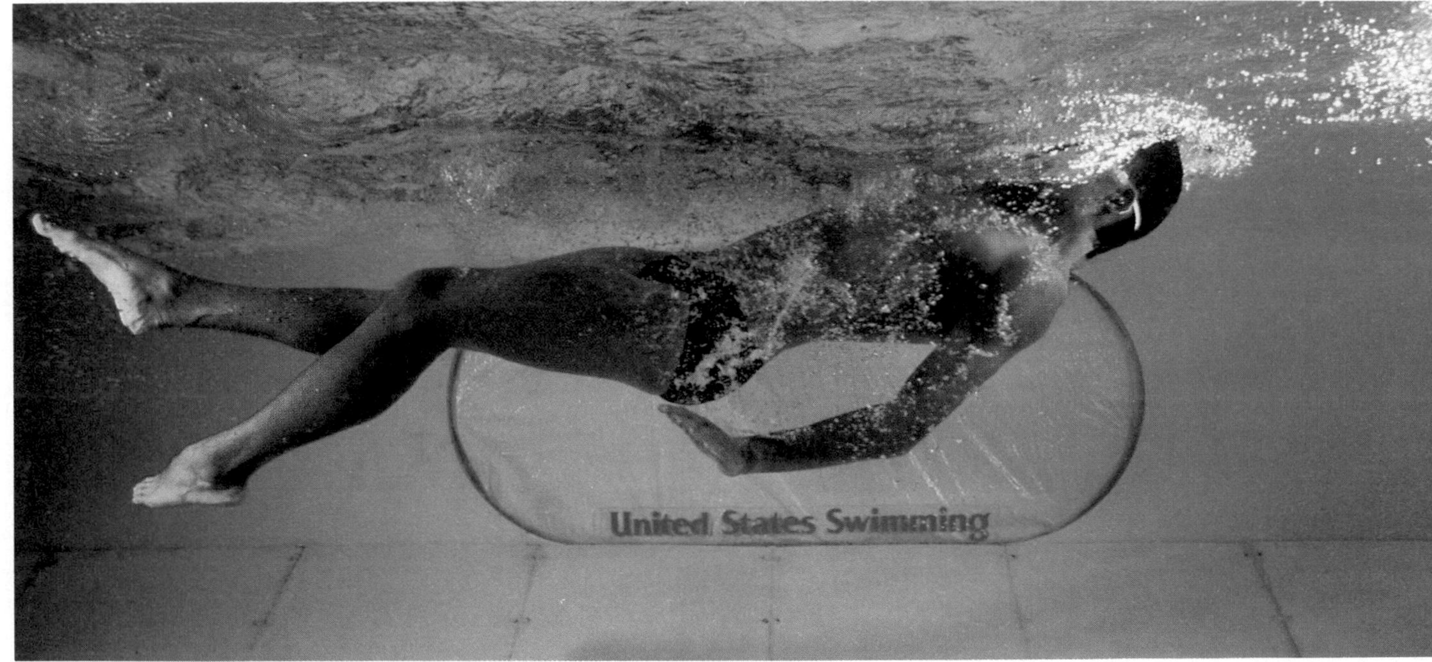


Fig. 1-7 Underwater photography has contributed valuable information to the study of swimming strokes.

This increased understanding of stroke mechanics has helped researchers and coaches improve swimmers' times in competition. American swim researchers include C. H. McCloy and Robert Kiphuth, who was awarded the Medal of Freedom, the United States' highest civilian award, by President Johnson in 1963. They and others have given swimmers new techniques, drills, and training methods based on these scientific principles.

## Diving and Other Water Sports

### *Competitive Diving*

Although it is a water sport, competitive diving is closer to gymnastics and tumbling than to swimming. In fact, competitive diving grew out of the gymnastic movement in Germany and Sweden. People may have been diving throughout history, but written reports date from 1871 when divers plunged from London Bridge and other high places.

Springboard diving began as an Olympic event in the 1904 games in St. Louis. American Jim Sheldon won gold medals in the 1-meter and 3-meter events. An event called distance plunging also was held. Each diver performed a racing dive into the pool followed by a prone glide for distance. W. E. Dickey won the gold with a plunge of 62 feet, 6 inches in the only Olympics that included this event.

Men's platform diving (10 meters) began in the 1908 games in London, and women's diving events started in the next two Olympic Games—platform diving in 1912 and springboard diving in 1920. The Olympic Games were not held in 1916 because of World War I.

Athletes. Since diving was an outgrowth of the gymnastic movement in Germany and Sweden, athletes from these countries won most of the early competitions. However, the United States has dominated Olympic diving competition since 1920, when Americans won gold medals in three events. In fact, the United States has enjoyed more success in Olympic diving than in any other sport, based on the number of medals awarded over time. The U.S. team has won 45 of the 70 gold medals and 121 of the 210 total medals awarded to date in Olympic diving competition.

Eight U.S. divers are responsible for winning 20 Olympic gold medals, each winning at least two. Al White (1924), Pete Desjardins (1928), and Victoria Draves (1948) won double gold medals in springboard and platform events at the same Olympics. In the platform event, Dorothy (Poynton) Hill (1932 and 1936), Sammy Lee (1948 and 1952), and Bob Webster (1960 and 1964) won gold medals in back-to-back Olympic Games. Most impressive, however, are Pat McCormick (1952 and 1956) and Greg Louganis (1984 and 1988) who are the only divers to sweep gold medals at consecutive Olympics. They are also the only four-time Olympic gold medalists to date.

Coaches. Several coaches also have helped the United States achieve supremacy in diving. Ernst Bransten is known as "the father of diving in the United States." He emigrated from Sweden just before 1920, bringing a thorough knowledge of diving fundamentals and revolutionary ideas for developing divers. One notable contribution was the construction of a "sand pit," a diving board mounted over sand (Fig. 1-8). This allows divers to practice basic diving movements such as approach and takeoff more efficiently.

Fig. 1-8

Mike Peppe, the swimming and diving coach at Ohio State University from 1931 to 1963, had a phenomenal coaching record. From 1938 on, his divers won 150 of 200 possible titles in the Big Ten Conference and in national competition of the National Collegiate Athletic Association (NCAA) and the Amateur Athletic Union. In two years (1947 and 1956), Peppe's divers placed 1-2-3-4 in both the 1-meter and 3-meter springboard events at the NCAA championships. His pupils did equally well in Olympic competition, winning two gold, five silver, and three bronze medals from 1948 through 1960.

FIG. 1-9

Peppe treated his divers and swimmers with equal importance and thus led other schools to emphasize diving more—just so they could compete with his teams. His influence led to improved diving facilities, more practice time, greater respect for the sport, and the birth of the diving coach. For this reason, Peppe might be designated "the father of collegiate diving in the United States."

Before 1960, college diving was strictly for men. Women trained at private clubs such as the Dick Smith Swim Gym in Phoenix, Arizona. In the Big Ten Conference, two coaches, Hobie Billingsley at Indiana University and Dick Kimball at the University of Michigan, opened the door for women in varsity diving programs.

Billingsley also contributed to diving by applying the principles of physics. He analyzed dives in terms of Newton's laws of motion. One of the divers he coached, Cynthia Potter, is a 28-time U.S. champion.

Kimball has been the foremost proponent of the overhead-mounted safety belt system for spotting divers over the trampoline and dry board (Fig. 1-9). This training aid allows the diver to repeat a dive many times in a short period of time.

Ron O'Brien followed in Peppe's footsteps at Ohio State University. He won the Mike Peppe Award for the outstanding Senior Diving Coach in the United States every year from 1979 to 1988. As the list of competitive dives evolved to add a third somersault and twist, O'Brien has been an advocate of maintaining aesthetic qualities of the sport. The stylized performance of his Olympic gold medalists Jennifer Chandler (springboard, 1976) and Greg Louganis (double gold medals, 1984 and 1988) defined the standard for grace.

DEVELOPMENT OF THE DIVING BOARD. Important in diving history is the evolution of the diving board. Changes improved safety and allowed for greater variety in dives. Before the mid-1940s, diving boards were wood planks covered with cocoa matting to prevent slipping. They were mounted on a fixed **fulcrum** and sloped upward. Since then, diving boards have become lighter and thinner and are made of an aluminum alloy with a nonskid surface. These are mounted level on movable fulcrums, which allows divers to achieve a greater height. Thus, divers can more easily complete rotations and travel a safe distance from the diving board.

The improved diving board enables divers to add more somersaults and twists to dives. In the early days there were only 14 platform and 20 springboard dives. Competitors and coaches have now assembled 87 different dives from the basic "ingredients": forward, backward, or inward takeoff; handstands and twists; somersaults and reverse dives—performed in a straight, pike, or tuck position from 1-meter or 3-meter diving boards or from platforms at various heights. Even the difficulty of dives has changed greatly. In 1904, a double somersault from a platform was considered dangerous; today, world-class divers routinely perform the reverse three-and-one-half somersault. What lies in store for tomorrow is anyone's guess, but millions of diving fans and enthusiasts are watching eagerly to see.

### *Water Polo*

Water polo combines soccer and rugby skills and is played in deep water. It requires tremendous stamina and skill. It was made a sport in 1885 by the Swimming Association of Great Britain and became an official Olympic sport in 1908. Today, it is a popular high school, college, and Olympic sport (Fig. 1-10). Water polo is described in more detail in Chapter 12.

*Courtesy of United States Water Polo*

FIG. 1-10

## *Synchronized Swimming*

***Synchronized swimming*** is a creative sport for swimmers at any level. It may be purely leisure swimming or competitive (Fig. 1-11). Beulah and Henry Gundling, founders of the International Academy of Aquatic Art, deserve much credit for its development. Esther Williams, who was inspired by Eleanor Holmes, popularized synchronized swimming in the movies (Fig. 1-12) and teamed with Johnny Weissmuller in the 1940 San Francisco World's Fair Aquacade. In competition, swimmers are judged on intricate skills and synchronization of routines set to music. In January 1991, the United States Synchronized Swimming National Team became the world champions. Chapter 12 discusses synchronized swimming as a competitive sport.

FIG. 1-11

*Archive Photo*

FIG. 1-12 Esther Williams (*center*) stars in "Million Dollar Mermaid."

**Sutro Baths**

*The increased popularity of swimming and diving in the early 1900s led to construction of water recreation facilities. The Fleishhacker Pool in San Francisco was the world's largest outdoor swimming pool. It was 1,000 feet long, 90 feet wide, and contained 800,000 gallons of water. The 450-foot bathhouse was designed in Italian Renaissance style.*

*In 1896, San Francisco Mayor Adolf Sutro opened a series of private swimming pools called Sutro Baths* (shown below). *The large, glass-roofed building has seven swimming pools with varying water temperatures, a skating rink, several restaurants, and a museum. The pool shells were 499.5 feet long and254 feet wide and contained 1,804,962 gallons of crystal clear water. Equipment included 9 diving boards, 7 slides, 3 trapezes, 30 swinging rings, a raft, and several high diving platforms. The bathhouse had 517 private dressing rooms. There were 7,400 seats for water shows. The Sutro Baths were said to be the largest glass-roofed building in the world. The admission price was 50 cents to swim or 10 cents to watch from the observation deck. The Sutro Baths were closed in 1966.*

*Courtesy of Recreonics Corp.*

*Courtesy of Indiana University Natatorium and IUPUI*

FIG. 1-13

## THE FUTURE: LEISURE AND COMPETITIVE TRENDS

An estimated 103 million people a year swim—for survival, leisure, or competition. Because of American Olympic swimming, the American Red Cross "Learn to Swim" and diving programs, and competitive swimming for all age groups and individuals, swimming and diving are more popular than ever. This popularity will continue into the twenty-first century. Comprehensive facilities, such as the Indiana University/Purdue University Natatorium in Indianapolis (Fig. 1-13), the King County Aquatic Center in Seattle, and the

Courtesy of the International Swimming Hall of Fame

FIG. 1-14

Swimming Hall of Fame in Fort Lauderdale (Fig. 1-14), demonstrate the public's diverse interests. Public and private facilities also are expanding the number and kinds of water activities available. Wave pools and water parks are enjoying a large share of the dollars spent on recreation (Fig. 1-15).

FIG. 1-15

Allsport USA

FIG. 1-16 1984 and 1988 Olympic diving champion Greg Louganis.

Aquatic research continues worldwide and will help develop swimming skills and techniques in the future. Competitive swimming will likely continue to refine and improve strokes.

Diving coach Ron O'Brien and diver Greg Louganis, among others, have set high standards for diving (Fig. 1-16). Research will continue to improve diving techniques, training, and safety.

Numerous organizations now govern the competitive aspects of aquatics. The Federation Internationale de Natation Amateur (FINA—the International Federation of Amateur Swimming) was founded in 1908 and continues as the world governing body for competitive swimming and diving. Many swimming and diving organizations support swimming and diving programs throughout the country. They are discussed in Chapter 12 and listed in Appendix A.

CHAPTER 2

# personal safety

## Key Terms

**Drift (side) currents:** Currents that move parallel to the shore.

**Hydraulics:** Whirlpools created as water flows over an object; they have a strong downward force that may trap an unwary swimmer.

**Hyperventilation:** A dangerous technique some swimmers use to stay under water longer by taking several deep breaths followed by forceful exhalations, then inhaling deeply before swimming under water.

**Hypothermia:** A life-threatening condition in which the body's warming mechanisms cannot maintain normal body temperature and the entire body cools.

**Rip currents:** Currents that move straight out to sea.

**SCUBA:** Self-Contained Underwater Breathing Apparatus.

**Undertows:** Currents that move down the slope of a beach.

# Objectives

***After reading this chapter, you should be able to—***

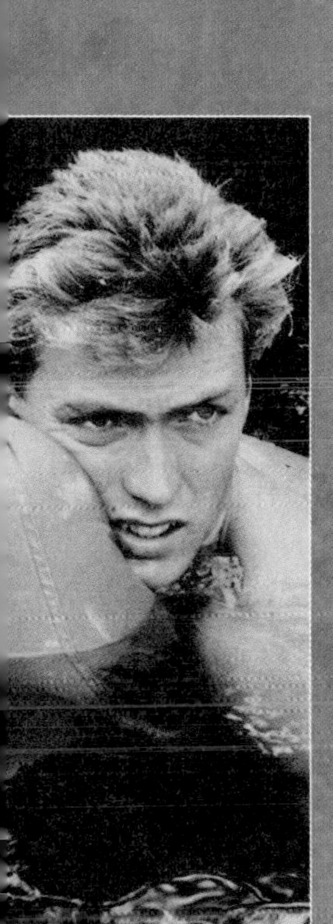

1. List at least five safety steps to take before starting any aquatic activity.
2. List at least eight basic safety tips for whenever you swim.
3. Describe how to care for a cramp.
4. Explain the dangers posed by waves and currents.
5. Describe a hydraulic and explain how to escape from one.
6. Explain the flag system for alerting swimmers about water conditions.
7. Describe three types of ocean currents and how to escape from two of them.
8. Name two forms of aquatic life that can be hazardous.
9. Explain the potential dangers of cold water and how to help yourself in a cold water emergency.
10. Explain what to do if you fall through ice.
11. Explain the basic rules for boating safety and how to care for yourself in a boating emergency.
12. List other activities in, on, or near water and the general safety precautions for each.
13. Define the key terms at left.

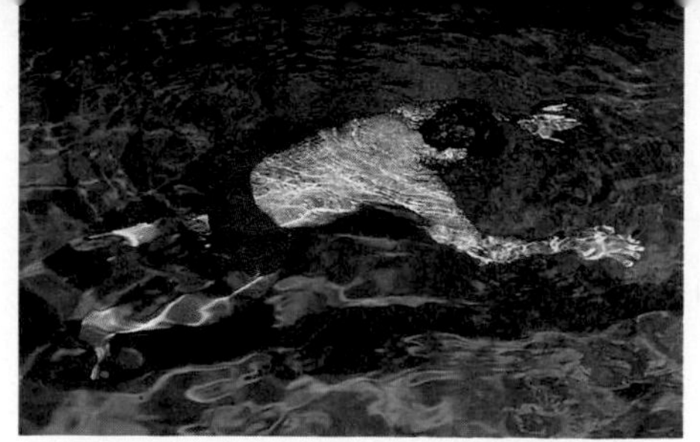

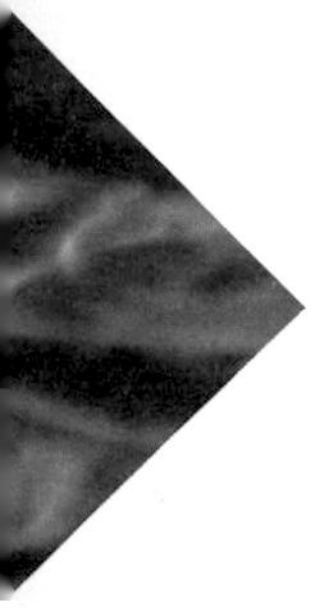

F O L L

IF YOU WATCH TELEVISION, listen to the radio, or read the newspaper, you know that people die while they are swimming or participating in other water activities. It is tragic that many of these deaths could have been prevented if the victim had followed basic rules of safety. Do not become one of these victims. Learn and follow the rules to enjoy aquatic activities safely.

THIS CHAPTER CONCERNS SAFETY ISSUES for swimming, boating, and other activities around ice and water. Diving safety is discussed in the next chapter and rescue techniques in Chapter 13.

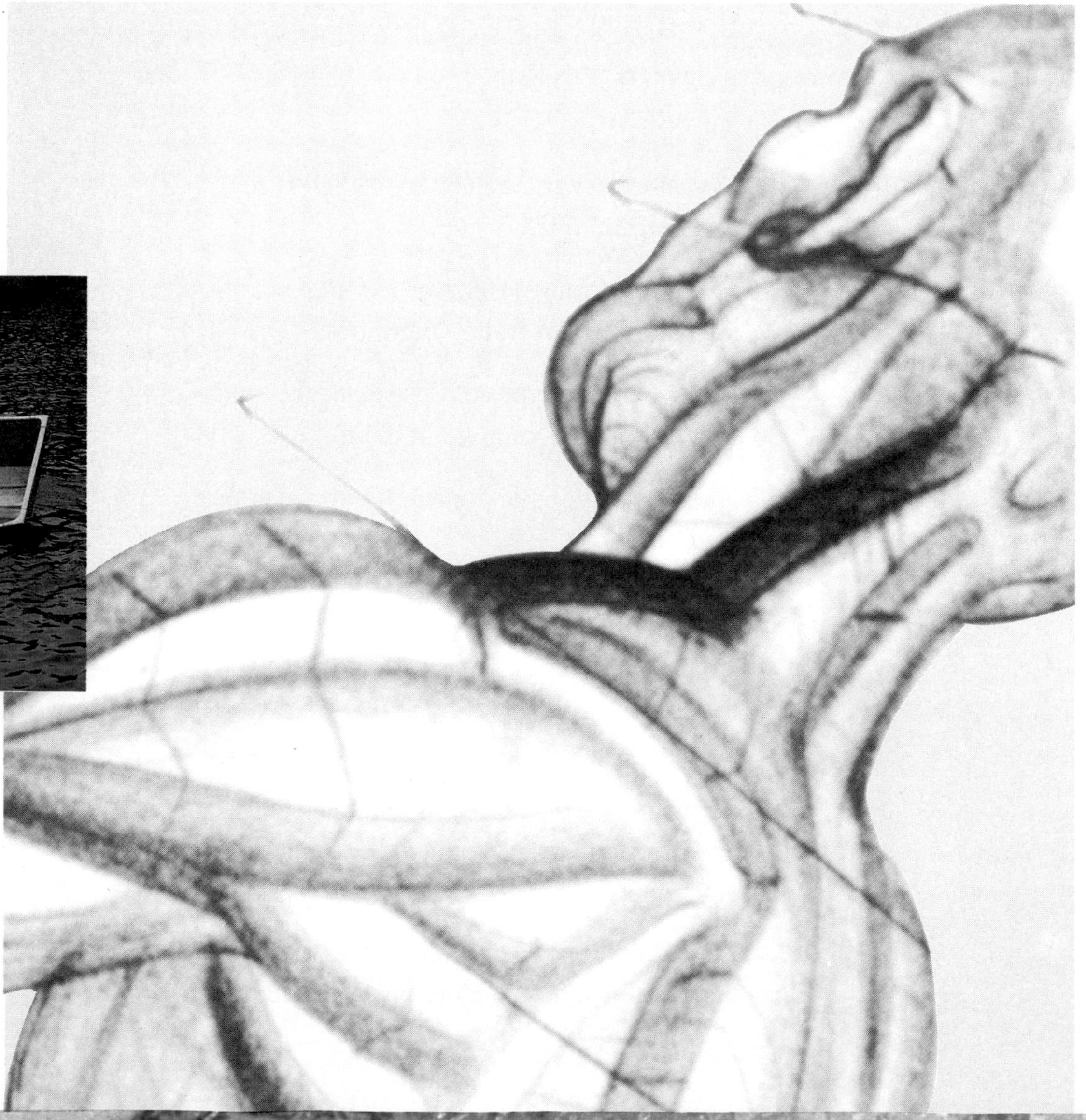

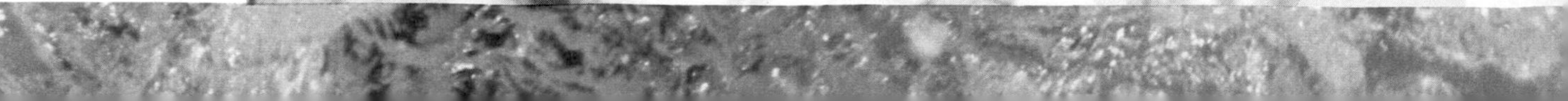

# PREVENT

OW BASIC RULES FOR SAFETY

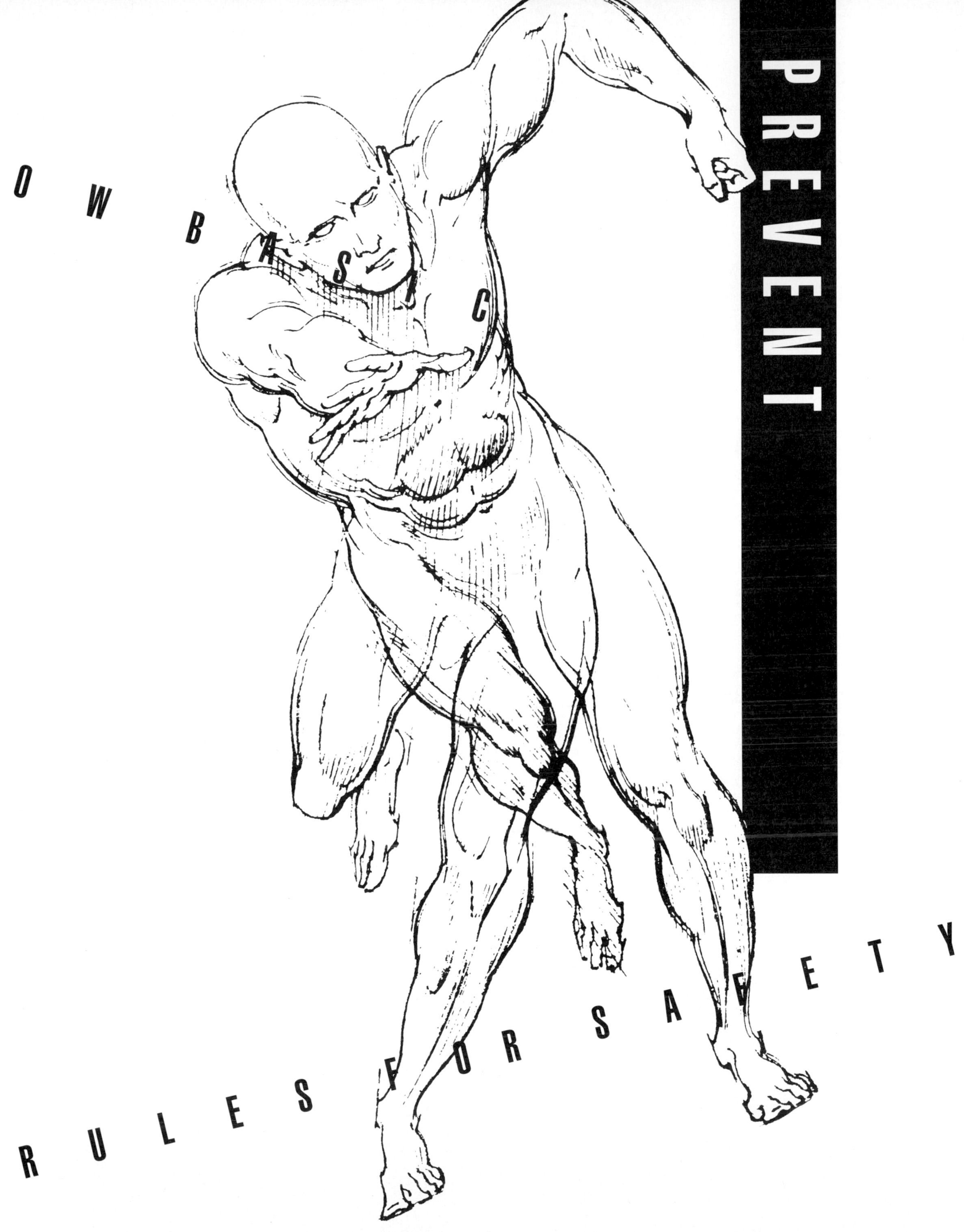

**Too Much of a Good Thing**

*Contrary to some beliefs, tan is not in. Although brief exposure to the sun stimulates your skin to produce the vitamin D necessary for the healthy formation of bones, prolonged exposure can cause problems such as skin cancer and premature aging—a classic case of too much of a good thing being bad.*

*There are two kinds of ultraviolet (UV) light rays to be concerned about. Ultraviolet beta rays (UVB) are the burn-producing rays that more commonly cause skin cancer. These are the rays that damage the skin's surface and cause you to blister and perhaps peel. The other rays, ultraviolet alpha rays (UVA), have been heralded by tanning salons as "safe rays." Tanning salons claim to use lights that only emit UVA rays. While UVA rays may not appear as harmful as UVB rays to the skin's surface, they more readily penetrate the deeper layers of the skin. This increases the risk of skin cancer, skin aging, eye damage, and genetic changes that may alter the skin's ability to fight disease.*

*How do you get enough sun without getting too much? First, avoid exposure to the sun between 10:00 A.M. and 2:00 P.M. UV rays are most harmful during this period. Second, wear proper clothing to prevent overexposure. Third, if you are going to be exposed to the sun at any time, take care to protect your skin and eyes.*

*Commercial sunscreens come in various strengths. The American Academy of Dermatology recommends year-round sun protection, including use of a high Sun Protection Factor (SPF) sunscreen, for all individuals, but particularly for those who are fair-skinned and sunburn easily. The Food and Drug Administration (FDA) has evaluated SPF readings and recognizes values between 2 and 15. It has not been determined whether products with an SPF rating higher than 15 provide any additional protection against sun damage.*

*Sunscreens should be applied before exposure to the sun and should be reapplied frequently. Swimmers should use sunscreens labeled as water-resistant and reapply them as described in the labeling.*

*Your best bet is to use a sunscreen that claims to be broad spectrum-protecting against both UVB and UVA rays. Carefully check the label to determine the protection a product offers. Some products only offer protection against UVB rays.*

*It is equally important to protect your eyes from sun damage. Sunglasses are a sunscreen for your eyes and provide important protection from UV rays. Be sure to wear sunglasses that are labeled with their UV-absorbing ability. Ophthalmologists recommend sunglasses that have a UV absorption of at least 90 percent.*

*The next time the sun beckons, put on some sunscreen and your sunglasses, go outside, and have a great time.*

FIG. 2-1

## PLANNING FOR SAFETY

### SAFETY STEPS

The following are safety steps you should take before starting any aquatic activity:

- Learn about swimming, boating, and first aid, and be sure that others in your group also are informed.
- Have an emergency plan in case of a water emergency, regardless of how well you swim.
- Choose a safe place for water recreation (Fig. 2-1).
- Use Coast Guard-approved life jackets.
- Check out potential water hazards.
- Know local weather conditions and how to find out what is forecast.
- Know how to prevent, recognize, and care for hypothermia.
- Know how to recognize and treat heat exhaustion and heat stroke.

These steps are discussed in detail in this chapter.

### BASIC SAFETY GUIDELINES

Follow these basic safety tips whenever you swim in any body of water (pools, lakes, ponds, quarries, canals, rivers, or oceans):

- Never swim alone.
- Swim only in supervised areas.
- Never drink alcohol or use drugs when you are swimming.
- Always check the depth before entering the water.
- Always enter feetfirst if you do not know the depth.
- Do not swim in a pool if you cannot see the bottom at the deep end or if the water is cloudy.
- Know your swimming limits and stay within them.
- Watch out for the "dangerous too's"—too tired, too cold, too far from safety, too much sun, too much hard playing.
- Stay out of the water when you are overheated or overtired.
- Do not chew gum or eat while you swim; you could easily choke.
- Learn the safe and proper way to dive and know when it is safe to do so. (See Chapter 3.)
- Use common sense about swimming after eating. In general, you do not have to wait an hour after eating before you may safely swim. However, if you have had a large meal, it is wise to let digestion get started before strenuous swimming.

### EMERGENCY ACTION PLAN

Wherever you swim, you should have an emergency action plan for responding to water accidents.

If you're using a community pool or supervised beach, look for information about the emergency action plan for that location. Follow the lifeguard's instructions if there is an emergency. If there is no emergency action plan displayed, get emergency information from your city, county, or state authorities.

It's best to swim at a supervised area, but if you're swimming at your own pool, a pond, or any unsupervised area, develop your own emergency action plan.

Here are the basic elements of an emergency action plan:

- An emergency signal. Blow a whistle or horn or wave a flag to alert swimmers that they should leave the water immediately. At a home pool or pond, the signal will tell other family members and neighbors that there is an emergency and help is needed quickly.
- Safety equipment for private swimming areas and other areas without lifeguards. Attach a ring buoy or other safety device to a white or yellow safety post close to the water. A well-stocked first aid kit also should be readily available.
- Emergency procedures. Develop and post procedures for what to do in a water emergency. All procedures must be carefully planned. At public facilities, follow the lifeguard's instructions during emergencies. At home pools or ponds, teach your family and friends the procedures. Tell your neighbors about your procedures so they can assist if necessary.

Conditions to Look for Before You Swim

| | **Swimming pools** | **Ponds, rivers, or lakes** | **Ocean beaches** |
|---|---|---|---|
| Lifeguards | X | X | X |
| Clean water | X | X | X |
| Clean, well-maintained beaches and deck areas | X | X | X |
| Nonslip surfaces | X | X | X |
| Free of electrical equipment or power lines | X | X | X |
| Emergency communication to get help | X | X | X |
| Safety equipment | X | X | X |
| Supervision for children and nonswimmers | X | X | X |
| Clearly marked water depths | X | X | X |
| Buoyed lines to separate shallow and deep water | X | X | X |
| Firm and gently sloping bottom | | X | X |
| No sudden drop-offs, large logs, submerged objects | | X | X |
| Well-constructed rafts, piers, docks | | X | X |
| Free of dangerous currents | | X | X |
| Free of dangerous aquatic life | | X | X |
| Signals for wave conditions | | X* | X |

*For very large lakes.

## Life Jackets

You should wear or have a life jacket immediately available whenever you are in, on, or around the water. Wear one whenever there is any chance you could fall or be thrown into the water. There are many types of life jackets, and they are rated for their buoyancy and purposes. How well you swim, what you are doing, and water conditions help you determine which type to use. For any type, be sure it is Coast Guard approved and in good condition. Local laws may require you to wear one. Be sure that the life jacket fits you or a person you are supervising correctly. Be sure that it is worn properly.

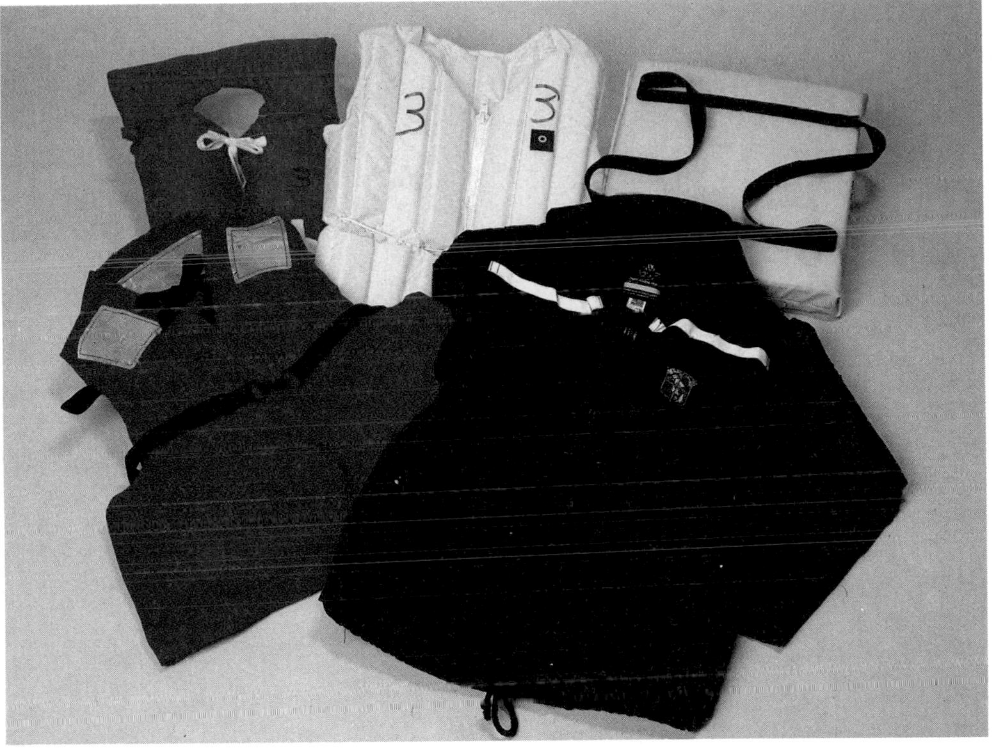

FIG. 2-2 Personal flotation devices, *clockwise from lower left:* Type I, Type II, Type III, Type IV, Type V.

Practice putting it on and swimming with it in shallow water. The life jacket must be easily accessible to you in an emergency or it has no value.

Life jackets are made to turn an unconscious person in the water from a face-down position to a vertical or slightly tipped-back position. Other flotation devices, such as buoyant cushions and ring buoys, do not take the place of life jackets, but they may be good throwing aids in an emergency (Fig. 2-2). They should also be Coast Guard approved.

**Life Jackets**

*You should wear a life jacket or have one available when you are in, on, or around the water. The United States Coast Guard has arranged personal flotation devices into five types. Four of these are life jackets:*

- *Type I (life preserver): Designed to turn an unconscious person in the water from a facedown position to a vertical or slightly tipped-backed position.*
- *Type II (buoyant vest): Designed to turn an unconscious person in the water from a facedown position to a vertical or slightly tipped-backed position. Buoyant vests offer less buoyancy than Type I life jackets.*
- *Type III (special purpose device): Designed to keep a conscious person in a vertical or slightly tipped-backed position. Type III is more comfortable for active water sports than Types I and II.*
- *Type V (restricted-use life jacket): A special purpose device approved for specific activities such as commercial white water rafting, where a life preserver device would interfere or when more protection is needed.*

*The buoyant cushion and the ring buoy (Type IV in the Coast Guard system) are flotation devices designed to be thrown to a victim in an emergency but are not designed to be worn. A buoyant cushion may be used as a seat cushion.*

*When you choose a life jacket—*

- *Make sure it's approved by the Coast Guard.*
- *Make sure it's the proper size.*
- *Practice putting it on in shallow water and swimming with it. When you practice, have a companion with you who can help you if you have difficulty.*
- *Wear the Coast Guard–approved life jacket whenever there's a chance that you could fall or be thrown into the water, for example, when you're boating, tubing or rafting, or walking alongside rapids.*

### Survival Floating and Survival Swimming

*Survival floating, also called "drownproofing," is a face-down floating technique that you can use if you end up in the water in an emergency. Use face-down floating only as a last resort to save yourself.*

*When you're face down in the water, your body tends to swing down into a nearly vertical position with your head just below the surface. Survival floating is based on this tendency. It was developed to help water accident victims in warm water conserve their energy while they waited to be rescued. Each move you make should be slow and easy.*

- *While your mouth and nose are above water, breathe in, hold your breath, put your face in the water, and let your arms and legs dangle. Keep the back of your head level with or just below the surface. Allow yourself to rest in this position for several seconds (Fig. 1).*
- *Slowly lift your arms to about shoulder height and separate your legs with one leg forward and the other back in a stride position.*
- *Tilt your head back to raise your face above the surface, but only high enough for your mouth to clear the water. As you raise your face, breathe out through your mouth or nose (Fig. 2). Keep your eyes open so you can make sure that you don't rise out of the water any farther than necessary for you to breathe.*
- *When your mouth clears the water, gently press down with your arms and, in the same motion, straighten your legs and bring them together. This helps keep your mouth above water while you take another breath with your mouth.*
- *Return to the resting position and repeat these movements.*

*If you sink too far below the surface while you're in the resting position, press down gently with your arms, or separate and then bring your legs together, as described above, to push yourself up toward the surface.*

*If you're so buoyant that your body remains on the surface, simply float in a position that is comfortable for you.*

*The survival stroke (survival swimming) is to be used in conjunction with the survival float in a warm water emergency only. It allows you, whether you're buoyant or not, to cover a considerable distance with a minimal use of energy. Remember that swimming long distances to safety should be used as a last resort only to save yourself.*

FIG. 1

FIG. 2

FIG. 3

FIG. 4

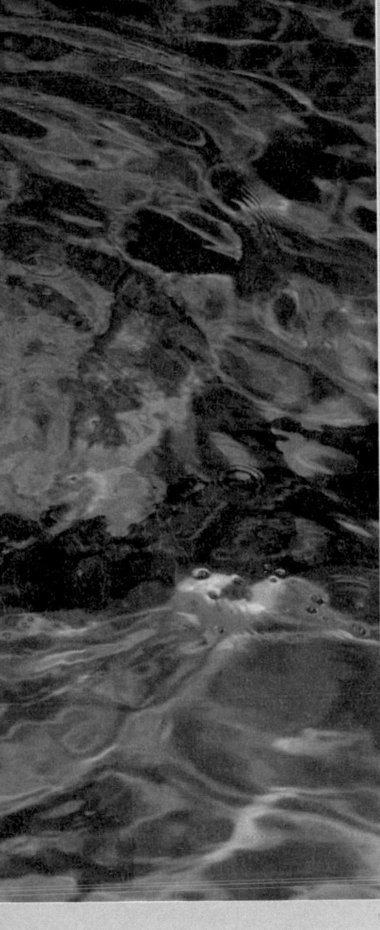

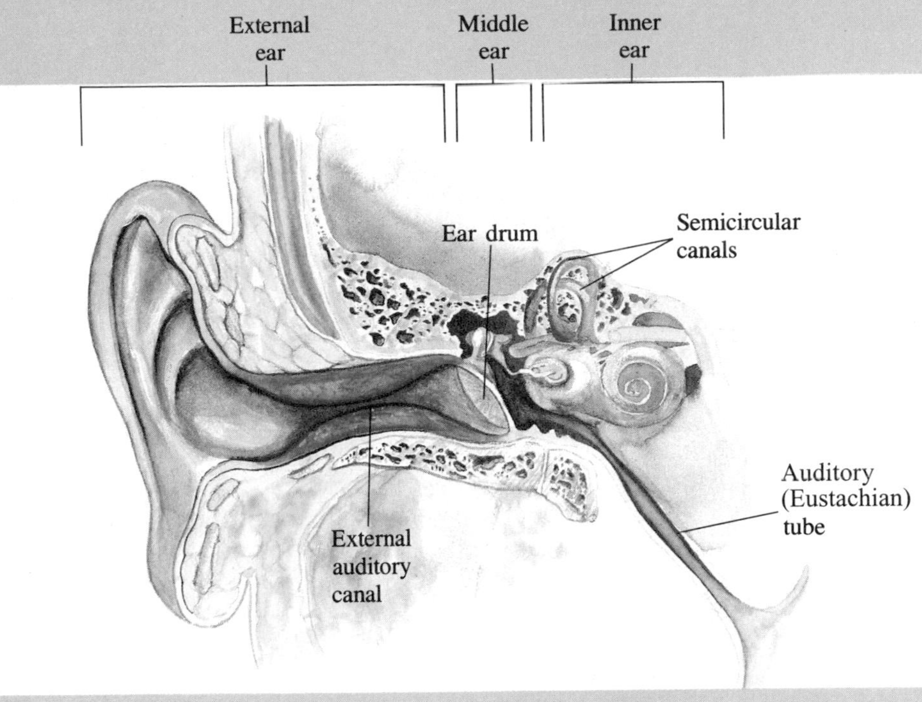


- *During the survival float (Fig. 3), after you take a breath, bend forward at your waist, bring your hands up alongside your head, separate your legs in the stride position, extend your arms forward, and then bring the legs together again, propelling yourself diagonally toward the surface (Fig. 4).*
- *Sweep your arms out and back to your thighs and glide easily near and almost parallel to the surface. When you feel like breathing, bend your legs and draw them toward your torso and bring your hands up again alongside your head. If you do not float well, you may need to pull harder with the arms and then quickly assume the body position just described to prevent the body from sinking.*
- *Extend the arms forward and separate the legs in the stride position once again. Tilt your head back and prepare to breathe out, as in survival floating. The full cycle is then repeated. If you are not very buoyant, these movements must be done more rapidly to prevent you from sinking before you breathe.*

**Swimmer's Ear**

*Chronic irritation of the outer ear caused by too much moisture is called "swimmer's ear." Moisture that remains in the S-shaped ear canal after swimming can cause this common ear infection. Pool water with too little chlorine and contaminated fresh water can cause the infection. Swimmer's ear may also depend on how long and how deep the swimmer or diver is in the water. If your ear is painful or swollen, or if you have a feeling of "fullness" in the ear or even mild hearing loss, see your doctor. These annoying symptoms could lead to a more serious inner ear infection and even long-term damage to the ear.*

***Tips to Prevent Swimmer's Ear***

- *After swimming, get the water out of your ears. Tilt your head and jump energetically several times, or use a towel to gently wipe the outer ear. Do not rub. You can also use a hair dryer on a low setting. Gently pull down your ear lobe and blow warm air into the ear from several inches away.*
- *Over-the-counter eardrops can help dry the ear canal after swimming. Ask your doctor to recommend a brand.*
- *Wear a swim cap or wet suit hood, especially for surfing or sailboarding. This can help slow or prevent the formation of bony growths in the ear's canal, which are thought to be caused by prolonged exposure to wind and cold water. These protrusions cause the ear canal's outer surface to become thin and inflamed. A properly fitted cap or hood keeps the ears warm and protects them from the wind.*
- *Do not use wax-type ear plugs. They may damage the ear-canal and make infection more likely. Silicone earplugs give better protection.*
- *Ask your doctor how to flush out your ears using warm water and an ear syringe.*
- *Do not scratch, touch, or put anything into your ears, since this may bring bacteria into the ear canal.*

## Swimming Fully Clothed

Aquatic emergencies can develop in situations where you did not intend to go into the water in the first place. The following information will help you prepare for those times when you might fall into the water fully clothed.

There are some advantages to keeping your clothes on if you fall into the water. Many types of clothing will actually help you float and will help protect you from cold water. If your shoes are light enough for you to swim comfortably, leave them on. If they're too heavy, remove them.

Use a swimming stroke that keeps the arms in the water, such as the breaststroke, sidestroke, or elementary backstroke. (For descriptions of strokes, see Chapter 6.) Whichever stroke you choose, swim in a way that is most comfortable for you. You do not have to swim a stroke perfectly for it to sustain you in the water.

Treading water will keep you in an upright position while you signal for help or wait for rescue. (For this skill, see Chapter 5.) You may need to tread water while you prepare to use your clothing for flotation.

Bobbing and floating are other safety techniques you can use if you accidentally fall into the water. (For these skills, see Chapter 5.) Even nonswimmers can quickly learn to bob in shallow water. When you practice, make sure you have a companion present who can help you if you have difficulty. However, if you end up in cool or cold water in an emergency, use bobbing only as a last resort to save yourself.

### *Using Your Shirt or Jacket for Flotation*

With air trapped in the shoulders of your shirt or jacket, you may be able to paddle toward safety. If you need one hand to hold your shirt or jacket closed, paddle with the other. There are two ways to use your shirt or jacket for flotation:

1. Tuck your shirt in or tie the shirttail ends together. Fasten the top button of the shirt up to the neck. Unbutton the second or third button, take a deep breath, bend your head forward, pull the shirt up to your face, and blow into the shirt (Fig. 2-3). The front of the shirt must be under water. The air will rise and form a bubble in the shoulders of the shirt, which will help you float.

2. Inflate your shirt or jacket by splashing air into it (Fig. 2-4). Float on your back and hold the front of the shirttail or jacket with one hand, keeping it just under the surface of the water. Strike the water with your free hand palm down from above the surface of the water to a point below the shirttail or jacket. The air, carried down from the surface, will bubble into the shirt or jacket.

Fig. 2-3

Fig. 2-4

## Safety at Residential Pools

Most swimming deaths occur in home pools. As more people have above-ground or in-ground pools, more small children have become drowning victims. To prevent drowning, constant supervision and physical barriers are best. In most drownings, the child was left alone for a moment or was thought to be in a safe area. A self-locking gate and a fence completely around the pool give the most security. The gate should have a latch at least 54 inches high to keep a small child from opening it. Often pool fencing uses the home as a part of the barrier, but this does not keep out a child who wanders out through an unlocked door or even crawls out through a pet door (Fig. 2-5). Many states have pool fence laws. Consult local agencies about regulations for your pool.

If you own a pool—

- Take a water safety course to learn more about pool safety and how to prevent swimming pool accidents.
- Find out about your state and community laws and regulations for residential pools.
- Never let anyone swim alone in your pool.
- Use buoyed lines to show where the depth changes from shallow to deep. Post depth markers.
- Set up a safety post with ring buoys or other safety equipment.
- Post the rules for your pool and enforce them without exception. For example, do not allow bottles or glass around the pool, do not allow running or pushing, and do not allow diving unless your pool meets the safety standards given in Chapter 3.
- Have a telephone near the pool with the emergency number posted. Also post your address and the nearest cross streets so that anyone can read them to an emergency dispatcher.
- Properly fence and secure the area to prevent people from entering without your knowledge and to keep out children, who may be drawn to the water.
- Store pool chemicals—chlorine, soda ash, muriatic acid, test kits—in childproof containers and out of children's reach. Clearly label the chemicals. Follow manufacturer's directions and safety instructions.
- Make sure all members of your family know how to swim.
- Put a cover on the pool when the family is away from home.
- Make sure neighbors and their children know when the pool is off limits.
- Make sure your homeowner's insurance policy covers the pool.

Two American Red Cross videos, *Home Pool Safety: It Only Takes a Minute* and *Water, The Deceptive Power*, may be available at your local Red Cross unit to help reinforce these safety principles. Public swimming facilities have the same potential hazards as home pools, but the consequences may be even greater because public pools are larger and there are more users.

Fig. 2-5

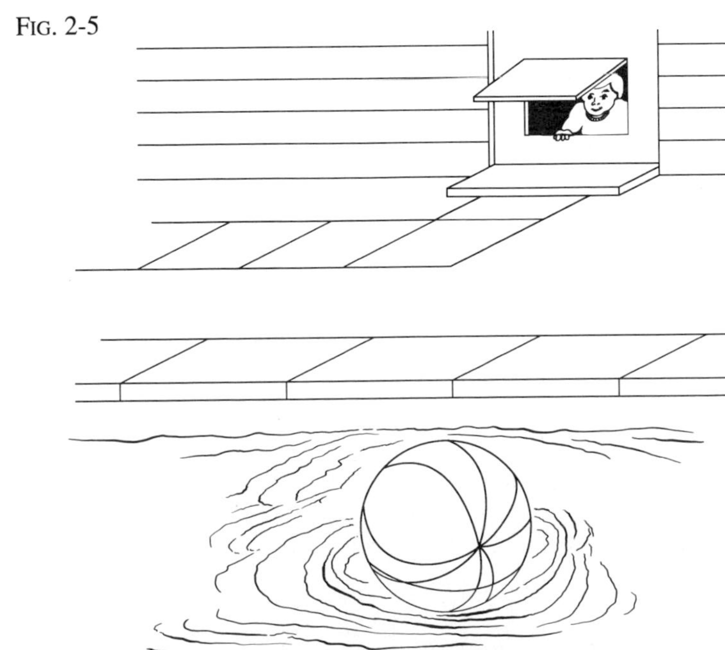

## Hazards in Open Water

Open-water areas usually have limited visibility in the water and may be more hazardous than pools. Even when a lifeguard is present, you must be more careful when swimming in open water. In an ocean, river, lake, or other open water, you may encounter potentially dangerous conditions that may differ from those you have seen in other waters. They may also change from hour to hour in some waters. Before swimming in a new area, check it out carefully and consider the hazards described in the next sections.

### Waves

Any open-water area may have dangerous waves (Fig. 2-6). The water surface also may change quickly with the weather. A sudden wave may carry or push a nonswimmer into deep water. Any swimmer can be knocked over by a wave breaking close to shore. A breaker may roll you under the surface or slam you into the sand. Children playing at the water's edge can be knocked down and pulled into the water by a sudden, large breaking wave.

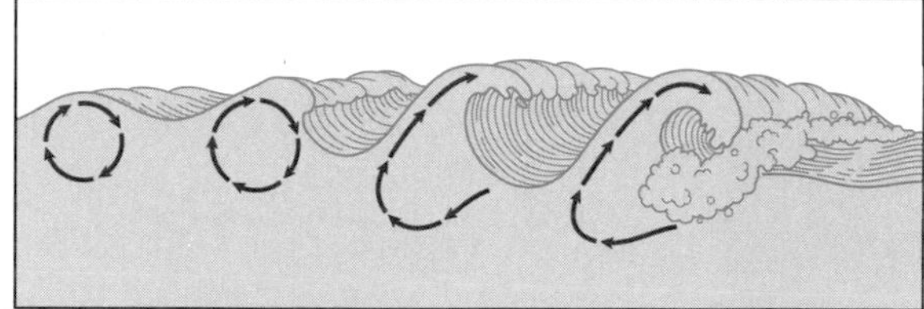

Fig. 2-6 Wave action.

### Currents

#### *Ocean Currents*

Guarded ocean beaches often use flags to alert you to water conditions. A green flag means the water is safe, a yellow flag means to be cautious when swimming because of currents or other conditions, and a red flag means the area is closed because conditions are unsafe. You should not swim at unguarded beaches because of the potential dangers.

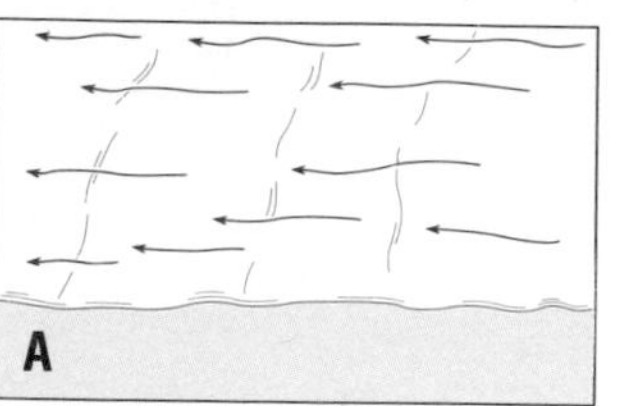


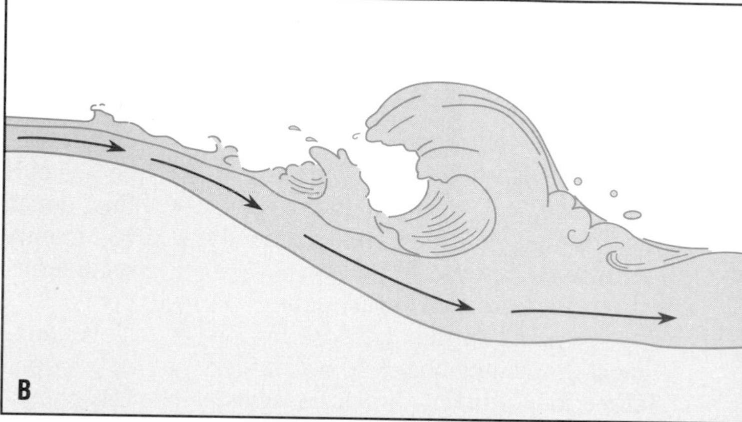


Fig. 2-7 *A,* Drift or side current. *B,* Undertow.

If you swim in the ocean, you should know the three types of currents that present danger. ***Drift or side currents*** move parallel to the shore (Fig. 2-7, *A*). ***Undertows*** move down the slope of the beach, straight out, and under incoming waves (Fig. 2-7, *B*). Undertows are common. Drift currents and undertows can be dangerous if you are not careful. An unexpectedly strong undertow can pull your feet out from under you, causing you to fall. They are especially hazardous to small children, who can easily fall into the water. Drift currents can move you rapidly away from the spot where you entered the water.

***Rip currents*** move straight out to sea beyond the breaking waves. They often occur if a sandbar has formed offshore. A band of water a few feet wide may rush back from the beach through a gap in the sandbar made by breaking waves. You can sometimes spot a rip current because of the narrow strip of choppy,

turbulent water that moves differently from the water on either side of it. A rip current can take you in over your head or move you a frightening distance from the beach.

Do not stand in breaking waves if the undertow is strong enough to knock you down. If a current carries you parallel to shore, try to swim toward shore while moving along with the current. If you are being carried away from shore, swim out of the current, not against it, by moving parallel to the shore. Once you are free, turn and swim toward shore (Fig. 2-8).

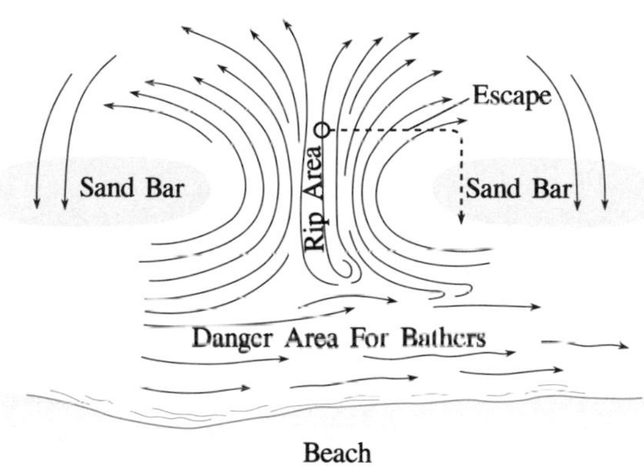


FIG. 2-8 Rip current and escape.

### River Currents

River currents are often unpredictable and fast moving. They may change direction abruptly because of bottom changes. You might not see the current on the water surface even though it may be strong below the surface. A current can slam you into an unseen object, such as a rock. If you are being carried by a river current, roll over onto your back and go downstream feetfirst (Fig. 2-9). This way, you can avoid crashing headfirst into a rock or other obstacle. When you are out of the strongest part of the current, swim straight toward shore. Because of the current you will actually move downstream at an angle toward the shore (Fig. 2-10).

FIG. 2-9 Travel downstream feetfirst in a river current.

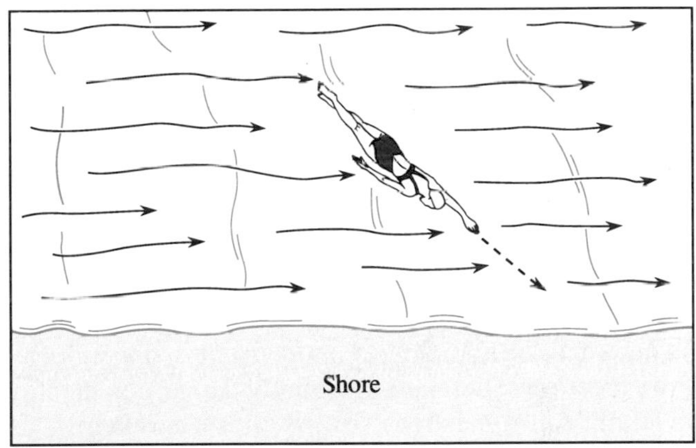


FIG. 2-10 Angle toward shore when in a current.

### HYDRAULICS

***Hydraulics*** are whirlpools that happen as water flows over an object causing a strong downward force that may trap a swimmer (Fig. 2-11). The water surface may look calm and fool you because the hydraulic does not show from the surface. To avoid this hazard, do not swim near areas where the water drops off. If you are caught in a hydraulic, instead of fighting it you should swim to the bottom and swim out with the current and then reach the surface.

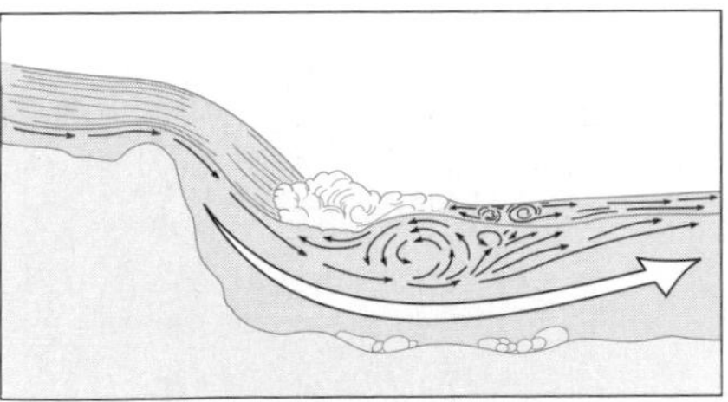

FIG. 2-11 Hydraulic current.

## Underwater Obstacles

There may be underwater obstacles like rocks, stumps, and remains of old structures in any open water. Even in some ocean waters there may be large unseen obstacles. With wind, currents, and heavy rains, some obstacles on the bottom may move or change shape. You can be seriously injured if you jump, slide, or dive into water and hit any object. Always enter open water slowly, carefully, and feetfirst.

## Dams

Dams are common on rivers or in large lakes or ponds. When the floodgates open, the water level can rise quickly below the dam, making a wall of water. If the dam is part of a hydroelectric power plant, the current made when the gates are open can pull swimmers and even boaters above the dam into danger. Therefore, always avoid both swimming and boating above or below a dam.

## Aquatic Life

There may be aquatic life in open water, depending on the location. There are potentially dangerous plants and animals in some areas. Weeds, grass, and kelp often grow thickly in open water and can entangle a swimmer. If you find yourself becoming caught, avoid frantic movements that may only entangle you more. Try to swim slowly and gently out of the plants, preferably along with a current. If you see or feel a patch of plants on the surface, avoid the area.

Aquatic animals seldom pose a danger to swimmers. In the ocean, however, you may be stung by a Portuguese man-of-war (Fig. 2-12, *A*), jellyfish (Fig. 2-12, *B*), or other aquatic life with less severe stings. A sting can be very painful and may cause illness or even death if the affected area is large. You may not see the tentacles of stinging jellyfish below the surface, and they may extend far from what you see on the surface. Even stepping on a dead jellyfish or Portuguese man-of-war can cause a sting. The stinging cells may be active hours after the creature dies.

Dave Fleeman/TOM STACK & ASSOCIATES

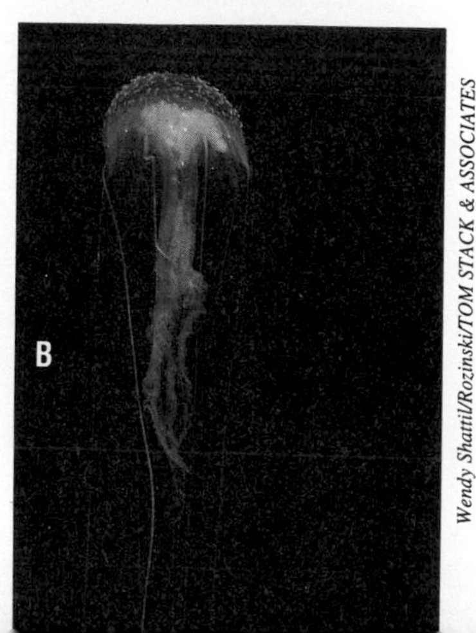

Wendy Shattil/Rozinski/TOM STACK & ASSOCIATES

Fig. 2-12 *A,* Portuguese man-of-war. *B,* Jellyfish.

A Sting can be treated by a simple method. First rinse the skin with sea water—not fresh water. Do not use ice and do not rub the skin. Soothe the skin by soaking it in vinegar or isopropyl alcohol. If these are not available, use a baking soda paste. Call for emergenc medical help if the victim—

- Does not know what caused the sting.
- Has ever had an allergic reaction to a sting from marine life.
- Is stung on the face or the neck.
- Develops any problem that seems serious, such as difficulty breathing.

In some ocean areas, there are sea urchins with spines that can break off in the foot and cause a painful wound. Another danger comes from coral that sting. Stingrays and other marine animals have stings that may be dangerous. Before going into any ocean, find out what local marine life may be dangerous, how to avoid it, and how to care for any injuries.

If you swim in fresh water, you might encounter snakes or leeches. Snakes rarely pose a threat. Leave them alone and swim slowly away. You will usually not see a leech but may come out of the water and find one on your skin. They can be pulled off and are not harmful.

## Bad Weather Conditions

Whether you are in a pool or in open water, your common sense tells you not to swim in storms, fog, or high winds. You should also not swim if bad weather is expected. Leave the water when rain starts or at the first sound of thunder or sight of lightning. Since water conducts electricity, being in the water during an electrical storm is dangerous. Get to an enclosed area if you can. Do not stay in an open area, under a tree, or near anything metal.

Do not swim after a storm if the water seems to be rising or there is flooding, because currents may become very strong. The clarity and depth of the water may change, and new unseen obstacles may become hazards.

Always try to stay aware of bad weather that may be coming. Television and radio stations broadcast weather reports all day. CB radios and scanners also can keep you informed. Many areas have 24-hour telephone service for weather reports. Watch the sky. Rolling, dark clouds or large clouds with cauliflower-like tops announce a storm.

## Water Emergencies

### Panic

Panic is a sudden and overwhelming terror. It occurs in most water accidents and can keep you from helping yourself or someone else. Many hazards, such as getting caught in weeds or suffering cramps, can cause the added danger of panic.

Even a skilled, experienced swimmer can panic. The more skilled you are and the more you know about water safety, however, the less likely you are to panic or react helplessly. Having a personal emergency plan is the best way to prevent panic and accidents.

Often a dangerous situation requires you to act quickly, but if you act too quickly and rashly, you could make the emergency worse. If you are suddenly in an emergency, remember that you may have more time than you think to plan what to do. For example, if you see someone struggling in the water, your first impulse may be to leap into the water to save that person. It is much better, however, to think for a moment and not put yourself in danger too. Instead, look around for a way to extend your reach to the victim to safely rescue him or her. (See Chapter 13 for more information.)

### Cramps

Cramps are common when a swimmer becomes tired or cold. A cramp is an involuntary muscle contraction, usually in the arm, foot, or calf. If you have a cramp, try to relax the muscle and change your swimming stroke. Changing the position of the muscle and massaging it often relieves the cramp. In deep water, you can release a leg cramp by taking a deep breath, rolling face down, extending your leg, flexing your foot, and massaging the cramp (Fig. 2-13).

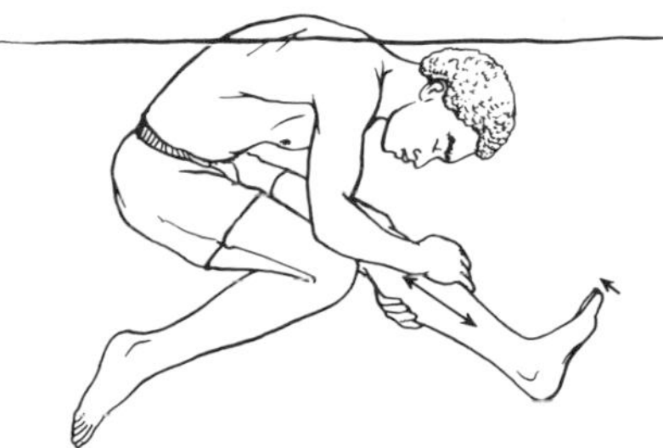

Fig. 2-13 Leg cramp release.

Abdominal cramps, although rare, can happen when you are tired and cold. They are *not* caused by swimming too soon after eating. If you have a mild cramp, try to relax and maintain your position in the water until the cramp passes. Someone with severe stomach cramps must be helped to safety as quickly as possible.

### Exhaustion

Exhaustion simply means that you no longer have the energy to keep swimming or floating. Exhaustion can occur—

- In reaction to cold water.
- From lying in the sun too long.
- From swimming when you're very tired.
- From swimming too long and too hard.

Fatigue early in the swimming season can be a serious problem. Exhaustion is more likely for younger swimmers who swim too much before they're really in shape.

Prevent exhaustion by resting often while you're swimming or doing other activities. Watch others in your swimming party for any sign of a chill—shivering, cold and clammy skin, or a bluish tinge to the lips. Especially look out for younger swimmers, who may become chilled or exhausted before they realize they're in danger.

### Hyperventilation

***Hyperventilation*** is a dangerous technique some swimmers use to try to stay under water longer. By taking a series of deep breaths and forcefully exhaling, you reduce the carbon dioxide in the blood. This delays the time when the carbon dioxide level triggers the demand for the body to take a breath. The practice is risky because the level of carbon dioxide in your blood is what signals your body to take each breath. If you hyperventilate and then swim under water, you could pass out before your body knows it is time to breathe. By the time your companions notice you've been under too long, it could be too late. If you enjoy underwater swimming, work on your skills with a certified Red Cross instructor. *Don't hyperventilate!*

### Submerged Vehicle

In most cases when vehicles plunge into the water, the occupants try frantically to open the doors but can't because of the external water pressure. They begin to panic and are unable to help themselves.

You can help yourself in this kind of emergency if you remain calm and remember the following guidelines:

- Wearing a vehicle safety belt will reduce your chances of being injured when the vehicle hits the water.
- Tests indicate that even a heavy vehicle, such as a station wagon, will float for about 45 seconds after entering the water. During this time, you should try to open the nearest window and immediately leave the car through that window.
- When your vehicle begins to sink, move to the higher end to breathe the trapped air.
- Use one of three routes to escape:
  —Open a window.
  —Open an undamaged door when the water pressure is equal inside and out (when the car is nearly full of water).
  —Break or push out a window. Vehicle windows are usually made of tempered glass.

If you witness a vehicle plunging into the water, get professional rescue assistance. Activate the EMS system. (See Appendix E.)

## Safety Around Cold Water

### Exposure to Cold Water

Falling off a dock, breaking through ice on a lake, being thrown into the water as your boat swerves—these accidents can suddenly put you in cold water. Exposure to cold water leads to the danger of immersion hypothermia (Fig. 2-14).

Fig. 2-14

***Hypothermia*** is a life-threatening condition in which the body's warming mechanisms cannot maintain normal body temperature and the body cools. Hypothermia occurs when cold or cool temperatures cause the body to lose heat faster than it can produce it.

Cold water is defined as being 70 degrees F (21 degrees C) or colder, but hypothermia can occur even in water near 80 degrees F (27 degrees C). As a general rule, if the water feels cold, it is cold.

Here's what happens when you fall into cold water:

- The temperature of your skin and of the blood in your arms and legs drops quickly.
- At first you may have trouble breathing and you may slowly become unable to use your hands.
- The temperature of your heart, brain, and other vital organs gradually drops.
- You start shivering.
- You may become unconscious. If your temperature drops more, you can die of heart failure.

### *Preventing Hypothermia*

Protect yourself from hypothermia in the following ways:

- When you're near cold water—playing, working, hunting, fishing—remember that cold water is dangerous even if you don't intend to go in.
- Join in water activities only when and where you can get help quickly in an emergency.
- Wear a Coast Guard–approved life jacket while boating. Have life jackets at hand whenever you're near cold water.
- If you will be near water in cooler weather, wear rain gear or wool clothes. Wool insulates you even when it is wet.
- Wear layers of clothes.
- Carry matches in a waterproof container. You may need to build a fire to warm up after a fall into cold water.
- Don't drink alcohol for the sensation of warmth. Alcohol actually increases loss of body heat.

### *Benefits of Winter Clothes*

People who fall into the water wearing winter clothes, especially heavy boots or waders, usually panic because they think they'll sink immediately. But winter clothes can actually help you float. Heavy clothes also help delay hypothermia. Tight-fitting foam vests and flotation jackets with foam insulation can double your survival time.

If you fall into the water wearing a snowmobile suit or other heavy winter clothes, air will be trapped in the clothes and help you float. Simply lie back, spread your arms and legs, and perform a "winging" motion with your arms to move toward safety (Fig. 2-15).

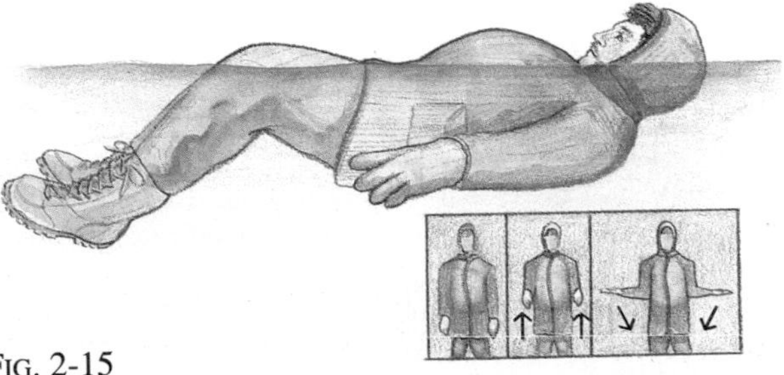

Fig. 2-15

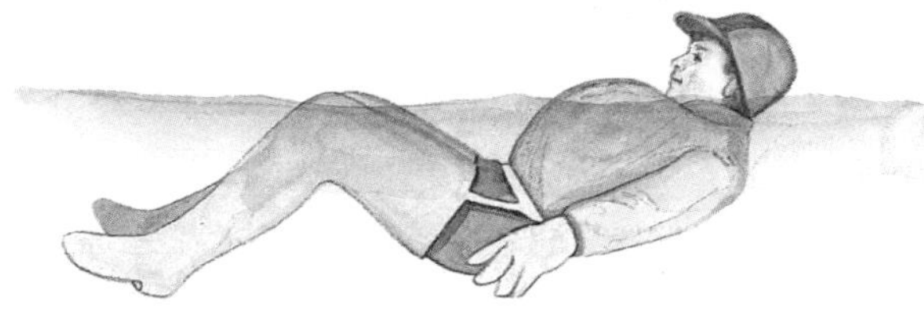

Fig. 2-16

Hip boots, waders, and rubber boots often trap air if you fall into water. Relax and bend your knees and let the trapped air in your boots bring you to the surface very quickly (Fig. 2-16).

While on your back, you can float in a tuck position. Bring your knees up to your chest, let your hips drop, and keep your head up and back. Then paddle backward with your hands to safety.

Fig. 2-17

You can also float on your front. Keep your head raised and bend your knees. Paddle forward with your arms in the water (Fig. 2-17).

#### If You Fall Into Cold Water With a Life Jacket

Even if the air is warm, wear a life jacket when you are near cold water, even if you are a good swimmer. If you fall into cold water wearing a life jacket—

- Keep your face and head above the surface. If you were in a boating accident, try to climb up onto the capsized boat to get more of your body out of the water.
- Keep all your clothes on, even your hat. Even wet clothes help you retain body heat.
- Swim to safety if a current is carrying you toward some danger. Unless you must swim away immediately, float on your back and go downstream feetfirst until you slow your breathing. Breathe normally for a few seconds before you start swimming to shore.
- If you are not in immediate danger but are far from shore, stay still and let your life jacket support you until help arrives.

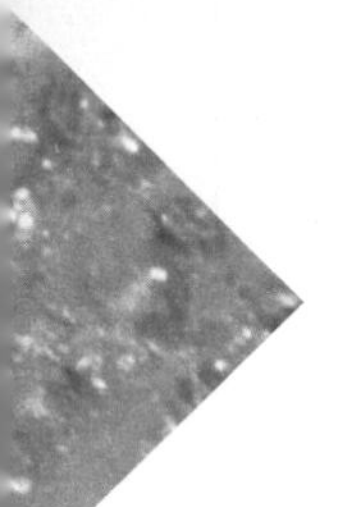

In cold water, you must decide whether to try to reach safety or float and wait for help. Remember that you can't swim as far in cold water as in warm water. Use only strokes with underwater arm recovery. If you can get to safety with a few strokes, do so. If not, float quietly and wait for rescue.

Treading water chills the body faster than staying still with a life jacket in the water. In cold water, tread water only if you cannot stay afloat any other way.

### If You're Waiting to Be Rescued

There are two positions for being in cold water in a life jacket. Because both of these positions are hard to maintain, you may want to practice them in warm shallow water. Practice only when supervised by someone with the water safety skills to help you if you have trouble.

Fig. 2-18 H.E.L.P. position.

#### *H.E.L.P. (Heat Escape Lessening Posture)*

In this position, draw your knees up to your chest, keep your face forward and out of the water, hold your upper arms at your sides, and fold your lower arms against or across your chest (Fig. 2-18). Do not use the H.E.L.P. position in swift river currents or white water.

#### *Huddle*

This position is for two or more persons. Put your arms over one another's shoulders so the sides of your chests are together. Sandwich a child between adults (Fig. 2-19).

Fig. 2-19 Huddle position.

### If You Fall Into Cold Water Without a Life Jacket

- Look around for a log or anything floating to support you. If you were in a boating accident, try to hold onto the capsized boat.
- Raise as much of your body as you can out of the water. Keep your face and head above the water. Turn your back to waves to help keep water out of your face.
- Keep all of your clothes on, even your hat. Even wet clothes help retain body heat.
- Don't splash around trying to warm up. The heat this movement creates will not stay with you. Splashing increases blood circulation in your arms and legs and may drain your last energy.
- Swim only if you are close enough to reach shore safely. How far you can swim depends on your swimming skill, the amount of insulation you're wearing, and water conditions. Remember, you can't swim as far in cold water as in warm water. Be careful not to underestimate the distance to shore. In emergencies it is hard to judge distance. When the water is 50 degrees F (10 degrees C) or colder, even a good swimmer may have difficulty reaching shore.

### Helping Yourself Once You're Ashore

You may still be at risk for hypothermia even after reaching safety. Follow these guidelines:

- Your clothes will be heavy with water. Stand still to let some of the water drain away before you try to move.

- Change into dry clothes right away if you can. If not, take off the wet clothes and wring them out. Put them back on, unless the air is unusually warm. Even damp clothes will help keep you warm, especially if they're wool.
- Get inside a building.
- If you can, get into a warm room, take a warm shower or bath, or start a fire to get warm quickly.
- As soon as you can, drink warm fluids such as hot broth or soup. Avoid caffeine or alcohol.
- When you've warmed up, start walking to safety if you know where you are and where you can get help. If you don't know which way to go, stay by the fire and wait for rescue. Its smoke will help rescuers find you.
- If you cannot build a fire and you don't know which way to go, stay out of the wind and cold as much as you can while you wait for help.

## Ice Safety

Outdoor ice sports and activities can be safe and enjoyable (Fig. 2-20). But first learn about ice and what precautions to take to protect yourself.

Fig. 2-20 Ice fishing.

Earth Scenes/Michael Gadomski

Ice over open water may be unsafe if any of the following are present:

- Springs or fast-moving water
- Wind and wave action
- Waterfowl and schooling fish
- Decomposing material in the water
- Water bubblers (devices designed to keep the water near boat docks from freezing thick)
- Discharge from an industrial site
- Objects protruding through the ice, such as tree stumps

### Preventing Ice Accidents

Follow these guidelines to avoid accidents when you are on or near ice:

- Check the ice thickness before you go out. To be safe, ice should be solid and at least 4 inches thick. Remember, the ice may not be the same thickness over the entire area of a lake or pond.
- Solid, 4-inch-thick ice is generally safe to walk on, but not thick enough to drive a vehicle on.
- To be safe, the ice should be thicker as more people are on it.
- Ice on smaller, shallower, and slower-moving bodies of water is more solid. Use these for ice activities.
- Look for objects sticking up through the ice and mark them as hazards.
- Don't go out on ice that has recently frozen, thawed, and then frozen again. This happens in the spring and early winter as temperatures change often. Wait until the outside temperature has been below freezing long enough that at least 4 inches of solid ice forms over the entire area.
- Always stay with at least one other person. (Remember, more people require thicker ice for safety.)
- Tell someone where you will be and when you intend to return.
- Wear warm clothes. Wool is best for holding warm air next to your body and for insulation, even when wet.
- Have something at hand to throw or extend to a person who needs help—a life jacket, a rope with a weighted end, a long tree branch, a wooden pole, a plastic jug with a line attached. (See Chapter 13 for more information on rescues.)
- Carry matches in a waterproof container. You may need to build a fire to warm up after a fall into cold water.

FIG. 2-21

### IF YOU FALL THROUGH THE ICE

- Resist the urge to try to climb out onto the ice. It is likely to be weak in the area where you fell in.
- Quickly get into a floating position on your stomach. Bend your knees to help trap air in your pant legs and boots.
- Reach forward onto the broken ice, but do not push down on it. Use a breaststroke or other kick to push yourself farther onto the ice.
- Don't stand up once you are on the ice. Crawl or roll away from the break area, with your arms and legs spread out as far as possible.
- Have your companion throw or extend something to you if needed. Remember not to stand on the ice.

Once safely out of the water, follow the guidelines for "Exposure to Cold Water" on page 38.

## BOATING SAFETY

Boats 16 feet or shorter are called small craft. Although they can be very enjoyable for recreation, small craft are more likely than large ones to be involved in accidents. The U.S. Coast Guard reports that U.S. waterways are second only to highways in transportation death rates.

Anyone going boating should know how to operate a boat safely and how to swim. No matter how well they swim, all passengers on small craft should wear a Coast Guard–approved life jacket at all times.

Take lessons in boat handling so you understand—

- Differences between types of craft.
- Effects of wind, water conditions, and weather.
- How to use boating equipment.
- Navigation rules and safe boat handling.
- Boat maintenance.
- Emergency procedures.

To find a boating course in your area, check with your local American Red Cross, the U.S. Power Squadron, the U.S. Coast Guard Auxiliary, United States Sailing, the American Canoe Association, or area marinas and recreational facilities. (See Appendix A for addresses.)

### DRINKING AND BOATING DON'T MIX

The U.S. Coast Guard says that more than 50 percent of the drownings from boat accidents involve alcohol. Even a little alcohol can be very dangerous (Fig. 2-21). Alcohol is dangerous in these ways:

- Alcohol affects your balance and makes you more likely to tumble off the boat.
- Alcohol makes it harder to stay warm—even though you might feel warm after your first drink.
- Alcohol affects your judgment.
- Alcohol slows down your movements and impairs your vision.
- Alcohol can reduce your swimming skills, even if you're an excellent swimmer.

Don't endanger yourself, your family, and friends. Stay sober and free of drugs while you're boating. Don't be embarrassed to refuse a boat ride from someone who has been drinking or using drugs. Don't let social pressure lead you to a possibly fatal mistake!

### CHOOSING A PLACE FOR BOATING

- Use a small boat well away from swimming areas.
- Choose docking facilities with separate areas for small boats, for safer maneuvering.
- Stay at least 100 feet from diving flags, which mean that divers are under water.
- Before you go boating, check the weather report from the local newspaper, radio, or television, or telephone the U.S. Coast Guard.
- Obey storm or gale warnings, small craft advisories, and warning flags (Fig. 2-22). Such warnings are given to alert boaters to hazardous weather and water conditions.

FIG. 2-22 Weather warning flags.

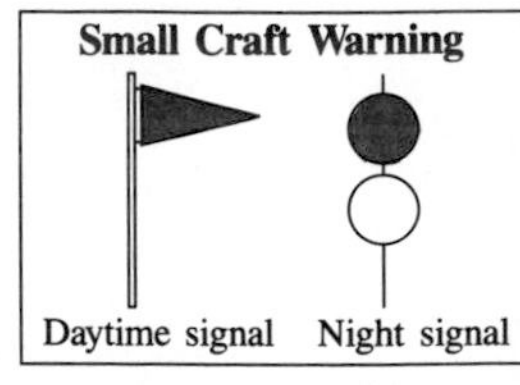


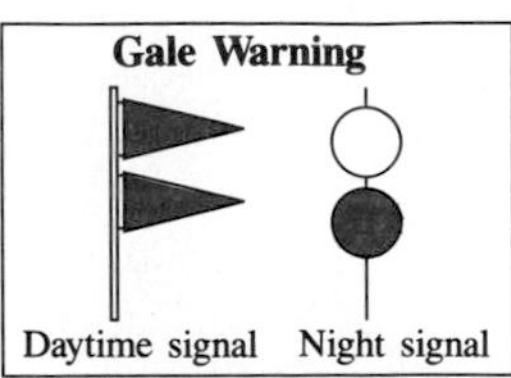


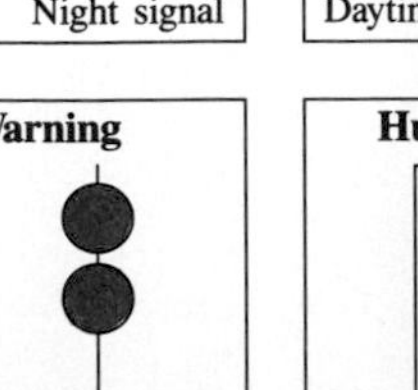


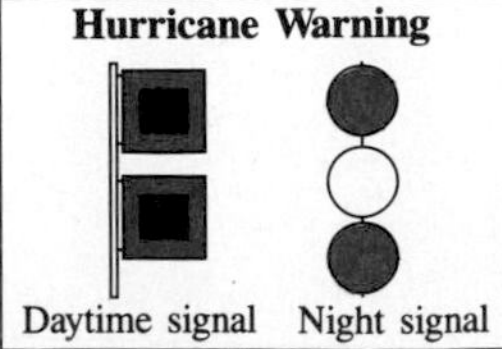

EQUIPPING YOUR BOAT

Check federal and state rules for equipment required for the type of boat you'll be using. The nearest U.S. Coast Guard station, Coast Guard Auxiliary, or U.S. Power Squadron can give you information.

For safety you should equip your boat fully, not only as required. Ideally, have the equipment listed below.

- Coast Guard–approved life jacket for each person aboard, in good condition. Nonswimmers *must wear* life jackets at all times.
- Sound-signaling device—whistle, horn, or bell.
- Visual distress signaling devices—flares or flags for daytime, flares or electrical lights for nighttime. Check the U.S. Coast Guard requirements and recommendations.
- Extra oars or paddle to maneuver the boat or to reach to a victim in the water.
- Fire extinguisher.
- Running lights.
- Anchor.
- Extra line.
- Throw bag.
- First aid kit.
- Bailing device.
- Flashlight.
- Tool kit and spare parts for the boat.
- Charts.
- Compass.
- Radio for listening to weather reports.
- Extra throwable safety equipment.

Check your equipment often for wear or damage. Store each piece of equipment in a well-ventilated place after each use.

The U.S. Coast Guard requires only that each boat carry one life jacket for each person on board. For safety, however, every passenger should wear the life jacket at all times.

The Coast Guard approves different types of life jackets for use on recreational boats. (See page 29 for more information.) Regardless of the type you choose—

- Make sure it's the proper size.
- Practice putting it on in shallow water and swimming with it; always practice with a companion.
- Wear it at all times while boating. In an emergency, you won't have to worry about putting it on and you may not have the time.

NAVIGATION RULES

Boat operators must learn and obey navigation rules, also known as "rules of the road." These rules help keep boating safe and enjoyable. Navigation rules are made by a committee appointed by the U.S. Congress and are enforced by the U.S. Coast Guard. Your nearest Coast Guard station can give you complete information. Courses offered by the U.S. Power Squadron, the U.S. Coast Guard Auxiliary, and United States Sailing include information and training for navigation rules.

### *Right-of-Way*

Boats with motors must give the right-of-way to boats under sail or being rowed or paddled, except when a sailboat overtakes a motorboat. Even when you have the right-of-way, you should still operate your boat carefully and responsibly. Always signal other boats what you're going to do, following the navigation rules.

### *Meeting*

When you approach another boat head-on or nearly so, keep to your right, just as in an automobile (Fig. 2-23, *A*).

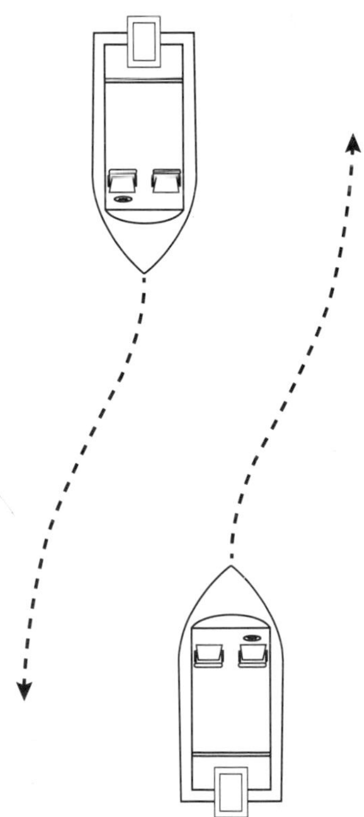

FIG. 2-23, *A*

FIG. 2-23, *B*

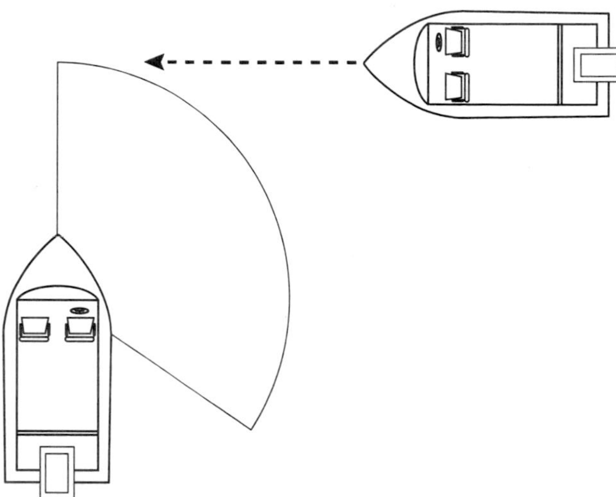

### *Crossing*

When two boats are crossing paths, the boat on the right has the right-of-way. The boat on the left must slow down, change course, or pass behind the other boat. The boat on the left must prepare to stop or reverse course to avoid a collision (Fig. 2-23, *B*).

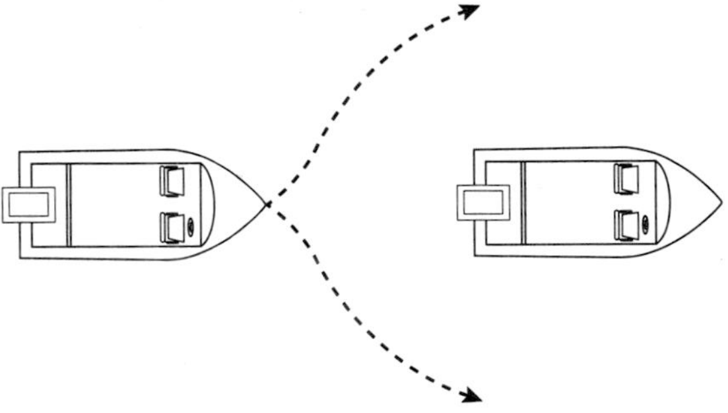

FIG. 2-23, *C*

### *Passing*

When one boat is overtaking another, the one being passed has the right-of-way. The boat that is passing may pass on either side after giving the proper signal, such as one horn blast to signal passing on the right, two blasts to pass on the left. The passing boat must keep clear of the boat being passed (Fig. 2-23, *C*).

### *Exiting and Entering the Marina*

Follow the rules governing right-of-way. Always go slow and stay under the posted speed limit, making a small wake, when you're near docks, piers, or congested boat ramp areas. Watch out for swimmers, other boats, and objects in the water.

## MOVING IN AND ONTO A BOAT

### *Keeping Your Boat Balanced*

Don't carry more people than recommended for your boat. Check the U.S. Coast Guard capacity information on your boat (Fig. 2-24). Trim the boat—that is, balance the weight from side to side (Fig. 2-25, *A* and *B*) and from front to back (Fig. 2-25, *C* and *D*).

FIG. 2-25, *A-D* Side-to-side trim: *A,* Incorrect. *B,* Correct. Front-to-back trim: *C,* Incorrect. *D,* Correct.

FIG. 2-24

C
Johnson 25
Cub Craft
548-R

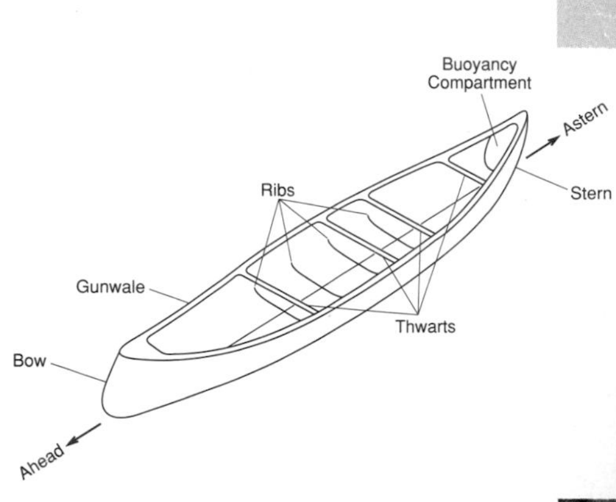


FIG. 2-26

### *Boarding a Boat and Disembarking*

Make sure all passengers know how to board (get on) and disembark (get off) the boat safely.

- Know the parts of a boat or canoe (Fig. 2-26).
- Wear nonskid deck shoes.
- Watch for waves or boat wakes that may throw you off balance.
- Alert those already on board that you are about to board or disembark.
- Have another person hold and help stabilize the boat while you board or disembark.
- Be careful not to step on equipment.
- Keep your weight low to the bottom of the boat to keep the boat stable.

FIG. 2-27, *A-B*

BOARDING AT A DOCK. Make sure the boat is tied at the front (bow) and the back (stern). The lines should be snug but not so tight that they keep the boat from settling when weight is added.

Step aboard as close to the center of the boat as you can. Reach down and grasp the side (gunwale) of the boat as you shift your weight to the foot in the boat. Then bring the trailing foot aboard. If the dock is much higher than the boat, sit on the dock and then move into the boat (Fig. 2-27, *A*).

BOARDING AT A BEACH OR SHORELINE. Make sure the boat is floating and not partly resting on the bottom. Step over the bow or stern while you grasp the sides with both hands (Fig. 2-27, *B*). Shift your weight to the foot in the boat. Keep your weight low to the bottom of the boat as you bring your trailing foot aboard.

DISEMBARKING. To disembark, reverse the steps used to board. Keeping your weight low, step ashore or onto the dock, carefully shift your weight to the leading foot, and then lift out your trailing foot.

### *Changing Positions*

If passengers have to change positions in a small boat—

- Only one person at a time should move.
- Keep the weight low and as near the center of the boat as possible.
- Keep the boat trimmed by balancing the weight of one passenger against the weight of another.
- In heavy waves, change positions only when needed to correct the balance.

FIG. 2-28, *A-B*

## IF YOUR BOAT CAPSIZES OR SWAMPS

- Stay with the boat. It will probably float and support you. Rescuers can find you more easily.
- Leave the boat only in case of fire or if you are near a waterfall, dam, or other hazard.
- Hold onto the hull (the bottom of the boat) and wait for rescue. Two or more persons should be positioned on both sides of the hull. To rest, you can grasp each other's wrist across the keel (an edge that runs down the middle of the hull from front to back).
- Enter a swamped boat (Fig. 2-28, *A*) and hand-paddle to shore (Fig. 2-28, *B*).

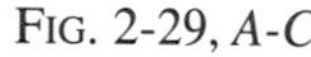

FIG. 2-29, *A-C*

## IF YOU FALL OUT OF A CANOE OR IF THE CANOE SWAMPS

- Stay with the canoe unless you are in fast water and you are sure you can reach shore safely and quickly. It will probably float and support you. Rescuers can find you more easily by spotting the canoe.

- If the canoe is upright and not completely swamped, place your hands at the bottom of the canoe (Fig. 2-29, *A*). Kick vigorously to raise your hips to the gunwale (Fig. 2-29, *B*). Rotate your hips to sit on the bottom of the canoe, and bring your legs into the canoe (Fig. 2-29, *C*). Paddle or hand-paddle to shore.

FIG. 2-30, *A-C*

- If the canoe is completely swamped, lie across the middle of the canoe to keep it from turning side to side (Fig. 2-30, *A*). Once the canoe is stabilized, rotate your body (Fig. 2-30, *B*). Turn to a sitting position and hand-paddle to safety (Fig. 2-30, *C*).

## OTHER ACTIVITIES IN, ON, OR NEAR WATER

### INFANT AND PRESCHOOL SWIMMING

Even though a child may demonstrate some swimming ability, no child should ever be considered totally safe around the water. Children must be carefully supervised by an adult at all times.

Anytime you take a child swimming, remember that infants and young children are very susceptible to hypothermia, even at relatively warm temperatures. Water temperatures should be a minimum of 82 degrees F (28 degrees C). Air temperature should be 3 degrees higher than the water temperature. You should limit the child's swimming time to 30 minutes in the water. If the child shivers or has blue lips or fingernails, take the child out of the water immediately. Remember, watch children in, on, or near the water at all times, and carefully supervise their water play.

### SAILBOARDING

To be safe when sailboarding, wear a Coast Guard–approved life jacket and make sure the water and weather conditions are safe. You need to have good physical strength and swimming ability. You will enjoy sailboarding more and be safer if you take lessons from a qualified teacher. Sailboarding hazards include falling off the board when you are too exhausted to swim back to it, being struck by the board, and colliding with another object. Also, if you do not take lessons, you might move far away from shore and be unable to turn back.

### SNORKELING AND SCUBA DIVING

When snorkeling, the swimmer uses fins for propulsion, a snorkel for breathing, and a mask to observe the underwater world while swimming on the surface. The snorkeler can dive under water by holding the breath and then blowing water out the snorkel upon returning to the surface. Snorkeling is relaxing and requires little equipment. It also promotes cardiovascular fitness and breath control and shows the swimmer the exciting world under water. Snorkelers often go on to take up ***SCUBA*** diving.

FIG. 2-31

Brian Parker/TOM STACK & ASSOCIATES

To snorkel safely, you should first—

- Practice in shallow water.
- Check the equipment carefully and know how it functions.
- Be able to clear water from the snorkel and to put your mask back on when treading water, should it allow water in.
- Be careful not to swim or be carried by a current too far from shore or the boat.

Some 3 to 4 million SCUBA divers enjoy the beauty and excitement of our underwater world (Fig. 2-31). SCUBA divers wear a mask and fins and carry a compressed air supply and regulator for breathing under water for extended periods of time. SCUBA divers must never hold their breath under water. SCUBA divers also use buoyancy compensators, weights, wet suits, and a variety of instruments to monitor depth, time, and direction under water. Divers enjoy a variety of underwater activities like shore diving, boat diving, reef diving, night diving, underwater photography, and underwater archeology.

SCUBA diving is a very safe sport for the certified diver. Recreational SCUBA diving has a good safety record because of the comprehensive training required. Some 40 hours of instruction in the pool and the classroom is required before the student starts supervised training in open water.

A medical examination and a swim test are strongly recommended and often required before learning SCUBA. Most SCUBA accidents can be easily avoided. Hazards include running out of air and diving in rough or dangerous waters or in environments for which the diver has not trained. Ice, cave, and shipwreck diving are very dangerous for novices. One can easily get lost and then run out of air. Panic on the surface or under water can be disastrous for any diver, but poorly trained divers are the most likely to feel panic.

Lung overexpansion, caused by an uncontrolled, rapid ascent to the surface, can result in **arterial gas embolism (AGE)**. Although this is a serious problem, it does not happen to well-trained divers.

Decompression sickness, or **"the bends,"** results from diving too deep and/or too long. It is seldom fatal. One can easily avoid it by using simple no-decompression tables and meters. Equipment failures and dangerous marine life attacks, which may scare the nondiver, are very rare.

### Water Skiing

Boat operators who tow skiers should know the area very well because hidden stumps or other obstacles can cause severe accidents. The skier should wear a Coast Guard–approved life jacket. Someone other than the boat operator must watch the skier at all times to allow the operator to focus on driving. Many areas have specific regulations for skiing you must know and follow. Follow these guidelines for safety:

- Be sure the boat and ski equipment are in good repair.
- Always turn the boat motor completely off when you approach a fallen skier.
- Watch for other boats and skiers in the area and avoid getting too close.

### Surfing

Before trying to surf, take lessons from a qualified instructor. Be sure water and weather conditions are safe. Because surfing moves you through the water very quickly, watch out for your board and other surfers. If a board hits you, you could be injured seriously or knocked unconscious. Wear a Coast Guard–approved life jacket.

### Rafting

When rafting on your own or with a guide, always wear a Coast Guard–approved life jacket. Monitor water and weather conditions for possible problems. Do not overload a raft. Follow the general safety rules applicable to all water activities. When rafting with a tour company, make sure the guides are qualified (Fig. 2-32).

Fig. 2-32

### Fishing and Hunting

When fishing or hunting near water, dress properly for the weather and have some type of reaching device nearby. Watch your footing when you walk next to water. In most drownings, the victim never intended to get in the water. When fishing or hunting from a boat, guard against losing your balance and wear a life jacket. Remember that alcohol is a cause of many hunting and fishing mishaps. Do *not* mix alcohol with any activities near the water.

### Summer Camp

Water activities are a major attraction of many summer camps. Before you enroll a child, check the condition of the waterfront and find out how it is supervised. Look for hazards such as underwater obstacles and unsafe structures. The area should be well marked, and enough certified lifeguards should be on duty at all times. The camp should have a system that ensures supervisors can account for all swimmers at all times. Such systems include roll call, colored swimming caps, and buddy systems. Make sure only qualified staff teach and supervise other water activities such as boating, waterskiing, and SCUBA diving.

*Spencer Swage/TOM STACK & ASSOCIATES*

### Group Trips

Before taking a group to a water recreational facility, plan in advance. Most facilities appreciate knowing when you will be coming, the names of contact persons, and the general age range and size of the group. The facility manager can thus ensure adequate supervision and help make your visit safer and more enjoyable.

Before the trip, talk to the group about what behavior is or is not allowed at the facility. If you are not sure of the swimming abilities of some in your group, you can pretest their skills to be sure they use only the appropriate parts of the facility. If you can, visit the site in advance and look for ways to help the group prepare for the outing. Review the rules and regulations and study a diagram of the facilities. Do not take a group, especially children, to open water unless you are sure there is enough supervision.

### Spas and Hot Tubs

Spas and hot tubs in the home or at a facility are often not guarded. According to the National Spa and Pool Institute (NSPI), the maximum safe water temperature is 104 degrees F (40 degrees C). Soaking too long at too high a temperature can raise your body temperature over safe limits. Limit soaking to 15 minutes. When not in use, a tub should be securely covered to prevent anyone from falling in. People with heart conditions and other medical conditions like diabetes, epilepsy, and high blood pressure should not use a spa or hot tub without their physician's approval. Never use a spa or hot tub when drinking or using drugs. NSPI suggests that pregnant women not use a spa without their doctor's permission. Children under 5 years of age should not go in water above 102 degrees F (39 degrees C). After using a spa, always wait at least 5 minutes before swimming. A sudden change in temperature can cause shock.

## Summary

Swimming and other water activities can be challenging sports or relaxing forms of leisure, but any activity in or near the water can be dangerous. For all water activities, always learn and follow the appropriate safety rules. Water is safe only when you respect its power, regardless of your abilities and the setting.

3

CHAPTER

# diving safety

## Key Terms

**Above-ground pool:** A portable pool that has water 36 to 48 inches deep at the wall. The wall is positioned on the ground and may be disassembled and stored.

**Breakpoint:** The area of the pool where the depth changes from shallow to deep.

**Diving board:** A diving apparatus that consists of a flexible board secured at one end and a fulcrum below the board. Also called a springboard.

**Diving platform:** A stationary structure for diving.

**Diving tower:** A structure used for diving that includes diving platforms at several heights. Towers used for competitive diving often have platforms that are 1 meter, 3 meters, 5 meters, 7½ meters, and 10 meters high.

**Fulcrum:** The part of a diving apparatus under the center of a diving board that lets the board bend and spring.

**Hopper bottom pool:** A pool with a bottom that angles sharply up on all four sides from the deepest point.

**Jumpboard:** A recreational mechanism with a spring beneath the board that is activated by jumping on the board.

**Plummet:** A line from the midpoint at the tip of a diving board to the bottom of the pool.

**Safe diving envelope:** The area of water in front of, below, and to the sides of a diving board that is deep enough that a diver will not strike the bottom, regardless of the depth of the water or the design of the pool.

**Spinal cord:** The bundle of nerves from the brain at the base of the skull to the lower back, inside the spinal column.

**Spoon-shaped pool:** A pool with a bottom that is rounded upward from the deepest point to all the sides.

**Starting blocks:** Raised platforms on the pool deck to add height for competitive swimming starts.

# Objectives

***After reading this chapter, you should be able to—***

1. Describe potentially dangerous areas for diving.
2. Name the most common causes of diving injuries.
3. List safe diving tips for all situations.
4. List safety rules for water slides.

5. Describe potential dangers of diving in open water and ways to avoid them.
6. Define the key terms at left.

# JUMP

AT ANY BUSY POOL ON A HOT SUMMER DAY, you will see a line of people at the ***diving board.*** Many of these children and adults will jump or dive, swim to the side, and do it again and again. Some are mastering their dives; others are just having fun.

THOUSANDS OF PEOPLE ALSO ENJOY RECREATIONAL swimming and diving in open water. Think of the adventurers who dive or jump from heights into lakes and rivers or swing from a rope into the old swimming hole. The thrills of height and the fall appeal to the daredevil in many of us. All too often, however, the thrill-seeker does not think of safety, but when a diving injury happens, it can be very serious. The person who hits his or her head or back against something while diving may suffer permanent catastrophic damage.

DIVING CAN BE AS SAFE AS MOST OTHER ACTIVITIES. Knowing how to recognize a safe place for diving, using good equipment, and applying a heavy dose of common sense are the keys to preventing injury. Equipment standards, pool standards, supervision, and teaching have come a long way since the early 1900s. Before you use a diving board, it is important to have instruction from a competent instructor. All diving should be carefully supervised.

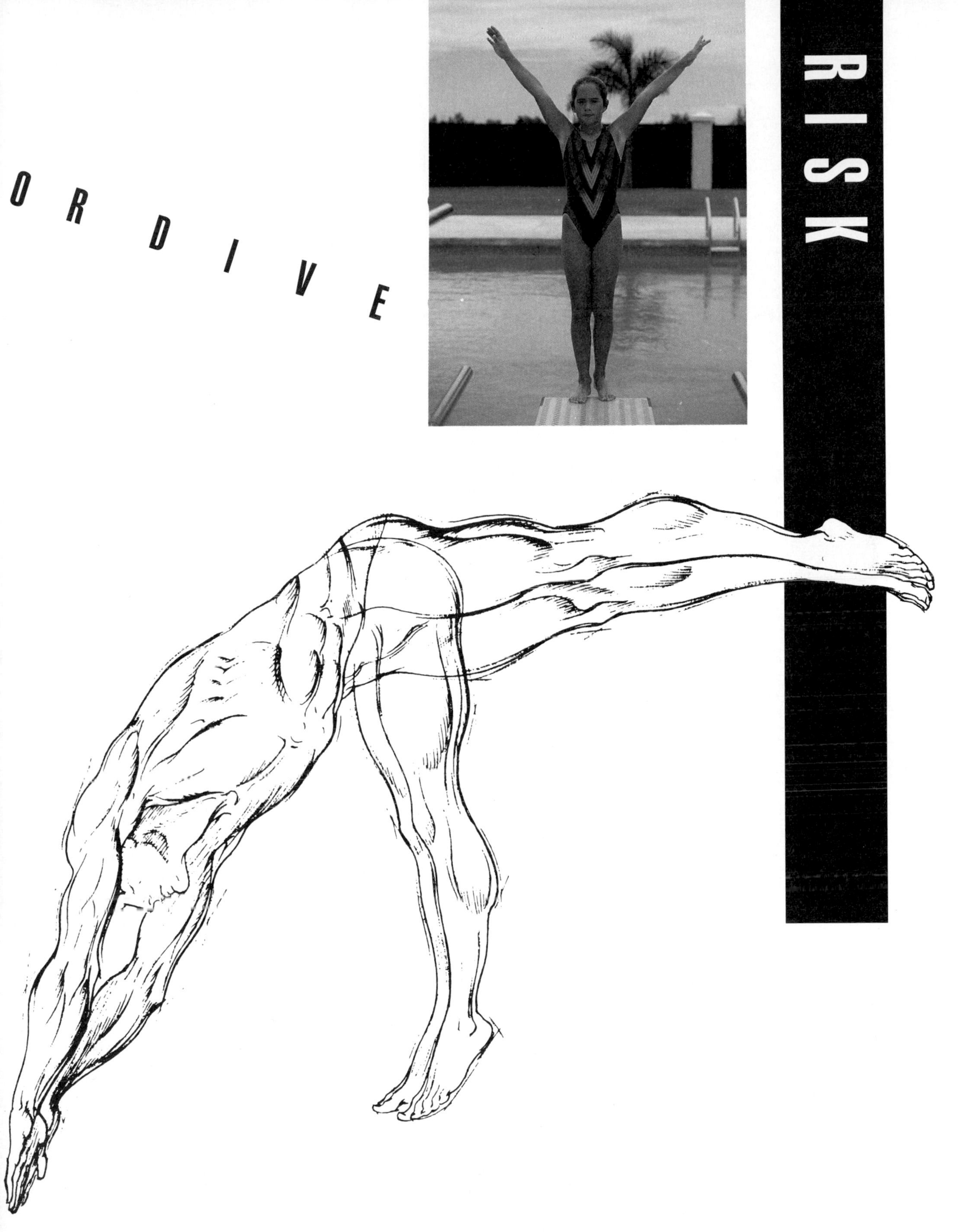
O R D I V E
RISK

## Risks of Diving

**Trauma** is a physical injury caused by a violent action. In 1990, sports injuries made up 13 percent of all ***spinal cord*** traumas.* Of these sports-related injuries, 66 percent were a result of diving into shallow water. Injuries occur from diving into surf, lakes, rivers, quarries, and swimming pools. Of those diving injuries, 95 percent occurred in water 5 feet deep or less. Very rarely does a spinal injury occur from supervised diving or from diving off diving boards into water 9 feet or deeper. Only a small percentage of diving injuries occur when divers are using diving boards. Several studies have revealed a profile of where, how, and to whom diving injuries occur most often.

Even an experienced diver can be seriously injured by diving improperly, diving into water of unknown depth, sliding down a water slide headfirst, falling off a diving board, or diving from ***starting blocks*** without proper training and supervision. You may hit the bottom, an underwater object, or another swimmer. Many diving accidents result in quadriplegia—total paralysis from the neck down.

## Causes of Injuries

Most spinal cord injuries happen in shallow water. Some involve the use of alcohol and/or drugs. Diving into open water that is shallow, diving from the deck into the shallow end of a pool, diving into above-ground pools, and unsupervised diving from starting blocks cause most diving accidents. No swimmer can be completely safe in poorly supervised or improperly maintained swimming areas. Some areas simply are not safe for diving, and the experienced diver recognizes the dangers and does not dive.

A spinal injury can also happen in the deep end of a pool. Injuries have been associated with dives or falls from diving boards, ***jumpboards,*** 3-meter stands, and from the deck into spoon-shaped pools or hopper bottom pools.

**Typical Diving Injuries**

***Who is the average spinal cord injury victim?***

- *Male, 18-31 years old, and athletic*
- *6 feet tall*
- *Over 175 pounds*
- *No formal training in diving*
- *First-time visitor to the location*
- *Making his first dive in the location*
- *Was not warned, by word or sign, about dangers*
- *Had been using alcohol and/or drugs*

***How does the accident occur?***

- *Diving into shallow water (95 percent)*
- *Diving from a deck or adjacent structure into an in-ground pool*
- *Diving without supervision or training from starting blocks into shallow water*

***What is the situation?***

- *No lifeguard on duty*
- *Water depth where the victim hit the bottom was less than 5 feet*
- *Water was cloudy or murky*
- *The bottom had no markings*
- *No warning signs prohibited diving*

---

*National Spinal Cord Injury Center. *Annual Report.* Birmingham Alabama: A Spinal Cord Injury Data Base at the University of Alabama at Birmingham, 1990.

## Principles of Diving Safety

The following guidelines are recommended for safe diving:

- Learn how to dive properly from a qualified instructor. The self-taught diver is much more likely to be injured.
- Follow safety rules at all times—never make exceptions.
- Do not wear earplugs; they can add dangerous pressure as you descend.
- Obey "No Diving" signs. They are there for your safety.

**The Old Swimming Hole**

*"Not too bad! The storm didn't do as much as I'd guess," said Joey to Jim as they reached their favorite swimming spot. They had been coming here for years, ever since Jim spotted the rock ledge on a canoe trip. The river was wide and deep here, in the middle of a bend that made the place very private. It was all the more special because it was hard to get to. To make it "their place," they had built a fireplace for cookouts and made a swing of heavy rope from the high oak tree branches overhanging the water. They had great fun diving into the river from the ledge and swinging in with the rope.*

*"I thought the damage would be much worse here," Jim said. Heavy storms that week had damaged their "road" to the site. Even with their four-wheel drive, it had been rough going, but the campsite and swimming hole looked pretty much the same as usual. A few tree limbs had blown down and part of the bank had been washed away, but everything else looked okay.*

*"Last one in's a rotten egg!" they said almost at the same time. They had been playing this game since they were kids, anytime they got near water. Joey ran for the rock ledge, tearing off his tee-shirt and kicking off his shoes as he went. They were already in their swimming suits.*

*"No! Wait!" commanded Jim. There was an authority in his voice that told Joey this was not just a trick to slow him down. Joey stopped at the ledge and looked down at the murky water passing swiftly below. The river was also considerably higher than usual.*

*Jim was making his way down the bank to the place they usually climbed* out *of the water, not* in. *He carried a long branch. Then he poked the branch into the water, starting in the area below the rope swing.*

*"You chicken!" Joey teased. He had always been more of a daredevil than his older brother—and he had the scars to prove it. But this time he had to admit Jim had a point. He soon found a branch of his own and helped Jim search for something they both hoped wasn't there.*

*But it was there. An old tree trunk, heavy from being in the water for years, had washed down the river in the rains. It had come to rest again just beneath the rock ledge. "Maybe it's the bend in the river," said Jim. "You know, currents and such. Anyway, I'm glad we checked."*

- Be sure of water depth. *The first time in the water, ease in or walk in; do not jump or dive.*
- Never dive into an above-ground pool or the shallow end of any in-ground pool.
- Never dive into cloudy or murky water.
- In open water, always check first for objects under the surface, such as logs, stumps, boulders, and pilings.
- Check the shape of the pool bottom to be sure the diving area is large enough and deep enough for the dive you plan to make.
- Remember that the presence of a diving board doesn't necessarily mean it is safe to dive. Pools at homes, motels, and hotels might not have a safe diving envelope.
- Dive only off the end of a diving board. If you dive off the side of a diving board, you might hit the side of the pool.
- Do not bounce more than once on the end of a diving board. You could miss the edge or slip off the diving board.
- Do not run on a diving board or attempt to dive a long way through the air. The water might not be deep enough where you enter it.
- Swim away from the diving board. Don't be a hazard for the next diver.
- Do not use drugs or alcohol when diving.

**Déjà Vu**

*When Liz Linton scanned the beach from her lifeguard tower at Newport Beach, she saw a man bobbing awkwardly just beyond the surf. She swam out toward the victim with an uneasy sense of deja vu. In her two summers as a lifeguard, Linton had already saved one victim of spinal cord injury from drowning. The memory reminded her how quickly a serious injury can occur.*

*As she swam, she marked the victim's position, fearful he would sink before she got there. Fortunately, she reached him in time. She held him carefully to protect his neck and back from movement and moved in to shore. The man was partially paralyzed. His head and shoulders had hit the bottom when he dove through a wave.*

*The man Liz Linton rescued was lucky. After many months of rehabilitation, he regained full use of his body.*

## Pool Safety Guidelines

Records maintained by United States Diving, the national governing body of competitive diving, show that there have been no fatalities or catastrophic injuries during practices or sanctioned competitive diving events. This safety record is mostly a result of careful training and supervision. It is also a result of the proper construction and maintenance of safe swimming pools that meet approved minimum standards for the depth and width of the diving area and proper locations of diving boards and ***diving towers***. (For more information on United States Diving and other groups that sponsor competition, see Chapter 12.)

## Pool Dimension Guidelines

Authorities continue to disagree about the recommended depth of water needed for safe diving from a deck or from a diving board. This difference of opinion especially concerns pools not designed for diving competition such as those at homes, hotels, and apartments.

Several studies have been conducted regarding the appropriate depth for safe diving. Some people and organizations take issue with the research design and findings. However, few disagree that no one should perform any type of dive in water 5 feet deep or less. For 1-meter springboard diving, the often-reached conclusion is that the minimum depth of water at the ***plummet*** (a line from the midpoint at the tip of a diving board to the bottom of the pool) should be 11 feet 6 inches and preferably deeper. This minimum 11 feet 6 inches depth should be carried forward and far enough to the sides that, regardless of pool design, a diver will not strike the bottom. This underwater area is often called the ***safe diving envelope.***

The National Spa and Pool Institute (NSPI) and the National Swimming Pool Foundation (NSPF) are the trade associations representing the pool and spa industry. They recognize and endorse the American National Standards Institute (ANSI) guidelines for pool design. Regardless of

Fig. 3-1

FIG. 3-2

FIG. 3-3

FIG. 3-4

the pool design, the American Red Cross recommends that you check the depth of the water. If the water is not at least 11 feet 6 inches deep at the point where you might hit the bottom, do not dive unless you have been trained in shallow water diving.

"NO DIVING" SIGNS

The American Red Cross recommends that any swimming area (pool or open water) with water less than 5 feet deep have signs reading "Danger—Shallow Water, No Diving" to ensure safety. Since most spinal injuries occur to people visiting an area for the first time, it is very important to warn everyone of the hazards.

Placing several signs in key locations may help prevent injuries. Suggested locations are the deck near the edge of the pool and walls or fences by shallow water. Signs should be visible to anyone entering the pool or approaching shallow water.

Many kinds of warnings can be used, such as the following:

- "No Diving" painted on the deck in contrasting colors (Fig. 3-1).
- Tiled lettering embedded into the deck in contrasting colors (Fig. 3-2).
- Universal "No Diving" tiles embedded into the deck.
- Plastic signs mounted on the walls, fences, or stands (Figs. 3-3 and 3-4).

FIG. 3-5

## POOLS WITH DIVING FACILITIES

Regardless of a pool's location, there may be some diving hazard. Pool owners should ensure that their pools meet minimum standards for safe diving. Public and private facilities with 1-meter or 3-meter diving boards and/or towers suitable for competition must meet more stringent pool design standards. Such standards are set by the National Collegiate Athletic Association (NCAA), the Federation Internationale de Natation Amateur (FINA), United States Diving, and other organizations that sponsor diving competition.

All swimming pools with diving boards and towers should display their diving rules near the diving board or tower (Fig. 3-5). These rules should be strictly enforced. Such rules include—

- Use the ladder to climb to the diving board or tower. Climbing in any other way is prohibited.
- You are allowed only one bounce on the end of the diving board.
- Only one person is allowed on the diving board at a time.
- Dive or jump only in a straight line out from the end of the diving board or tower.
- Look before diving or jumping to make sure no one is in the diving area.
- Swim to the closest ladder or wall immediately after diving or jumping.
- Your hands must enter the water first when performing a headfirst dive.
- The tower can be used only with supervision from a qualified instructor or coach.
- Learn or practice twisting, somersaulting, inward, and reverse dives only under close supervision.

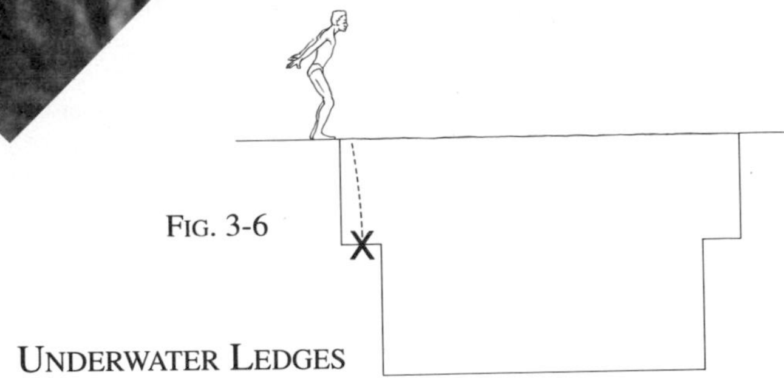

Fig. 3-6

## Underwater Ledges

Some swimming pools have underwater ledges (sometimes called safety ledges) that may present a diving hazard (Fig. 3-6). If the ledge is hard to see, you might dive into what seems to be deep water, hit the ledge, and injure the spine. To reduce this risk, black stripes should be painted on the ledge border to clearly show where the ledge is (Fig. 3-7).

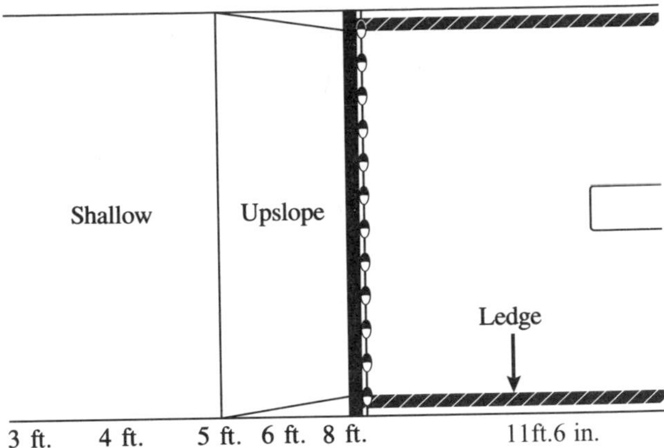


Fig. 3-7

## Diving Equipment

Diving equipment varies greatly at different facilities. Years ago, a diving board was just a long wooden plank crudely attached to a stand. It angled upward, making the diver's approach uphill. The stiffness and angle of the board limited the dives that could be done from it and sometimes made the diving board unsafe.

Some older diving boards have a wooden core surrounded by a fiberglass outer surface, with a top made of nonslip material. The stand for this kind of diving board generally secures the back end of the board and has a stationary ***fulcrum*** (the part of a diving apparatus under the center of a diving board that lets the board bend and spring) (Fig. 3-8). Diving facilities

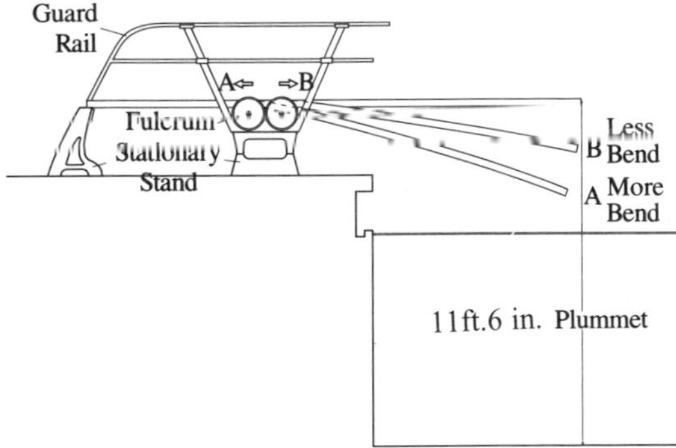


Fig. 3-8 Parts of a diving board.

not built to minimum standards may have different board lengths, fulcrum placement, height of the board over the water, and board resiliency. These inconsistencies could be dangerous, since a diver cannot tell if the equipment is reliable. You should learn more advanced dives on equipment that meets the standards for competitive diving.

Equipment for competitive diving has evolved into an advanced system of diving board, movable fulcrum, and stationary stand. Diving boards used for competition are made of aluminum and coated with an abrasive surface. They are 1 meter and 3 meters in height over the water.

The quality of the stand is important. The stand has a solid base and a movable fulcrum. The movable fulcrum lets you make adjustments according to your strength, weight, and timing. Proper adjustment for your abilities is very important for your performance. The diving board should stay level when the fulcrum is moved. A level board helps you reach the proper distance from the board in flight and entry. There should be a guard rail on each side of the board to prevent a fall onto the deck. Steps or stairs of nonslip material should give easy access to the diving board from the deck.

Some diving facilities have ***diving platforms*** (stationary structures for diving), which are constructed in various ways. Proper construction provides a solid foundation and a nonskid surface. State-of-the-art diving facilities include 1-meter, 3-meter, 5-meter, 7½-meter, and 10-meter platforms (Fig. 3-9). Use diving platforms only under the direct supervision of a qualified diving coach or instructor.

Courtesy of Indiana Natatorium and IUPUI.

Fig. 3-9

The depth of the water for springboard diving is an important safety factor. Competitive divers may vary in the depth they need to maneuver safely under water. For beginning diver, the water underneath and in front of a 1-meter diving board should be at least 11 feet 6 inches.

## Residential Pools

### In-Ground Pools

In-ground residential pools at homes, apartments, and condominiums come in many sizes and shapes. They generally range from 3 to 8 feet in depth. Since most spinal injuries in residential pools come from dives into shallow water, the American Red Cross recommends that pool owners take these precautions:

- Do not allow any diving unless the water is 11 feet 6 inches deep and there is at least 16 feet 6 inches from the plummet to the upslope in front of the diving board.
- Clearly mark depths on the deck near the edge of the pool and on the side coping.
- Clearly mark the location of the ***breakpoint*** between shallow and deep water by placing a float line there and marking the deck with signs that indicate depth.
- Place "No Diving" signs on the deck near shallow water and on the fence or wall around the swimming pool or on a stand at the entry to the swimming pool.

Even deep water in home pools may be dangerous because of the shape of the bottom and sides of the pool or the placement of the diving board. The average home pool is not long enough or deep enough for safe springboard diving.

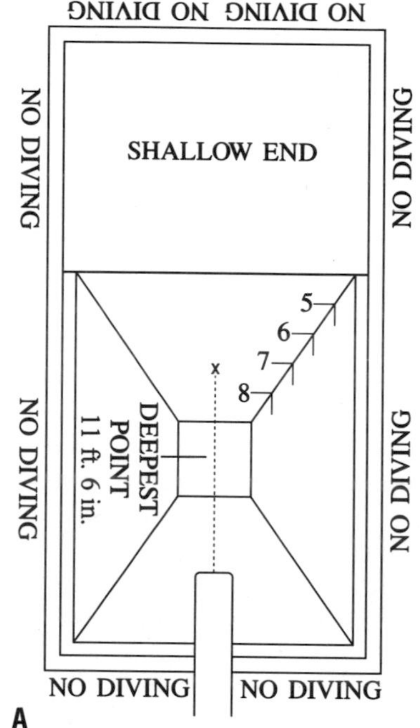


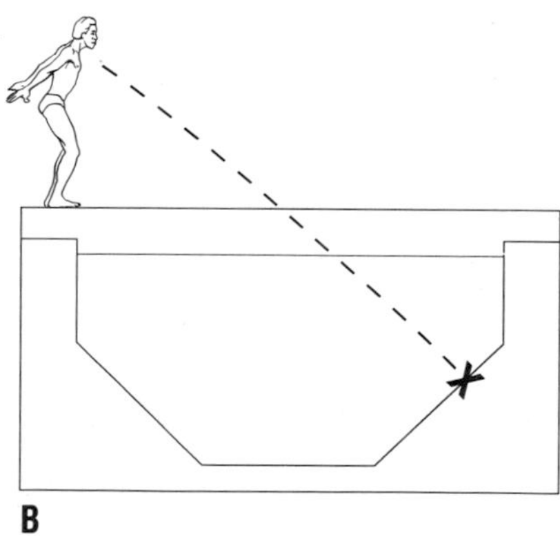


FIG. 3-10, *A-B* *A,* Top view of hopper bottom pool. *B,* Cross section of hopper bottom pool.

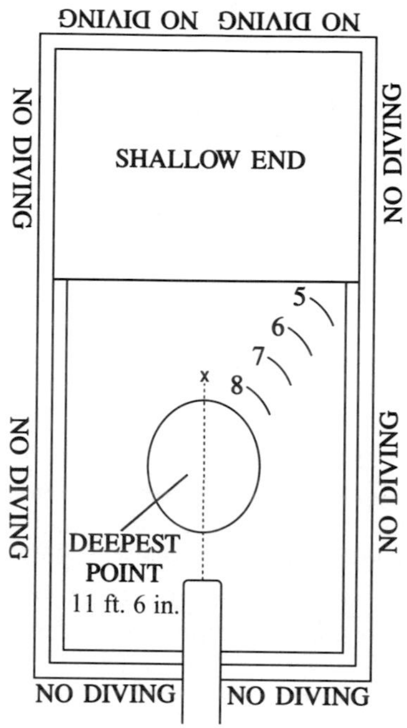


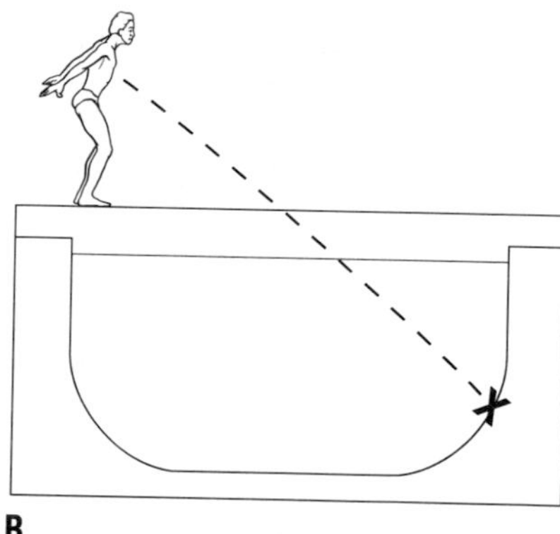


FIG. 3-11, *A-B* *A,* Top view of spoon-shaped pool. *B,* Cross section of spoon-shaped pool.

Two common designs for in-ground residential pools are the hopper bottom pool and the spoon-shaped pool. A ***hopper bottom pool*** has a bottom that angles sharply up on all four sides from the deepest point up to the breakpoint (Fig. 3-10). Thus, the safe diving envelope is much smaller than it appears. Diving into a hopper bottom pool may be like diving into a funnel. If the depth markers give only the depth at the deepest point, a diver may think the area for safe diving is larger than it actually is. Diving from either a diving board or the deck, the diver may hit the bottom.

The *spoon-shaped pool* also may present risks to safe diving because the distance from the end of the diving board to the slope of the bottom is greatly reduced (Fig. 3-11). The bottom contour of the spoon-shaped pool may give a false sense of depth and bottom area throughout the deep end.

### Above-Ground Pools

No one should ever dive into an ***above-ground pool.*** People have been injured by diving from the deck, the rim, or a structure above the edge. Swimmers must use the ladder to enter or ease into the pool to be safe.

## Public and Private Pools

Hotel/motel, apartment, and public pools may have the same diving hazards found in residential pools. The lack of supervision at many facilities also adds to potential hazards. Before diving, carefully check the pool to make sure it is safe. Check the depth of the water, the length and height of the diving board, and the shape of the bottom.

### Starting Blocks

Pools designed for competitive swimming are equipped with starting blocks, which can be permanent or removable. Starting blocks at the shallow end of a pool may be a hazard. Competitive swimmers are trained for correct diving from blocks. People without training who dive from blocks are at risk. An improper dive could lead to injury. Therefore, the American Red Cross recommends that racing starts, from starting blocks, be taught in water at least 9 feet deep. If this is not possible, *the blocks should be restricted to supervised competitive swimming* (Fig. 3-12). At all other times, "No Diving" signs should be posted on each block, the block removed, or access prevented.

Fig. 3-12

**C5 Quadriplegia**

*Bill Brooks, a 29-year-old man from Davidsonville, Maryland, was diving through an inner tube into a pool on a Sunday afternoon. His neck hit the tube. He later remembered how, as he floated in the water, he was aware of everything yet powerless to move.*

*At the hospital, doctors told Brooks he was a "C5" quadriplegic, referring to the fifth cervical vertebra, the area of the neck he had damaged. In college Brooks had played baseball, and then he had played slow-pitch softball. He had enjoyed his active life, but in one afternoon he lost control of his legs, chest, and arms. He couldn't dress himself, feed himself, go to the bathroom by himself, or even hold a softball in his hands.*

*Months of rehabilitation gradually improved Brooks's life. Although his right hand remains paralyzed, Brooks can use his left hand to hold a telephone and control a computer mouse. With the computer, he is learning to design the sprinkler systems he once installed as the foreman for a sprinkler company. Brooks is learning to get by with his injury, but his spinal nerves will never regenerate. He has little hope to be able to walk again.*

## Water Parks and Water Slides

Water parks and water slides have become very popular. Water park pools and slides are built in many sizes and shapes (Fig. 3-13). Slides vary in length, height, and angle and direction of descent. With the proper precautions, they can be very enjoyable and safe.

Fig. 3-13

To reduce the possibility of injury when using a water slide, follow these guidelines:

- Follow all posted instructions.
- Always slide feetfirst (Fig. 3-14).
- Keep the landing area in front of the slide clear of people.
- Do not try deep entries on purpose.
- Be sure the slide is anchored securely to the deck.
- If the slide has a lip that is higher than the deck or the surface of the water, be sure there is sufficient water depth to keep you from striking the bottom.
- On speed slides, cross your legs to help prevent injuries.

Fig. 3-14

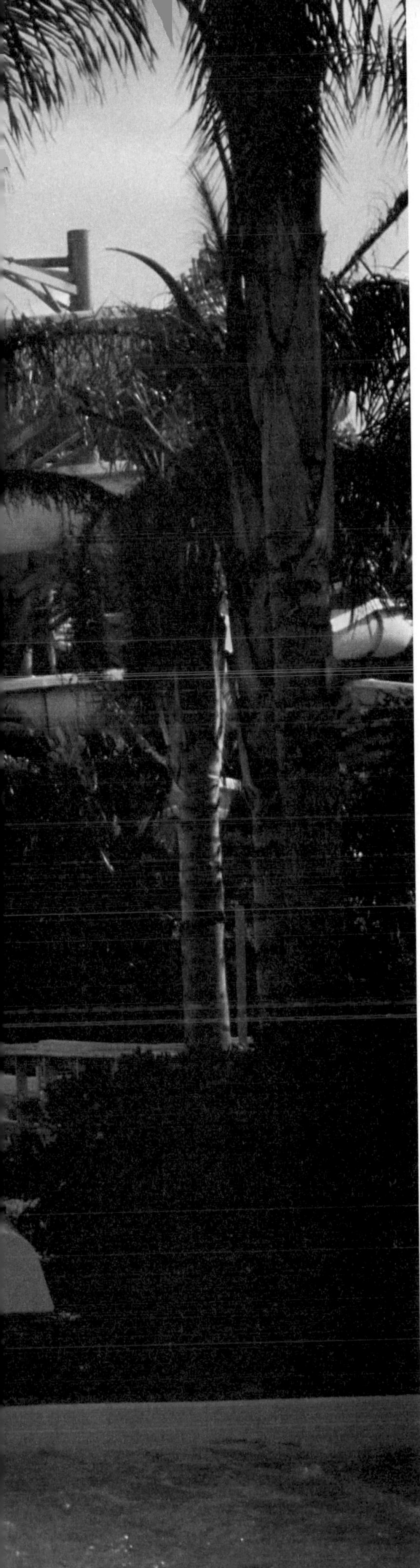

## Open Water

### Oceans and Rivers

Currents and tides can cause the bottom contour of oceans and rivers to change very rapidly. Sunken logs, debris, and built-up silt or sand are risks for swimmers who run and dive into the water. Any object under water, even another swimmer, could be a major hazard.

Take care to enter the water safely. Check for "No Diving" signs on the beach or on floats in the water. Never run and dive into an area of moving water. Even when the area seems clear, the current can bring an underwater obstruction into the area within minutes. Wade into the water until it is chest-deep. Then, if you want to dive in, do a shallow dive with your hands overhead and your head between your arms. Steer up to the surface immediately.

### Lakes and Quarries

Although lakes and quarries have less water movement than oceans and rivers, the bottom may present hazards. Wind and waves can move submerged debris close to shore. In man-made lakes, submerged tree stumps or logs may be close to shore. In lakes and especially in quarries, boulders may be hidden under water (Fig. 3-15).

Running and diving into a lake or quarry can be very hazardous. In supervised areas, the bottom should be surveyed for obstructions at the beginning of the season and daily thereafter. Any obstruction should be removed or marked with a buoy and a warning sign. Diving should be prohibited in the area. Unless you know what safety precautions have been taken in an area, do not assume it is safe. Never run and dive in an unsupervised area. Wade until the water is chest-deep before swimming. Any headfirst entry could cause injury.

Never dive from a dock into water less than 9 feet deep. If you are unsure of the depth and bottom contour, do not dive. The water may be shallower than you expect. Each time you swim in open water, lower yourself into the water feetfirst or wade in from shore the first time you go in the water.

Never dive into a quarry. Often there are underwater obstacles, such as boulders, ledges, and equipment from excavation operations. Carefully check the bottom and depth before entering from *any* height. Ease in feetfirst to check the bottom and depth. If you cannot ease into the water, try another entry point.

Fig. 3-15

## Summary

Most spinal injuries happen when a person dives into water less than 5 feet deep. Injuries can result from running and diving into open water, diving from docks, diving into quarries, and diving from a deck or a diving board into a pool with insufficient diving area or depth. Jumping, falling, or being pushed against a solid object also can injure the spine. Most spinal injuries happen at the pool's shallow end, in a corner, or where the bottom slopes up toward shallow water.

In open water, such as lakes or rivers, spinal injuries can occur in shallow areas and where the water level varies because of tides or currents. Areas with underwater hazards, such as rocks and tree stumps, also cause injuries.

The incorrect use and placement of water slides and starting blocks present risks. Never slide headfirst on a water slide.

When you arrive at any swimming area, look carefully for "No Diving" signs and potential diving hazards. By systematically checking the diving area for any potential hazards, you can avoid catastrophic injury. By being safety-minded, you can protect yourself, your family, and your friends from severe injury.

Chapter 13 describes the basic methods to care for someone with a spinal injury from swimming or diving. You can learn more in these American Red Cross aquatics courses: Community Water Safety, Lifeguard Training, and Safety Training for Swim Coaches. Contact your local American Red Cross unit for information about these courses.

# 4

# hydrodynamics

CHAPTER

## Key Terms

**Adipose tissue:** Body tissue that stores fat.
**Buoyancy:** The upward force a fluid exerts on bodies in it.
**Center of buoyancy:** The point around which the buoyant properties of the body are evenly distributed.
**Center of mass:** The point around which the weight of the body is evenly distributed.
**Displacement:** The volume or weight of the fluid displaced by a floating or immersed body.
**Drag:** The resistance of water on a body moving through it.
**Dynamic inertia:** The tendency of a body in motion to stay in motion.
**Equilibrium:** A state of balance between opposing forces.
**Force of gravity:** The pull of the earth on a body.
**Form drag:** The resistance caused by an object's shape and profile as it moves through a fluid.
**Frictional drag:** The resistance caused by an object's surface texture as it moves through a fluid.
**Hydrodynamics:** The science that studies the motion of fluids and forces on solid bodies in fluids.
**Laminar flow:** The principle by which the molecules of a fluid that is moving around an object speed up or slow down to stay parallel to each other.
**Law of acceleration:** The principle by which a body's speed depends on how much force is applied to it and the direction of that force.
**Law of action and reaction:** The principle that for every action there is an equal and opposite reaction.
**Law of inertia:** The principle that a force must be applied to move a body from rest, to stop a moving body, or to change the direction of a moving body.
**Law of levers:** The principle that movement of levers is related to the force applied, the resistance that occurs, the force arm (the distance from where the force is applied to the pivot point), and the resistance arm (the distance from where the resistance occurs to the pivot point).
**Lift:** A force created by a body's shape and motion through a fluid, acting perpendicular to the movement.
**Physics:** The science that studies matter and energy.
**Specific gravity:** The ratio of the weight of a body to the weight of the water it displaces.
**Static inertia:** The tendency of a body at rest to stay at rest.
**Streamlined position:** A body position with hands interlocked, arms straight and stretched overhead, head centered between arms, legs together, body straight, and toes pointed.
**Wave drag:** The resistance caused by turbulence in a fluid.

# OBJECTIVES

***After reading this chapter, you should be able to—***

1. Describe how buoyancy works.
2. Explain the effects of the three types of drag on motion through the water.
3. Describe the law of inertia and its effects on aquatics.
4. Explain how Newton's law of acceleration affects swimming efficiency.
5. Give two examples of action and reaction.
6. Explain why circular motions are more effective for swimming than linear motions.
7. Describe the application of the law of levers in swimming.
8. Define the key terms at left.

***After reading this chapter and completing appropriate course activities, you should be able to—***

1. Demonstrate the jellyfish float to determine your own buoyancy.
2. Demonstrate how controlling your breath and changing body position can affect how you float.
3. Do a simple experiment to experience how lift forces work.

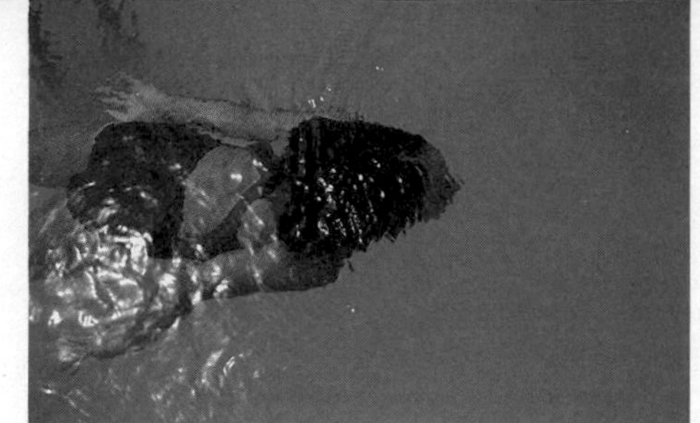

THE

"PHYSICS IS PHUN!" students used to write on the chalkboard before class. After the teacher's moans, the teacher and students with very different motives ended up with the same objective—to keep the students awake for the whole period. Many people find the mere mention of science sleep-inducing. The concepts seem too hard, too confusing, or simply irrelevant to what matters to them.

YOU MIGHT EVEN BE ASKING YOURSELF, "Why do I have to know anything about physics to be a good swimmer?" In some ways you don't. To be a better swimmer, you can simply use trial and error and practice, practice, practice. But good swimmers do not rely on practice alone. They mix practice with a basic knowledge of ***physics,*** the science of matter and energy. Combining practice with knowledge allows you to learn something more easily than with practice alone.

RESEARCH HAS LONG SOUGHT TO IMPROVE how the human body moves through the water. Researchers have spent years trying to find ways to help people gain even a small advantage in swimming. Their study builds on a long history of exploring the world of ***hydrodynamics,*** as the physics of fluids is called. In this chapter you will read about these discoveries, some clearly related to aquatics, others indirectly relevant. All of them are important because they affect the way you swim.

# PHYSICS OF SWIMMING AND DIVING

# SCIENCE

THE MORE YOU UNDERSTAND *WHY* THINGS HAPPEN in the water, the better you will be at *what* you do in the water. This chapter describes 10 principles related to being and moving in the water. It also has exercises to help you understand and get a "feel" for the principles. These exercises are intended mostly for beginners, but even experienced swimmers and divers might want to do them for fun or to review these basic principles.

## Why Some Things Float

### Archimedes' Principle

Imagine you have three glass bottles the same size. Each one weighs 1 pound and can hold 10 pounds of water. Leave the first bottle empty, seal it, and put it in water. It floats high in the water, with most of the bottle above the surface. Now put 8 pounds of pebbles in the second bottle, seal it, and put it in water. This bottle also floats, but it is low in the water; most of it is submerged. Finally, put 11 pounds of pebbles into the third bottle, seal it, and put it in water. It sinks—even with air inside. If you lifted the third bottle while it was still under water, however, it would seem to weigh only 2 pounds (Fig. 4-1).

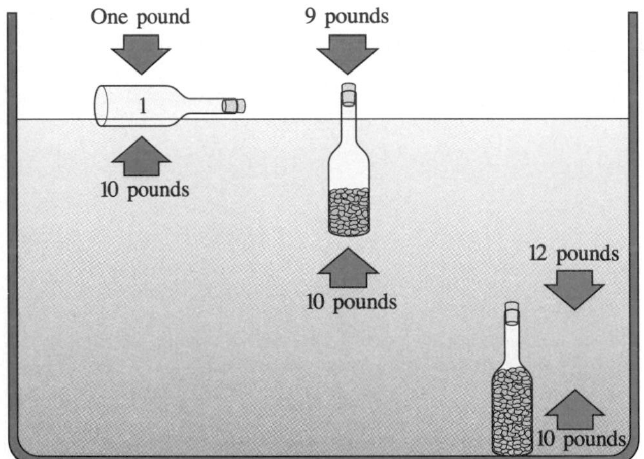


Fig. 4-1

What is going on with these three bottles? The first floats because it weighs only 1 pound but would have to push aside 10 pounds of water (the amount of water it could hold) for it to sink. Thus, it would take some effort to push the empty bottle under water. This is called ***buoyancy,*** which means that the water exerts an upward force against an object equal to the weight of the water that would be pushed aside by the object. Since, in this case, this amount, called ***displacement,*** is more than the weight of the first bottle, the bottle floats.

The second bottle also floats, and for the same reason. The 9 pounds pushing down is still less than the force needed to displace 10 pounds of water. Since only 9 pounds of the buoyancy is used to lift the 9 pounds of glass and stone, part of this bottle—1/10 of it—floats above the water.

Even though the third bottle sinks, buoyancy is still a factor. The 10 pounds of water displaced by the sunken bottle is still pushing upward, so the bottle seems to weigh only 2 pounds in the water—even though it weighs 12 pounds out of the water.

The effect shown with all three bottles is called *Archimedes' principle:* a body in water is buoyed up by a force equal to the weight of the water displaced (Fig. 4-2).

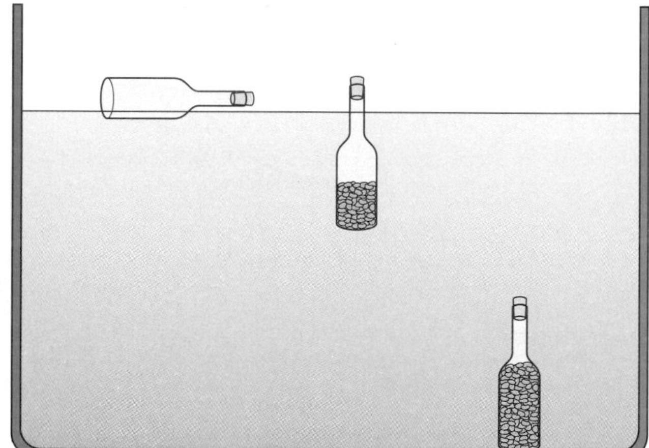

Fig. 4-2

How does this affect swimming and other water activities? This principle explains why most people float. Like the bottles, your body displaces water. You can see this when you sit in a bathtub and the water level goes up. (In fact, this is just what Archimedes was doing when he discovered his famous principle [Fig. 4-3]!) When the weight of the water you displace is more than your weight, you float. The force of buoyancy in this case is greater than the ***force of gravity.***

Eureka!

Fig. 4-3

Because of buoyancy, you weigh very little, if anything, in the water. You can put most of your energy into movement because you need very little to "carry" yourself. This is especially valuable for persons with physical disabilities. Those who find it hard to move on land or who depend on a wheelchair can get around in the water much more easily because the buoyancy of water does most of the work of carrying the person.

### Specific Gravity

The two bottles that floated were at very different heights in the water, even though buoyancy pushed both up. The reason is related to Archimedes' principle. This is known as ***specific gravity.*** The ratio of the weight of a body to the weight of the water it displaces is its specific gravity. Pure water has a specific gravity of 1.0 and is the standard against which other objects are compared. A body with a specific gravity less than 1.0 floats; one with a specific gravity greater than 1.0 sinks. The first bottle, which weighs 1 pound but displaces 10 pounds of water, has a specific gravity of 0.1 and floats high on the surface. The second bottle, which weighs 9 pounds with its pebbles but displaces 10 pounds, has a specific gravity of 0.9 and floats with only a small part above the surface. The third bottle, which weighs 12 pounds but displaces 10 pounds of water, has a specific gravity of 1.2, so it sinks.

What does all this mean for swimming? For one thing, it explains why some people can float easily while others do not. A person's specific gravity depends mostly on how much muscle mass, fat, and bone density he or she has. ***Adipose tissue*** (body fat) has a specific gravity less than 1.0; bone and muscle tissue have a specific gravity slightly greater than 1.0. People with lots of muscle and a heavy bone structure, or with little body fat, do not float easily. Those with more body fat and less muscle usually float more easily. Because the average female has 21 to 24 percent body fat and the average male has 15 to 20 percent body fat, females generally float more easily than males.

Body composition also changes with age. For example, very young children tend to have more fat weight and less muscle. Their specific gravity is usually less than 1.0 and they float easily. Young adults tend to have more muscle and less fat, and in general they do not float very well. Older people often have more fat and less muscle and float more easily. The old saying that everyone can learn to float is not entirely correct because a person cannot easily change his or her body composition.

Fig. 4-4

You can use an easy test, called the *jellyfish float,* to see how buoyant you are. In chest-deep water, submerge to the neck, take a deep breath of air, bend forward at the waist, put your head in the water, and flex your knees slightly to raise your feet off the bottom. Your arms and legs hang from your body (Fig. 4-4). Hold your breath and relax as much as you can. If you sink, your specific gravity is greater than 1.0. If part of your head or back stays above the surface, you can learn to float on your back with at least part of your face out of the water.

You can also use the jellyfish float to see how you can change your own specific gravity. Do the float the same way, but this time while floating exhale some air and see whether you start to sink or float lower in the water. With a friend, you can watch how high you each float when your lungs are full of air and how low you float (or whether you sink) with less air in your lungs.

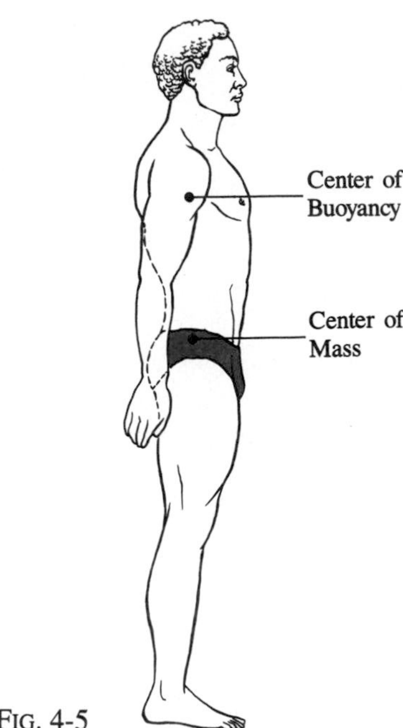


FIG. 4-5

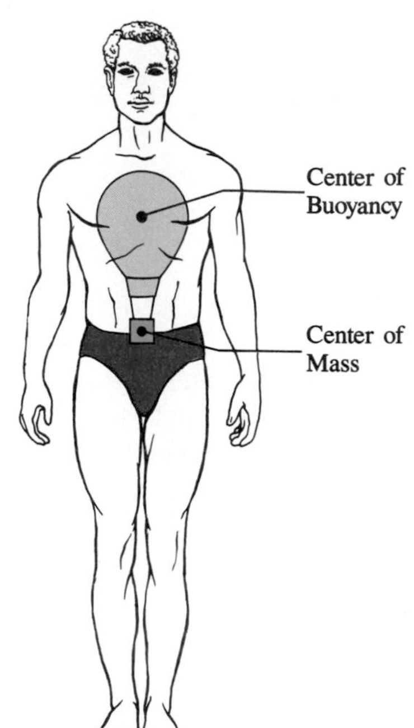


FIG. 4-6

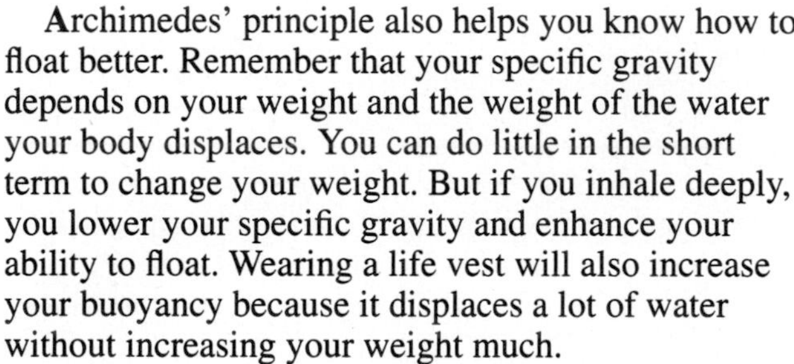

Archimedes' principle also helps you know how to float better. Remember that your specific gravity depends on your weight and the weight of the water your body displaces. You can do little in the short term to change your weight. But if you inhale deeply, you lower your specific gravity and enhance your ability to float. Wearing a life vest will also increase your buoyancy because it displaces a lot of water without increasing your weight much.

People with great buoyancy can breathe normally when they float. If you have marginal buoyancy, you can stay afloat if you control your breathing. To keep your face above water when you float on your back, exhale rapidly and then rapidly inhale, to keep your lungs full and your chest expanded as much as possible.

A body's specific gravity is not the only factor that affects buoyancy. The water's specific gravity also makes a difference. Salt water has a slightly higher specific gravity than fresh water, so it has more buoyant force. If you float easily in fresh water, you will float slightly higher in salt water. If you have trouble floating in fresh water, you might really float for the first time in salt water.

## CENTER OF MASS AND CENTER OF BUOYANCY

We have seen how the specific gravity of a body affects how high it floats. Two other factors affect the position a floating body takes in the water: the center of mass (sometimes called the center of gravity) and the center of buoyancy.

A body's ***center of mass*** is the point around which its mass is evenly distributed. Imagine it as a single spot where all of the body's weight is concentrated. For a baseball, a body of even shape and density, the center of mass is its center. For the human body, location of the center of mass is affected by the weight and positions of different parts of the body. One way to imagine the center of mass of the human body is to see the body like a seesaw in every direction (from bottom to top, side to side, and front to back), with both sides of the balance point weighing the same. For most people, the center of mass is somewhere in the pelvic region (Fig. 4-5).

The ***center of buoyancy*** is the point around which the body's buoyancy is evenly distributed. Its location is also affected by the buoyancy and position of all body parts. The center of buoyancy is also affected by the lungs because of their great ability to expand and change a person's specific gravity. For most people, the center of buoyancy is in the chest region.

On land and in the air, keeping your balance in any position or movement depends on keeping your center of mass balanced and supported. You usually do this unconsciously, except when you move in an unfamiliar way or assume an awkward or unusual position. In the water, however, your position and motion are also related to your center of buoyancy. When you float, your center of mass is below your center of buoyancy. Think of this like a hot-air balloon. The basket (where the center of mass is) always hangs below the center of the balloon (where the center of buoyancy is) (Fig. 4-6).

When a person of average build tries to float on his or her back with arms along the sides of the body, the center of mass is nearly level with the center of buoyancy. Most people have more body weight in their legs and hips because of the high proportion of muscle tissue there, so their center of mass is near the hips. Thus, when trying to float in a horizontal position, gravity pulls the hips and legs downward while the buoyant force of the water pushes the chest area (center of buoyancy) upward. The body rotates until the center of mass is directly below the center of buoyancy. At that point, the person should float motionless. (However, the momentum of the legs moving downward may cause the body to submerge because the force of buoyancy is not enough to overcome this momentum.)

A person's final floating position (vertical or diagonal) in the water depends on the position of the center of mass relative to the center of buoyancy. Indirectly, this position is related to the person's specific gravity. A person with a specific gravity of 0.9 is likely to have more weight in the hips and legs than a person with a lower specific gravity; therefore he or she will float in a vertical position (Fig. 4-7, *A*). This person will not be able to float horizontally. This would be like trying to lift the basket of a hot-air balloon up alongside the balloon.

Someone with a specific gravity of 0.8 might float diagonally (Fig. 4-7, *B*). This person has more buoyancy than the person with a specific gravity of 0.9, and that buoyancy is probably distributed more evenly between the upper and lower body. Thus, less rotation is needed to bring the center of mass below the center of buoyancy.

A person with a specific gravity of 0.7 tends to float nearly horizontally because in that position the center of mass is below the center of buoyancy (Fig. 4-7, *C*). A person with a specific gravity of 1.0 is suspended between the surface and the bottom; this person is said to have reached ***equilibrium*** with the water and neither floats nor sinks.

It is important to realize that you can alter the position of both the center of mass and the center of buoyancy. You can shift the center of mass by moving your arms and legs. You can change your center of buoyancy by inhaling or exhaling. This means that if you float diagonally when your arms are at your side and your legs are straight out, you might be able to float horizontally with a few changes. Your goal is to move your center of mass toward your head and your center of buoyancy toward your feet.

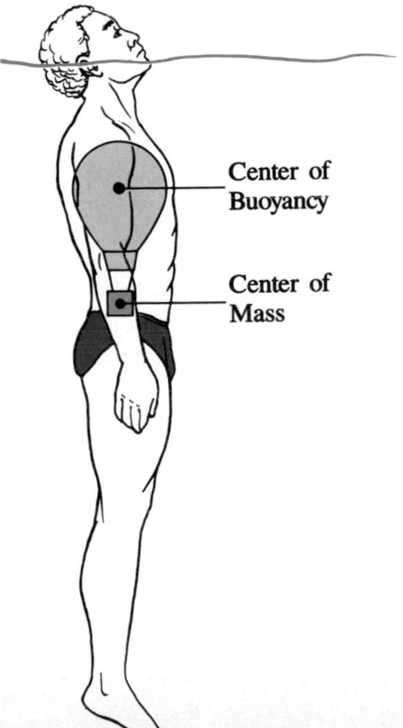


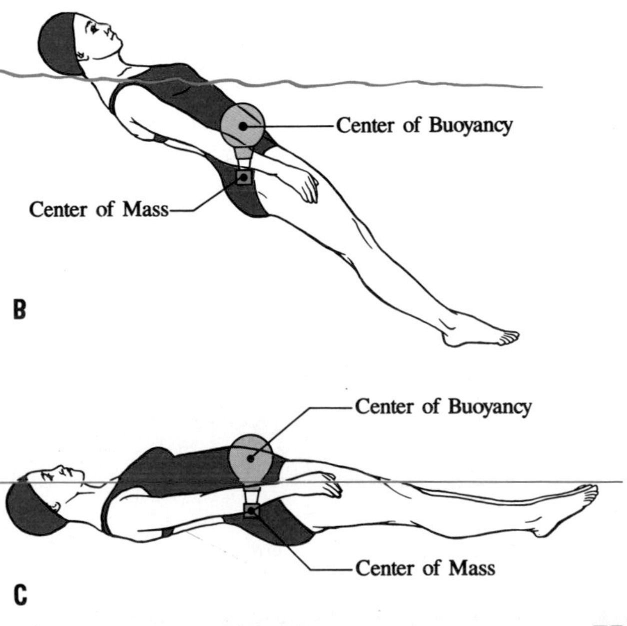


FIG. 4-7, *A-C*

FIG. 4-8

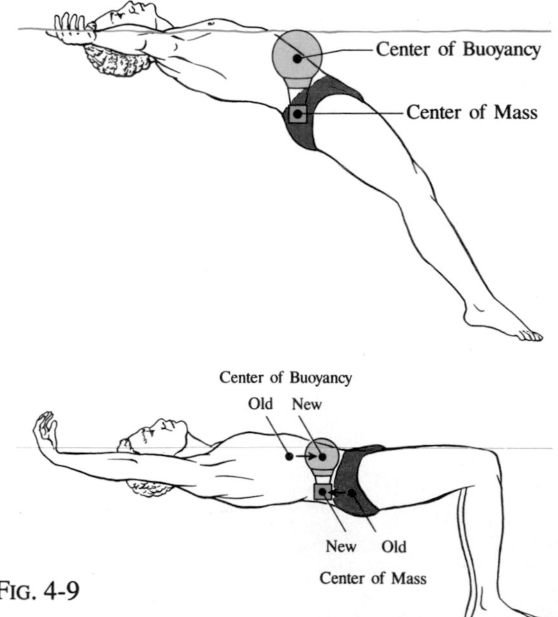


FIG. 4-9

To move your body's center of mass toward your head, you can do three things:

1. Slowly move your arms through the water to a position above your head. In this position you have more mass higher up, and your center of mass thus moves up.
2. Bend your knees. This means that the mass of your lower legs is closer to your head.
3. Flex your wrists to bring your hands out of the water (Fig. 4-8). This makes your hands "heavier" because they are no longer held up by the buoyancy of the water.

To move your center of buoyancy, you can inhale more air. As you fill your lungs, air moves down against your diaphragm in the direction of your feet. Thus, your center of buoyancy also moves toward your feet (Fig. 4-9).

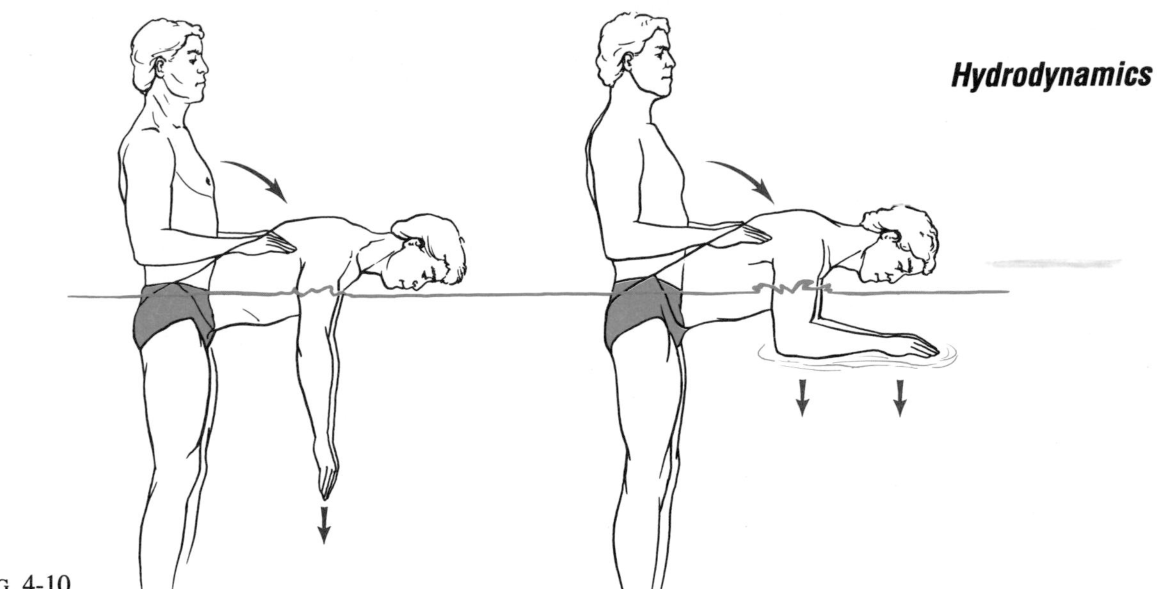
FIG. 4-10

To see how your body position changes your ability to float, start in a floating position on your back with your arms over your head, hands out of the water, and knees bent. Then relax your wrists so your hands are not out of the water and move your arms to your sides. (Your legs will sink a little.) Next, straighten your legs. (Your lower body will sink more. You might have to control your breathing, as described earlier, to stay afloat.) If you are still diagonal, exhale some air until you are floating in a vertical position with only your face out of the water. Slowly reverse these measures (inhale deeply, bend your knees, extend your arms over your head, and raise your hands out of the water) to go back to your original floating position.

## MOVEMENT IN THE WATER

### THE PROBLEM: RESISTANCE

Any object moving through water meets resistance from the water. This is known as ***drag.*** There are three types of water resistance: form drag, wave drag, and frictional drag.

#### *Form Drag*

***Form drag*** is resistance related to the object's shape and profile to the water. A tight, narrow shape experiences less form drag as it passes through water than a broad shape. Think of a sleek, narrow boat slicing through the water and compare it to a wide tugboat pushing through. The narrow shape has to push less water aside. To experience this yourself, stand in waist-deep water and thrust your hands, fingers first, down to touch your knees. You can do this quickly and easily. Now bend forward and put both your arms, palms down, on the surface of the water. Try to touch your knees quickly by bringing your arms down through the water with your palms still flat. This motion is slower and much harder than the first. In the second movement, your arms present a much larger profile to the water, so you feel much more resistance (Fig. 4-10).

To reduce form drag, therefore, keep your body in a ***streamlined position.*** To feel the difference, push off from the wall of the pool and try gliding in various positions: streamlined (but with your arms at your sides), with your arms out to the sides, and with your knees flexed. As you increase the surface area the water must pass around, you increase form drag and you cannot glide as far (Fig. 4-11).

FIG. 4-11

### *Wave Drag*

***Wave drag*** is resistance caused by water turbulence, including the turbulence made by the swimmer moving through the water (Fig. 4-12). Wave drag is directly proportional to swimming speed. The faster you swim, the more wave drag you make. You can reduce wave drag with smooth, even strokes and by not using splashing arm entries. Avoiding too much side-to-side and up-and-down body motion also helps reduce wave drag. Wave drag is also caused by other sources of water movement . Other swimmers can cause wave drag for you. Lots of activity in the water increases the turbulence. Lane lines have been designed to reduce turbulence (Fig. 4-13). Wave drag is also reduced, but not completely eliminated, when you move under water, for instance, during starts and turns and in underwater swimming.

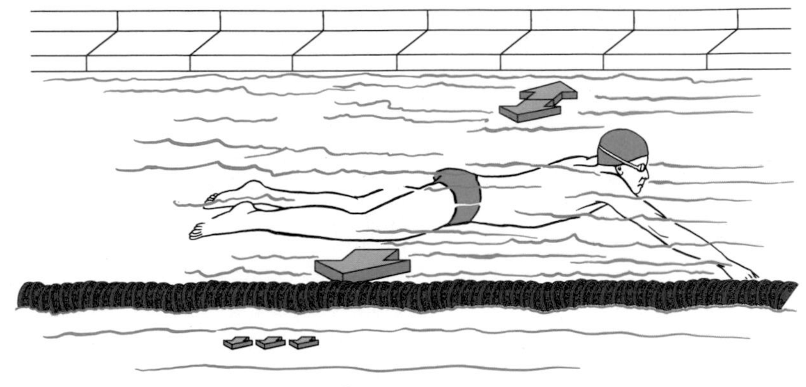

FIG. 4-13

FIG. 4-14

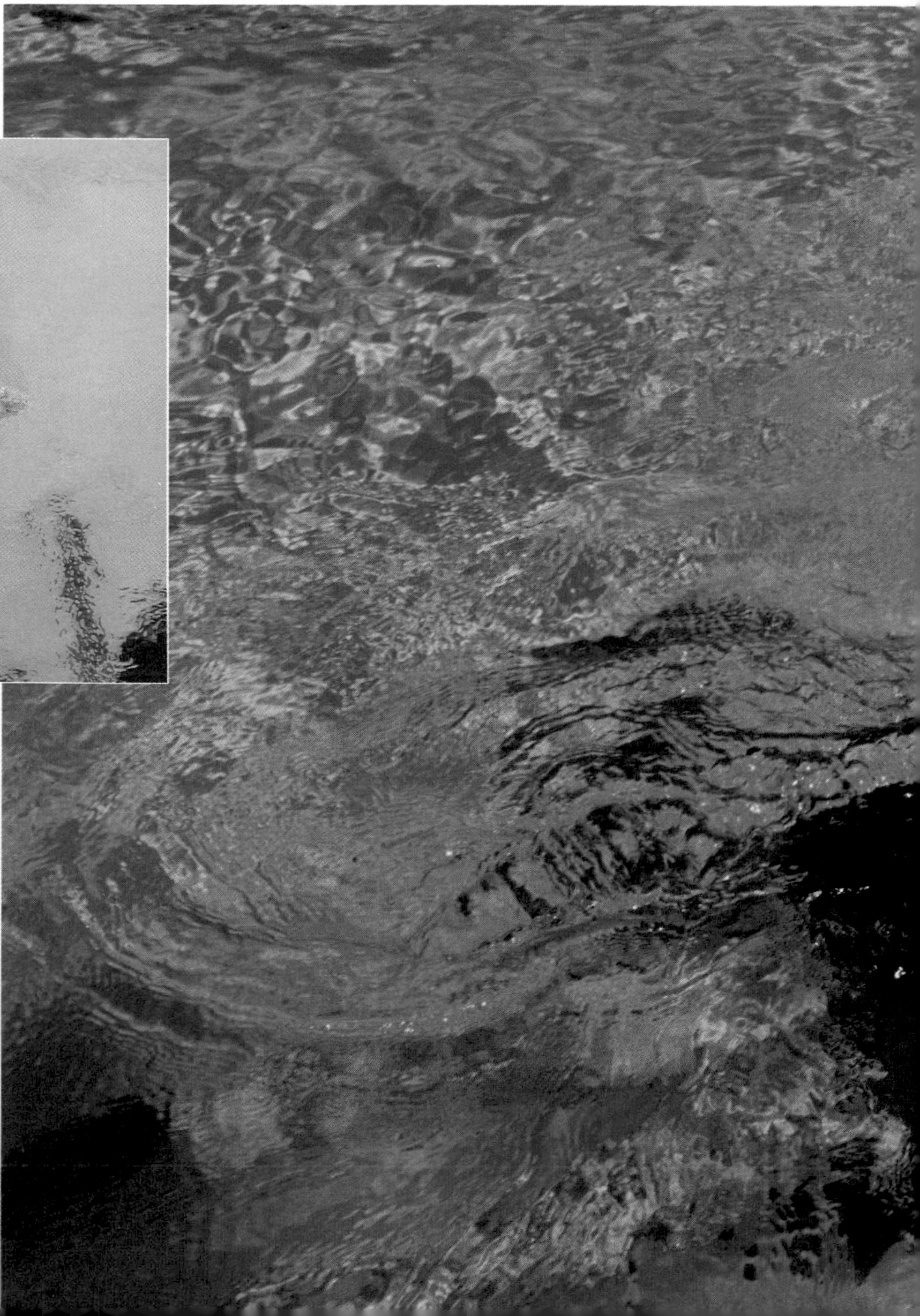

FIG. 4-12

### *Frictional Drag*

***Frictional drag*** is resistance caused by the surface texture of the body as it moves through the water. The major factor is how smooth the surface is. To reduce frictional drag, swimmers wear swimming caps and smooth, tight-fitting swimsuits. Some competitors even shave their body hair to reduce friction. Of the three forms of drag, frictional drag has the least effect. You can feel frictional drag by wearing a tee-shirt when you swim and noticing how much it slows you down (Fig. 4-14).

Drag
Moving Water
Buoyancy
Motion of Hand
Moving Water
Lift

FIG. 4-15

FIG. 4-16

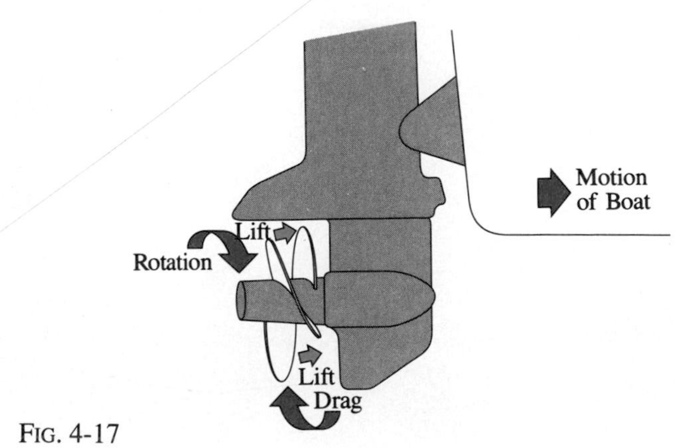


FIG. 4-17

## BERNOULLI'S THEOREM AND LAMINAR FLOW

The principle of ***laminar flow,*** discovered by Daniel Bernoulli, has been the foundation of fluid mechanics for over 250 years. The basic principle is that as a fluid moves around an object its molecules either speed up or slow down so that they stay parallel to the molecules on the other side of the object. Molecules that slow down, because of drag, create pressure against the object, while those that speed up pull the object toward them with a force called ***lift.***

These two forces, lift and drag, combine to move the object through the fluid. In the air, lift on the upper side of an airplane's wing pulls the wing up. In swimming, lift helps the swimmer move forward through the water. Drag forces oppose movement through the water, and lift forces always act perpendicular to drag forces. The result of these two forces propels a body through the water (Fig. 4-15).

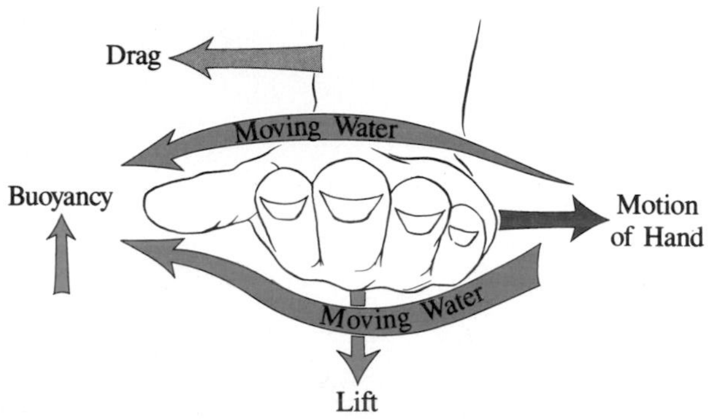

A simple way to experience lift is to stand in chest-deep water (or kneel in shallow water) with one arm extended forward from your elbow and your palm cupped and facing upward. First, relax your arm muscles. You will feel some buoyancy, making your hand drift upward. Next, bring your forearm back down to the horizontal position and, with your palm cupped, sweep your hand several times, at different speeds, horizontally through the water. You will feel your hand pulled deeper into the water (Fig. 4-16). Lift forces from the water passing over the back of your hand draw your hand down into the water. This is sometimes called the "propeller" effect because it acts in the same way that a propeller slices through the water to push a boat forward (Fig. 4-17).

The experiment with your hand in the water shows you that "lift" forces do not always act in an upward direction. Actually, they can act in any direction. A swimming stroke is made up of many different slicing motions, some outward and downward, some inward and upward. These combine to make a horizontal force that moves you forward when you swim.

A second aspect of this principle is that the force of lift is proportional to the speed of motion. In the previous experiment, you felt this when you moved your hand faster and felt the pull downward get stronger.

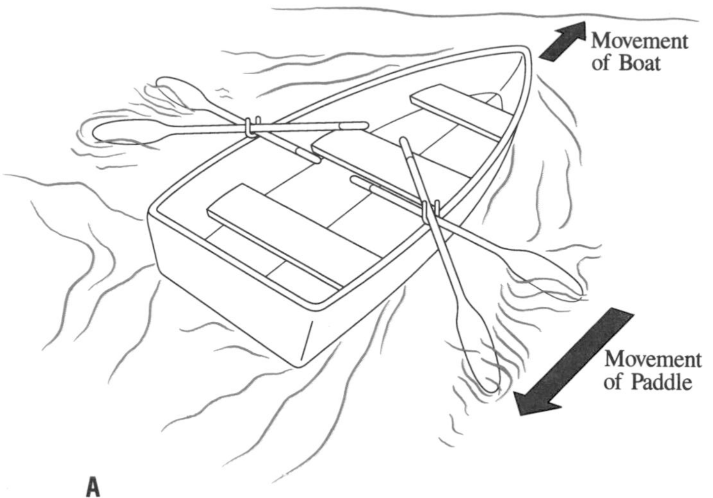


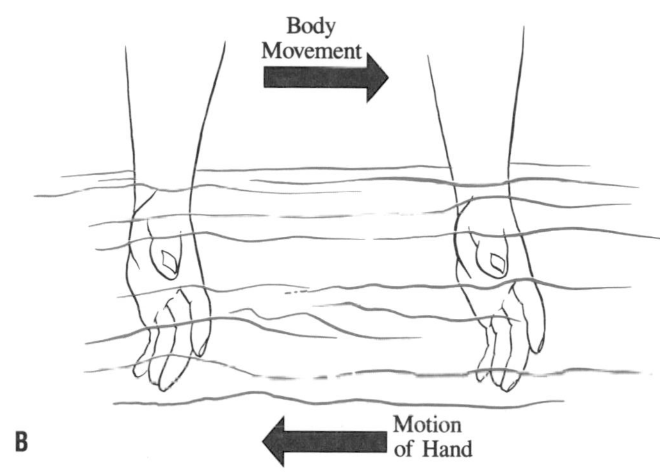


FIG. 4-18, *A-B*

In addition to this *propeller* form of propulsion, there is another, more familiar form known as *paddle* propulsion. This is how oars propel a rowboat through the water. Until recently, swimmers were thought to propel themselves best with paddle propulsion. They were said to be pulling their body through the water with their arms and hands. The analysis of stroke mechanics, however, has shown that propeller propulsion is far more effective for swimming, although paddle propulsion is still used in swimming. Sometimes paddle propulsion is used in an entire stroke, such as the arm stroke in the elementary backstroke (Fig. 4-18, *A-B*). At other times, paddle propulsion is very brief, such as the moment after one slicing movement has ended and the next has not yet begun. In this moment, your arms and legs rely on paddle propulsion and form drag to keep their position in the water. The combination of the two forms of propulsion enables a swimmer to move through the water.

## Newton's Laws of Motion and Swimming Efficiency

Isaac Newton discovered three laws of motion: the laws of inertia, acceleration, and action and reaction. These are also important for swimming efficiency. To understand how using them can improve your swimming, you first need to see how each works and how they interact to help you swim.

### *The Law of Inertia*

The ***law of inertia*** states that a force is needed to move a body at rest, to stop a body that is moving, or to change the direction of a moving body. All three parts of this law affect swimming in positive or negative ways.

***Static inertia*** is the tendency of a body at rest to stay at rest. You must overcome this every time you start to move in the water. Static inertia resists any effort to change position. ***Dynamic inertia*** is the tendency of a moving body to keep moving. This principle helps you once you've started moving. If it were not for drag, dynamic inertia would keep a body moving through the water forever.

To experience the law of inertia yourself, push off on your back from the side of the pool and glide on your back as long as you can. As you push off, you feel static inertia that makes you use force to get moving. But once you are moving, you will experience dynamic inertia, which keeps you moving, however slowly, until drag forces slow you to a halt.

Two aspects of inertia relate to swimming efficiency. First, a swimmer needs more energy to start a stroke than to keep moving. Thus, it is more efficient to keep moving than to stop and start repeatedly. At the same time, dynamic inertia lets you rest during some strokes. With the sidestroke, breaststroke, and elementary backstroke, dynamic inertia keeps you moving forward and gives you some time to rest between strokes. But if you rest too long, you may slow down so much that you have to overcome static inertia with your next stroke. The effort to start up again cancels out the benefits of the rest. The challenge of these strokes is to balance the strokes with short rests to keep static inertia from increasing the energy you expend swimming.

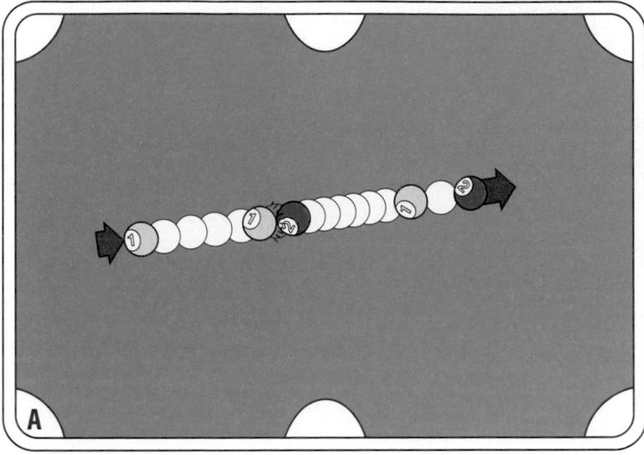

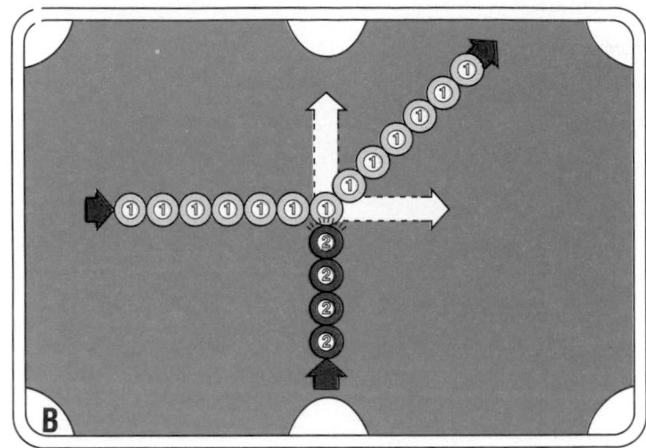

FIG. 4-19, *A-B*

The second aspect of inertia related to swimming involves how dynamic inertia can work for you. The more streamlined your body, the more benefit you get from dynamic inertia. A swimmer who keeps a streamlined position needs less force to keep moving than one who makes more form drag. This is true for every aquatic skill.

The third part of the law of inertia states that force is needed to change the direction of a moving body. This can have both positive and negative effects on swimming. When you are swimming in the direction you want, with your body aligned well for your stroke, inertia works to keep you in line. This is true because force is needed to change your direction. The faster you are going, the more force it takes to push you off track. But this aspect of inertia can work against you, too. If you are not swimming in the right direction or if your body is not aligned, you have to use force to get back on course or to realign your body.

## THE LAW OF ACCELERATION

The ***law of acceleration*** states that the speed of a body depends on how much force is applied to it and the direction of that force. There are two aspects of this law: force and direction.

If a certain amount of force produces a certain amount of speed or movement, then twice the force will produce twice the speed or movement. For example, if you push off from the wall with a certain force, you will travel a certain distance. If you push off with twice as much force, you will go twice as far, assuming you glide the same way each time. Your speed right after pushing off, before drag starts to slow you down, will be twice as fast when you use twice the force.

Second, the law of acceleration means that the effect of a force occurs in line with the direction in which the force is applied. For example, when you push a ball floating on the water, it moves in the direction you push it. With a body at rest, this principle is simple.

When the body is already in motion, the situation is more complicated. To understand it, imagine two billiard balls. If one ball is already moving and another one moving faster strikes it directly from behind, the first ball keeps moving in the same direction but faster. In this case, the force of the second ball acts in a direction *in line* with the first ball's direction, so that direction does not change (Fig. 4-19, *A*). But if the force is applied in a direction different from the body's line of movement, the body's direction is changed. The new direction will result from the body's initial direction and the direction of the force. Imagine a moving billiard ball struck from the side by another ball moving at the same speed. In this case, the first billiard ball will not go faster, but it will go in a new direction (Fig. 4-19, *B*).

This law has relevance for swimming in two ways. The first is that the more force you use in a stroke in the direction you are going, the faster you will swim. Second, your swimming is more efficient when you stay in your chosen direction and when all your propulsive force is in that direction. If you must correct your direction, you use energy for that motion instead of for moving forward. Likewise, if you exert force at an angle away from the direction you intend, you will push your body somewhat off course, and you will have to use more force to get back on track.

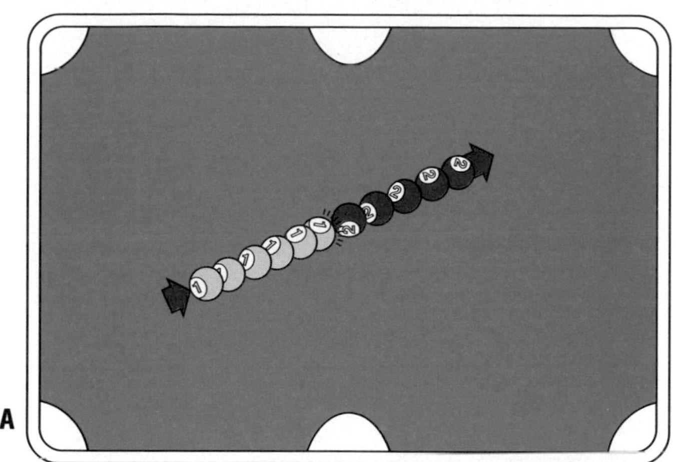

FIG. 4-20, *A-B*

To experience this law for yourself, swim the elementary backstroke across the pool, and then swim the same distance with only one arm for each stroke. (Alternate arms, keeping the arm you are not using in the glide position along your body.) Note how much more effort and time it takes swimming with one arm at a time. This is because you are applying less force and the force you are using is not parallel to your line of travel since alternating arms creates a zigzag pattern. This exercise demonstrates both aspects of the law of acceleration.

### THE LAW OF ACTION AND REACTION

The ***law of action and reaction*** states that for every action there is an equal and opposite reaction. For example, if a moving body such as a billiard ball strikes one that is standing still, two things happen. The moving ball transfers some of its motion and direction to the one that is not moving. But the second ball, the one that is at rest, "pushes back" by transferring some of its static inertia to the first ball. This might even cause the first ball to stand still after the collision (Fig. 4-20, *A*). When you dive from a diving board, the board *reacts* to the force of your feet *acting* against it, so you can take off for the dive (Fig. 4-20, *B*). Likewise, during paddle propulsion in swimming strokes, as your arm pushes (acts) against the water, the water pushes back (reacts), providing resistance to let you move forward.

### CONSERVATION OF MOMENTUM

Conservation of momentum is an application of Newton's laws. To produce an efficient stroke, circular stroke patterns are more effective than linear movements. When you use back-and-forth linear movements in your strokes, you use some force to stop moving in one direction (overcoming dynamic inertia) and then use more force to start moving again in another direction (overcoming static inertia). The abrupt changes of linear motion may also throw your body out of alignment, requiring even more energy to overcome the increased drag.

To experience the conservation of momentum, stand in waist-deep water and bend over to submerge your forearm. First move your forearm back and forth in a straight line so the water presses first against the palm and then against the back of your hand. Then make the same motion in a circular or oval path. This circular pattern will take much less effort because you are not starting and stopping your arm. One application in swimming involves the flutter kick. If you keep your ankles stiff, your kick will not be as powerful because they will be using a back-and-forth, linear motion. If you relax your ankles, they can follow a more efficient "rounded" path at the top and bottom of the kick.

### THE LAW OF LEVERS

A lever is one of the six basic tools. It consists of a pivot point and one or two rigid parts called arms. A common example of a lever is a seesaw. The pivot point is in the center, and the arms extend on each side. The weights of two children riding the seesaw are the forces acting on the lever. The ***law of levers*** relates four components: the force applied (the weight of the first child), the resistance encountered (the weight of the second child), the force arm (the distance between the first child and the pivot point), and the resistance arm (the distance between the second child and the pivot point). The law of levers states that the product of the force and force arm is equal to the product of the resistance and resistance arm:

$$F \times FA = R \times RA$$

In the seesaw example, if the two children weigh the same and sit at the same distance from the center, the seesaw will be balanced (Fig. 4-21, *A*). (The seesaw will move only if the children push off the ground.) If one child is heavier than the other, the heavier child must sit closer to the pivot point for the seesaw to be balanced (greater weight × less distance = same effect) (Fig. 4-21, *B* and *C*).

The relevance of the law of levers for swimming can be seen in the arm stroke of the front crawl. The shoulder is the pivot point. The arm muscles supply the force. The force arm is the length of bone between the shoulder and where the muscle is attached. Resistance comes from the water acting on the arm. The resistance arm is the distance from the shoulder joint to the middle of the forearm (Fig. 4-22, *A*).

The only practical way to improve your leverage and thus use less force when swimming is to reduce the length of the resistance arm. With the front crawl, you can do this by bending the elbow (Fig. 4-22, *B*). This reduces the force needed to move you

FIG. 4-21, *A-C*

through the water. The length of the force arm is nearly constant in this situation. (The muscle does contract slightly but this has almost no effect.)

**B**e careful not to confuse the word *resistance* in speaking of levers with the drag on a body moving through the water. Any technique that reduces drag on the body improves a swimmer's performance. The resistance being discussed here is necessary for the propeller and paddle functions of the hand and arm in strokes. Without such resistance, it would be like trying to swim through the air!

**A**pplying the law of levers has helped swimming researchers analyze all types of strokes to find the best limb positions and motions for each. These results are part of the description of swimming strokes in Chapter 6.

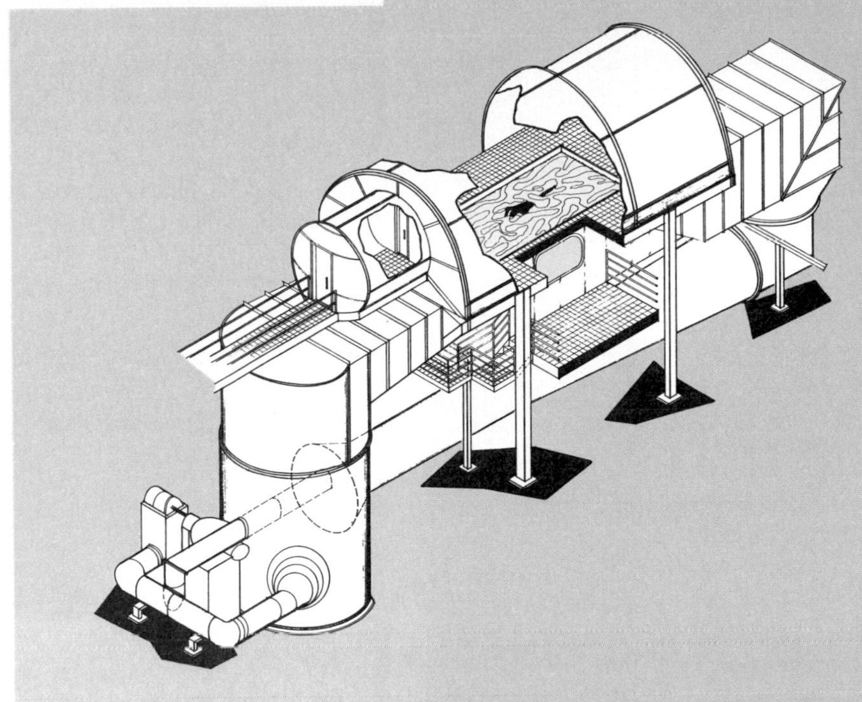

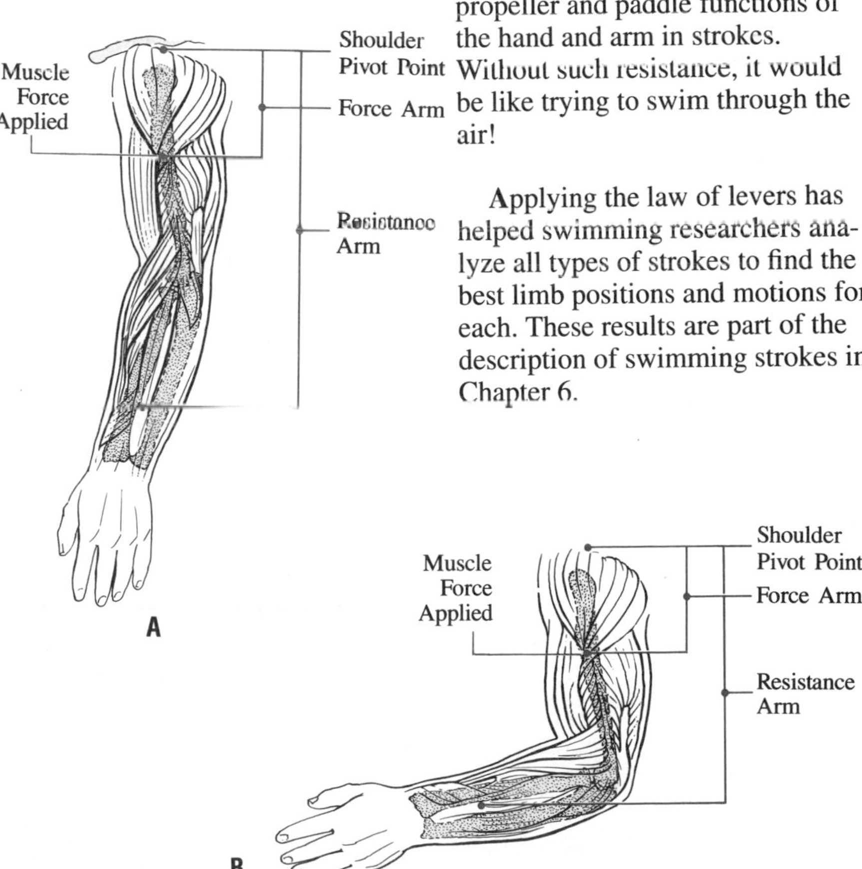


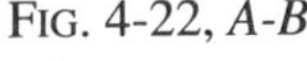
FIG. 4-22, *A-B*

**The Swimming Treadmill**

*The swimming treadmill, or "flume," in the International Center for Aquatic Research at the United States Olympic Training Center in Colorado Springs, Colorado, is the centerpiece of research for evaluating swimming technique. The steel flume is the only one of its design in the world and weighs nearly 1 million pounds. It is 25 meters long, is 4 stories high, and holds 50,000 gallons of water. Its 265-horsepower pump moves the water at speeds up to 3.0 meters per second, which is equal to a 33-second, 100-meter freestyle swim. Since the world record for this event is 48.2 seconds, the flume will still be able to test swimmers for years to come.*

*The environment of the swimming channel can be fully controlled. Scientists can simulate altitudes from sea level to 8,000 feet above sea level and regulate the temperature between 65 and 104 degrees F (18 to 40 degrees C).*

*With this impressive treadmill, coaches and scientists run controlled tests on swimmers for training and research purposes. Often swimmers work on their technique in the flume. Using computers and the latest video imaging technology, coaches and scientists can evaluate the motion of an athlete within an hour of a test. This study has helped improve our understanding of how physical principles affect stroke mechanics.*

## Summary

Even after reading this chapter, you might not be interested in the discoveries of Archimedes, Bernoulli, or Newton, but whether you are a beginner or an experienced swimmer, you probably are interested in swimming faster and more efficiently and not being as sore or tired afterwards.

Being aware of and understanding the forces that act on you in the water and knowing how to overcome them will help you improve your swimming skills. Consider one principle at a time and the way it applies to your strokes. Just as swimming researchers do, watch swimmers with good technique to see how these scientific principles are working as they swim. What researchers have learned through their curiosity you will learn in the following chapters.

5

CHAPTER

# basic AQUATIC SKILLS

## Key Terms

**Back glide:** A technique for moving through the water in a supine position.

**Bobbing:** The skill of submerging and pushing off from the bottom to return to the surface.

**Feet-first scull:** A sculling technique for moving the body feetfirst in a supine position on the surface of the water using only the arms and hands.

**Feet-first surface dive:** A technique for moving under water from the surface with the feet leading.

**Flat scull:** A technique using basic sculling motions to stay floating supine on the surface.

**Headfirst scull:** A technique for moving headfirst in a supine position on the surface of the water using only the arms and hands.

**Long shallow dive:** A dive for entering the water headfirst at a shallow angle with great forward momentum.

**Pike surface dive:** A technique for moving under water from the surface by bending at the hips and descending headfirst with legs kept straight.

**Prone float:** A stationary and face-down position in the water.

**Prone glide:** A technique for moving through the water in a prone position.

**Rotary kick:** A kicking technique used for treading water; sometimes called the eggbeater kick.

**Sculling:** A technique for moving through the water or staying horizontal using only the arms and hands.

**Supine float:** A stationary and face-up position in the water.

**Treading water:** A skill using arm and leg movements to stay stationary and vertical with the head out of the water.

**Tuck surface dive:** A technique for moving headfirst from the surface with the hips and knees flexed to under water with the hips and knees extending.

# Objectives

*After reading this chapter, you should be able to—*

1. Name two kicks used to tread water.
2. Describe stationary, headfirst, and feet-first sculling.
3. Describe the feet-first, tuck, and pike surface dives.
4. Describe turns for the front crawl, back crawl, elementary backstroke, sidestroke, and breaststroke.
5. Define the key terms at left.

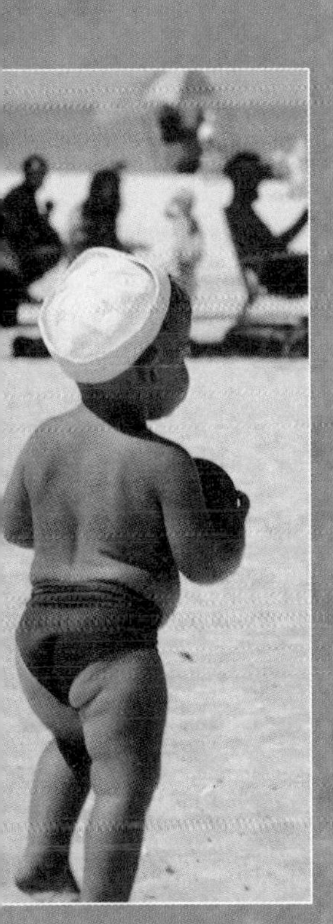

*After reading this chapter and completing appropriate course activities, you should be able to—*

1. Demonstrate prone and supine floats.
2. Demonstrate how to tread water using two different kicks.
3. Demonstrate stationary, headfirst, and feet-first sculling.
4. Demonstrate rolling over in the water from prone position to supine and supine to prone.
5. Demonstrate changing direction as you swim.
6. Demonstrate the feet-first, tuck, and pike surface dives.
7. Demonstrate swimming under water.
8. Demonstrate in-water starts from front and back positions.
9. Demonstrate a long shallow dive.
10. Demonstrate turns for the front crawl, back crawl, elementary backstroke, sidestroke, and breaststroke.

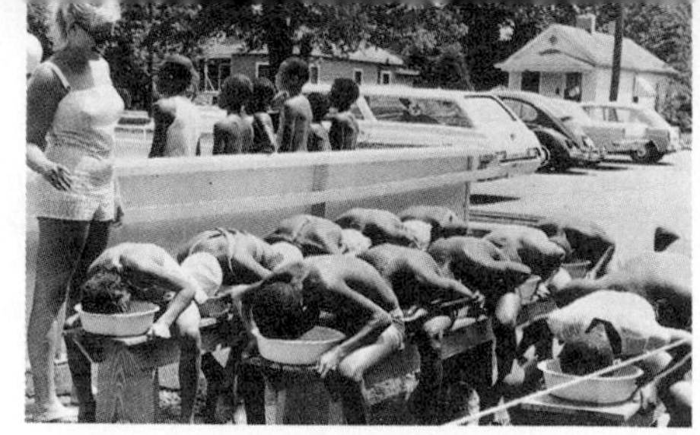

WHEN YOU THINK OF SWIMMING, what do you visualize? Some people imagine the arm-over-arm motion of the front crawl, while others envision the explosive power of the butterfly. Others recall how pleasantly they used the sidestroke to move peacefully through the water.

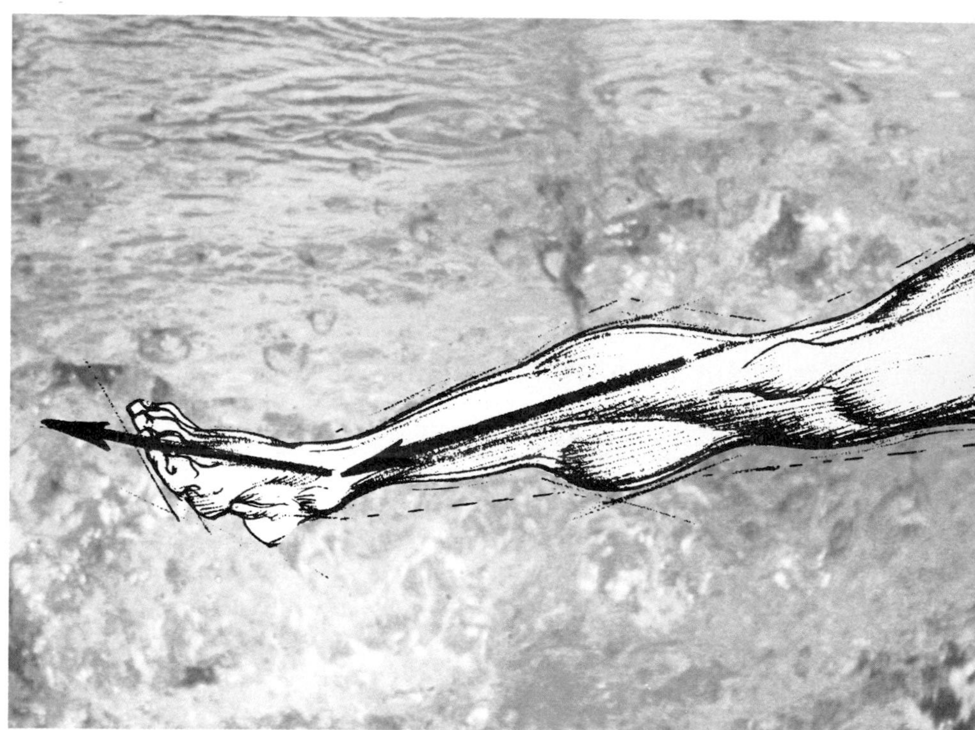

SWIMMING HAS MANY ASPECTS BESIDES STROKES. These include safety skills and turns. This chapter describes many of these basic skills, starting with entering the water and getting adjusted to it. It also treats different ways to float. As you become used to the water, you will learn skills for moving around. This will give you independence in the water. Treading water, surface diving, and sculling are basic ways to hold and change position and move in the water. Changing directions and rolling over to a supine float are important safety skills that also help build your confidence. Finally, you will learn how to start in the water and to turn when swimming laps in a pool.

# FLOAT

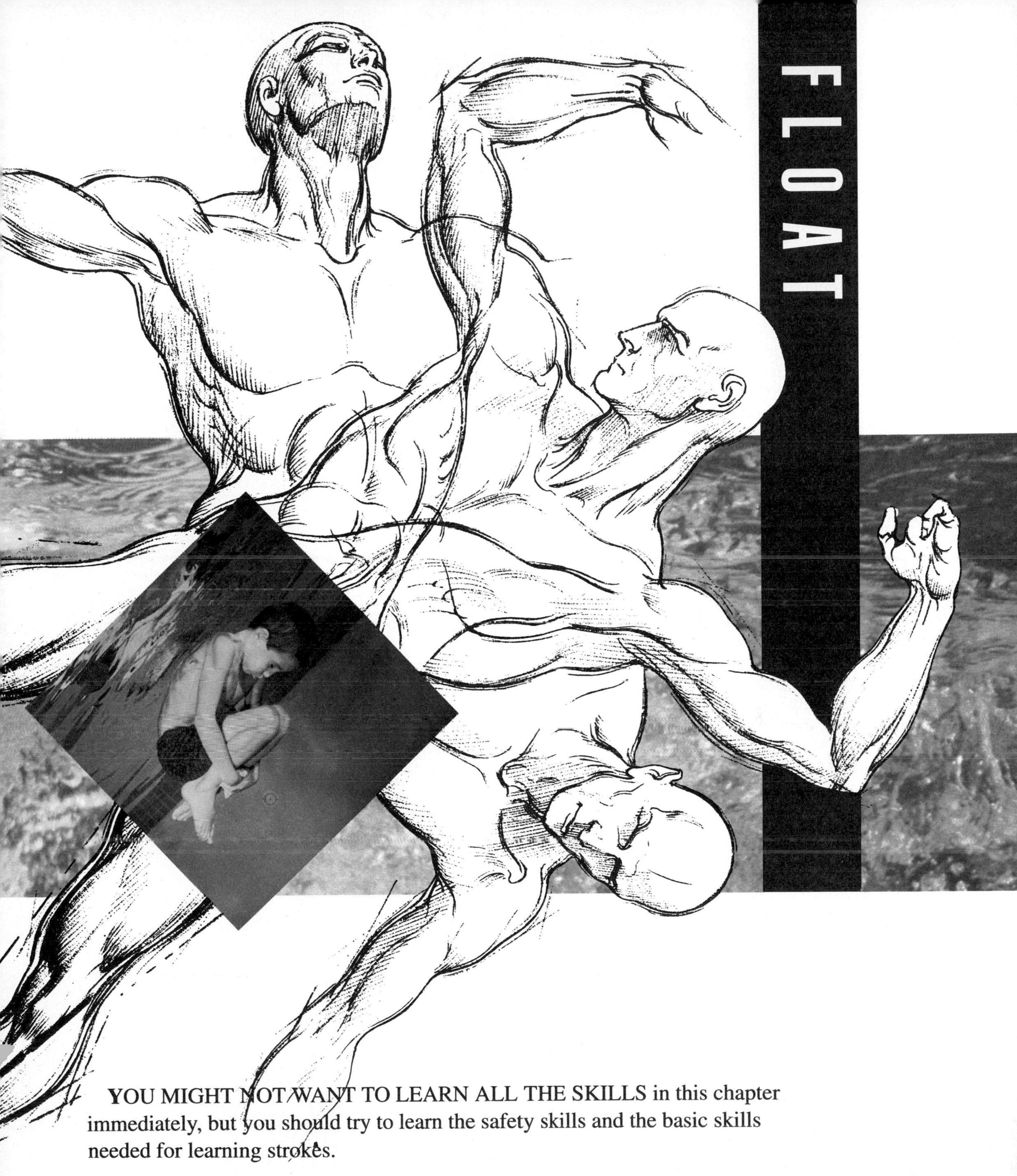

**YOU MIGHT NOT WANT TO LEARN ALL THE SKILLS** in this chapter immediately, but you should try to learn the safety skills and the basic skills needed for learning strokes.

# Basic Skills

## Physical and Mental Adjustment

When you enter the water the first time, you may need to get gradually adjusted physically and mentally. Swimming pool water is much cooler than bath water. Even relatively warm water (80 degrees to 82 degrees F, 26.7 degrees to 27.8 degrees C) may feel cool and make your breathing and pulse speed up. When you are in up to your neck, either wading or crouching, breathing may seem harder because of the added pressure of the water on your chest. You may also feel somewhat lighter because of the effects of buoyancy. (See Chapter 4.) Take the time to get used to the effects of temperature, pressure, and buoyancy. As you become more comfortable and relaxed, you will no longer notice these effects.

## Entering the Water

Getting wet gradually will help your body get used to the cooler water temperature (Fig. 5-1). Enter on the steps, ramp, or slope until you are thigh-deep and scoop water with your hands to wet your arms, chest, neck, and face. You may also sit on the edge of the pool and scoop water onto yourself. Be sure you are comfortable with the water temperature before getting in all the way.

Fig. 5-1

Fig. 5-2

## Bobbing and Breath Control

You must be able to control your breathing to swim well. You do not need to be able to hold your breath for a long time, but you should be able to breathe in and out rhythmically and steadily while swimming. A good method to practice breath control is ***bobbing*** (Fig. 5-2). To bob, hold onto the side of the pool in chest-deep water. Take a breath, bend your knees, and submerge your head. As you go down, gently exhale and then straighten your legs to return to the surface. Inhale when your mouth rises above the surface of the water. Exhale through your mouth and nose, and make the bobbing movement smooth and steady. Repeat this movement over and over until you are comfortable, then move to chin-deep water away from the wall and practice some more.

Deep-water bobbing is good to know as a skill for rescuing yourself. If you are suddenly in water over your head, you can keep breathing as you bob, pushing off of the bottom at an angle toward shallow water, until you are out of the deep water.

## Staying Afloat

Everyone needs to feel confident and safe in the water. Confidence helps you prevent panic and think clearly. This is even more important for the beginner or nonswimmer. You have to be able to stay on the surface and move calmly to safety, however slowly.

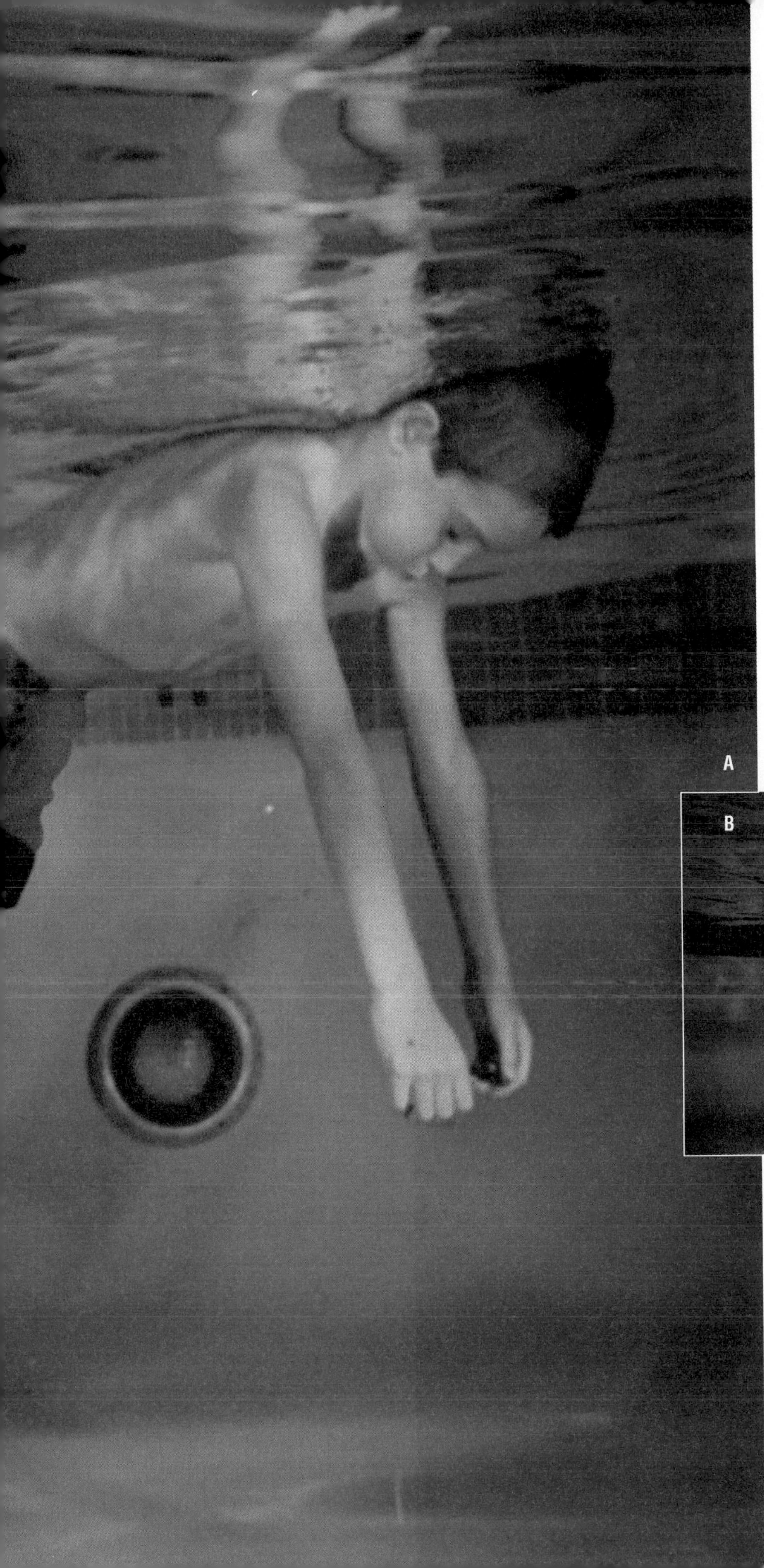

Floating is an easy way for many people to stay near the surface. Chapter 4 explains why we float. Learning to float is easier if you use those principles and if you feel comfortable in the water. Remember that not everyone floats easily. Reread Chapter 4 if you are having trouble with floating.

### *Jellyfish Float*

The jellyfish float is described in Chapter 4. Use this float to see how buoyant you are and to feel how water can support you (Fig. 5-3, *A*).

A

FIG. 5-3, *A-B*

### *Tuck Float*

The tuck float is similar to the jellyfish float, except that you flex your hips and knees and hold onto your legs at mid-calf. (This is the tuck position.) You can also use this float to see how buoyant you are (Fig. 5-3, *B*).

A

FIG. 5-4, *A-C*

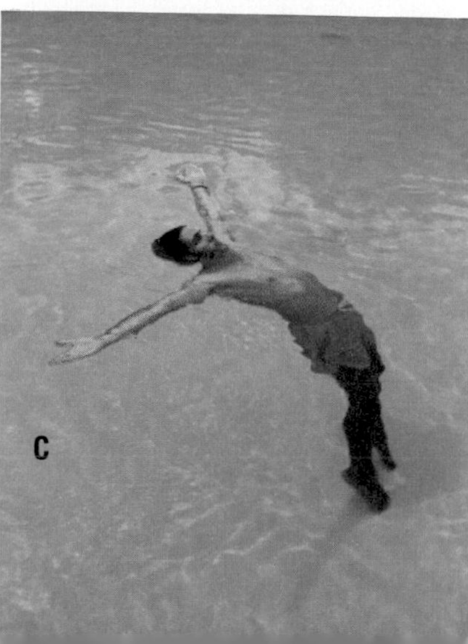

### Supine Float

You can learn the ***supine float*** if you let your body rise to its natural floating position. Stand in shoulder-deep water. Take a deep breath, lay your head back, arch your body gently, relax, bend your knees, and hold your arms out from the shoulders, palms up. The water will support your body as you lie all the way back. Do not push off the bottom but let your feet rise to the floating position that is normal for you—vertical, diagonal, or horizontal (Fig. 5-4, *A-C*). As you float, breathe in and out through your mouth every few seconds. As you learned in Chapter 4, filling your lungs will help you float.

If your natural floating position is diagonal or vertical, you can float more horizontally by moving your arms in the water above your head, lifting your hands out of the water, and bending your knees (Fig. 5-5). (See Chapter 4.) If you cannot float motionless, sculling motions can help you stay on the surface with only a little effort. (See page 98.) You can also stay at the surface by using a winging motion with your arms under water. This is called *finning.*

To recover to a standing position, exhale, tuck your chin toward your chest, and bring your knees forward. Sweep your arms back, down, and forward in a circular motion to bring your body back to vertical, and then stand. This motion is like pulling a chair up underneath you.

### Prone Float

The ***prone float*** helps you become comfortable in a position that involves holding your breath. It is easy to learn this skill in water shallow enough for you to put your hands on the bottom. Start by lying face down with your hands on the bottom. Take a breath and place your face in the water until your ears are covered. Relax and slowly lift your hands off the bottom. Extend your arms in the water above your head. To keep your nose from filling with water, lift your chin slightly and blow some air gently out through your nose. If your toes are still on the bottom, relax your legs and gently push up off the bottom to see if they will rise. Do not be alarmed if your toes return to the bottom. This only means that the water is not deep enough for your body to rotate to its normal (diagonal or vertical) floating position.

To recover, lift your head, bend your hips, and press your arms down until your hands and feet touch bottom.

You can also learn the prone float in chest-deep water. Flex your knees until your shoulders are submerged, extend your arms on the surface, take a deep breath, place your face in the water, lean forward, and gently push your toes up off the bottom. If your normal floating position is near vertical, your toes will return to rest on the bottom.

To stand from this floating position, pull your knees under your body and move your arms toward the bottom. Lift your head and stand up.

Another way to experience your buoyancy is to combine several face-down floats. In chest-deep water, begin with the jellyfish float, move to the tuck float, and extend to the prone float. Then reverse the process and recover to a standing position.

Fig. 5-5

## *Treading Water*

***Treading water*** keeps you upright in deep water with your head out of the water. This is an important personal safety skill for all swimmers. Swimmers must master treading water before taking a lifeguarding class. You can tread water using your arms only, your legs only, or arms and legs together. Use the scissors, breaststroke, or ***rotary kick*** along with sculling movements of the arms and hands, as described below. You should learn to tread water in a relaxed way with slow movements. Move the arms and legs only enough to keep your body vertical.

To tread water, stay nearly vertical with your upper body bent slightly forward at the waist (Fig. 5-6). Make continuous broad, flat, sculling movements with the hands a few inches below the surface in front of the body. Keep the elbows bent. Do the sculling movements with a much wider reach than you use to hold your position when floating on your back. Do the scissors or breaststroke kick with just enough thrust to keep your head above water (Fig. 5-7).

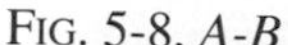

FIG. 5-8, *A-B*

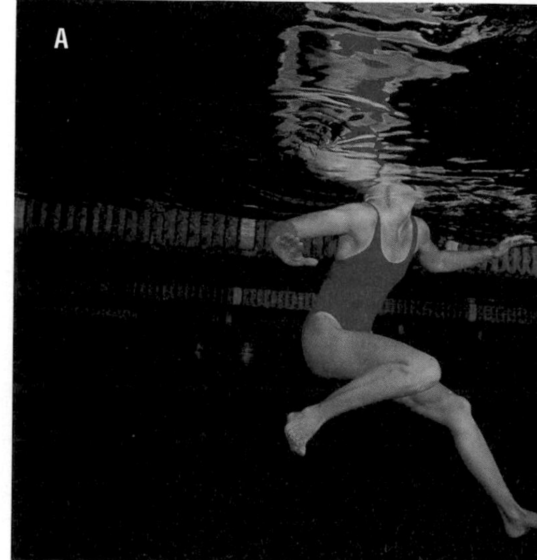

FIG. 5-6

FIG. 5-7

The rotary or "egg beater" kick is also effective for treading water. It gives continuous support because there is no resting phase. This strong kick is used in water polo, synchronized swimming, and lifeguarding.

To tread water with the rotary kick, stay in the same position as treading water with other kicks. Your back should be straight. Keep your hips flexed so your thighs are comfortably forward (Fig. 5-8, *A*). Flex your knees so your lower legs hang down at an angle of nearly 90 degrees to the thighs. With your knees slightly wider than hip distance apart, rotate your lower legs at the knees, one leg at a time. The left leg moves clockwise and the right counterclockwise. Make a large circular movement with the foot and lower leg. Reach as far sideways and backward as you can while keeping your body position. As you move each foot sideways and forward, extend it sharply

(Fig. 5-8, *B*). The power of the kick comes from lift forces created by the sweeping action of the leg and foot (Fig. 5-9). As soon as one leg completes its circle, the other starts. Kick just hard enough to keep your head out of the water.

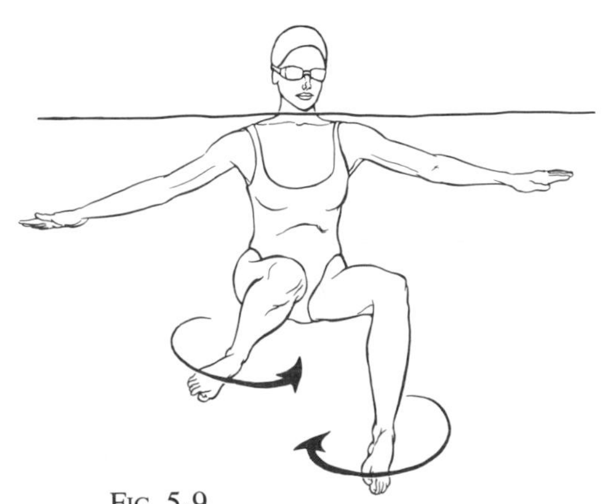

FIG. 5-9

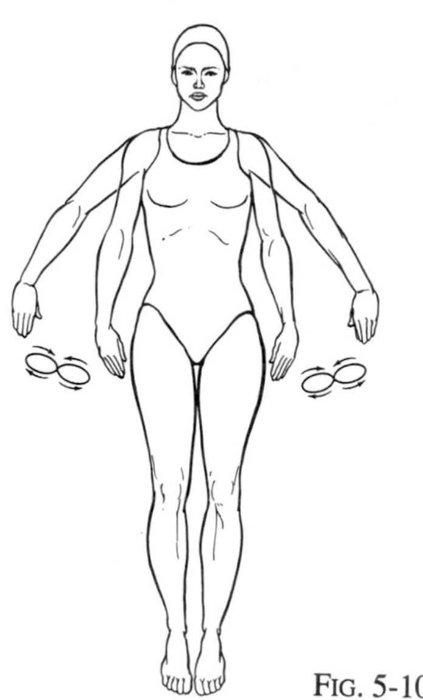
FIG. 5-10

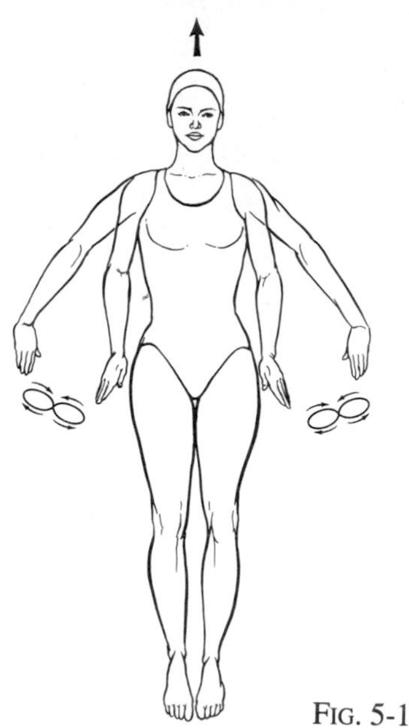
FIG. 5-11

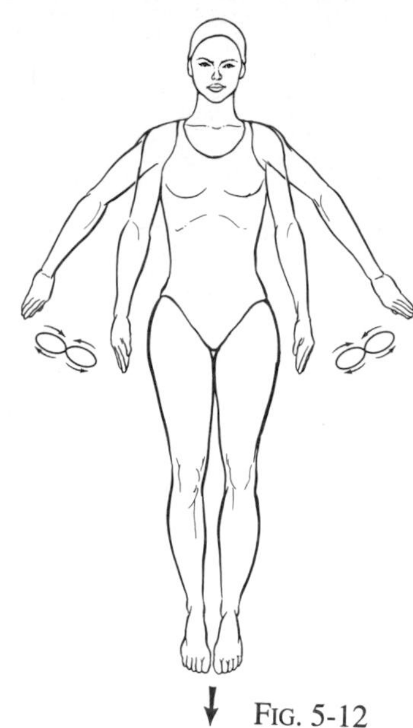
FIG. 5-12

MOVEMENT IN THE WATER

Once you feel comfortable floating or treading water, you can learn how to move in the water. The many swimming strokes you can use are described in Chapter 6. The following sections describe basic skills to help you move or change direction in the water.

## Sculling

***Sculling*** is a way to move through the water using only your hands and forearms. You can also use sculling to stay in position while floating on the back or treading water. On your back, you do sculling with your arms extended along the sides of your body, palms down under the surface of the water. Exert equal and constant pressure with continuous hand movements. In this starting position you can scull in three different ways: the flat, headfirst, and feet-first sculls.

FLAT SCULL. The ***flat scull*** is used to stay still when floating supine. From the starting position, rotate your hands slightly to put the thumb down and move your hands outward just beyond shoulder width. Keep your elbows bent the whole time. Then rotate your hands to put the thumbs up and palms facing inward. Move your hand toward your hips. The hands lead and the forearms follow. Make the motion into a smooth, continuous figure-eight pattern (Fig. 5-10). As you sweep each hand from side to side, water passing over the back of the hands creates lift that raises your hand in the water. (See Chapter 4.) This force, combined with the leverage of your shoulder, helps you keep your position in the water.

HEADFIRST SCULL. The ***headfirst scull*** is used when you are floating supine. The motion is similar to the flat scull, but a different pitch of the hands forcing water outward away from the body and inward toward the feet moves the whole body headfirst. Extend your wrists so your fingers point up slightly. Do the sculling motion with the thumb side of each hand pitched slightly toward the feet during the inward press and the little finger of each hand pitched slightly toward the feet during the outward press (Fig. 5-11).

FEET-FIRST SCULL. The ***feet-first scull*** is also used when you are floating supine. Flex your wrists so your fingers point slightly toward the bottom of the pool. Do the sculling motion with the thumb side of each hand pitched slightly toward the head during the inward press and the little finger of each hand pitched slightly toward the head during the outward press (Fig. 5-12).

## Turning Over

It is helpful to know how to turn over so you can change strokes. To turn over while swimming prone, lower one shoulder and turn your head in the other direction. To turn to the right, lower your right shoulder and turn your head to the left. To turn to the left, lower your left shoulder and turn your head to the right. The momentum from your stroke will help you complete the turn. If you are too tired to keep swimming, you can float or scull gently in the supine position.

To turn over while swimming in a supine position, lower one shoulder and turn your head in the same direction. Keep your arms under water while turning, and reach across your body in the direction of the turn until you are in a prone position.

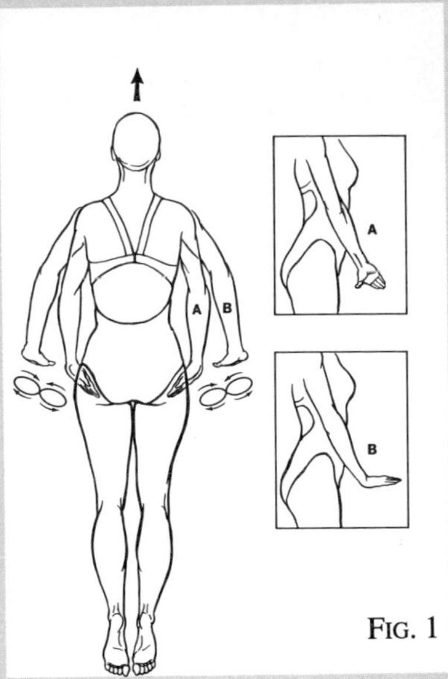

FIG. 1

FIG. 2

**Advanced Sculls**

*To perform the* canoe scull *(Fig. 1), the body is streamlined in the prone position. To maintain a horizontal position, the swimmer must slightly arch the back, press up gently with the heels, and press down gently with the shoulders. This will keep the heels, buttocks, and head at the surface of the water. The face may either be in or out of the water. The arms and hands move freely between the shoulders and hips either to propel the swimmer forward or to keep him or her stationary.*

*The swimmer leads with the wrists, palms outward, away from the body, sweeping the water out by outwardly extending the elbows 12 inches. He or she then immediately turns his or her palms inward and sweeps the hands back toward each other by bending the elbows. The hands are flat and fingers are close together with the thumb alongside the forefinger. This provides a constant and maximum pressure against the water. The movement of the arms and wrists resembles a figure eight.*

*The execution of the* torpedo scull (Fig. 2) *is similar, but the body is in the supine position, and the swimmer moves feetfirst. The body is streamlined, with the face, hips, thighs, and feet at the surface. The movement of the arms and wrists is identical to that of the canoe scull, but the swimmer gently slides the arms up the sides of the body to a position above the head, keeping the wrists and elbows relaxed.*

FIG. 3

*The* support scull (Fig. 3), *which is extremely important in synchronized swimming, is a stationary scull that allows the swimmer to lift the legs out of the water and maintain an inverted position. Once in the inverted position, the swimmer begins with forearms and hands at waist level and perpendicular to the body. The hands are flat and the palms almost face the bottom of the pool. The outward rotation is identical to that of the other sculls, but because of the inverted position, it is extremely difficult to do and creates a strain on the forearms. Even the strongest swimmers will have difficulty with the outward rotation. As with the other sculls, the movements of the hands and wrists also resemble a figure eight.*

### Changing Directions

**B**eing able to change directions while swimming is an important safety skill. When using the front crawl, reach an arm in the desired direction, look toward that arm, and pull slightly wider with the other arm in the new direction. To change directions while swimming on your back, tilt your head in the desired direction and stroke harder with the opposite arm.

## Underwater Skills

### Surface Diving

**S**urface diving is used to go under water when you are swimming on the surface. This skill is used to retrieve objects from the bottom, to rescue a submerged victim, and to go under water in activities such as skin diving. Surface diving is the quickest way to descend accurately under water.

**A** surface dive can be either feet first or headfirst. The headfirst dive may be in a tuck (curled) or pike (bent at the hips) position. To avoid injury by hitting an object as you go down or come back up, keep your eyes open and arms above the head. In all surface dives, exhaling while you go down prevents water from entering your nose.

*If you feel ear pain or uncomfortable pressure as you go deeper or swim under water, hold your nose and blow air out through the nose. If this does not relieve the pressure, you must swim to shallower water or to the surface to prevent damage to your ears.*

FIG. 5-13, *A-B*

### *Feet-First Surface Dive*

A ***feet-first surface dive*** is the only safe way to go down into murky water or water of unknown depth. Start by treading water vertically. Simultaneously press both hands down vigorously to the sides of the thighs and do a strong scissors or breaststroke kick. These movements help you rise in the water so you will have a better descent (Fig. 5-13, *A*). Take a deep breath at the top of the rise. As you start down, keep your body vertical and in a streamlined position. When your downward momentum slows, turn your palms outward, then sweep the hands and arms upward to get more downward propulsion (Fig. 5-13, *B*). When you are as deep as you want, tuck your body and roll to a horizontal position. Then extend your arms and legs and swim under water.

### *Tuck Surface Dive*

The ***tuck surface dive*** is a headfirst surface dive. First, get forward momentum with a swimming stroke or glide. Take a breath, sweep your arms backward to the thighs, and turn your palms down. Tuck your chin to your chest, bend your body at a right angle at the hips, and draw your legs into a tuck position (Fig. 5-14, *A*). Roll forward until you are almost upside down (Fig. 5-14, *B*). Then extend your legs upward quickly while pressing the arms and hands forward, palms down, toward the bottom (Fig. 5-14, *C*). For greater depth, do a breaststroke arm pull. If you do not know the depth of the water or it is less than 8 feet, keep one arm extended over your head toward the bottom.

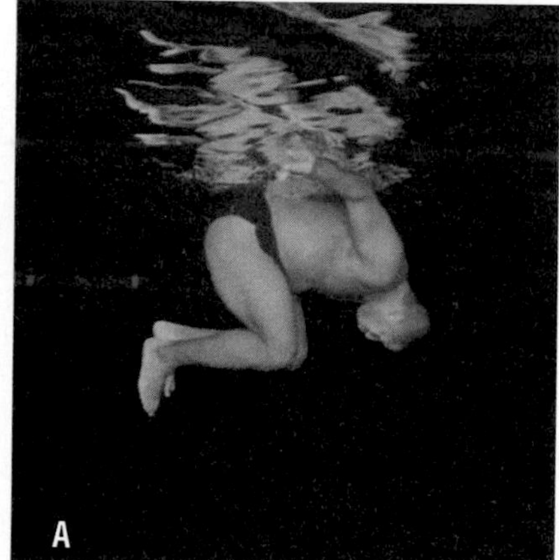

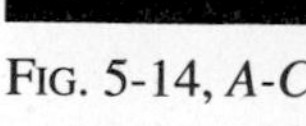

FIG. 5-14, *A-C*

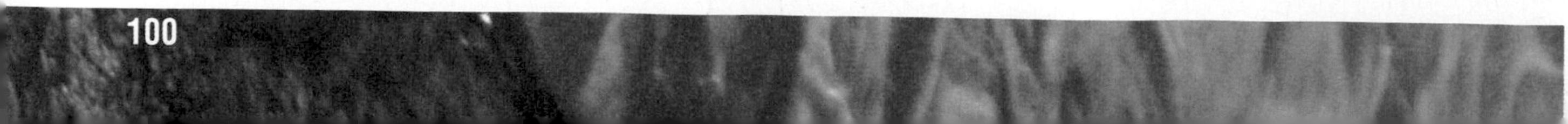

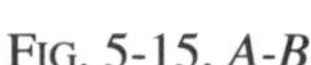

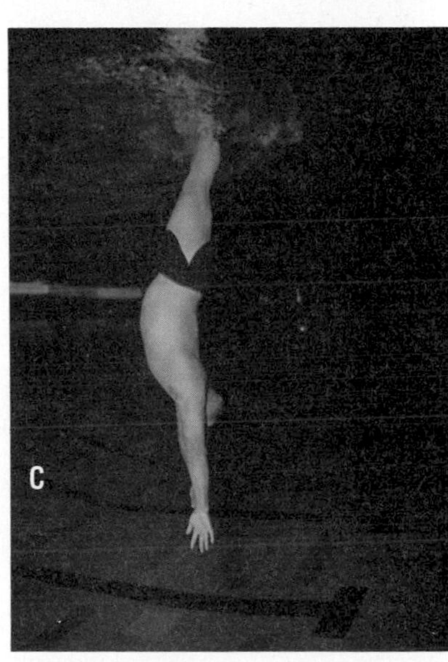

FIG. 5-15, *A-B*

### *Pike Surface Dive*

The ***pike surface dive*** is similar to the tuck surface dive, except the legs are kept straight and the pike position is used. Use a swimming stroke or glide to gain forward momentum. Sweep your arms backward to your thighs and turn them palm down. Tuck your chin to your chest and flex at the hip sharply while your arms reach forward and downward toward the bottom (Fig. 5-15, *A*). Lift the legs upward, straight and together. Your body is now fully extended, streamlined, and almost vertical (Fig. 5-15, *B*). The weight of your legs and the forward momentum usually take you deep enough without more arm movement.

## SWIMMING UNDER WATER

### *Safety Precautions*

Swimming under water lets you recover lost objects, avoid surface hazards, and explore the underwater world. You can easily learn this skill, but you must follow safety precautions to prevent injury. Keep at least one hand extended in front of you and always swim with your eyes. open. These precautions help you avoid obstructions and know how deep you are.

When you swim under water, do not hyperventilate. (See Chapter 2.) This is dangerous because even an accomplished swimmer may black out under water and possibly drown.

### *Underwater Strokes*

Although no one stroke is always best for underwater swimming, a modified breaststroke is generally used. You can modify the breaststroke for underwater swimming in several ways. Use a breaststroke kick or flutter kick (Fig. 5-16). Extend the arm pull backward to the thighs for a longer and stronger stroke. Another method is to use the arm pull and kick together followed by a glide with arms at the sides. If you cannot see very far in the water, shorten the arm pull or do not use it at all. Keep your arms stretched out in front to feel for obstructions.

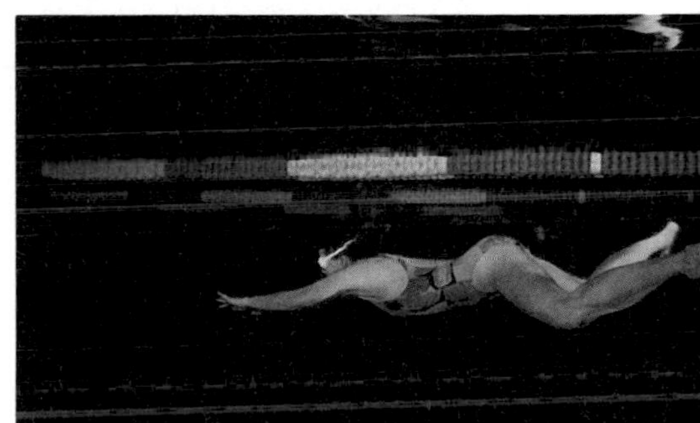

FIG. 5-16

To change direction or depth while swimming under water, raise or lower your head and reach your arms in the desired direction while pulling. Flexing or extending the hips directs the body up or down.

## Starting and Turning

### Starting in the Water

When first learning strokes, most people prefer to start in the water. If the pool is too shallow for safe diving or you do not know how to dive, you will start from poolside.

#### *Starting Facedown*

To start facedown, grasp the overflow of a pool wall or the pool side with one hand. If holding on with the right hand, rotate your body and lean forward slightly so that your left shoulder and arm are under the surface. Hold your feet together and place them against the pool wall, with the right foot closer to the surface (Fig. 5-17, *A*). As you push off the wall with both feet, lift your right hand up and extend your arm above the head. As your right arm extends, rotate your body to a prone position and submerge so that both arms are under water and extended over your head (Fig. 5-17, *B*). Interlock your thumbs or index fingers or overlap your hands to stay safe and streamlined. Glide until your momentum slows to your swimming speed and then start swimming. You can use this technique with the front crawl and the breaststroke. This start is better than just plunging forward in the water because it helps you assume a streamlined position for starting the strokes. You can use this start regardless of the pool depth.

Prone glide. Use the ***prone glide*** to start from a standing position in open water or when you are not near poolside. Begin as you would for a prone float, but push off the bottom with your feet so you move forward in a prone streamlined position. Then begin your swimming stroke.

Fig. 5-17, *A-B*

FIG. 5-19, *A-C*

### *Starting on Your Side*

To start a sidestroke, use the same body position as for face-down strokes but do not rotate your body. Extend in front of you the arm closer to the bottom of the pool. Push off with both feet and place your other arm against your thigh. Glide until your momentum slows and then start the sidestroke.

FIG. 5-18, *A-B*

### *Starting on Your Back*

To start swimming on your back, hold the pool wall with both hands about shoulder-width apart. Tuck your body and put your feet about hip-width apart against the wall just under the surface. Bend your arms slightly and put your chin on your chest (Fig. 5-18, *A*). Pull your body closer to the wall, take a breath, and lean your head backward to slightly arch your body. Then, all in one motion, let go, bring your hands close to your body, reach your arms over your head with hands touching, and push strongly off the wall (Fig. 5-18, *B*). Keep your body stretched and streamlined as it pushes into the water. As soon as your face submerges, tuck your chin slightly and start to lift your arms toward the surface. Glide just under or at the surface of the water until your momentum slows. Then start the flutter kick followed by the first arm pull.

BACK GLIDE. You may also use the ***back glide*** to start from a standing position. Begin as you would a supine float, but push off the bottom with your feet so you move in a streamlined position. Start the flutter kick followed by the first arm pull.

STARTING OUT OF THE WATER

The ***long shallow dive*** is a low-projecting dive done in a streamlined body position. You enter the water at a controlled, shallow angle with great forward momentum. It is used to dive in shallow areas and in rescues when speed is urgent. You should do this dive only in clear water of known depth. *Do not try to learn this dive in less than 9 feet of water. Never do it thereafter in water shallower than 5 feet.* Misjudging the depth or angle of your entry could lead to hitting the bottom and injuring your spine.

Start on the edge of the pool with your feet about shoulder-width apart and your toes gripping the edge. Flex your hips and knees and position your back nearly parallel to the pool deck. To gain momentum for the dive, draw the arms backward and upward, letting the heels rise and the body start to move forward (Fig. 5-19, *A*). Immediately swing your arms downward and then forward. As you lose balance, extend your hips, knees, ankles, and toes forcibly to drive forward in a line of flight over and nearly parallel to the surface of the water (Fig. 5-19, *B*). Keep your body stretched and your hands interlocked and out in front of you.

During the flight, drop your head slightly between your outstretched arms, which should be angled downward slightly (Fig. 5-19, *C*). Make your entry at a slight angle to the surface to avoid a painful flat landing. Steer upward toward the surface with your hands and head once under water. Keep your body fully extended and streamlined as you glide under water. When your speed slows, start the leg kick to rise to the surface and start swimming.

As you become a more proficient swimmer, you may want to progress to the competitive starts described in Chapter 7.

## TURNS

Most people swimming for general fitness use pools. Since you usually swim back and forth, being able to turn easily at the wall is important. This chapter describes basic turns called *open turns.* Flip turns, used by more advanced swimmers, are described in Chapter 7.

### *Front Crawl Turn*

As you approach the wall, keep your leading arm extended until you touch the wall. Then bend the elbow of the leading arm and drop that shoulder slightly as you rotate your body to move your back toward the wall. Tuck your body, turn, and spin away from the leading hand, ending with your feet against the wall, one above the other (Fig. 5-20, *A*). (If the right hand is the leading hand, the right foot will be on top.) During the spin, lift your face and take a breath. Return your face to the water as your leading hand recovers over the surface (Fig. 5-20, *B*). Extend both arms in front of you as your legs push off. Keep your body in a streamlined position on one side. Rotate in the glide until you are face down. As your momentum slows, start kicking to rise to the surface and resume the arm stroke.

FIG. 5-20, *A-B*

Fig. 5-22, *A-C*

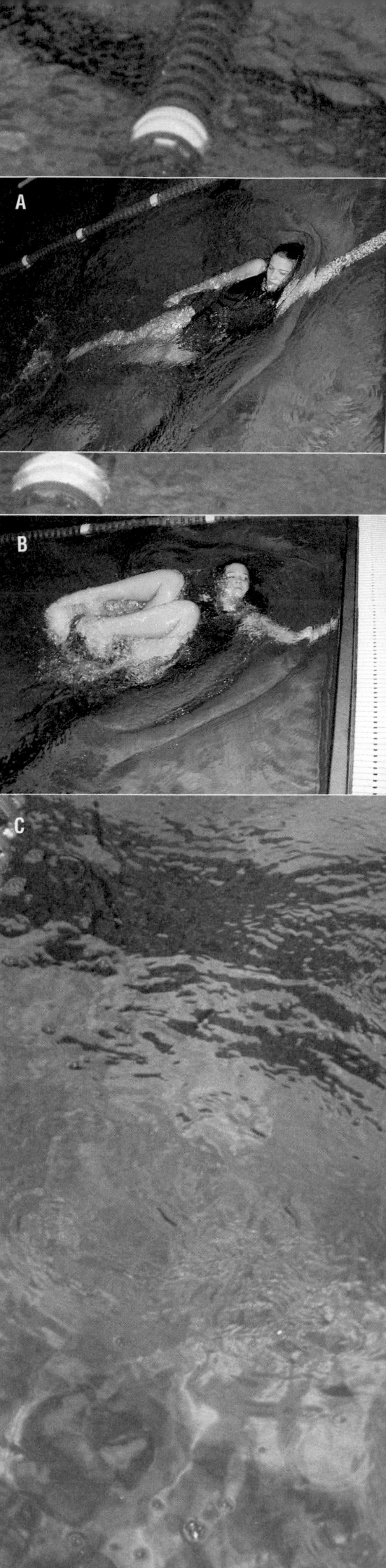


### *Sidestroke Turn*

For a sidestroke turn, vary the front crawl turn slightly. Touch the wall with your leading (bottom) arm, and do the whole turn as previously described. In the glide, stay in the side-lying position from the push-off and pull your trailing arm to the thigh ready for the next stroke.

### *Breaststroke Turn*

As you come to the wall, reach to touch the wall with both hands (Fig. 5-21, *A*). Tuck your body, turn your head in the chosen direction, and swivel your hips to bring your feet to the wall, one above the other. (With a spin to the right, your head turns right and your left foot is on top.) Push off with your right hand to help the spinning action. Raise the left hand over the surface toward the other end of the pool. Submerge your hands, arms, and head as you strongly push off the wall with your body in a side-lying position (Fig. 5-21, *B*). This turn is deeper and the underwater glide longer than in the front crawl turn. Rotate until your body is face down, and glide with arms and legs extended until your speed slows. Do a full arm pull to your thighs, then a breaststroke kick and glide. Then raise your head and return to the surface and start your strokes. To turn to the left, simply reverse these directions.

### *Backstroke Spin Turn*

With the elementary backstroke or back crawl, gauge your approach to the wall with the backstroke flags, the color change of the lane lines, or a glance backward. Fully extend one arm behind your head and take a breath as your palm touches the wall (Fig. 5-22, *A*). Bend the elbow of the leading arm and let your head come near the wall as you tuck your body and spin the hips and legs toward the leading hand (Fig. 5-22, *B*). You can keep your head above water if you choose, although submerging it allows for a smoother, more efficient turn. Sweep the trailing hand toward your head to help the spinning and put both feet on the wall, assuming a sitting position in the water.

Push off with the top of your head facing the other end of the pool. Assume a streamlined position with your arms fully extended over the head (Fig. 5-22, *C*). As you begin to lose speed, tuck your chin, angle your hands and arms slightly toward the surface, and start kicking. As you come to the surface, start the first arm pull. Breathe out slowly through the nose during the push-off to keep water from entering the nose.

Fig. 5-21, *A-B*

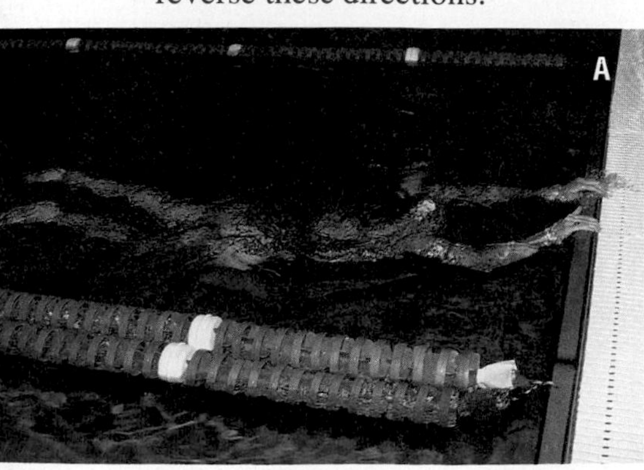

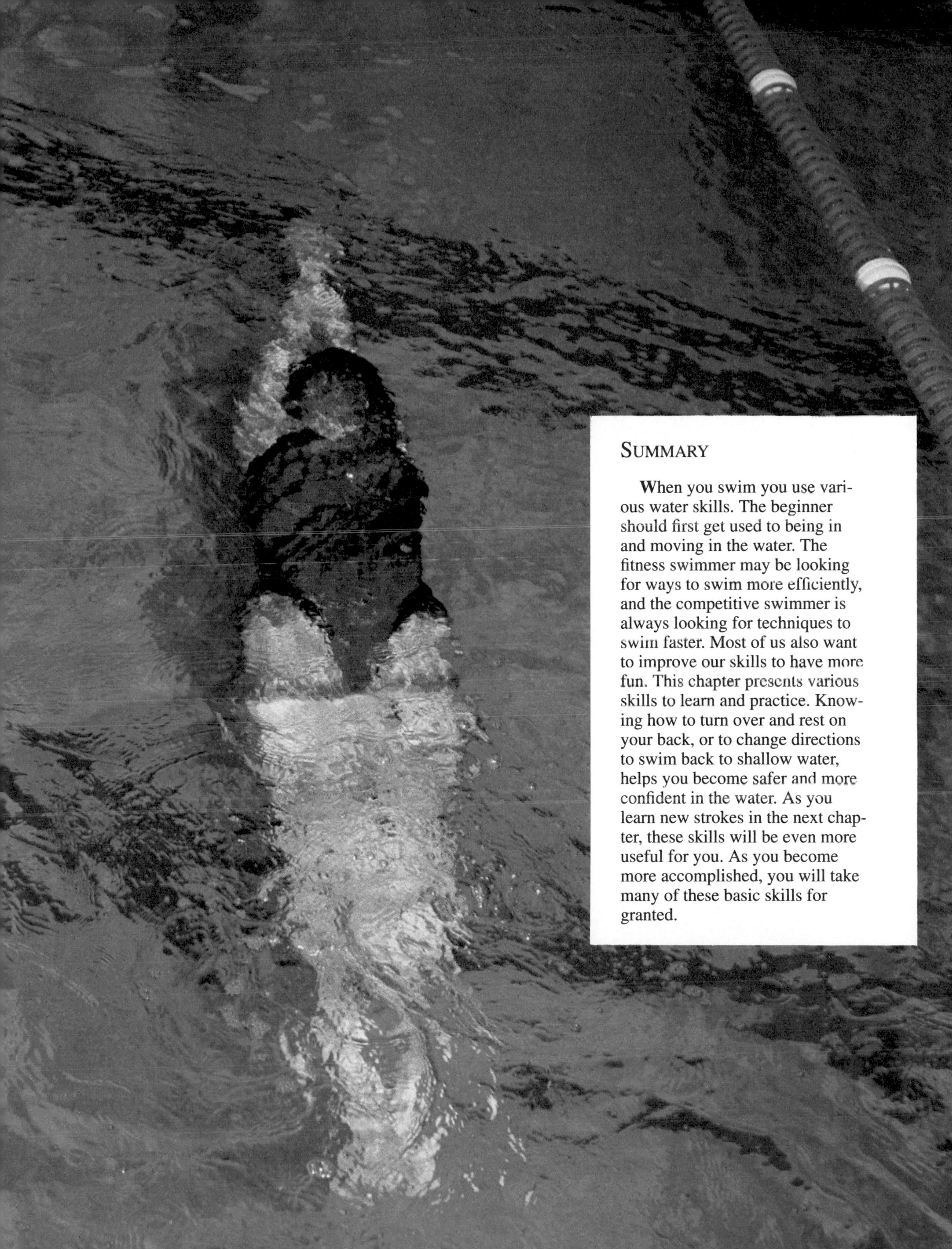

## Summary

When you swim you use various water skills. The beginner should first get used to being in and moving in the water. The fitness swimmer may be looking for ways to swim more efficiently, and the competitive swimmer is always looking for techniques to swim faster. Most of us also want to improve our skills to have more fun. This chapter presents various skills to learn and practice. Knowing how to turn over and rest on your back, or to change directions to swim back to shallow water, helps you become safer and more confident in the water. As you learn new strokes in the next chapter, these skills will be even more useful for you. As you become more accomplished, you will take many of these basic skills for granted.

6

CHAPTER

# stroke mechan

## KEY TERMS

**BODY ROLL:** A rotating movement of the body around the midline.

**CATCH:** The stage in a stroke when the swimmer first engages the water in a way to start moving; the start of the power phase.

**GLIDE:** The stage of a stroke after the power phase when the body keeps moving without any swimmer effort.

**LEADING ARM:** The arm reaching beyond the head when in the glide position. In the sidestroke, this is also called the bottom arm.

**POWER PHASE:** The stage when the arm or leg stroke is moving the body in the desired direction.

**PRONE:** On the front, face down.

**PROPULSIVE:** Causing motion.

**RECOVERY:** The stage of the stroke when the arms and/or legs relax and return to the starting position.

**SUPINE:** On the back, face up.

**TRAILING ARM:** The arm that rests on the hip in the glide phase of the sidestroke. Also called the top arm.

ics

# Objectives

***After reading this chapter, you should be able to—***

1. Describe the front crawl.
2. Describe the elementary backstroke.
3. Describe the breaststroke.
4. Describe the sidestroke.
5. Describe the back crawl.
6. Describe the butterfly.
7. Define the key terms at left.

***After reading this chapter and completing the appropriate course activities, you should be able to—***

1. Perform the front crawl.
2. Perform the elementary backstroke.
3. Perform the breaststroke.
4. Perform the sidestroke.
5. Perform the back crawl.
6. Perform the butterfly.

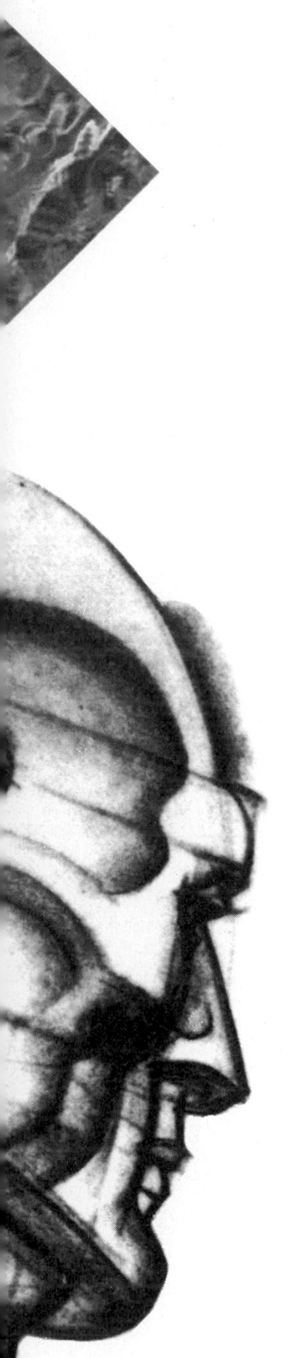

I M P R

THROUGHOUT HISTORY, swimmers have developed many strokes to improve their speed and mobility in the water. (See Chapter 1.) Although new developments still occur, the focus in recent years has been on improving the basic swimming strokes that have endured over time. The science of stroke mechanics has led to new and more efficient ways to propel ourselves through the water.

IN THE PAST, SWIMMERS AND THEIR COACHES used trial-and-error methods to improve their performance, but now stroke mechanics has become a sophisticated science. It has advanced with a greater understanding of hydrodynamics (Chapter 4) and the use of underwater video and computer analysis.

THIS CHAPTER DESCRIBES IN DETAIL the six basic strokes: front crawl, elementary backstroke, breaststroke, sidestroke, back crawl, and butterfly. Less frequently used strokes are described in summary form: trudgen, trudgen crawl, double trudgen, overarm sidestroke, and inverted breaststroke. Each stroke is described simply enough for the beginner to learn and in enough detail for an experienced swimmer to benefit.

A CLEAR, CONSISTENT APPROACH is used to describe all strokes. The different movements that make up each stroke are analyzed in their different aspects and phases:

- Body position/motion
- Arm stroke
- Kick
- Breathing and timing
- One or two hydrodynamic principles involved in the stroke

THE PURPOSE OF THIS CHAPTER is to help you improve your strokes. Whether you swim for leisure or competition, propelling yourself easily and efficiently through the water is the goal. Thus, this chapter focuses on how to propel yourself in the best manner with each stroke. Other factors, such as your size, strength, body composition, and flexibility, influence how you do your strokes. This chapter does not try to give you the one "perfect" way to swim a stroke. Instead, it gives you the basics that you can adjust for your own circumstances. The better you understand the components of the strokes, the better swimmer you will be.

E F F I C

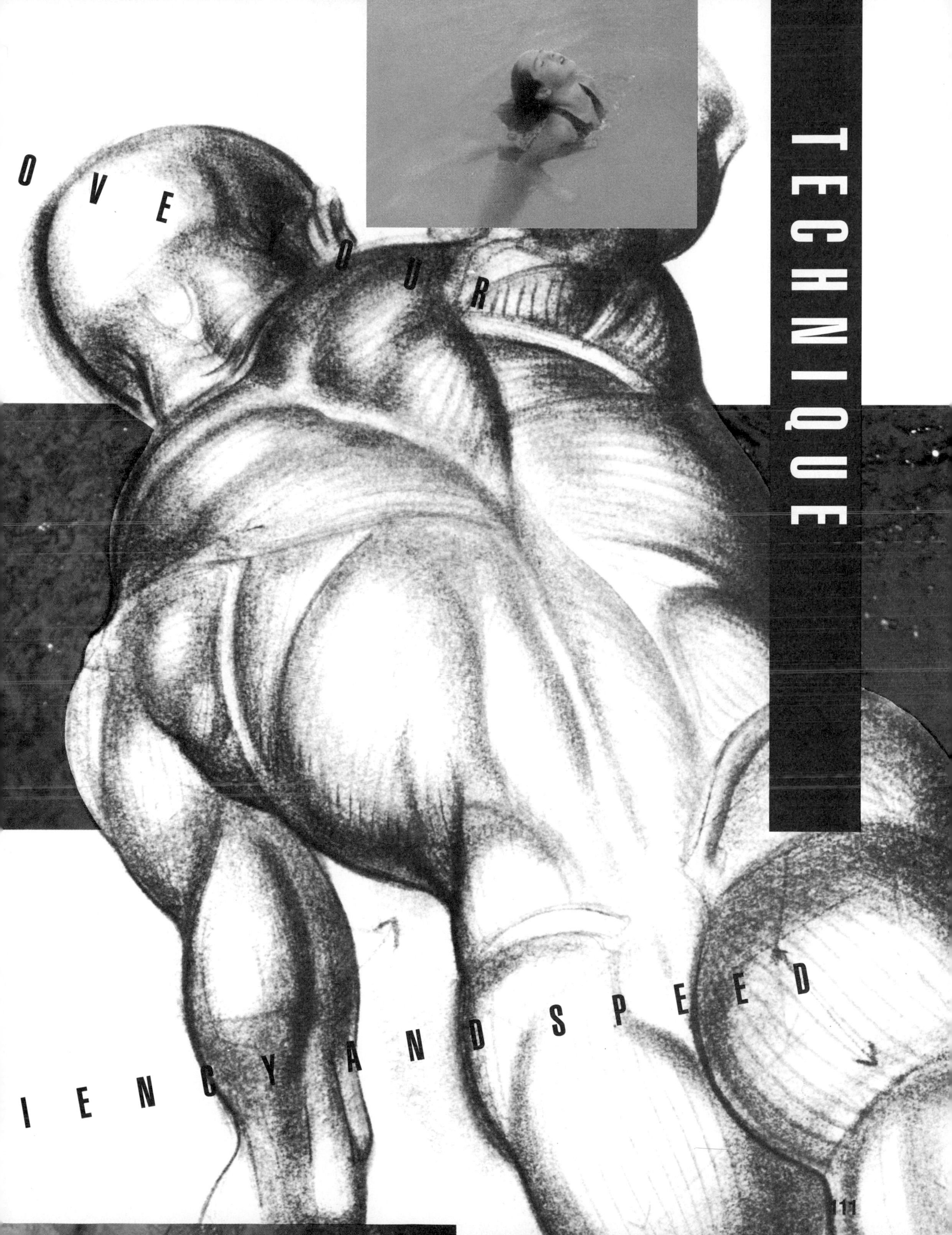
OVE YOUR
TECHNIQUE
IENCY AND SPEED

# FRONT crawl

The front crawl, sometimes called freestyle, is the fastest stroke. Most people think of the front crawl when they imagine swimming, and most are interested in learning it first. Like all strokes, it has three characteristics:

- The goal is efficiency of motion.
- The stroke depends on principles of hydrodynamics.
- Stroke components, such as body position, arm and leg action, and breathing, are critical for success.

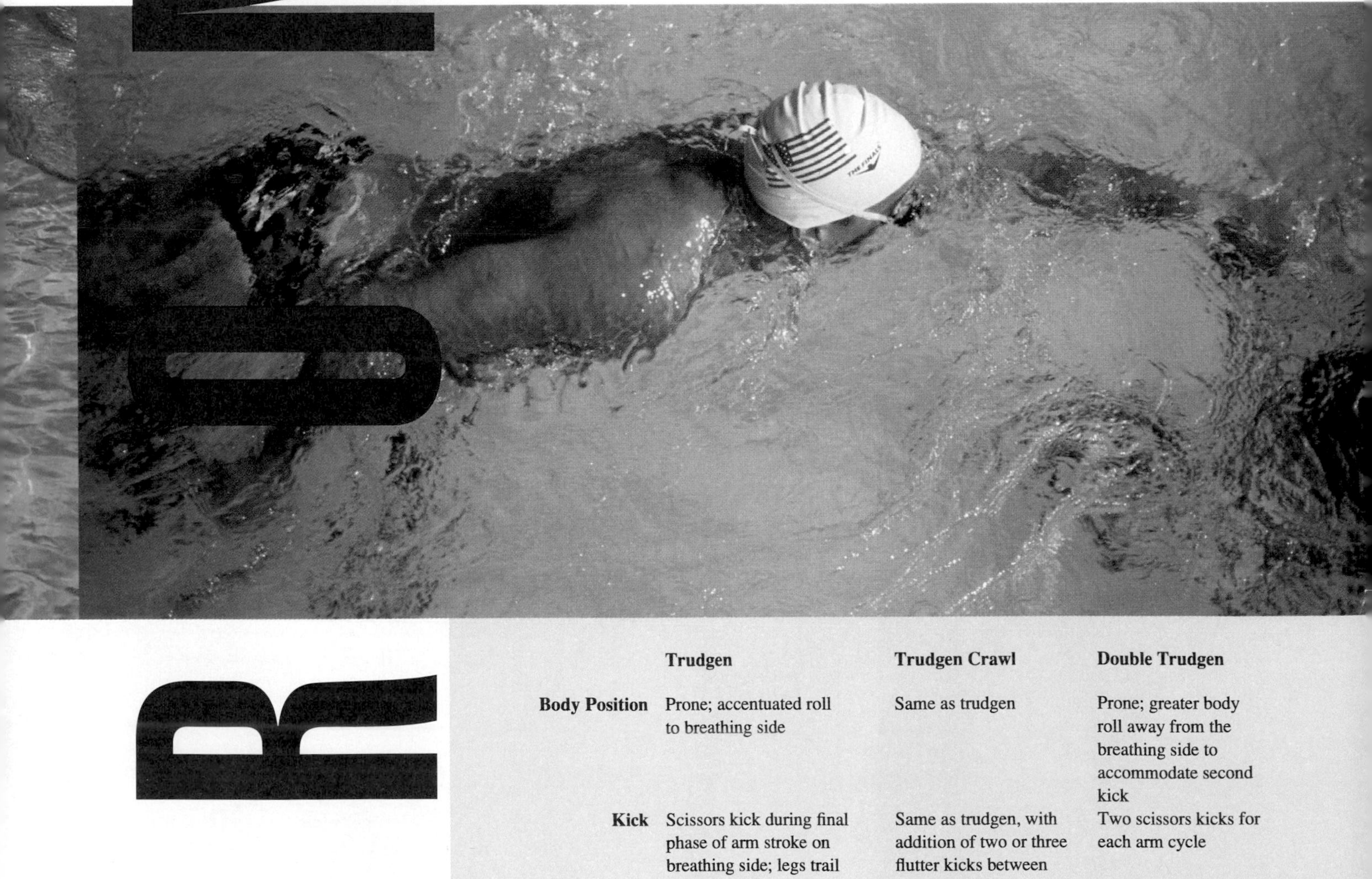

| | Trudgen | Trudgen Crawl | Double Trudgen |
|---|---|---|---|
| **Body Position** | Prone; accentuated roll to breathing side | Same as trudgen | Prone; greater body roll away from the breathing side to accommodate second kick |
| **Kick** | Scissors kick during final phase of arm stroke on breathing side; legs trail between kicks | Same as trudgen, with addition of two or three flutter kicks between scissors kicks | Two scissors kicks for each arm cycle |
| **Arm Stroke** | Similar to front crawl (more body roll to breathing side) | Same as trudgen | Catch-up stroke: each arm does a complete stroke and recovery before opposite arm strokes |
| **Breathing and Timing** | Leg on breathing side kicks as arm on breathing side finishes power phase; inhalation at start of arm recovery | Same as trudgen | Same as trudgen; may breathe to alternate sides |

# body POSITION/MOTION

FIG. 6-1

In this stroke, your body is ***prone*** and straight. The front crawl uses much ***body roll,*** however. Body roll is a rotating movement around the midline, an imaginary line from head to feet that divides the body equally into left and right parts. With body roll, the whole body rotates, not just the shoulders (Fig. 6-1). It results from three movements: (1) the high recovery of one arm, (2) the downsweep of the other arm, and (3) the sideways force of the kicks as the legs roll with the rest of the body.

**Trudgen, Trudgen Crawl, and Double Trudgen**

*The trudgen family of strokes uses a shortened scissors kick by itself or combined with a flutter kick along with the breathing and arm pull of the front crawl. In this scissors kick, the knees do not recover as far as in the sidestroke. An alternative is a wider flutter kick, as occurs naturally with greater body roll. The table at left presents the details of the three strokes.*

Body roll is important for almost all aspects of the front crawl. It helps you use a relaxed and high elbow ***recovery*** and improves arm propulsion. Body roll helps you keep good lateral body position (your position in relation to the midline). It also helps you breathe rhythmically and keep an overall rhythm in your stroke.

Your head position is an important part of overall body position. Most swimmers keep the water line between the eyebrows and hairline, depending on their buoyancy (Fig. 6-2). Someone with little buoyancy may have to lower the head a little to raise the hips to the best level.

FIG. 6-2

Head movement also is critical. As is commonly said, "Where the head goes, the body follows." If your head moves from side to side, as often happens if it is placed improperly for breathing, your body will move laterally. If your head bobs up and down, your hips will do the same. In both cases, the resulting body motion slows you down.

Finally, your legs also affect body position. Poor body position can cause a poor kick, and a poor kick can cause poor body position. In a correct kick, your heels just break the surface of the water. Your legs roll with the rest of your body.

# arm STROKE

### *Power Phase*

The front crawl, like other strokes, is a "feel stroke" in that the more you "feel" the water, the better you swim. You feel the resistance from lift forces (propeller propulsion) and action-reaction forces (paddle propulsion) of your arms and legs. (See Chapter 4.)

FIG. 6-3

To begin the ***power phase*** of the stroke, your hand enters the water in front of your shoulder, index finger first. Since you keep the elbow partly flexed, the point of entry is about three-fourths as far as you could reach with your arm straight. Use a smooth entry, with your elbow higher than the rest of your arm and entering the water last (Fig. 6-3). Think of it as your forearm going through a hole that your hand makes in the water's surface. Your hand is pitched (angled) out and down as you extend your arm fully under water to start the ***catch.*** It is called the catch because you feel as if you have grabbed a semi-solid mass of water—the effect of form drag and lift forces (Fig. 6-4, *A*).

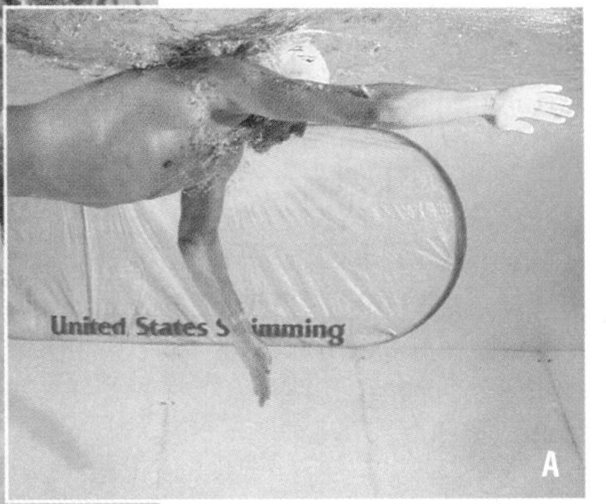

FIG. 6-4, *A-C*

Seen from above, your left hand traces an S-shaped pattern in the power phase (reverse-S for the right hand). The power phase starts with the catch. With your arm extended and your wrist slightly flexed, you sweep your hand down and slightly out to just outside the shoulder (the top of the S shape). If the arm made a good entry, your elbow will be higher than your hand at the start of the pull and will stay higher throughout. The catch feels like a natural motion to make to move forward. It happens automatically if your hand is pitched correctly and you let your shoulder roll properly. You feel tension in your wrist and pressure on your palm. This part of the power phase is dominated by lift forces.

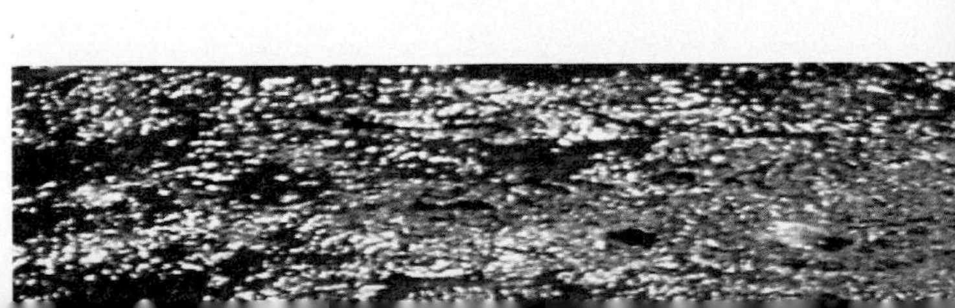

As the power phase continues, your elbow bends to a maximum of 90 degrees and your hand and arm sweep back toward your feet and up toward your chest (Fig. 6-4, *B*). (This is the diagonal part of the S shape.) Your hand should not cross the midline of your body. In this sweep, pitch your hand in instead of out and keep your wrist nearly flat. Your arm and hand move from the deepest point of the stroke (at the end of the catch) to the shallower mid-pull phase. The sweep of your hand from deep to shallow produces lift forces. The press of your arm and hand against the water in the backward direction produces propulsion with action-reaction forces.

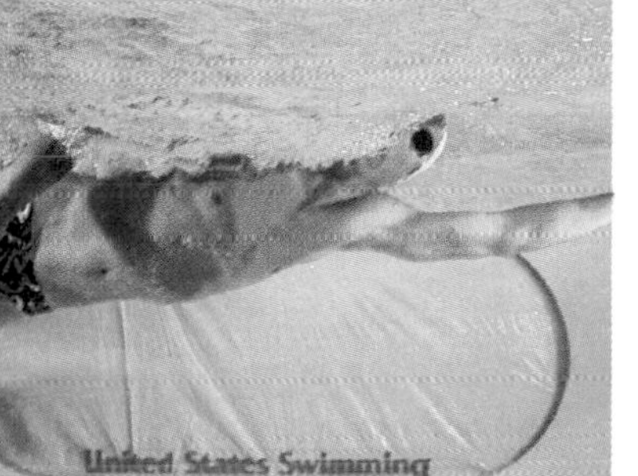


In the finish of the stroke, straighten your arm and press your hand straight back toward your feet while moving it to the side of your body. (This is the bottom of the S shape, which is not as broad as the top of the S shape.) Extend your wrist (bend it back) to keep your palm pressing toward your feet. Keep this pull going to the full extent of your reach, until your thumb brushes your thigh (Fig. 6-4, *C*). Your hand has accelerated from the catch through the finish of the stroke and is at its highest speed. The finish is dominated by action-reaction forces (Fig. 6-5, *A-E*).

FIG. 6-5, *A-E*

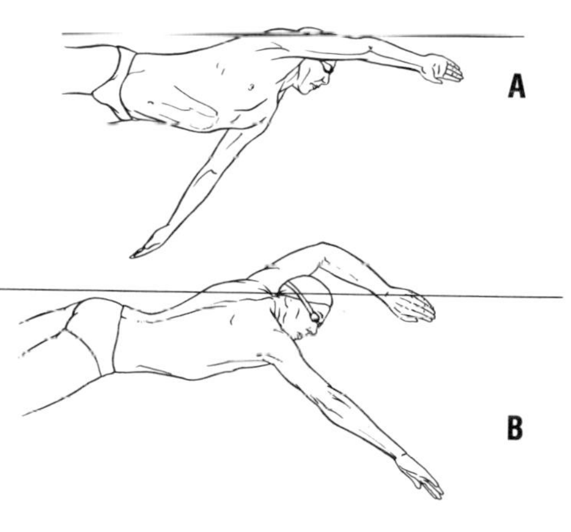


C

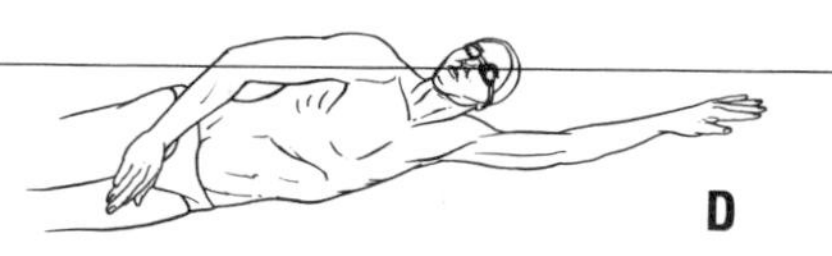


E

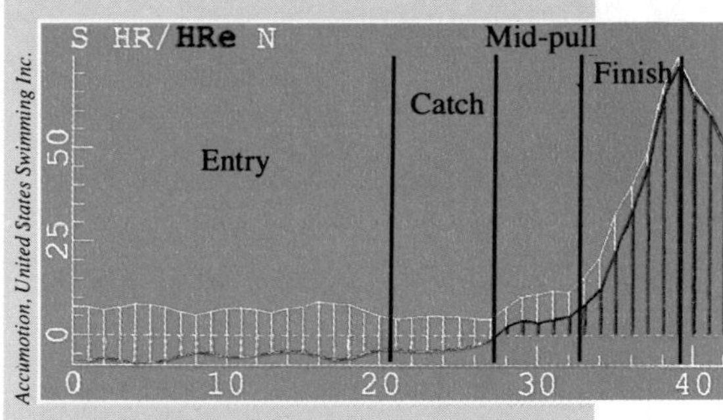


**Technology Innovations: Computer Analysis of Swimming Strokes**

*Images created by computer can tell us more than meets the eye about our strokes. These images, called "Hand Force Curves" give you detailed information about your stroke. They can also help you understand the overall patterns of strokes and how to make them more efficient.*

*The hand force curves shown in this chapter are part of a series of images generated by computer analysis of videotape. The total force produced is shown in yellow. The force used to produce forward motion, the effective force, is shown in black. The closer these two lines are to each other, the more efficient the swimmer. Points where the line drops below the bottom axis of the graph indicate drag and are red.*

*Examining the graph from left to right you see that the entry not only produces no forward motion, it creates drag decreasing the efficiency of the swimmer. The first "peak" is the catch, where you begin to move forward. Each peak and valley represents changes in hand pitch and motion. The highest peak represents the finish, the most powerful part of the stroke.*

*The differences between swimmers give each force curve a slightly different shape, but the overall patterns remain the same. Graphs for each competitive stroke are placed throughout the chapter. Examine each one carefully, comparing the image you see to the information in the text. You will find that they are very similar. This knowledge can assist you in making your stroke as efficient as possible.*

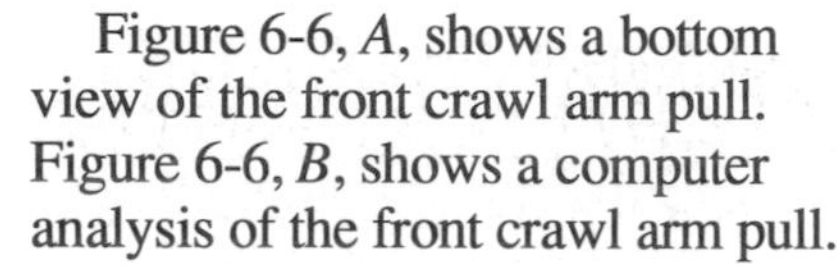

Figure 6-6, *A*, shows a bottom view of the front crawl arm pull. Figure 6-6, *B*, shows a computer analysis of the front crawl arm pull.

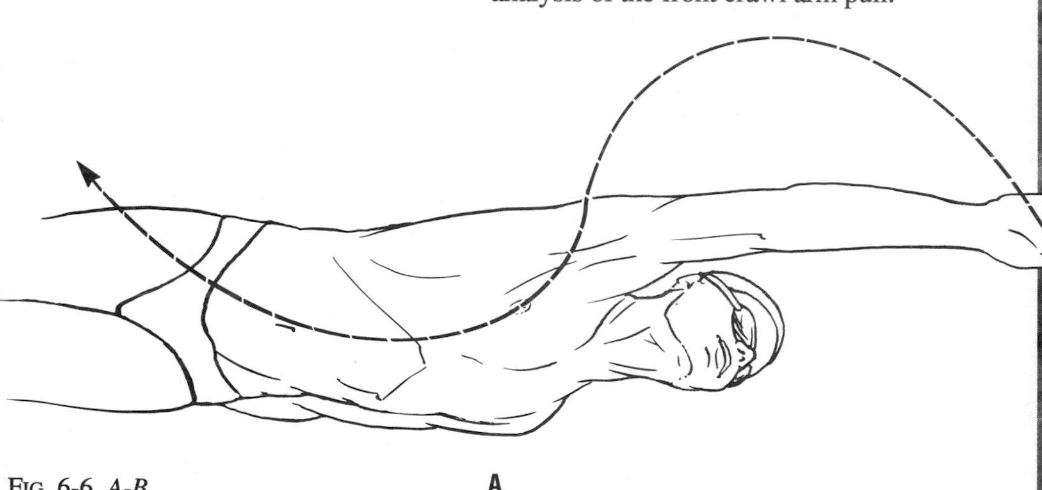

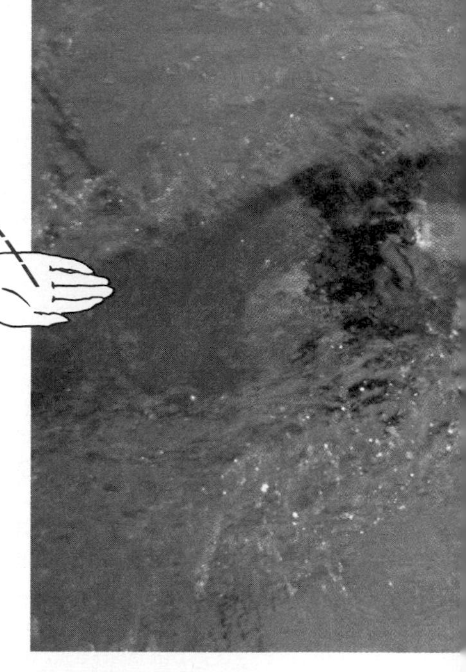

FIG. 6-6, *A-B*

**A**

**B**

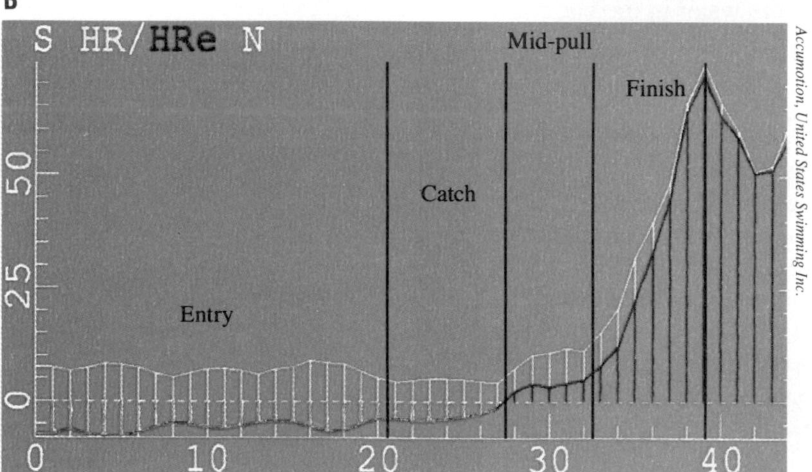


*Accumotion, United States Swimming Inc.*

FIG. 6-7, *A-C*

### *Recovery*

The recovery is not ***propulsive;*** it simply puts your hand in a position to pull again. The most important point is that the recovery should be relaxed. While your arm recovers to the starting position, its muscles can rest. If you do not let your arm, hand, and fingers relax, they do not benefit from this brief rest, and you will tire more quickly. Your recovery will also be stiff and mechanical.

Make a smooth transition from the finish of the power phase to the beginning of the recovery. In the recovery, lift your elbow high out of the water. Turn your palm toward your leg so that your hand exits the water little finger first (Fig. 6-7, *A*). Your body roll is at a maximum. Lift your elbow high and relax your arm with your forearm hanging down (Fig. 6-7, *B*). As your hand passes your shoulder, let it lead the rest of your arm until it enters the water (Fig. 6-7, *C*). Your arms at this point are not completely opposite each other. Instead, the recovering arm starts to catch up with the stroking arm.

# kick

The propulsion from the kick (called a *flutter kick*) is less than from the arms, but the kick is still important. In fact, without a good kick, you won't have proper stroke mechanics.

The way you hold your ankles is essential in this kick. They must be relaxed and "floppy" to be effective. Even if you have perfect mechanics, the kick will be ineffective if your ankles are either stiff (with toes pointed) or flexed. On the other hand, if your ankles are loose and relaxed, you can have a moderately effective kick even if other aspects of your kick need work (Fig. 6-8).

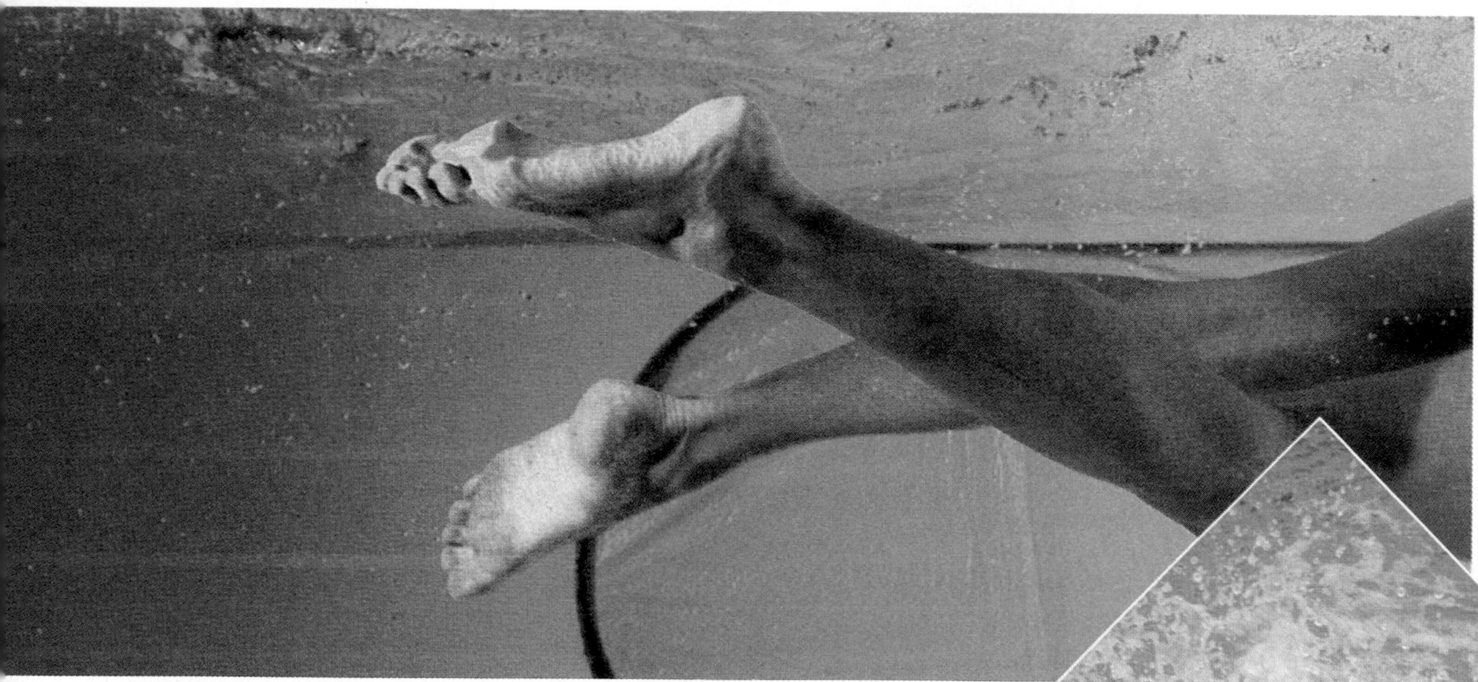

FIG. 6-8

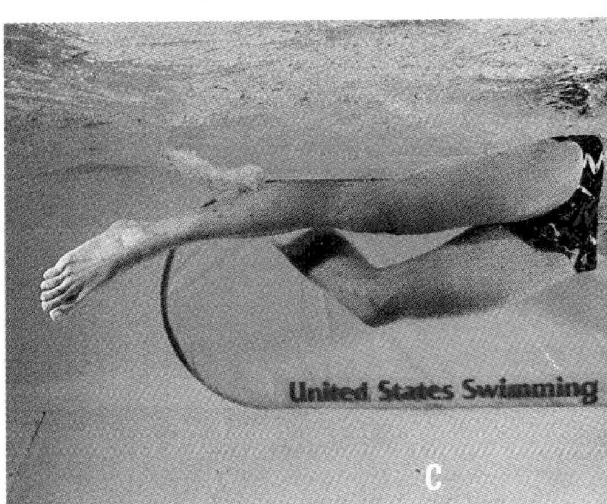


FIG. 6-9, *A-C*

The power part of the kick is the downbeat. The motion starts at the hip, with your thigh starting downward even while your calf and foot are still moving upward. For most of the downbeat, keep your knee slightly flexed (Fig. 6-9, *A*). The propulsion occurs when you straighten your leg. This motion continues through the whole leg, and the feet follow through. The feet are turned slightly inward (pigeon-toed). Your foot snaps downward, completing the motion, as though you were kicking a ball (Fig. 6-9, *B*).

In the upbeat (recovery), raise your leg straight toward the surface with little or no flexion in your knee (Fig. 6-9, *C*), until your heel just breaks the surface. A common error is to bend the knee and thus pull the heel toward the buttocks. Your leg must stay straight in the recovery. Your knee is flexed for most of the power phase, and extends forcefully at the end of the kick.

The size of the flutter kick, the distance the leg moves up and down, is not great. Depending on how tall you are, it ranges from about 12 to 15 inches. The overall leg movements of the flutter kick are illustrated in Fig. 6-10, *A* and *B*.

You can use different cadences or "beats" with the front crawl. The number of beats is measured for one arm cycle: from the time one arm starts to pull on one stroke to the time it starts to pull on the next stroke. Cadences vary from a six-beat kick to a two-beat kick. One way is not more correct than another. They are used at different times and at different speeds. Usually more beats are used for shorter distances, fewer for a longer swim. All kicks have a rhythm corresponding to the arm stroke, and most swimmers fall into a cadence that suits them.

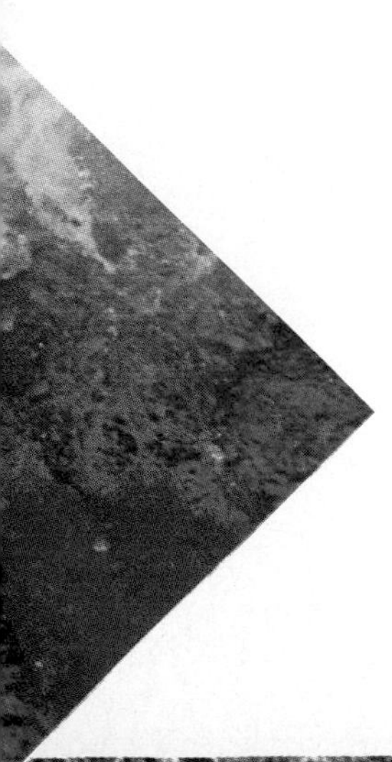

FIG. 6-10, *A-B*

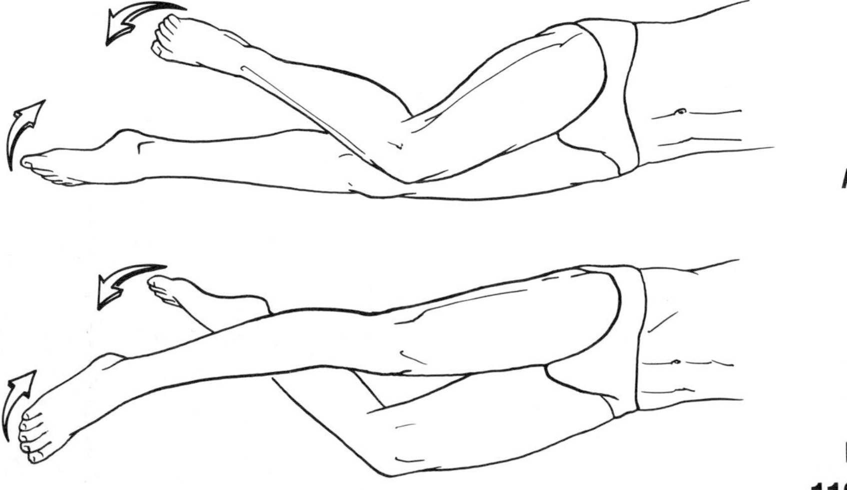

# breathing AND TIM

Most swimmers breathe each arm cycle (e.g., each time their right arm recovers) or every $1^1/_2$ arm cycles (alternating the side on which they breathe). Either method is correct, although most people learn this stroke by breathing every cycle. Coordinate your breathing so that you do not pause in the stroke to breathe. You do not need to inhale a large amount of air with each breath because the next breath is coming soon.

Start turning your head to the side as that arm starts its pull. Your mouth clears the water at the end of the pull, and you inhale just as the recovery starts. Body roll makes it easier to turn your head to the side. Look to the side and slightly back, keeping your forehead slightly higher than your chin. The opposite ear stays in the water. In this way you breathe in a trough made by your head as it moves through the water (Fig. 6-11). After inhaling, return your face to the water.

FIG. 6-11

I N G

Proper head motion for breathing lets you keep your head low in the water, which helps you keep good body position. Return your face to the water as you move your arm forward. Exhale slowly through your mouth and nose between breaths. Exhale completely underwater so you are ready to inhale at the next breath.

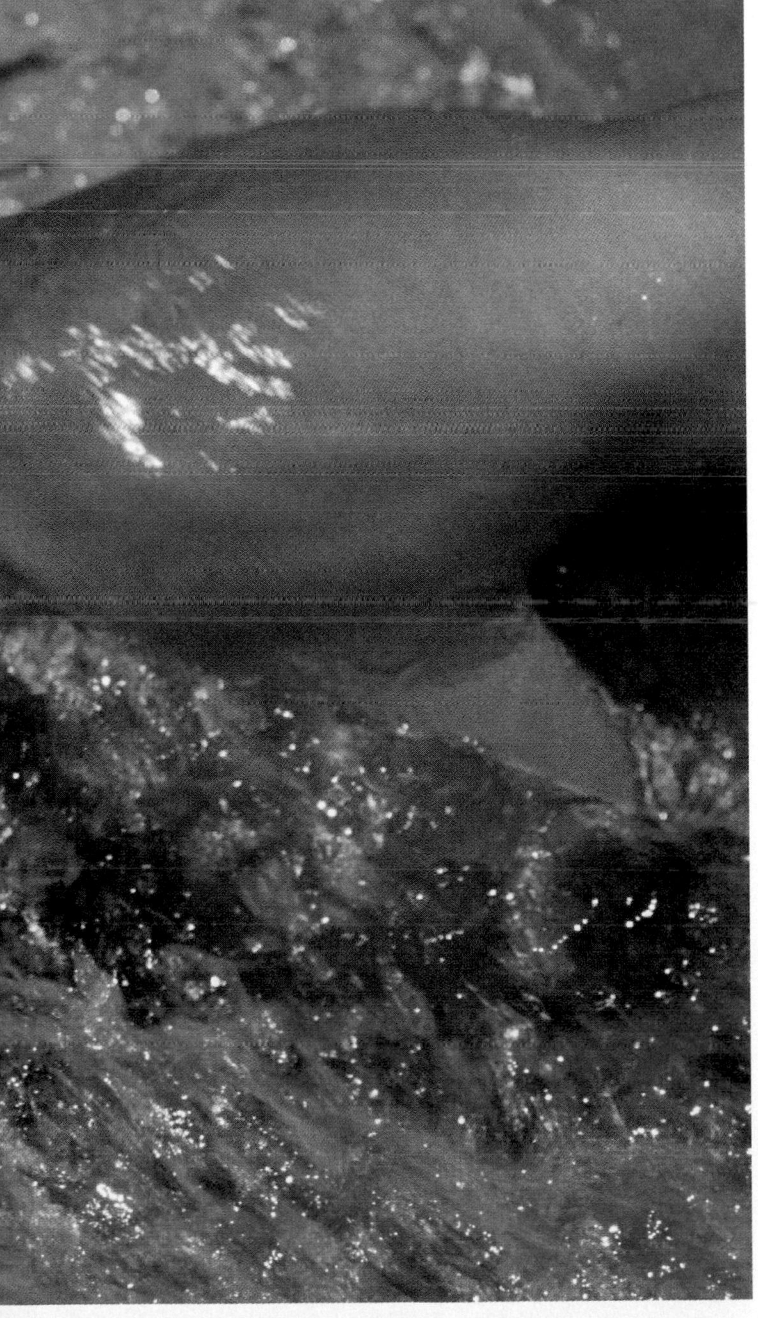

# hydroDYNAMIC PRINCIPLES

Almost all hydrodynamic principles are involved in the front crawl, but two are prominent. First, it has been discovered that lift propulsion is more important in the crawl than action-reaction propulsion. Thus the focus of stroke mechanics is on sweeping arm motions, which use lift forces, rather than pushing arm motions, which use action-reaction forces. Still, the front crawl uses both kinds of propulsion, as explained earlier.

Second, it is important to keep the body aligned in this stroke because of Newton's laws of inertia and acceleration. Good body alignment makes strokes much more efficient. Any lateral movement of part of the body away from the midline increases the resistance of the water against the body. An improper body position caused by holding your head too high has a similar effect. In either case you expend energy to correct your body position instead of using it to propel yourself forward.

# ELEMENTARY backSTROKE

The elementary backstroke was mentioned in one of the earliest swimming books. The elementary backstroke is used for leisure, for survival swimming, and for exercising muscle groups not used in other strokes. Swimmers also use this stroke to recover from strenuous effort while still making slow but effective progress through the water. Breathing is easy because the face stays out of the water.

FIG. 6-12

# body POSITION/MOTION

This stroke uses symmetrical and simultaneous movements of the arms and legs. In the ***glide,*** your body is in a streamlined, ***supine*** position (Fig. 6-12). Most swimmers keep their head submerged to the ears only, with the face always out of the water. The back is kept almost straight, with hips and legs slightly lower than head and shoulders. The arms extend along the body with palms against the thighs, and the legs are fully extended and together. The hips stay near the surface at all times in this stroke.

*Fig. 6-13, A-C*

# arm STROKE

### *Recovery*

Move your arms continuously and smoothly from the start of the recovery to the completion of the power phase. Keep your arms and hands just below the surface throughout the stroke. From the glide position, recover your arms by bending your elbows so your hands, palms down or in, slide along your sides to near your armpits (Fig. 6-13, *A*).

### *Power Phase*

Point your fingers outward from your shoulders with palms facing back toward your feet. With fingers leading, extend your arms out to the sides until your hands are no farther forward than the top of your head (Fig. 6-13, *B*). Imagine a clock with your head at 12:00 and your feet at 6:00; your hands should extend no farther than 2:00 and 10:00. Without pause, press your palms and the insides of your arms, at the same time and in a broad sweeping motion, back toward your feet (Fig. 6-13, *C*). Keep your arms straight or slightly bent in the propulsive phase. You end this motion with arms and hands in the glide position.

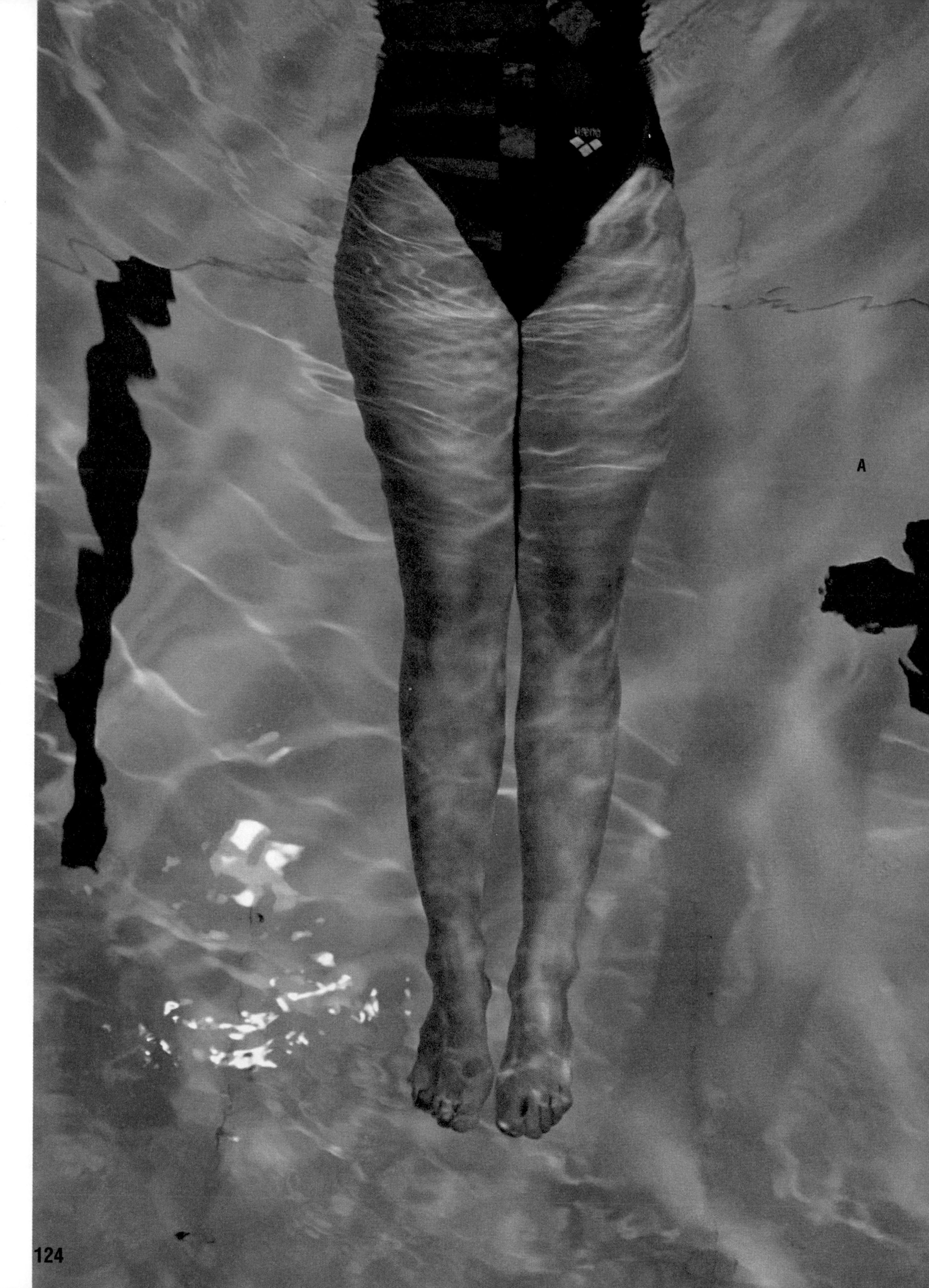
A

# kick

In the kick for the elementary backstroke, both legs bend at the knee and circle around in a kind of whipping action. The kicking action is continuous and smooth, without a pause between the recovery and the power phase. From the glide position—legs together and straight, toes pointed (Fig. 6-14, *A*)—recover your legs by bending and slightly separating your knees and drawing your heels downward to a point under and outside your knees (Fig. 6-14, *B*). The knees are spread as wide as the hips or slightly wider, with variations among swimmers. The recovery uses an easy, rhythmical motion, with back, hips, and thighs kept nearly straight. At the end of the recovery, rotate your knees inward slightly while flexing your ankles and rotating your feet outward. Then press your feet backward with a slightly rounded motion (Fig. 6-14, *C*), ending with legs in the glide position. In this action, your feet move into a pointed position. The pressing action of this kick starts slowly and speeds up to completion where the feet touch. The entire motion of the elementary backstroke kick is illustrated in Figure 6-15, *A-E*.

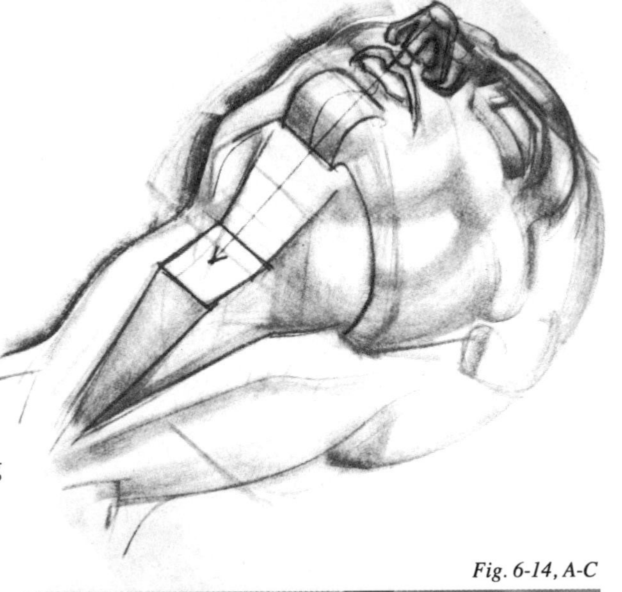

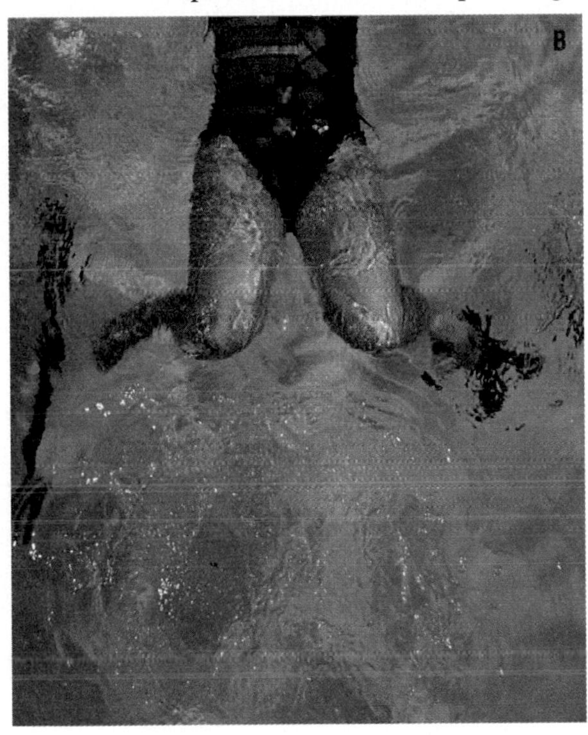


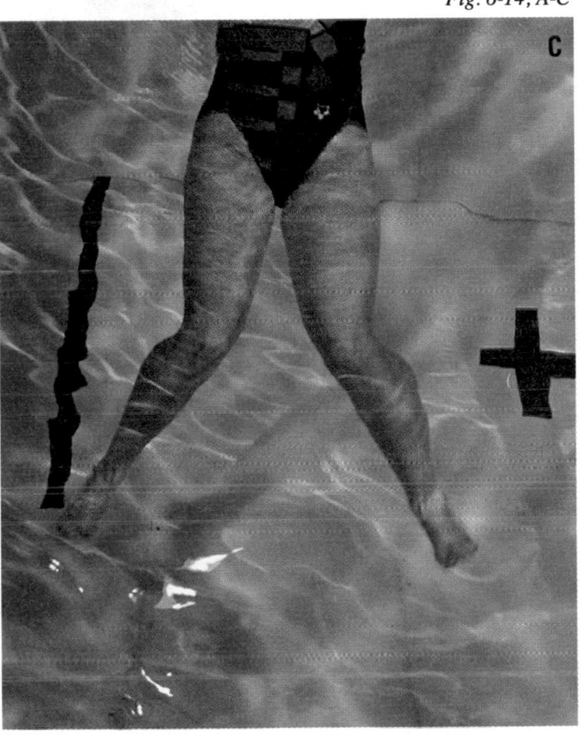


*Fig. 6-14, A-C*

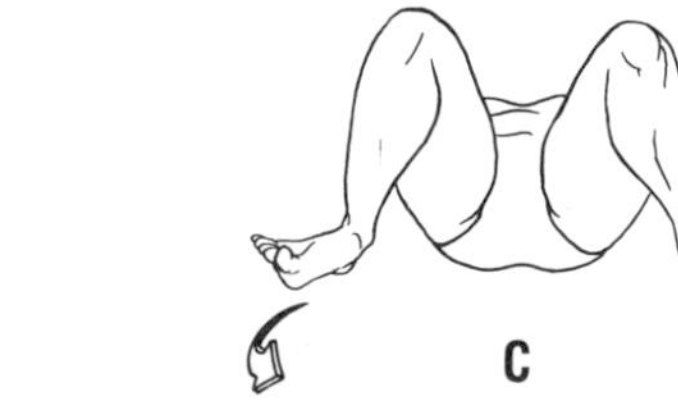


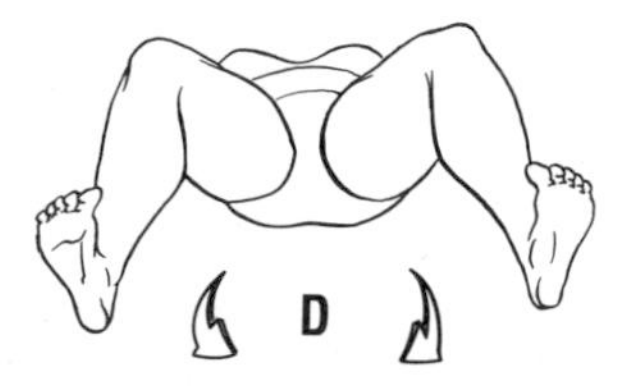


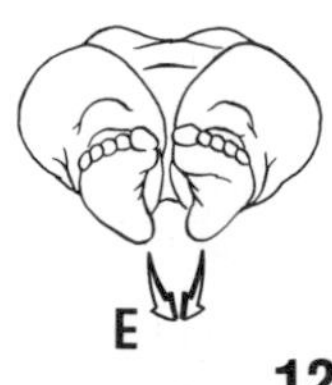


FIG. 6-15, *A-E*

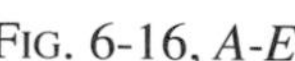

FIG. 6-16, *A-E*

# breathing

## AND TIMING

**I**n this stroke, you breathe during each arm stroke. Since your face is always out of the water, breathing is very easy. Inhale as you recover your arms up your sides and exhale as your arms press backward during the power phase. Exhaling in the power phase keeps water from entering your nose during the forceful part of the stroke. Remember to relax and to exhale slowly throughout the arm action.

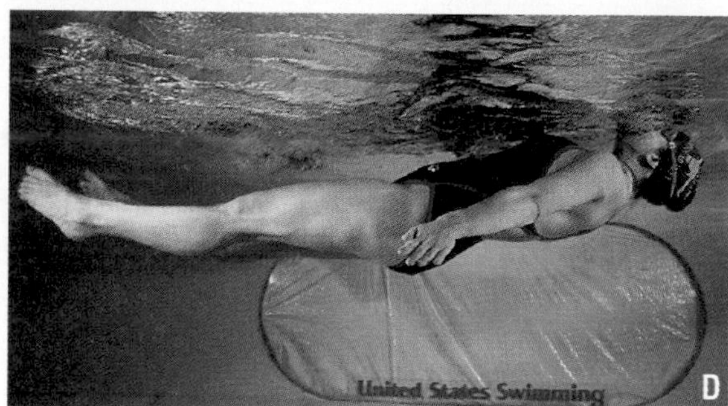


**Y**our arms start their recovery just ahead of your legs. However, because of their shorter movement and greater strength, the legs finish their thrust at the same time as the arms (Fig. 6-16). After this combined propulsion, glide with your body streamlined. Start the next stroke as your momentum slows. Do not let yourself come to a complete stop from the drag of the recovery of the arms and legs.

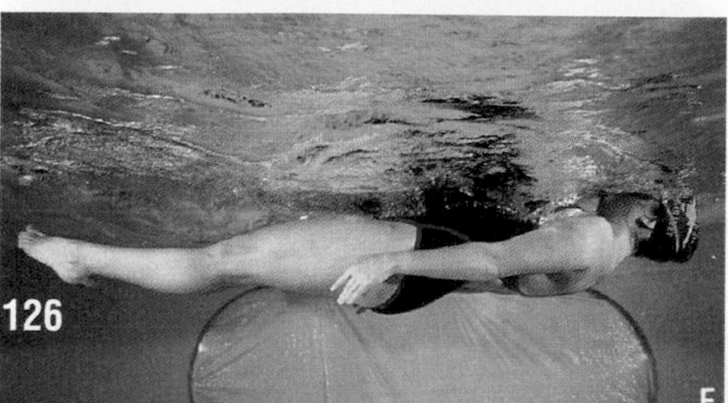

# hydro-
## DYNAMIC PRINCIPLES

The most obvious feature of this stroke is the way the arms function as levers in the power phase. The resistance on the whole surface of the arms and hands is overcome by the muscles rotating the arm at the shoulder, using action-reaction propulsion to drive the body forward. Leverage is also used when the knees are extended and when the ankles move from flexed to toes pointed.

**Inverted Breaststroke**

*The inverted breaststroke evolved from the breaststroke and elementary backstroke. It is a relaxed style of swimming on the back, especially for those with good buoyancy. It has the following characteristics:*

- *The glide position is streamlined, horizontal, and on the back, with arms extended beyond the head and legs straight.*
- *The kick is the same as in the elementary backstroke.*
- *The arms, with elbows slightly bent, press outward and back toward the feet until the palms are along the thighs. Without pause, the arms recover along the body to the armpits, where the palms turn up as the hands pass over the shoulders. Fingers first, the hands slide under the ears and extend to glide position.*
- *The swimmer inhales during arm recovery and exhales during the power phase.*
- *The legs recover as the hands move under the ears. The arms are two thirds of the way through the recovery when the propulsive phase of the kick starts, and they reach the thighs just before the kick is finished.*

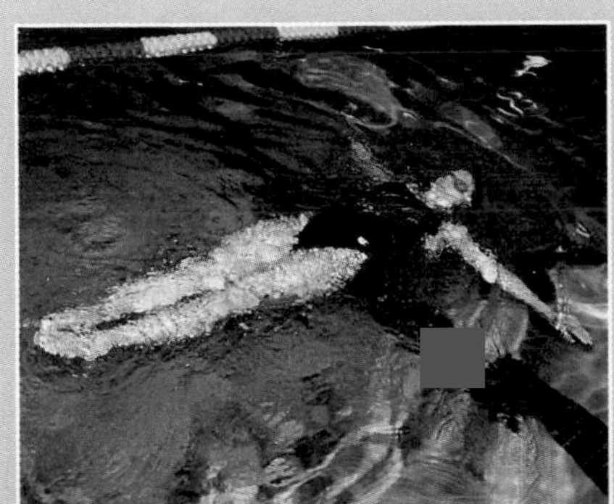

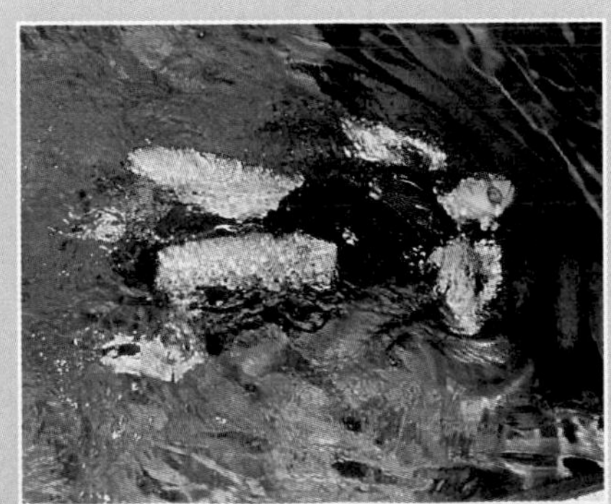

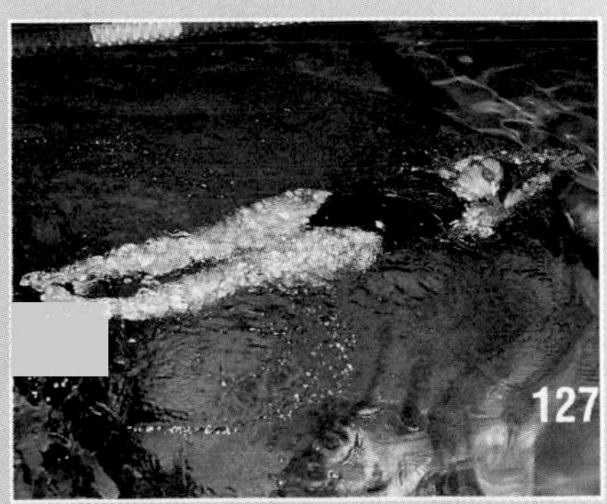

# breast STROKE

The breaststroke is the oldest known swimming stroke. For many centuries it was thought the best stroke to teach beginners. It is one of four strokes used in competitive swimming, but it is also very popular for leisure swimming because the head can be kept up, making vision and breathing easy, and because the swimmer can rest momentarily between strokes. Swimmers can use it for survival swimming and in modified form in some lifesaving situations.

## body POSITION/MOTION

In this stroke, the arms and legs move symmetrically. In the glide, your body is flat, prone, and streamlined, with legs together and extended. Extend your arms in front of your head. Keep your palms down and 6 to 8 inches below the surface. Position your head with the water line near your hairline. Keep your back straight and your body nearly horizontal, with hips and legs just below the surface.

The stroke uses a rocking action that comes from lifting the hips as you extend the hands in front and then lifting your upper body as your hands finish and start to recover. The final lift from the kick adds to this rocking action.

FIG. 6-17, *A-D*

FIG. 6-18, *A-G*

A

# arm STROKE

## *Power Phase*

In the glide position, angle your hands slightly downward and turn your palms outward at 45 degrees to the surface of the water. With your arms straight, press your palms directly out (Fig. 6-17, *A*) until your hands are spread wider than your shoulders. From this catch position, bend your elbows and sweep your hands downward and outward (Fig. 6-17, *B*) until they pass under your elbows with forearms vertical. At this point, rotate your wrists and sweep your hands inward, upward, and back slightly toward your fcct (Fig. 6-17, *C*), until your palms are below the chin, facing each other and almost touching (Fig. 6-17, *D*).

Elbow position is important for good propulsion. Throughout the power phase, your elbows should be higher than your hands and lower than your shoulders. They should also point outward, not backward, and should not pass back beyond your shoulders.

## *Recovery*

Start to recover your arms immediately after the power phase. After you sweep your hands in together, keep squeezing your elbows toward each other. Then, with palms angled toward each other, extend your arms forward to a glide position below the surface and rotate your wrists until your hands are palms down. The entire breaststroke pull pattern is illustrated in Figure 6-18, *A-G*. Figure 6-19 shows a computer analysis of the breaststroke arm pull.

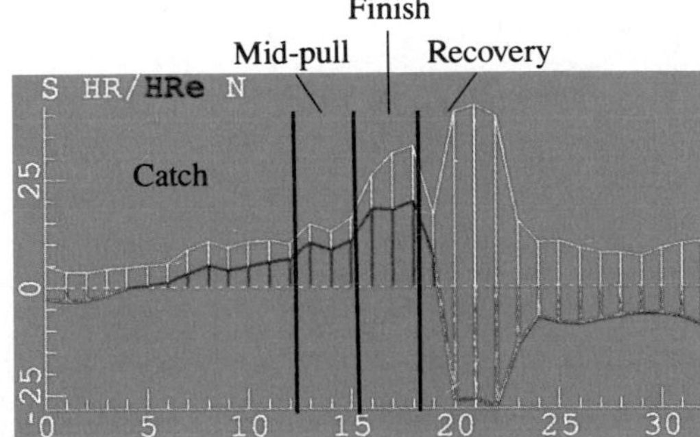


FIG. 6-19

Accumotion, United States Swimming Inc.

A
B

# kick

The kick for this stroke is like the kick used in the elementary backstroke. From the glide position, start to recover your legs by bending your hips and knees and bringing your heels up toward your buttocks (Fig. 6-20, *A*). With this action, you gradually separate your knees and heels until your knees are hip-width apart and your feet are outside your knees. Keep your heels just under the surface. At the end of the recovery, flex and rotate your ankles outward (Fig. 6-20, *B*) to engage the water with the soles when you start the propulsive action. The strongest propulsion comes from drawing your feet as far forward as you can without upsetting good body position. The ideal distances between the knees and between the heels and buttocks at the end of the recovery vary among swimmers.

Fig. 6-20, *A-D*

With a continuous whipping action, press your feet outward and backward until feet and ankles touch (Fig. 6-20, *C* and *D*). Extend your ankles and lift your legs and feet slightly. Lift forces on your feet moving outward give some forward propulsion. The pressing action also gives your feet some momentum for their thrust backward. The pressing action starts slowly, then speeds up to the completion of the kick. Propulsion results from the pressure of the water against the soles of your feet and the insides of your feet and lower legs (Fig. 6-21, *A-E*).

Fig. 6-21, *A-E*

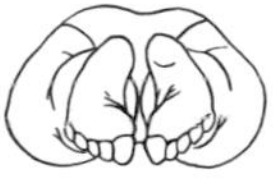


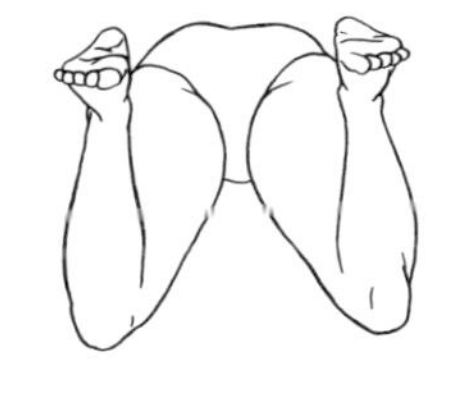


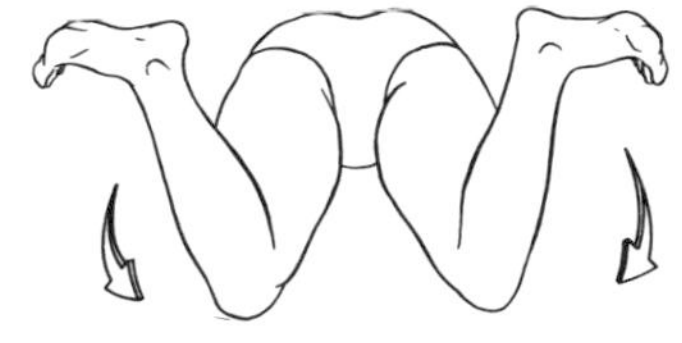

# breathing AND TIM

As your arms and hands start to pull backward, start lifting your head to breathe. Near the end of the arm pull, with your jaw jutting forward, your mouth just clears the water and you inhale. As your arms start to recover, lower your face into the water. Exhale in a slow, steady manner, mostly through your mouth, from the arm recovery until just before the next breath. At that point, explosively exhale the last of your breath and start lifting your head for the next breath. Breathe during each armstroke.

From the glide position, start the propulsive phase with your arms (Fig. 6-22, *A*). Near the end of the arm pull, take a breath and start to recover your legs (Fig. 6-22, *B*). Without pause, put your face in the water, start to recover your arms, and start the kick with your feet positioned properly (Fig. 6-22, *C*). Your arms reach about two thirds of their extension forward when you start to press backward with your feet. Your arms reach full extension just before your kick ends (Fig. 6-22, *D*). Glide briefly and start the next stroke before losing forward momentum. Remember the timing of this stroke with the phrase, "Pull and breathe, kick and glide" (Fig. 6-23, *A-D*).

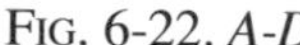

FIG. 6-22, *A-D*

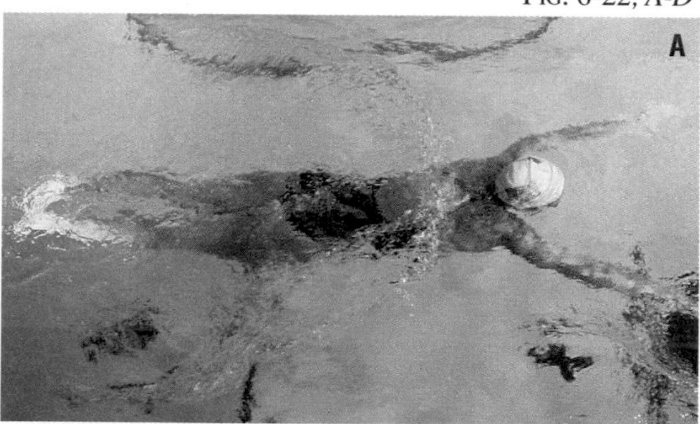


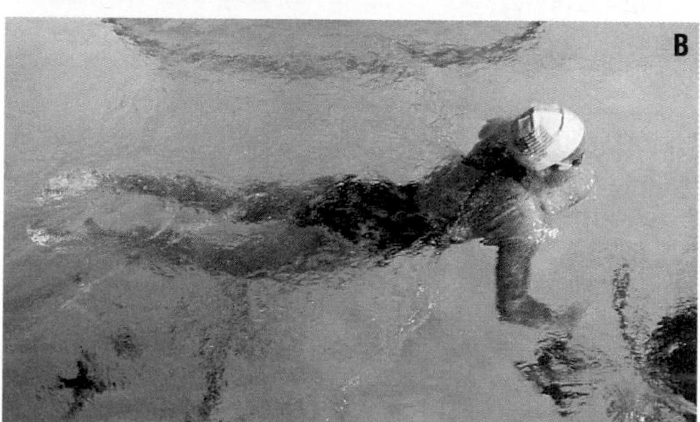

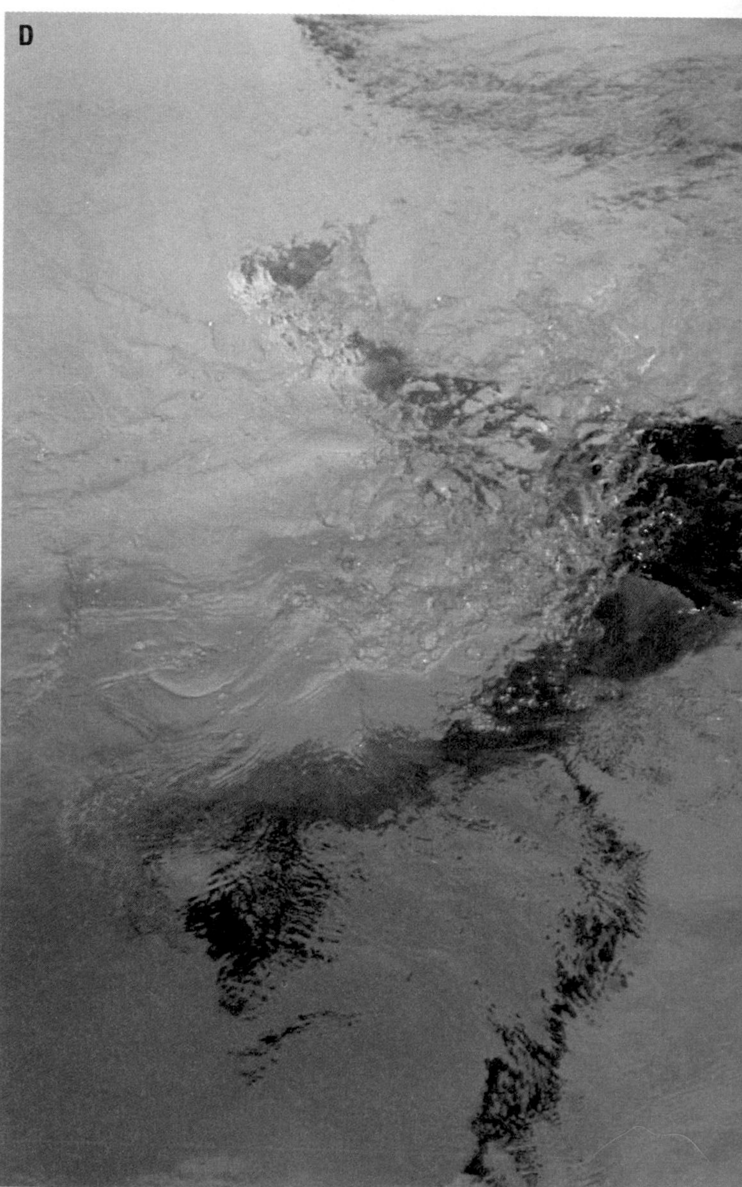

FIG. 6-23, *A-D*

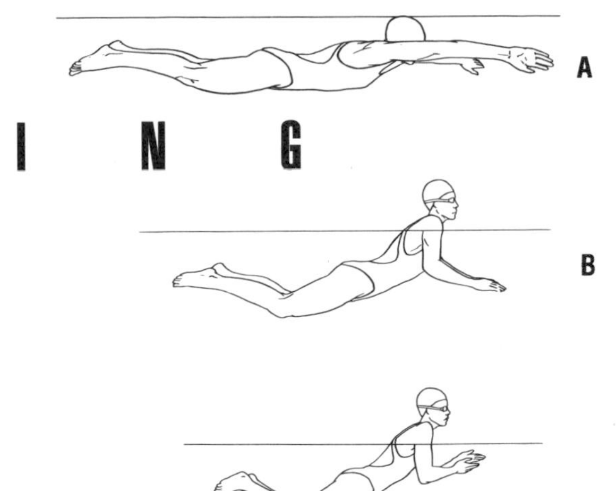

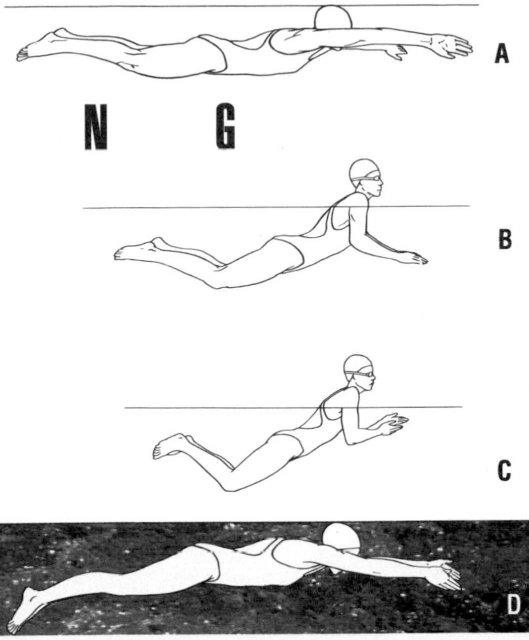

# I N G

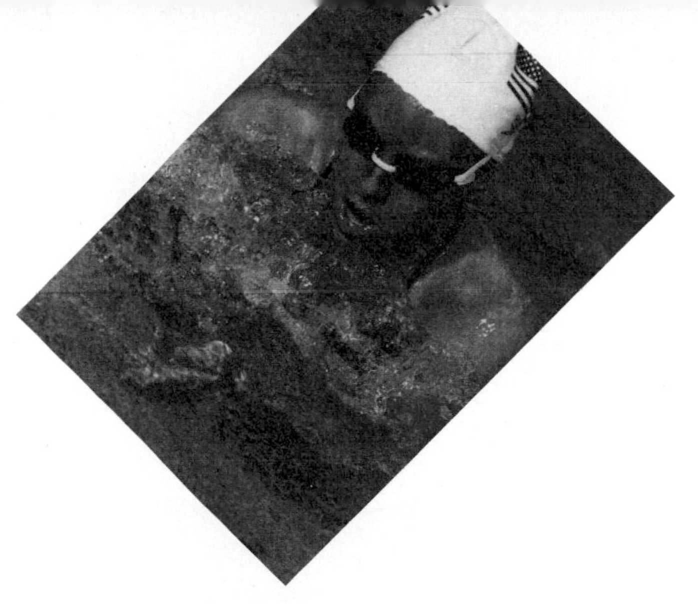

## hydro-DYNAMIC PRINCIPLES

Correct body alignment is important for all strokes. It is easier to keep aligned with the strokes that involve symmetrical movements (breaststroke, elementary backstroke, and butterfly), because of the law of acceleration. Because the arm and leg actions of both sides are performed together, forces that would otherwise push the body out of line (accelerate it in one direction) are counteracted by the same forces from the other side of the body. (Do not confuse these counteracting forces with the law of action and reaction.)

The propulsive force of this stroke is almost all from lift, more than in any other stroke.

# side STROKE

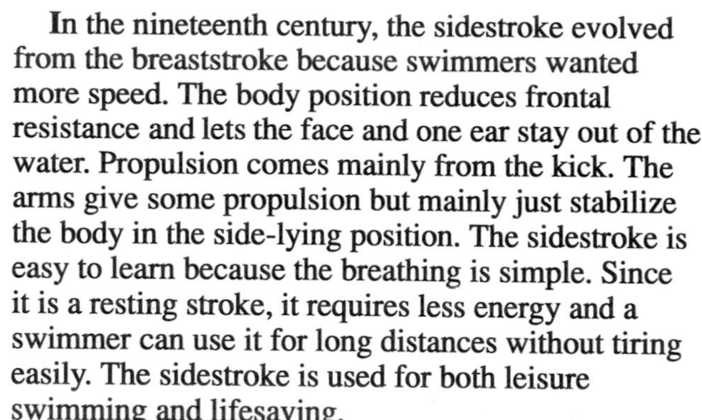

In the nineteenth century, the sidestroke evolved from the breaststroke because swimmers wanted more speed. The body position reduces frontal resistance and lets the face and one ear stay out of the water. Propulsion comes mainly from the kick. The arms give some propulsion but mainly just stabilize the body in the side-lying position. The sidestroke is easy to learn because the breathing is simple. Since it is a resting stroke, it requires less energy and a swimmer can use it for long distances without tiring easily. The sidestroke is used for both leisure swimming and lifesaving.

United States Swimming

# body
## POSITION/MOTION

In the glide, your body is nearly horizontal on its side. Keep your head, back, and legs in a straight line, your legs fully extended and together, and your toes pointed (Fig. 6-24). Your ***leading arm*** (or bottom arm) is extended in front of you, parallel to the surface, palm down and in line with your body, 6 to 8 inches below the surface of the water. Your ***trailing arm*** (or top arm) is fully extended toward your feet, hand above the thigh. Your lower ear rests in the water close to your shoulder. Your face is just high enough to keep your mouth and nose above the water for easy breathing. In general, you face across the pool but can occasionally glance to the front to see where you are going. Keep your head and back aligned throughout the stroke.

FIG. 6-24

**Overarm Sidestroke**

*This stroke evolved from the sidestroke in 1871. It differs from the sidestroke in that the trailing arm recovers out of the water. This reduces the drag of the water on the swimmer. This stroke is sometimes used for leisure swimming. It has the following characteristics:*

- *Body position, kick, leading arm action, and breathing are the same as the sidestroke.*
- *The trailing arm recovers out of the water with a "high" elbow, and the hand enters just in front of the face, similar to the front crawl.*

- *The trailing hand enters the water as the leading arm finishes its power phase and the legs recover.*
- *As the trailing hand starts its power phase, the legs extend and the leading arm recovers.*

# arm S T R

FIG. 6-25, *A-C*

### *Leading Arm*

The power phase of the leading arm uses a shallow pull. From the glide position, rotate your leading arm slightly to put your palm down and angled slightly outward (the way you are facing). From this catch position, bend your elbow and sweep your hand downward slightly and then back toward your feet, until your hand almost reaches your upper chest (Fig. 6-25, *A*).

Without pausing after the power phase, recover your leading arm by rotating the shoulder and dropping the elbow. Pass your hand under your ear until your fingers point forward (Fig. 6-25, *B*). Thrust your leading arm forward, rotating it so your palm is down for the glide position (Fig. 6-25, *C*).

FIG. 6-26, *A-C*

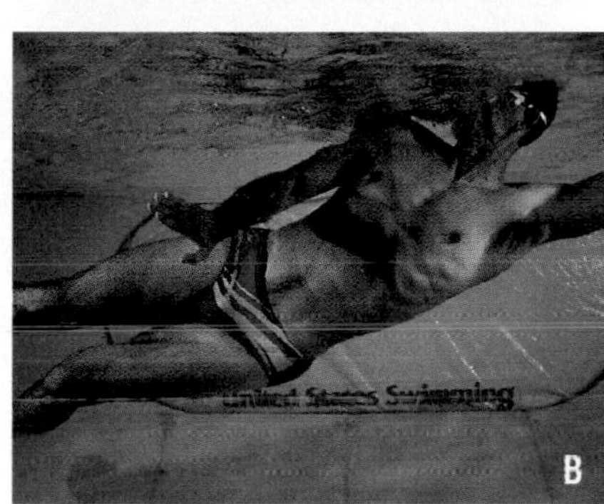


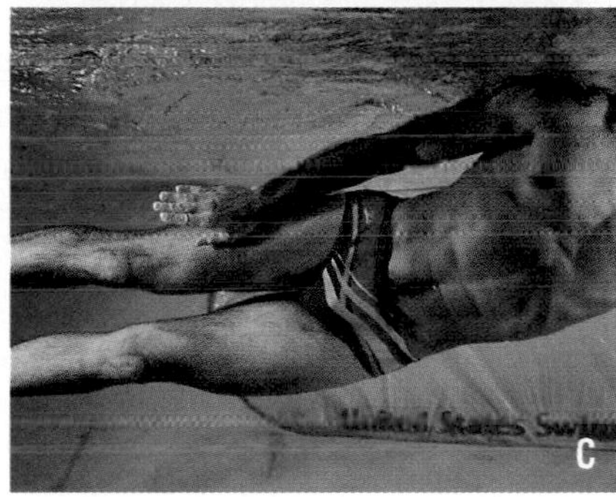


### *Trailing Arm*

During the power phase of the leading arm, recover the trailing arm by drawing the forearm along your body until your hand is nearly in front of the shoulder of your leading arm (Fig. 6-26, *A*). Keep the palm down and angled slightly forward. This creates lift to help keep your face above water. In the power phase, sweep your trailing hand downward slightly and then backward close to your body to the glide position (Fig. 6-26, *B* and *C*). Start this phase with your wrist flexed but finish with it extended, so your palm is always toward your feet. The pull pattern for both arms is illustrated in Figure 6-27.

FIG. 6-27

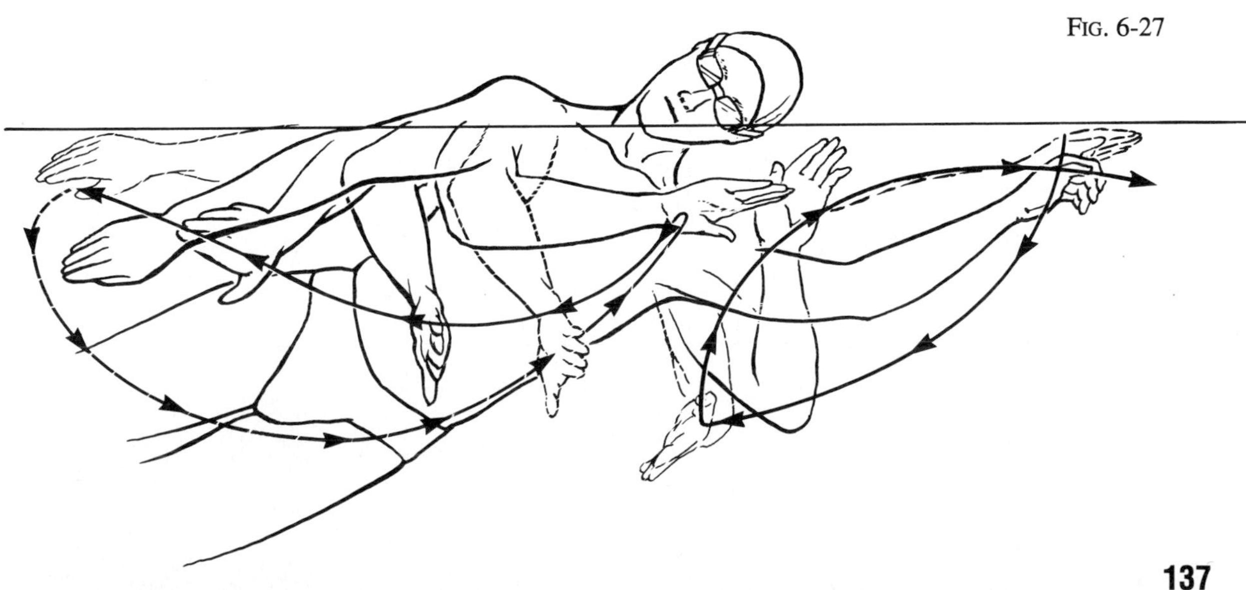

# kick

The sidestroke uses the scissors kick. When done well, this kick is propulsive enough to give a good rest between strokes. In the kick, the legs move smoothly in a plane nearly parallel to the surface. Avoid rolling your hips forward and backward as you recover and kick. In contrast to the flutter kick, in which the legs move constantly, this kick lets the legs rest during the glide. This kick and its alternate, the inverted scissors kick, are also used for lifesaving carries, treading water, underwater swimming, and the trudgen strokes.

FIG. 6-28, *A-D*

From the glide position, recover your legs by flexing your hips and knees and drawing your heels slowly toward your buttocks. Keep your knees close together in this movement (Fig. 6-28, *A*).

At the end of the recovery (Fig. 6-28, *B*), to prepare for the kick, flex your top ankle and point the toes of your bottom foot. Move your legs to their catch positions, top leg toward the front of your body, bottom leg toward the back. When extended, your top leg is almost straight (Fig. 6-28, *C*). Your bottom leg extends the thigh slightly to the rear of your trunk, with that knee flexed.

Without pause, press your top leg (which stays straight) backward while extending your bottom leg (like kicking a ball), until both legs are fully extended and together in the glide position (Fig. 6-28, *D*). You push the water with the bottom of your top foot and the top of your bottom foot. As you move your top foot backward, move that ankle from a flexed position to a toes-pointed position to let the sole of the foot press with greatest pressure against the water. Do not let your feet pass each other at the end of the kick. Keep your toes pointed in the glide to reduce drag.

The inverted scissors kick is identical to the scissors kick, except that it reverses the top and bottom leg actions. The top leg (with toes pointed) moves toward the rear of the body and the bottom leg (with ankle flexed) moves toward the front of the body.

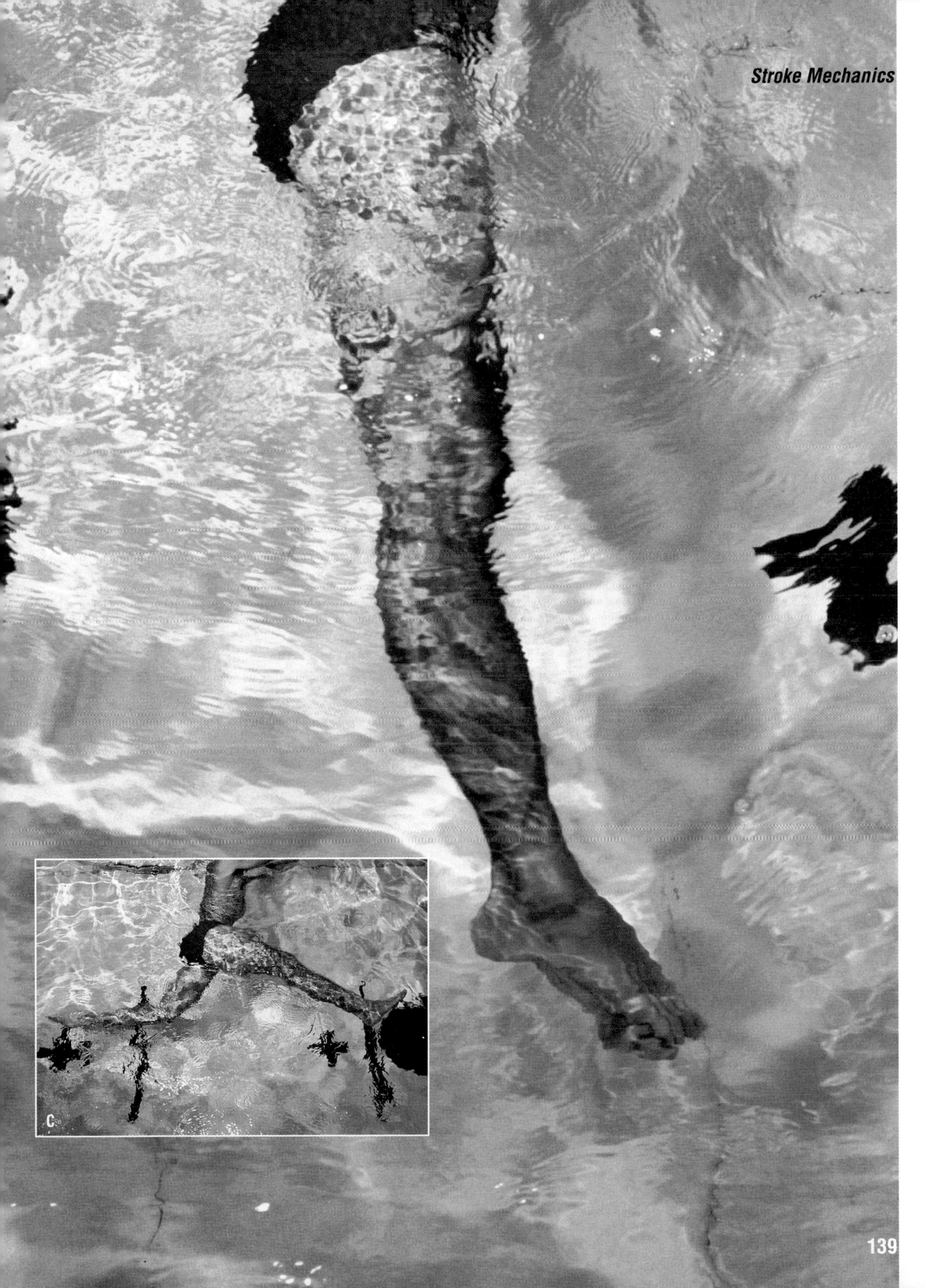
C

# breathing AND TIM

With the sidestroke you breathe with each stroke. Inhale through the mouth while you recover your trailing arm and exhale in the power phase of your trailing arm.

From the glide position, start the stroke with the sweep of your leading arm. Then recover your trailing arm and your legs and kick and stroke with your trailing arm as your leading arm recovers (Fig. 6-29, *A* and *B*). Your arms and legs are fully extended when you complete the kick and the stroke of your trailing arm (Fig. 6-29, *C*). Glide until your momentum slows. Remember not to glide too long, since it takes more energy to start and stop than to keep moving. Figure 6-30, *A-E*, shows the coordination of the arms and legs in the sidestroke.

FIG. 6-29, *A-C*

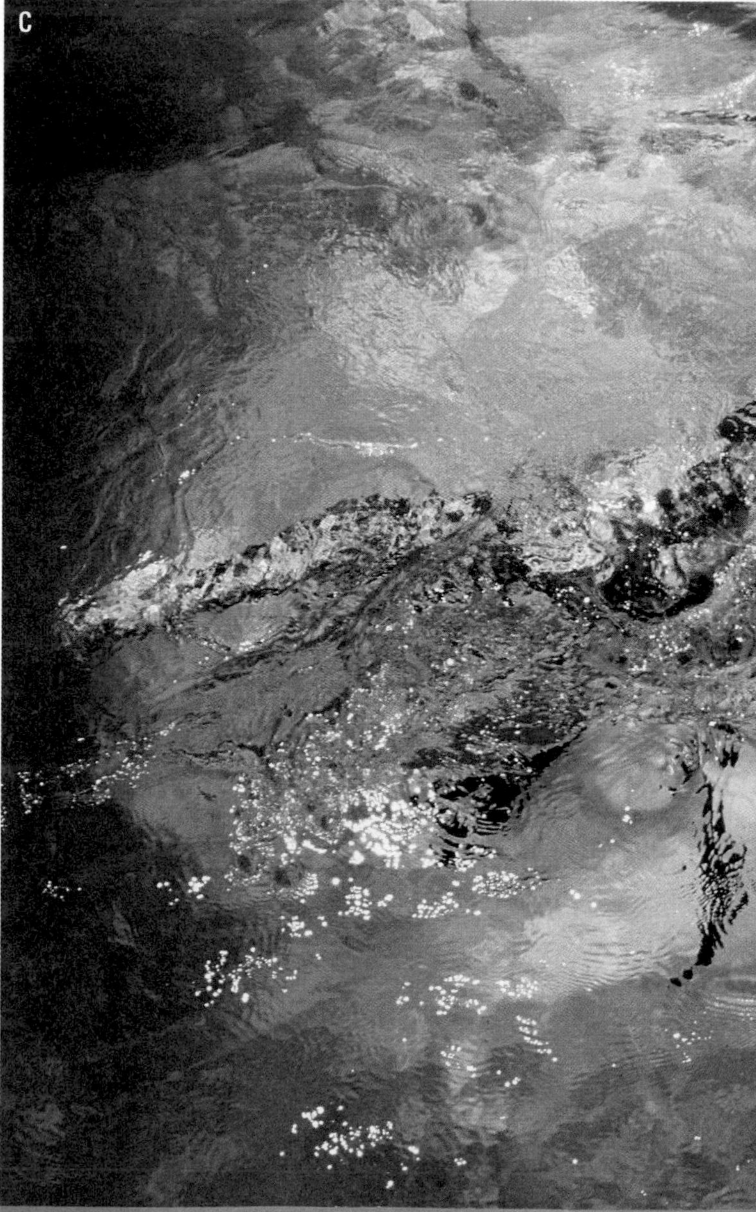


FIG. 6-30, *A-E*

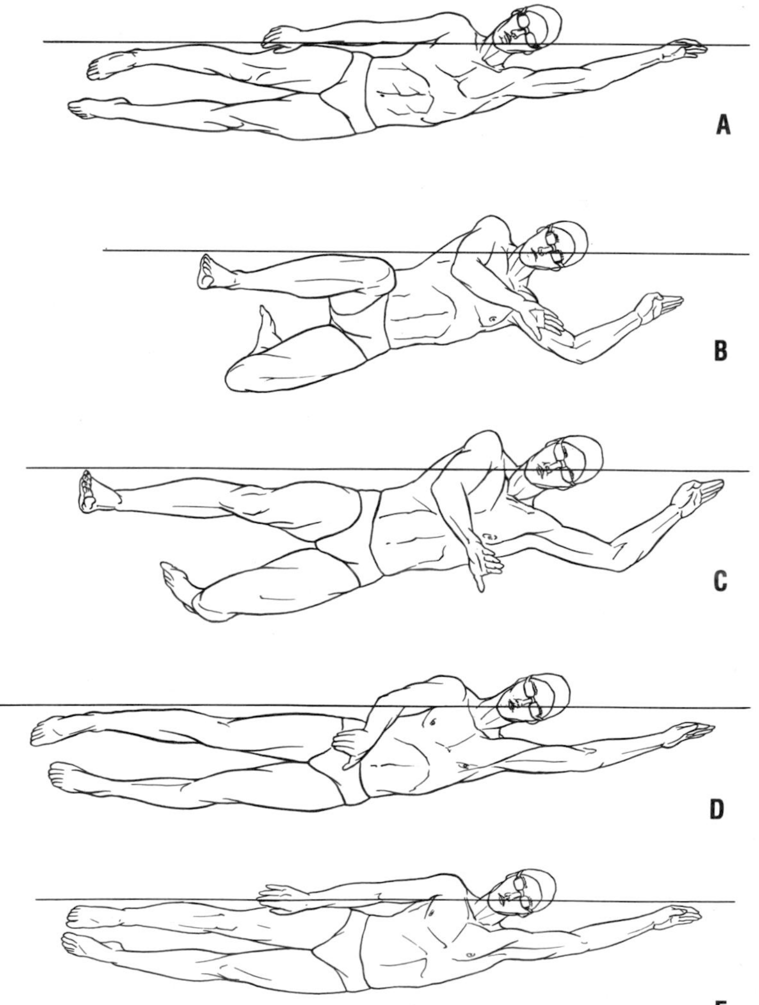

I N G

# hydro-
## DYNAMIC PRINCIPLES

Two principles are important in this stroke. The first has already been mentioned: this stroke was developed from the breaststroke to reduce form drag. Offering a smaller shape as you move through the water, with part of your head and one shoulder out of the water, reduces the water resistance to your movement.

Second, remember the relationship between dynamic inertia and static inertia. If you glide too long and use almost all of your dynamic inertia, your stroke loses efficiency because of the effort needed to start moving again. This principle is important for all strokes with a gliding phase.

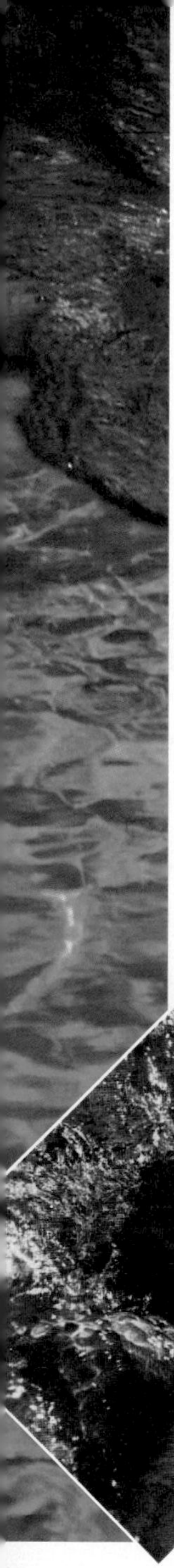

# BACK crawl

This stroke, which developed from the inverted breaststroke and the trudgen, was introduced in 1902. The body position generally allows unobstructed breathing and clear vision above water. It is one of the four competitive strokes and is the fastest stroke on the back. For this reason, it is frequently called the backstroke. It is also used in leisure swimming.

# body POSITION/MOTION

In this stroke, you lie on your back in a flat, streamlined, horizontal position. As in the front crawl, there is a lot of body roll. It is important to keep your head still and aligned with your spine. Since your face is out of the water, you do not have to roll your head to breathe. For most swimmers, the water line runs from the middle of the top of the head to the tip of the chin, with the ears under water. The best head position depends on your proficiency, speed through the water, body composition, and buoyancy. Keep your back as straight as you can. Flex your hips slightly to let your feet churn the surface (Fig. 6-31).

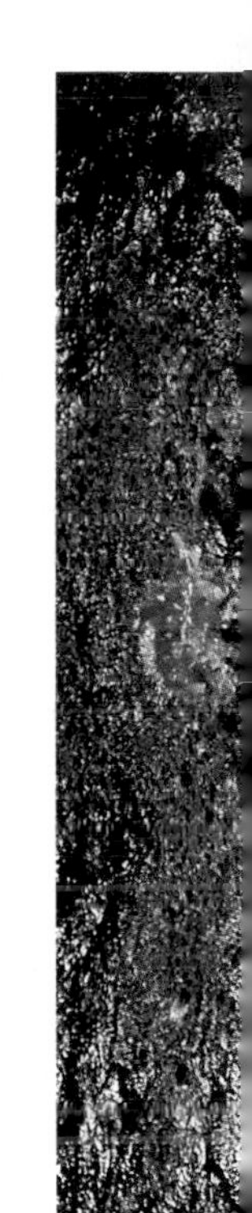

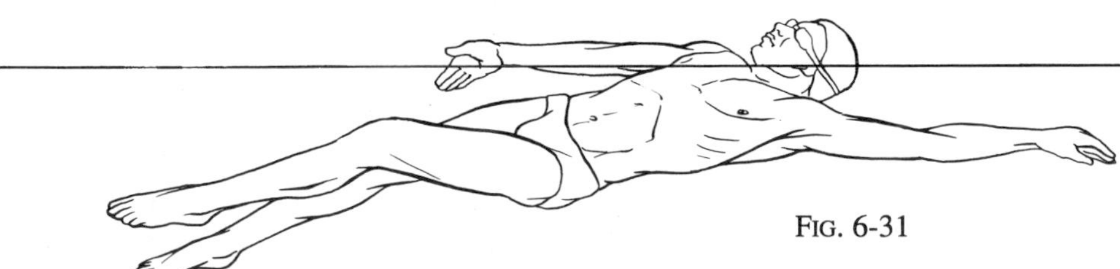

FIG. 6-31

# arm S T R

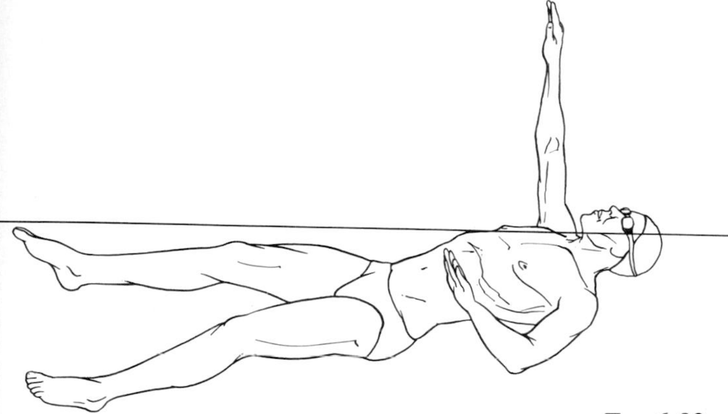

FIG. 6-32

**Y**our arms move continuously in constant opposition to each other; one arm recovers while the other arm pulls (Fig. 6-32). This is called *opposition rhythm* and looks like a windmill. Except for differences of speed between the power phase and the recovery, each arm is always opposite the other arm.

FIG. 6-33, *A-D*

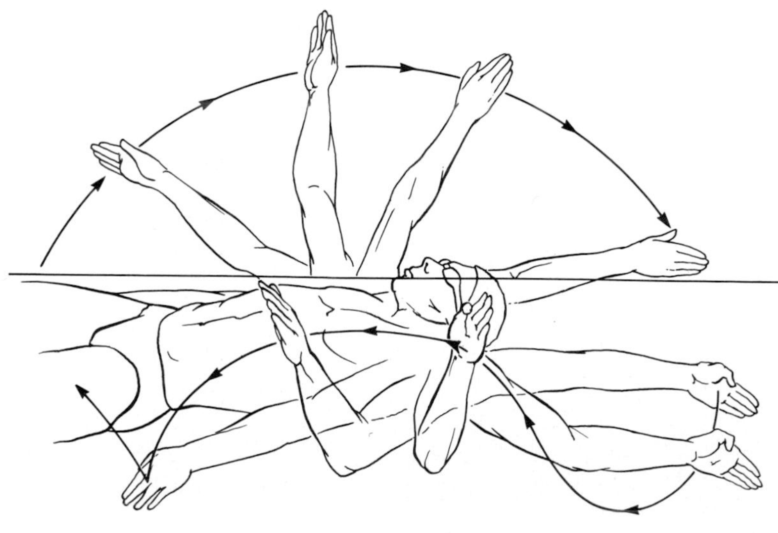

A

FIG. 6-34, *A-B*

# O K E

### *Power Phase*

With the arm straight, one hand enters the water just outside the shoulder, little finger first. The palm is to the outside and the wrist angled slightly down (Fig. 6-33, *A*). Keep your body streamlined. With your head steady, roll your body to the side of your entry arm just before your hand enters the water. At the same time, lift the other arm toward the surface to start its recovery.

Your entry hand slices downward 8 to 12 inches and slightly outward to the catch, where the propulsive action starts (Fig. 6-33, *B*). Sweep your hand outward and downward as you start bending the elbow. This elbow must point down for the same reason that it is held high in the front crawl. "Dropping" the elbow and letting it lead the hand greatly reduces the propulsive forces.

About one quarter through this sweep, the mid-pull starts. Keep bending the elbow and rotate your wrist slightly so your hand presses upward and inward. Your elbow is bent most (about 90 degrees) at the midpoint of this movement as your forearm is passing your chest (Fig. 6-33, *C*).

For the finish of the power phrase, your hand speeds up as you sweep it downward and toward the feet, with wrist extended so your palm faces your feet. This phase ends with your arm straight and your hand below your thigh (Fig. 6-33, *D*). The finish gives propulsion and helps overcome the tendency of the body to sink from the weight of the recovering arm. The entire arm pull of the back crawl is illustrated in Figure 6-34, *A*. Figure 6-34, *B*, shows a computer analysis of the back crawl arm pull.

B

C

D

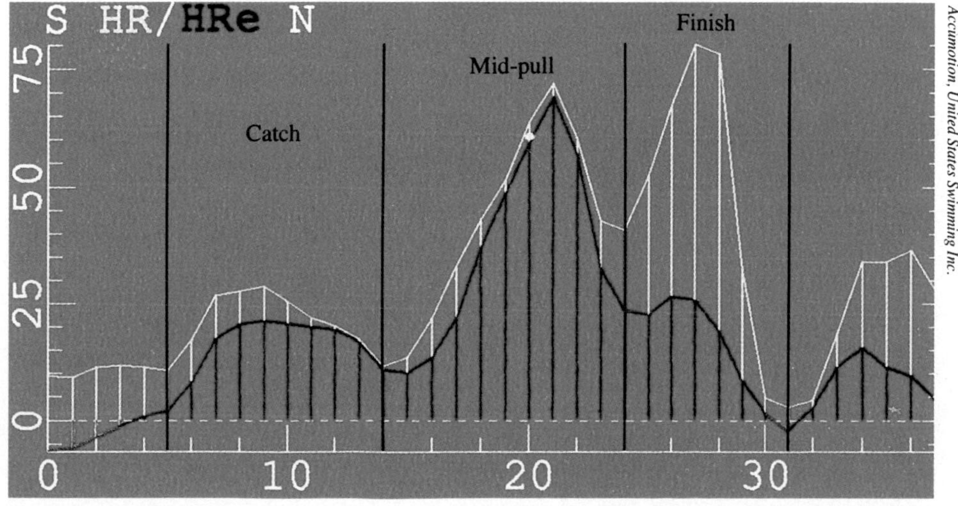

Accumotion, United States Swimming Inc.

B

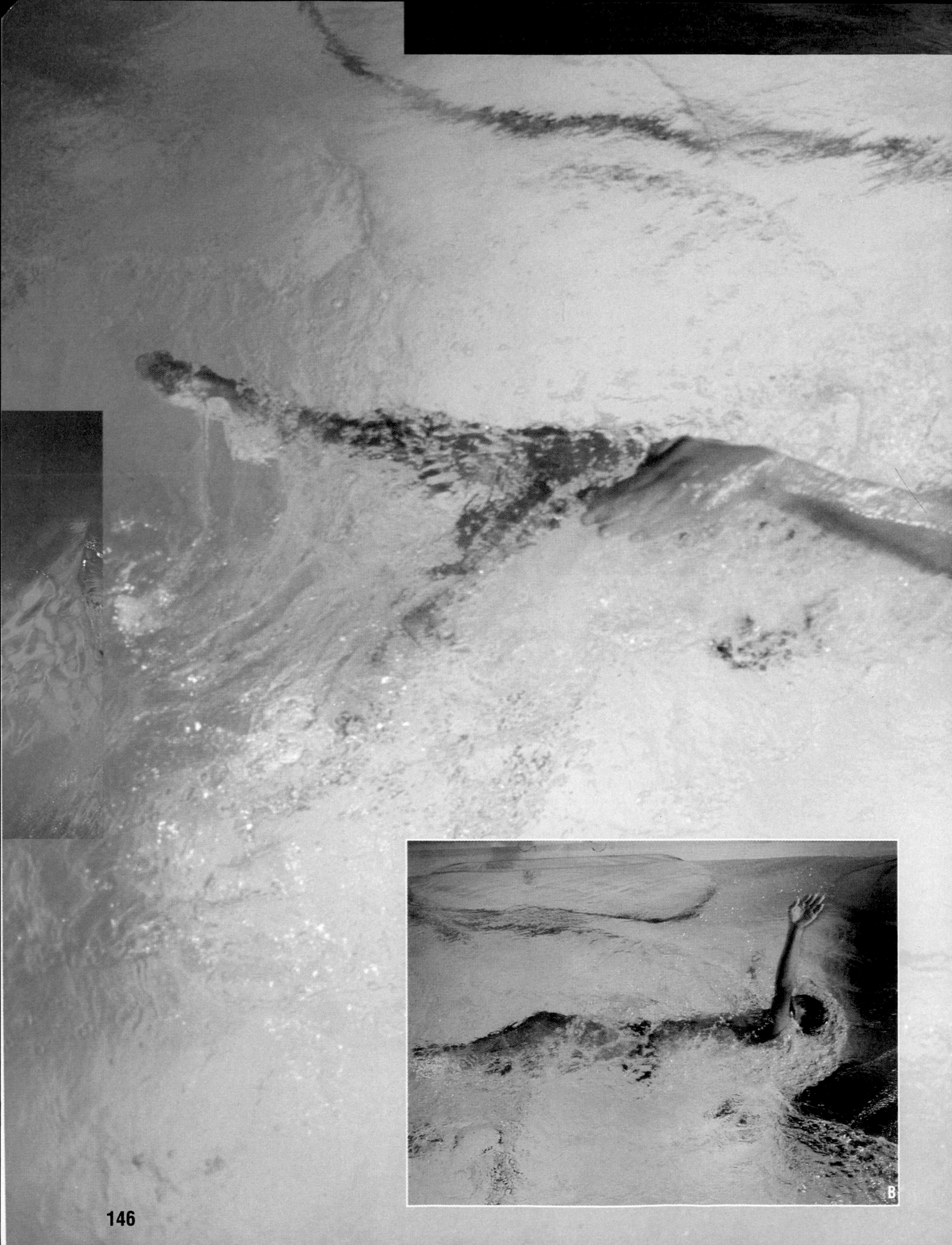
B

### *Recovery*

Start the recovery by lifting your arm from the water, shoulder first, palm inward (Fig. 6-35, *A*). Relax your wrist so that your thumb and the back of your hand leave the water first. This position of the arm when it leaves the water allows the large muscles on the back of your upper arm to relax more. In the recovery, your arm moves almost perpendicular to the water (Fig. 6-35, *B*). Body roll makes this easier. Keep your arm straight but relaxed in the recovery. Rotate your hand so the little finger enters the water first (Fig. 6-35, *C*). Remember that your arm muscles should rest in the recovery.

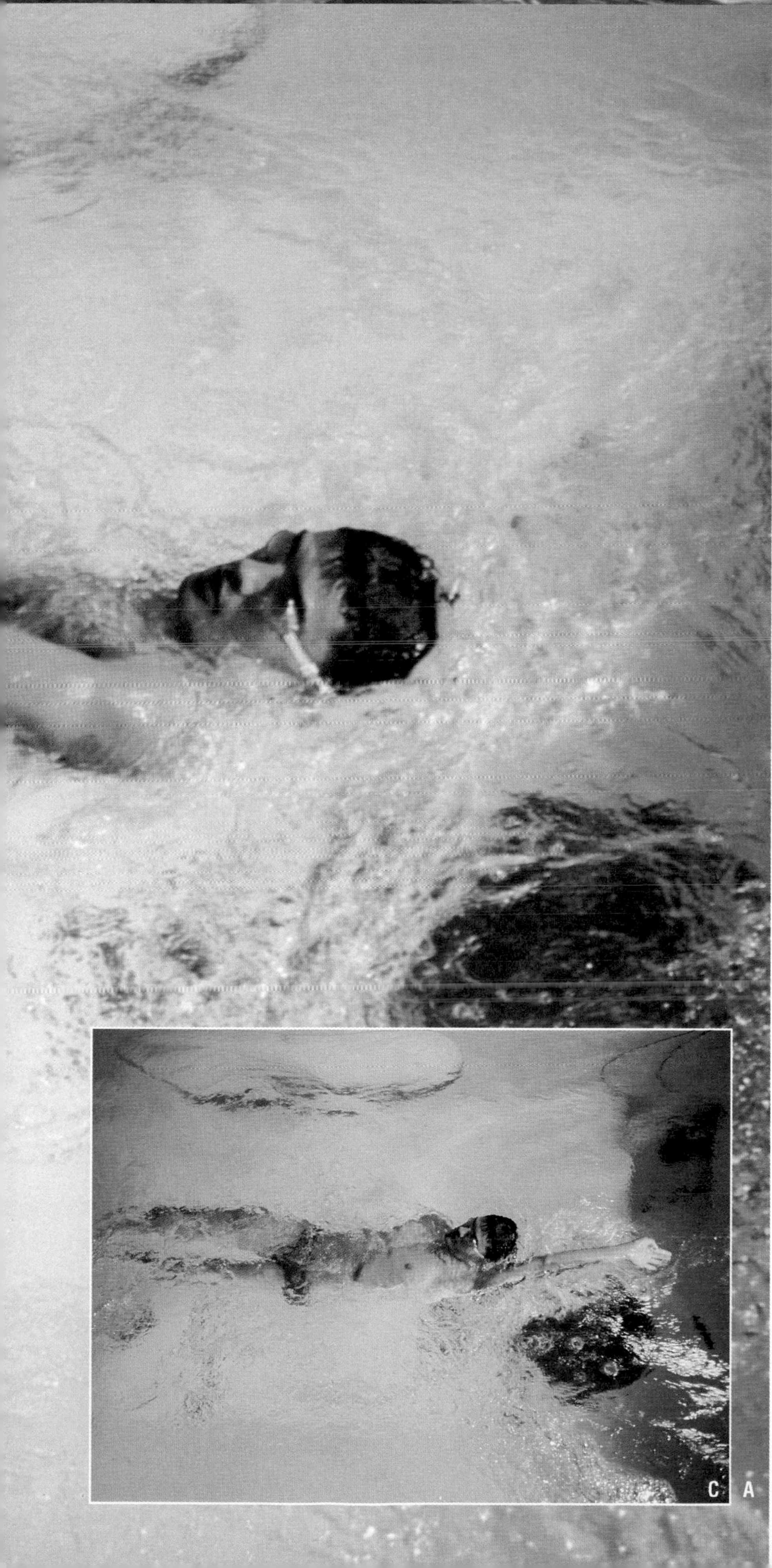

FIG. 6-35, *A-C*

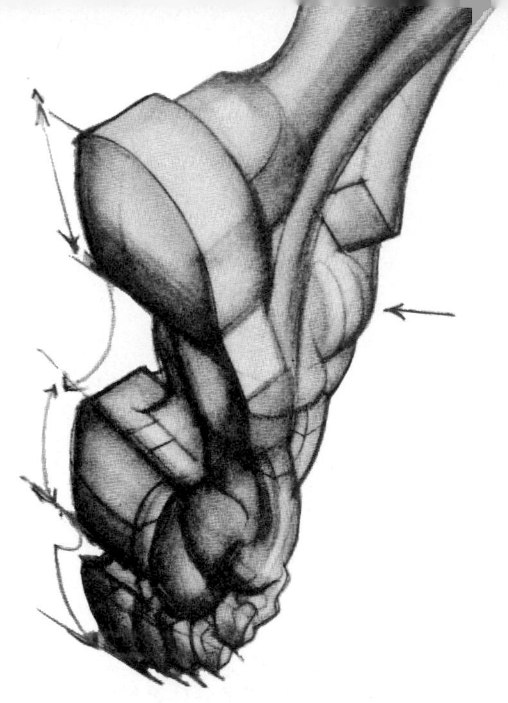

# kick

The kick is like the flutter kick used in the front crawl but is a little deeper in the water. It is a continuous, alternating, up-and-down movement that starts from your hips. Keep the ankles loose and floppy, your feet slightly pigeon-toed, and your legs separated slightly so that your big toes just miss each other. Most of the propulsive force comes from the upward kick, which is like punting a football with the tip of your foot. The downward movement of the sole of your foot against the water also helps propel you. The kick also helps stabilize you by counteracting the motion of your arms and the rolling of your body.

FIG. 6-36, *A-B*

At the start of the upward kick, flex your knee to gain the most propulsion from the upper surface of your lower leg and foot. Bring your thigh and knee near the surface, but keep whipping your foot upward until your leg is straight and your toes reach the surface. Keep your leg nearly straight in the downward kick. At the end of the downward movement, bend your knee and start your upward kick. Your thighs should pass each other and your knees should stay relaxed (Fig. 6-36, *A-B*).

The depth of your own kick depends on the length of your legs, your hip and ankle flexibility, your pace with the stroke, and the amount of body roll. Remember that if you kick too deep the greater form drag will cancel out the kick's added propulsion.

# breathing AND TIMING

Use a regular breathing pattern during each stroke. Inhale when one arm recovers and exhale when the other arm recovers.

Start your body roll to the side of your entry arm as it starts to enter the water. Your body continues to roll as the entry hand reaches the catch and the other arm lifts toward the surface to start its recovery. The propulsive action of one arm and the recovery of the other arm start at the same time. Keep an opposition rhythm as described earlier.

This stroke uses a continuous kick. Although most swimmers use a six-beat kick for each full arm cycle, the beat depends on the individual. You can find your own best timing by slightly adjusting your stroke mechanics until the stroke is smooth and effective.

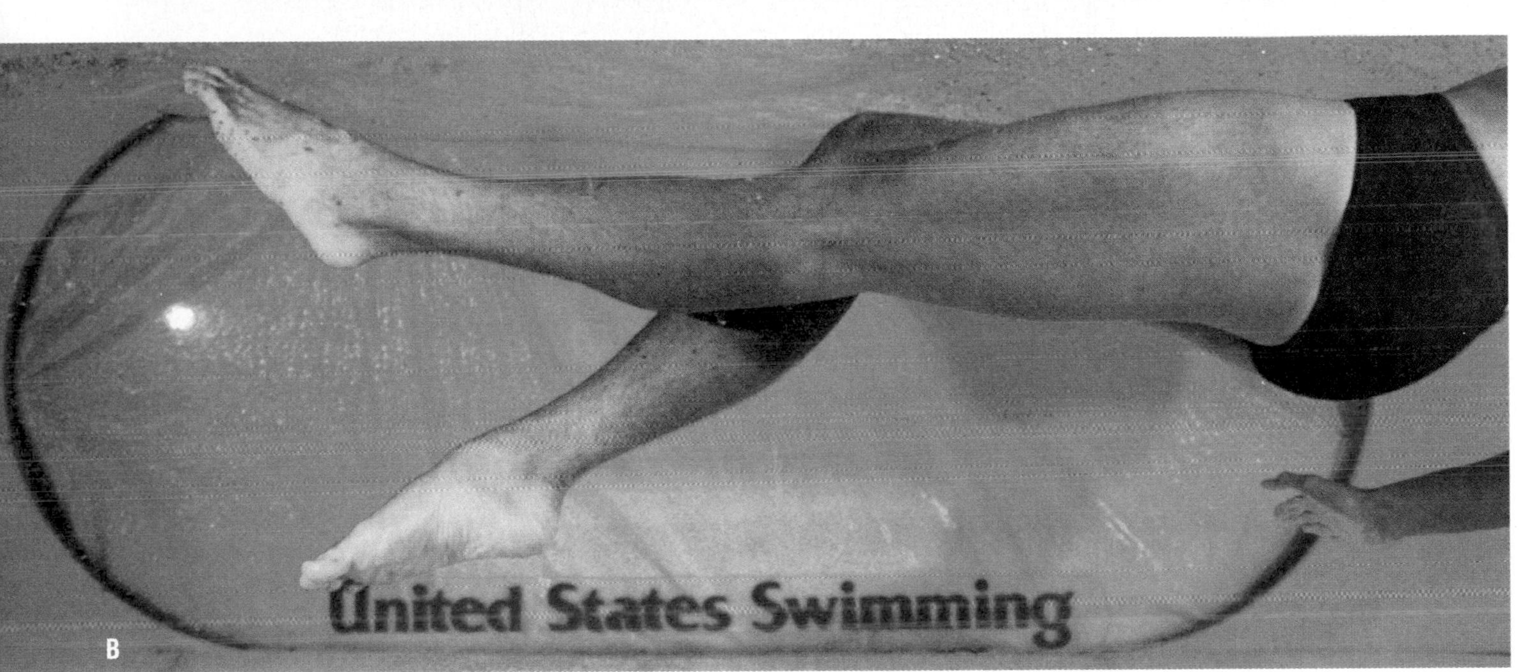

B

# hydroDYNAMIC PRINCIPLES

The flutter kick in the back crawl, as in the front crawl, takes advantage of the conservation of momentum. The loose ankles in the upsweep and downsweep actually travel in circular patterns that efficiently maintain momentum. Holding the ankles stiff would force the feet to use a linear start-and-stop motion that would have to overcome inertia with each kick.

# BUTTERFLY

Many people think of the butterfly as a difficult stroke that is used only for competition. Thus many swimmers, even those good at other strokes, do not try to learn it. But even beginning swimmers can learn the butterfly by practicing timing and technique. A trained instructor can teach you the butterfly. The key to this stroke is relaxing and using your whole body in a flowing motion. This stroke gives you a rewarding feeling of power and grace.

# body POSITION/MOTION

Leg and body motions give this stroke a unique dolphin-like feeling. In a prone position, the body moves in a constantly changing, wave-like motion in which it rolls forward through the water. The wave motion starts with the head and continues to the ends of the feet. The kick, breathing, and pull are very closely related. For this reason, body motion is described in the section on breathing and timing, after you understand how the kick and pull are done.

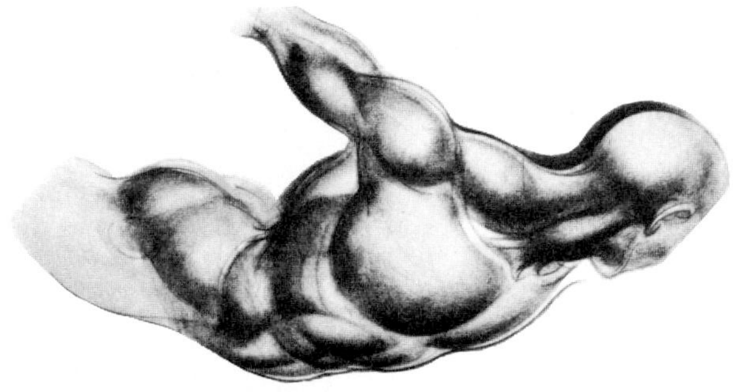

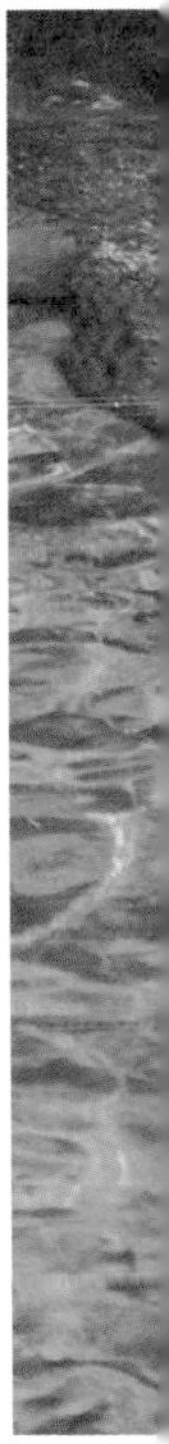

# arm S T R

### *Power Phase*

The power phase of the butterfly arm stroke consists of the catch, the mid-pull, and the finish. The arm stroke is like the front crawl, except that the arms move together and the sweep out and sweep in are exaggerated, tracing a pattern like a key hole (Fig. 6-37, *A*). The press back is very much like the front crawl. The sweep in and sweep out create lift forces,

which give most of the propulsion of this stroke. Figure 6-37, *B*, shows a computer analysis of the butterfly arm pull.

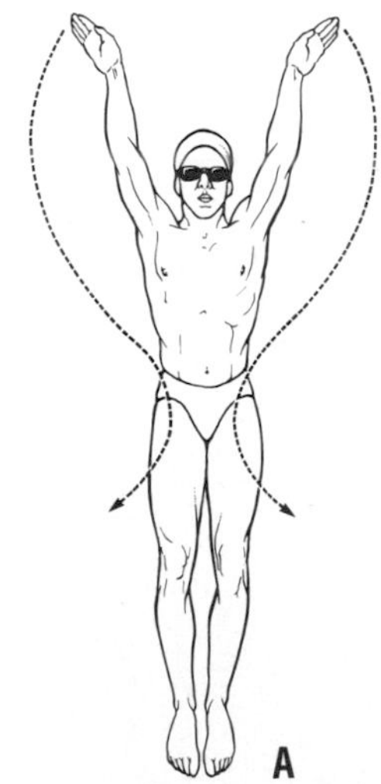

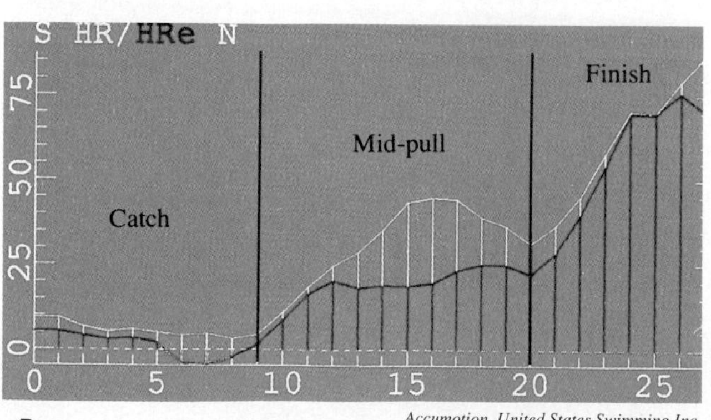


FIG. 6-37, *A-B*

A

B

Accumotion, United States Swimming Inc.

FIG. 6-38, *A-E*

O K E

The catch is an outward sculling motion that starts with your arms extended in front of your shoulders. It ends with your hands spread slightly wider than your shoulders (Fig. 6-38, *A*). Flex your hands slightly down and pitch them to the outside in this phase.

In the mid-pull, continue the sculling action and sweep inward and backward from the end of the catch to a point near the midline of your body. Change the

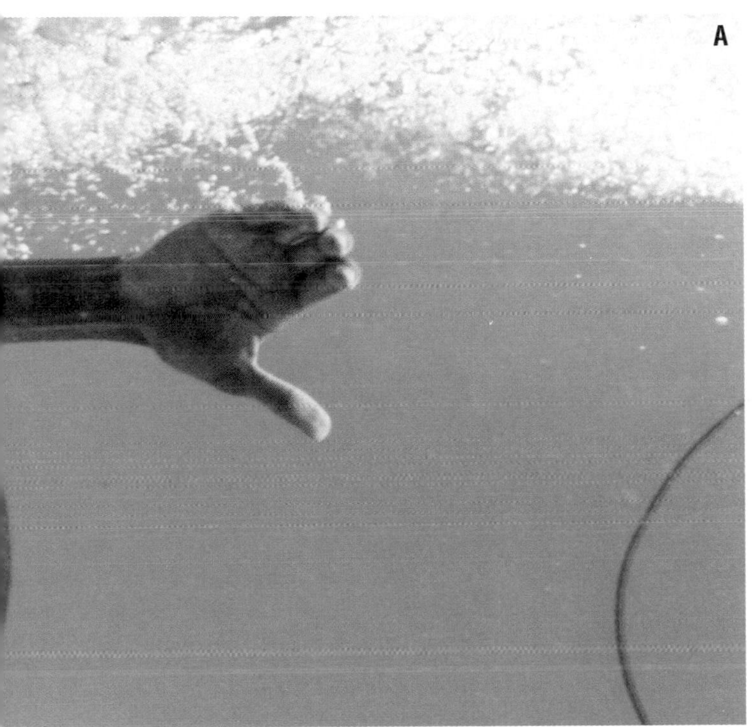

pitch of your hands from outward to inward (Fig. 6-38, *B*). Start to bend your arms after the catch to a maximum of about 90 degrees at the finish of the arm pull. As your arm reaches this maximum bend, your hands are very close together under your shoulders (Fig. 6-38, *C*). As your hands sweep together, your elbows stay higher than your hands, as in the front crawl. Action-reaction forces increase in this phase, but most of the propulsion still comes from lift.

As you end the inward sweep of the hands and start a backward press toward your feet, you do the finish of the power phase (Fig. 6-38, *D*). Continue to press your hands back toward your feet, past your hips to near the sides of your thighs (Fig. 6-38, *E*). As in the front crawl, speed up this motion from the start of the stroke to the finish, especially here at the end. Action-reaction forces are dominant in the end of the power phase.

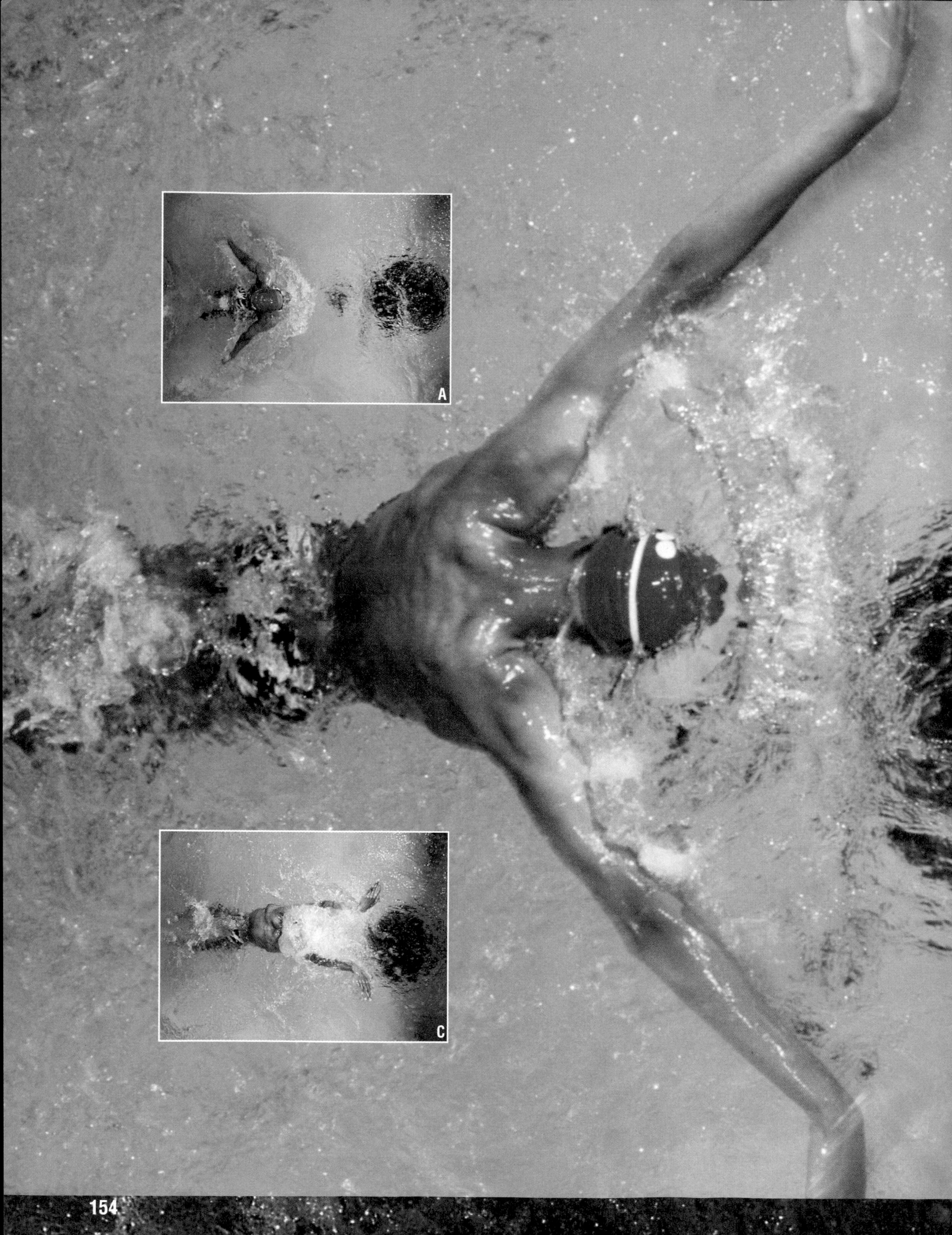
A
C

B

### *Recovery*

A relaxed arm recovery is important but takes more effort than in the front crawl because you can't roll your body to help and your arms stay nearly straight. The recovery is easier if you accelerate hard through the finish of the stroke and then lower your head as your arms recover.

The recovery starts as your hands finish their press toward your feet and your palms turn toward your thighs. Bring your elbows, slightly bent, out of the water first (Fig. 6-39, *A*). Then swing your arms wide to the sides with little or no bend in your elbows (Fig. 6-39, *B*). Move your arms just above the surface to enter in front of your shoulders (Fig. 6-39, *C*). Keep your wrists relaxed and your thumbs down through the recovery.

The entry ends the recovery. With your elbows still slightly flexed, your hands enter the water directly in front of or slightly outside of your shoulders. After the entry, extend your elbows to prepare for the next arm stroke. Pitch your hands out and down for the catch of the next stroke.

Fig. 6-39, *A-C*

# kick

The power of the dolphin kick, the kick used in this stroke, comes from the same dynamics as the flutter kick. The leg action is the same as in the front and back crawl, but the legs stay together in the dolphin kick. The kick starts at the hips and makes the same whip-like motion as the front crawl. Most of the power comes from the quick extension of the legs. Bend the knees slightly through most of the downbeat and straighten them on the upbeat (Fig. 6-40, *A-B*). Relax your ankles. Let your heels just break the surface at the end of the recovery.

Compared to the front and back crawl, you use your hips much more in the dolphin kick, moving up and down in the stroke (Fig. 6-41, *A-B*). Raising your hips at the right time in the stroke makes the follow-through of the legs a natural continuation of the motion. Thus, the dolphin kick involves your whole body, not just your legs.

FIG. 6-40, *A-B*

Fig. 6-41, *A-B*

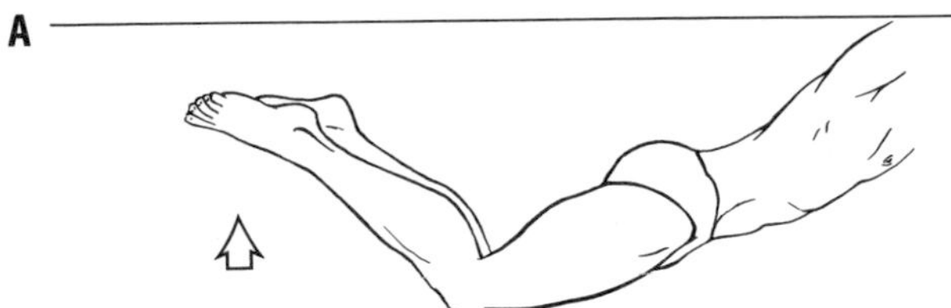


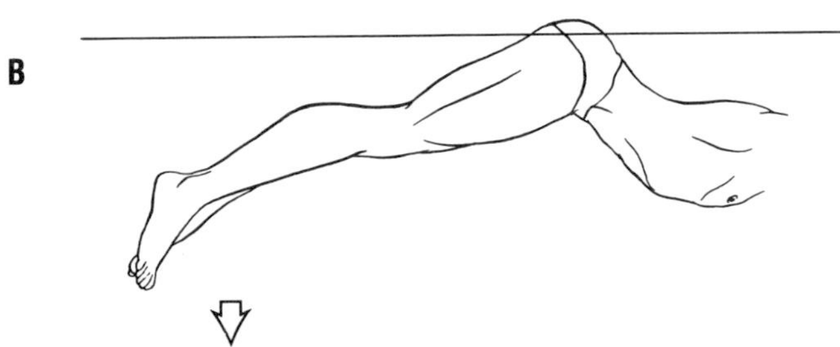

# breathing

The butterfly uses two kicks at specific moments in each arm stroke. With the right timing, this stroke is graceful and looks effortless. With the wrong timing, the stroke is very difficult. The timing of the butterfly depends on the relation of the kicks to the entry and finish of the arm stroke. As you move your hands into the water to start the catch, raise your hips and start the downbeat of the first kick (Fig. 6-42, *A*). As you press your hands through the finish of the power phase, start the downbeat of the second kick (Fig. 6-42, *B*). You should end the second kick just as you finish the pull (Fig. 6-42, *C*).

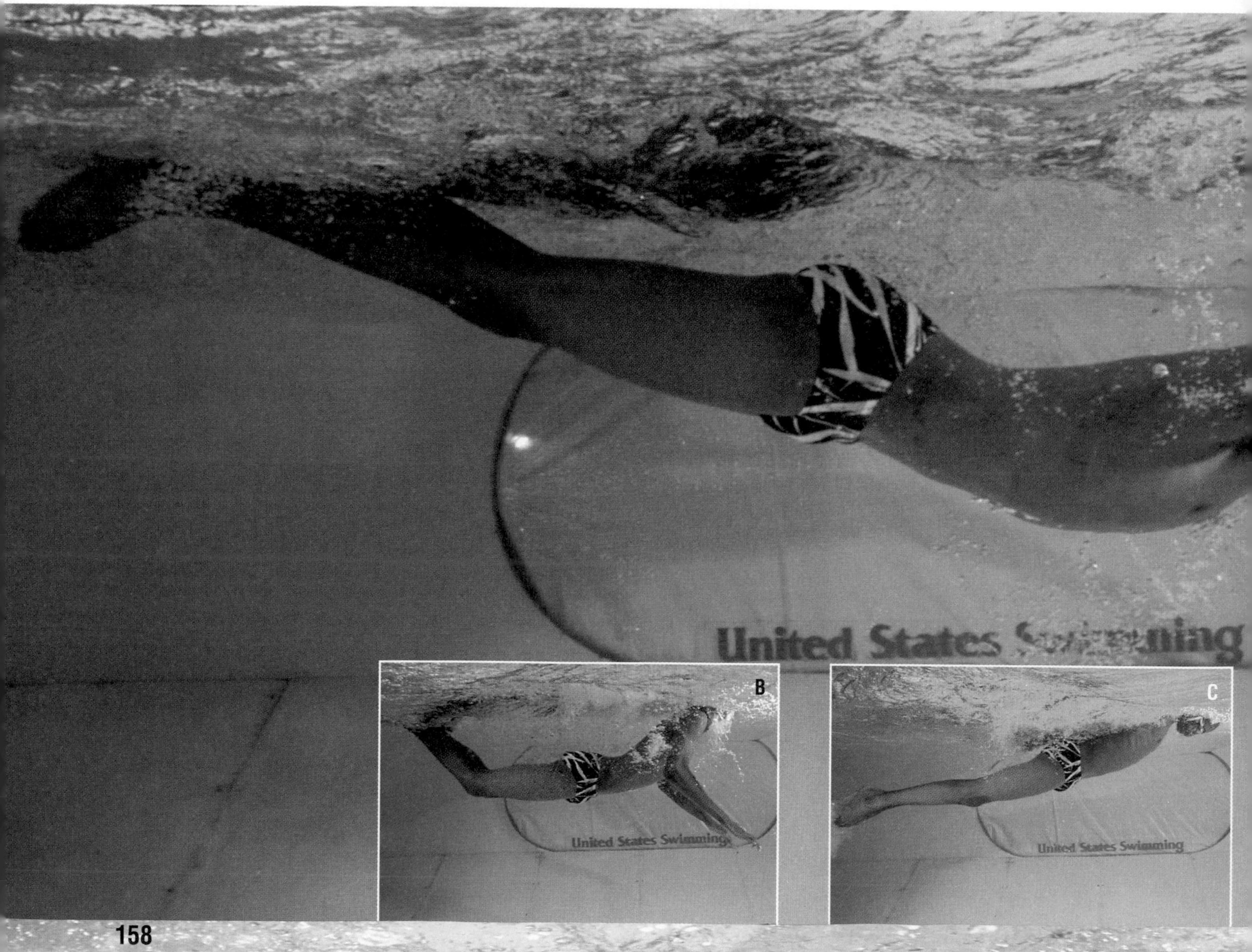

B

C

## AND TIMING

Inhale at the end of the second kick, before your arms start their recovery. To be ready, exhale fully during the underwater pull and raise your head as your hands press toward your hips (Fig. 6-42, *D*). Thrust your chin forward (not upward) as your face just clears the water (Fig. 6-42, *E*). As soon as you inhale and start your arm recovery, lower your head to return your face under water (Fig. 6-42, *F*). Some swimmers learn to breathe only every two or more strokes to gain efficiency in the stroke.

For the butterfly, one learns to use a wave-like movement of the body. In the downbeat of the first kick, the hips go up and the head goes deeper. As the head comes up during the mid-pull phase, the hips drop and the legs recover. As the arm stroke finishes, the hips go up again and the head and shoulders go down to help the arms clear the water in recovery. With good rhythm and timing, this stroke is very graceful and fluid.

## hydroDYNAMIC PRINCIPLES

Many hydrodynamic principles make the butterfly work. Dynamic inertia is one of the important ones. In the stroke as a whole, the power of each stroke maintains the speed and momentum of the body. But in the wave-like motion, the separate actions of the head, torso, hips, and legs each build on the dynamic inertia of the preceding part in forward progress. If the swimmer does not use this inertia well, the stroke becomes awkward or does not work at all.

Fig. 6-42, *A-F*

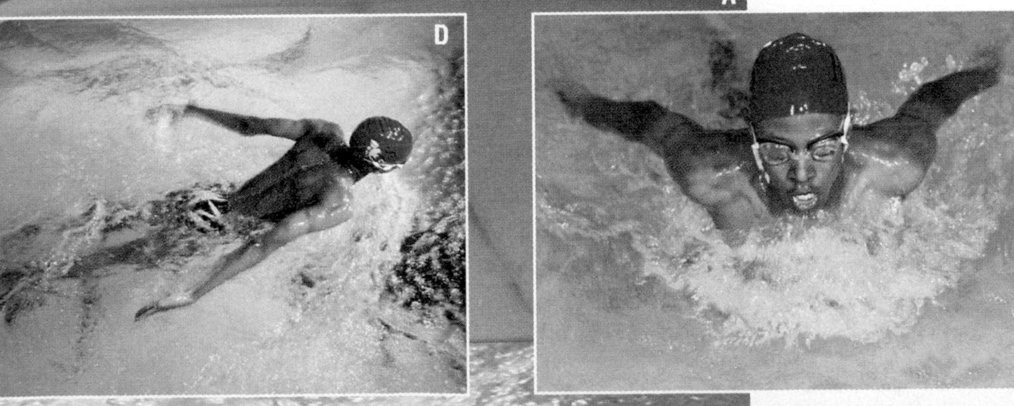


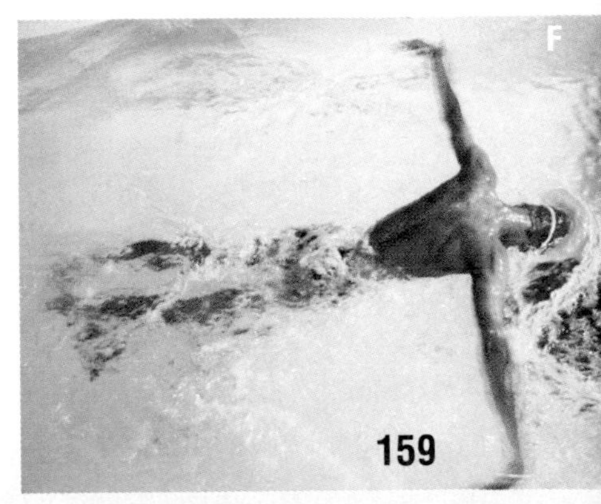

## SUMMARY

We have come a long way since our ancestors found they could propel themselves safely through the water. New swimming techniques have been invented, improved, adapted, and sometimes abandoned. Swimmers, coaches, and researchers constantly examine new ways to swim. There is no doubt that the continuing study of biomechanics, using the latest technology, will lead to faster and more efficient strokes in the years to come.

7

CHAPTER

# starts and tur

## KEY TERMS

**FLIP TURN:** A fast and efficient turn done in a tuck position; used in lap swimming and in the freestyle and backstroke events in competition.

**GRAB START:** A competitive start often used from starting blocks for the fastest takeoff.

**STARTING BLOCK:** A platform competitive swimmers dive from to start a race. A bar or handhold is usually attached for backstroke starts.

ns

# OBJECTIVES

***After reading this chapter, you should be able to—***

1. Discuss when and how starts and turns can be safely learned and practiced.
2. Describe a grab start.
3. Describe a backstroke start.
4. Describe a flip turn for the front crawl.
5. Describe speed turns for the breaststroke and butterfly.
6. Describe a backstroke flip turn.
7. Define the key terms at left.

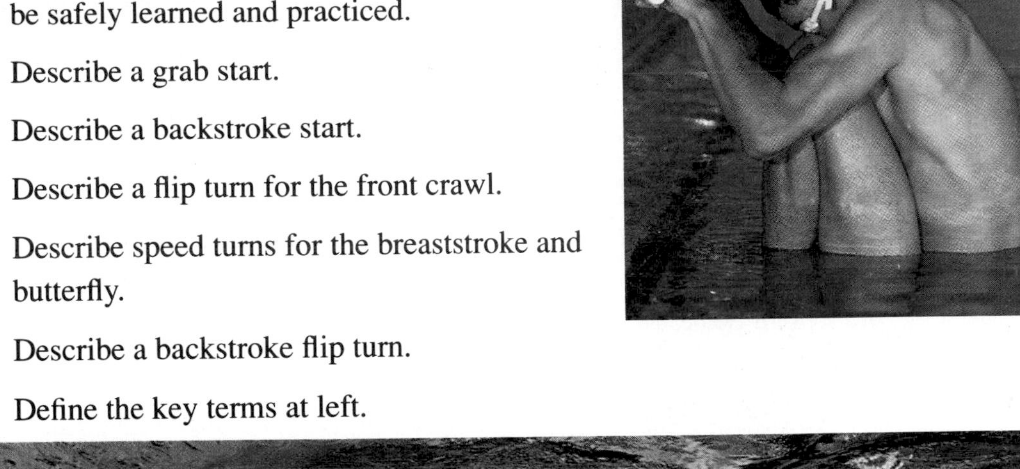

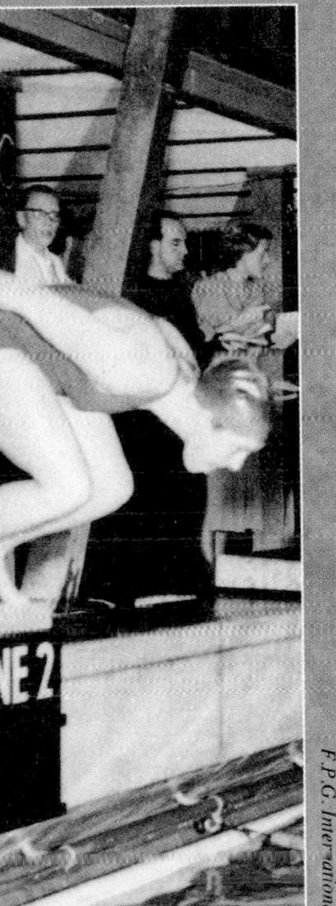

F.P.G. International

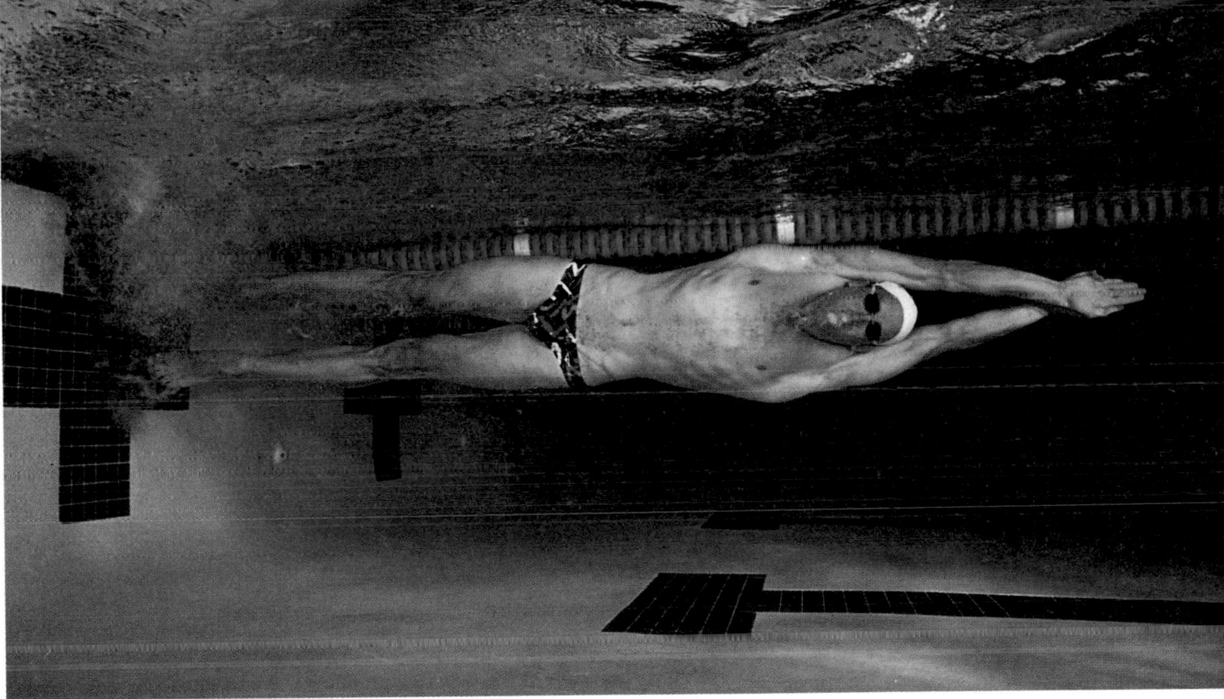

***After reading this chapter and completing appropriate course activities, you should be able to—***

1. Demonstrate a grab start.
2. Demonstrate a backstroke start.
3. Demonstrate a flip turn for the front crawl.
4. Demonstrate speed turns for the breaststroke and butterfly.
5. Demonstrate a backstroke flip turn.

F A S

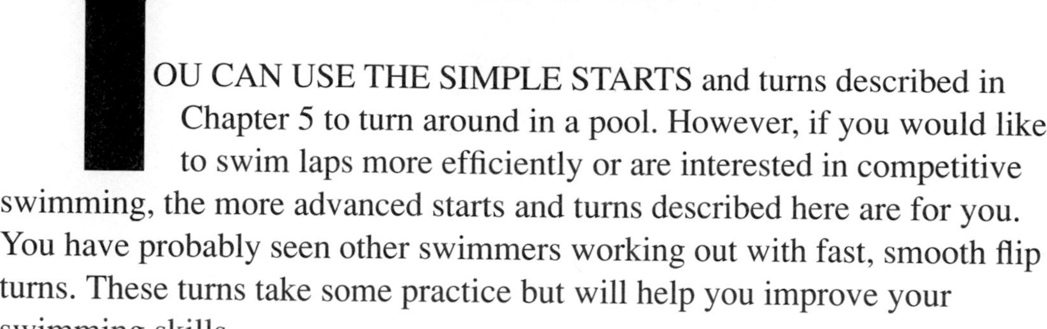

YOU CAN USE THE SIMPLE STARTS and turns described in Chapter 5 to turn around in a pool. However, if you would like to swim laps more efficiently or are interested in competitive swimming, the more advanced starts and turns described here are for you. You have probably seen other swimmers working out with fast, smooth flip turns. These turns take some practice but will help you improve your swimming skills.

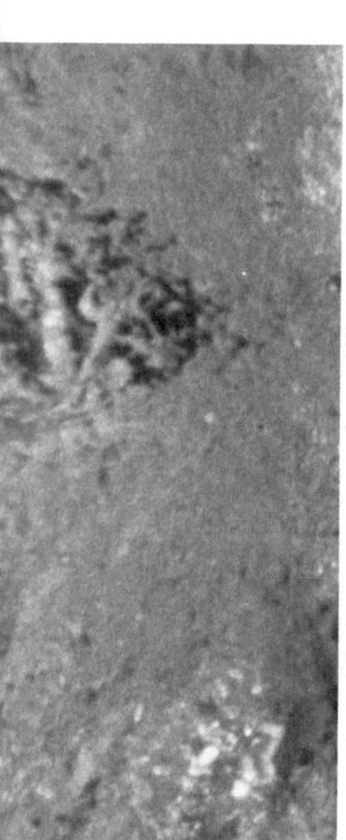

THE GRAB START AND THE BACKSTROKE START described in this chapter are usually used in competition. Chapters 11 and 12 describe competitive programs and training techniques in more detail.

YOU SHOULD HAVE GOOD TRAINING AND SUPERVISION when learning or practicing these skills. Otherwise, you might experience the following problems:

- If you try to use a ***starting block*** without proper training, you face the risk of spinal injury.
- Using a starting block that is not anchored securely can lead to injury.
- If you misjudge your distance from the wall, you could be hurt by swimming into the wall or by hitting your head in the backstroke.
- You may hit your heels on the wall during a flip turn.
- You might push off at the wrong angle, which is especially dangerous in shallow water.

F

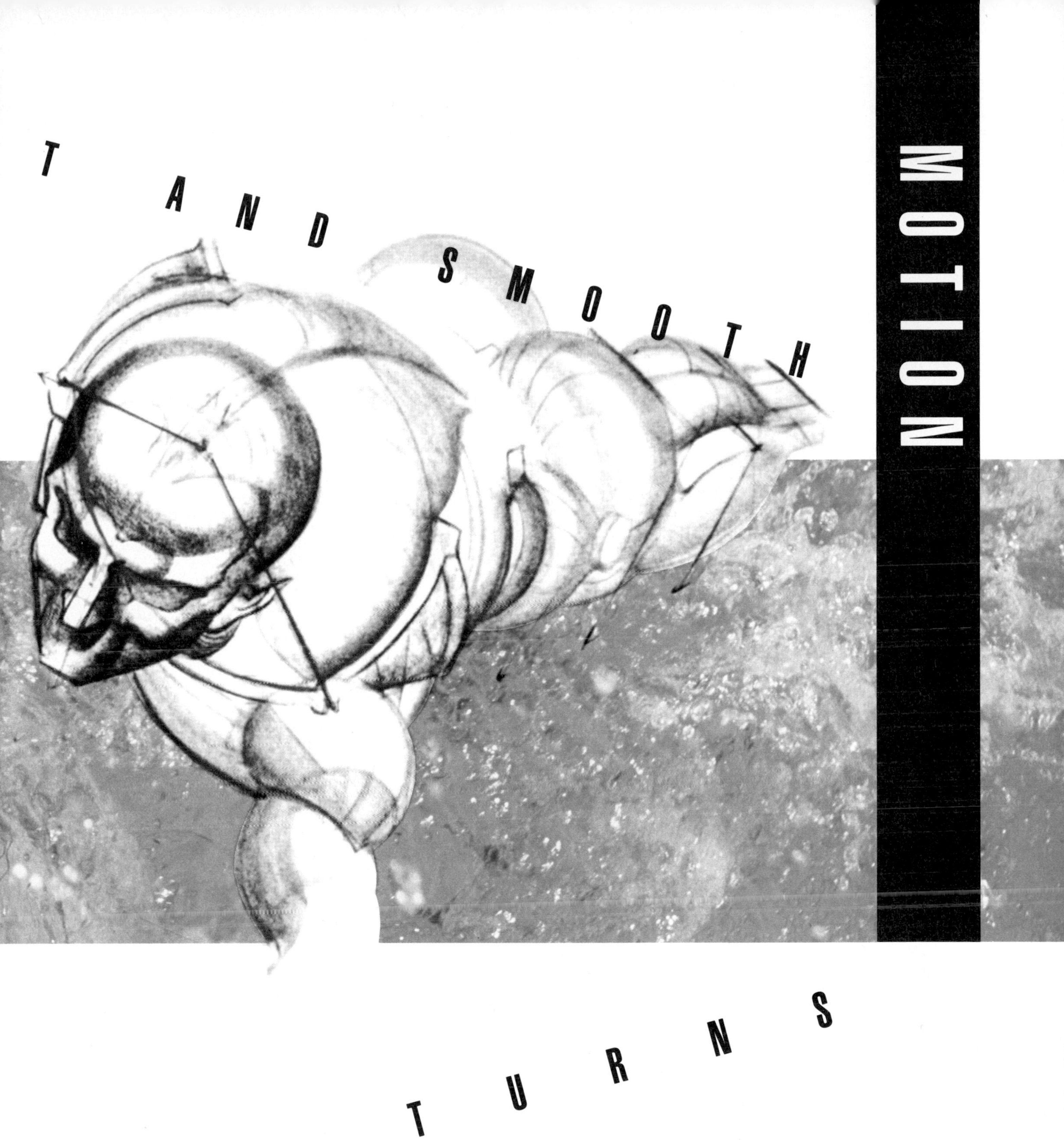


LIP TURNS

# grab START

FIG. 7-1

**M**ost swimmers think the ***grab start*** is the fastest start for competition for all strokes but the backstroke. Before trying the grab start, you must be able to do a long shallow dive safely (Chapter 5).

**T**o position for the start, curl your toes around the starting block with your feet about shoulder width apart (Fig. 7-1). On the command, "Take your mark," grasp the front edge of the starting block. Put your

FIG. 7-2, *A-F*

hands either inside or outside your feet, whichever feels more comfortable. Lower your head and bend your knees slightly (Fig. 7-2, *A*). On the starting signal, pull against the starting block and bend your knees further, so your body starts moving forward. Look forward, release the block, and quickly extend your arms forward to lead your body's flight. As your hands release the block, increase your knee bend still further and then push off by driving your feet against the block and forcefully extending your hips, knees, and ankles (Fig. 7-2, *B*).

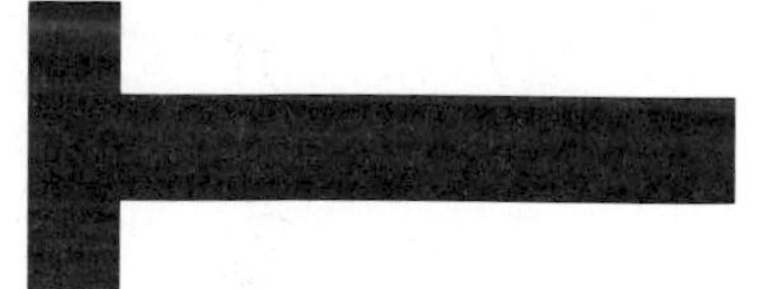

As your feet leave the block, focus your eyes on and aim your arms and hands at the entry point (Fig. 7-2, *C*). Just before hitting the water, lock your head between your arms and enter smoothly, as if going through a hole in the water (Fig. 7-2, *D* and *E*).

Once in the water, angle your hands up toward the surface to decrease your downward motion. Glide in a streamlined position, hands out in front, until you start to slow down (Fig. 7-2, *F*). Then start your kick and follow immediately with your first arm pull. Do not take a breath until you finish your first arm cycle.

C

D

E

F

# backstroke START

FIG. 7-3, *A-F*

The rules for the backstroke start have changed several times in the past few years, and different governing bodies may have different rules. Before your race, check with the meet official about the rules for your particular event.

To get in position for the backstroke start, grasp the starting block with both hands and put your feet parallel on the wall. (FINA and NCAA rules currently require the toes to be under the surface.) Move your feet a comfortable distance apart.

When the starter says "Take your mark," bend your arms and pull your body up and out of the water into a crouched position. Bring your head close to your knees and tuck your body as much as possible (Fig. 7-3, *A*). At the starting command, throw your head back and push your arms out and around with palms outward (Fig. 7-3, *B*). Push forcefully with your legs as you arch your back and drive your body, hands first, up and out over the water (Fig. 7-3, *C*). Tip your head back and look toward your entry point. Your whole body should enter smoothly through a single point in the water (Fig. 7-3, *D* and *E*). Once in the water, adjust the angle of your hands for a good glide (Fig. 7-3, *F*). When you start to slow down, kick and use your first arm pull to come to the surface. Then start stroking.

*Note:* Many swimmers prefer to do several quick dolphin kicks after the start and each turn instead of the flutter kick. If you have a strong dolphin kick, you may wish to try this. First check with the meet official to see what distance you can travel under water before surfacing to start stroking (Fig. 7-4, *A* and *B*).

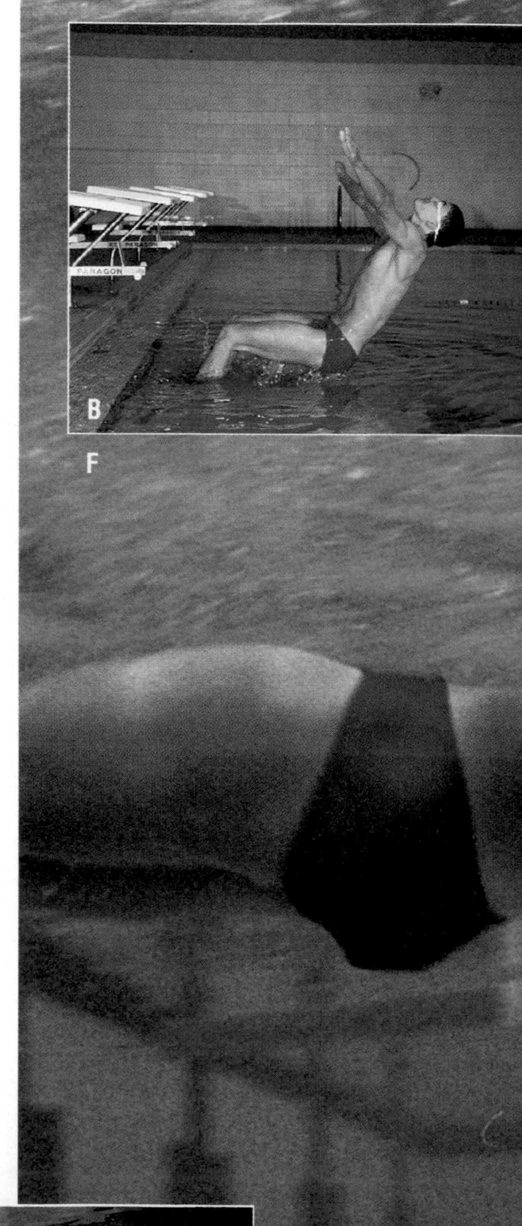


FIG. 7-4, *A-B*

C
D
E

# TURNS

FIG. 7-5, *A-F*

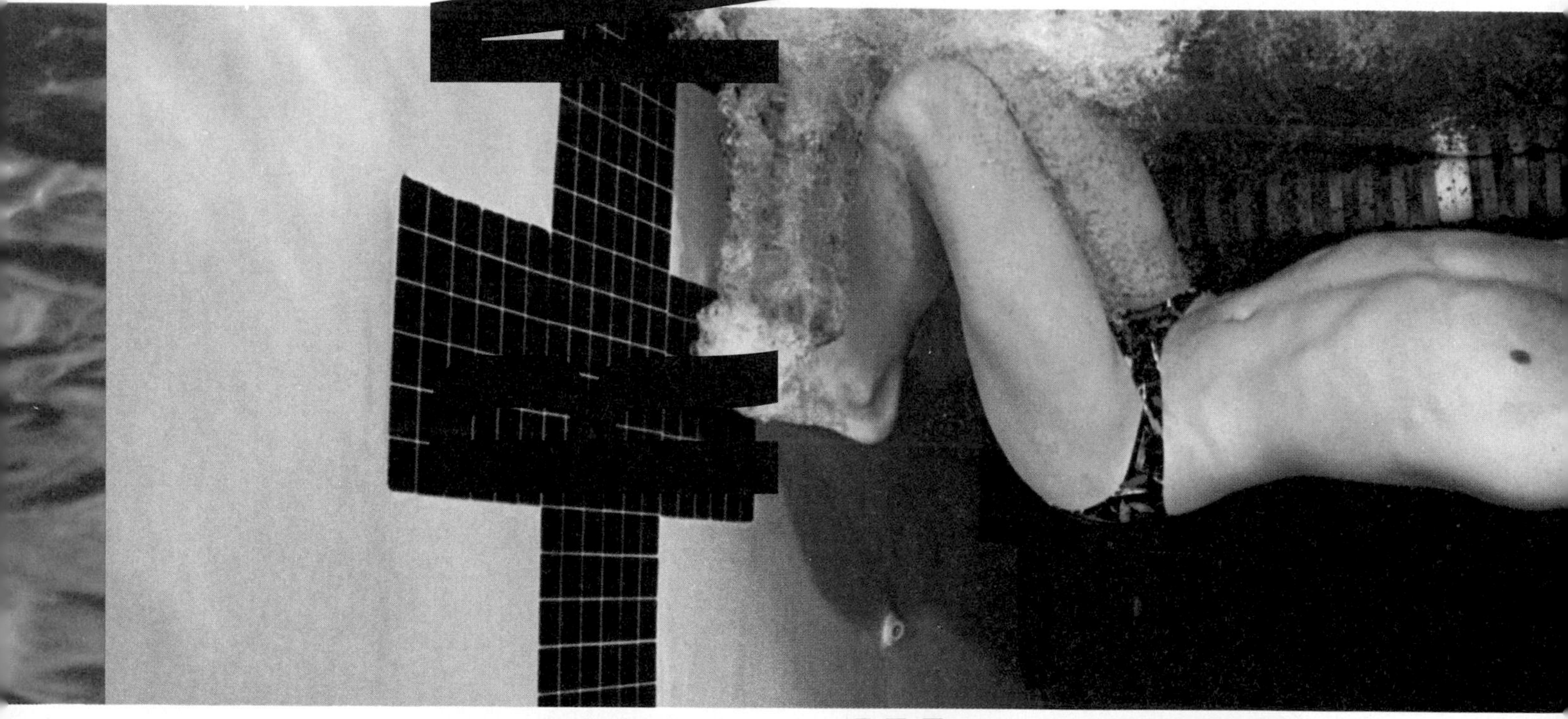

## flip turn

The ***flip turn*** is a fast and efficient turn for the front crawl. Watch the bottom markings to help judge your distance from the wall. When you are one stroke ($3^1/_2$ to 4 feet) from the wall, keep your trailing arm at your side while you take the last stroke with your lead arm (Fig. 7-5, *A*). Both hands are at your thighs. With both arms straight, turn your hands palms down and use a dolphin kick to push your hips forward and upward (Fig. 7-5, *B*). Then drive your head downward and go into a tuck position so your body does a somersault. During the somersault, flex both elbows so your palms push toward your head (Fig. 7-5, *C*); this helps complete the rotation. Plant your feet on the wall with your toes pointed up or slightly to

FIG. 7-6, *A-F*

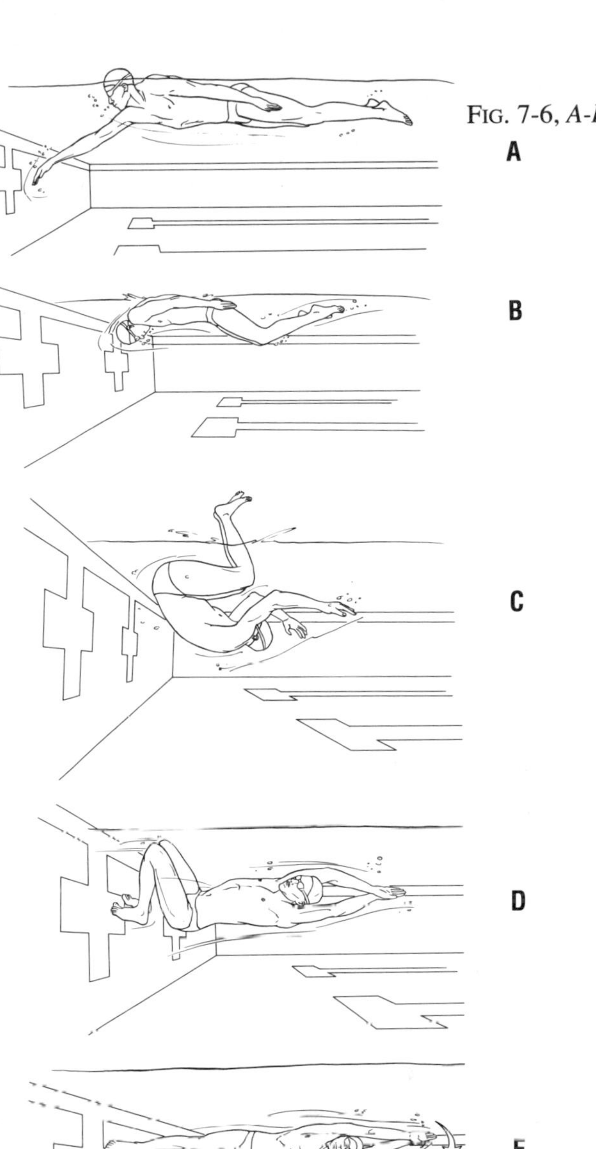


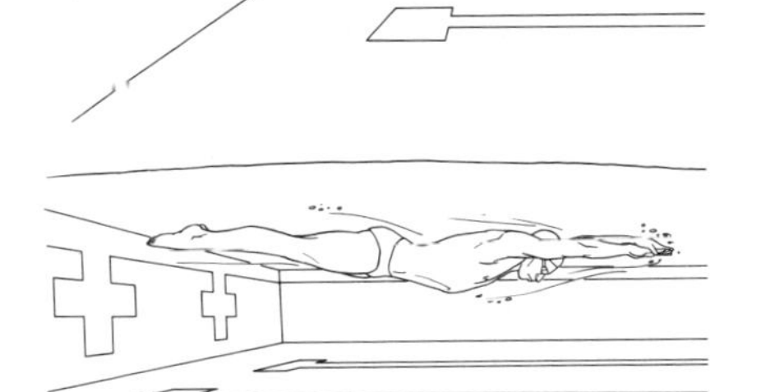


the side and your knees bent (Fig. 7-5, *D*). Push off in a face-up or side-lying position and rotate to a face-down position in the glide (Fig. 7-5, *E* and *F*). Your initial speed when you push off is faster than your swimming speed. When you slow to swimming speed, take one or two kicks and resume the arm stroke. Figure 7-6, *A-F*, illustrates the entire sequence of the flip turn.

*Note:* Some swimmers prefer to rotate into a side-lying position as they plant their feet on the wall, but the push-off on the back is generally considered to be the faster method of turning.

B

# speed turns

## FOR BREASTSTROKE AND BUTTERFLY

The turns used for the breaststroke and butterfly are faster variations of the open turns described in Chapter 5. Time your last stroke so that you are fully stretched as you reach the wall. After both hands touch the wall, dip the shoulder on the side to which you will turn. The example here starts with dipping the left shoulder to turn left. Touch the wall with both hands and tuck your hips and legs tight as they continue to move toward the wall (Fig. 7-7, *A* and *B*). As your hands touch the wall, move your head away from the wall, bend your left elbow, and move your left arm backward as close as possible to your body (Fig. 7-7, *C*). When your legs pass under your body, move your right arm over your head, keeping it close to your head. Take a deep breath before your head submerges. Plant both feet on the wall with toes pointing toward the side, knees bent. Extend your arms as you push off in a side-lying position (Fig. 7-7, *D*). Rotate to a prone position while gliding about 1 foot below the surface. This helps reduce wave drag.

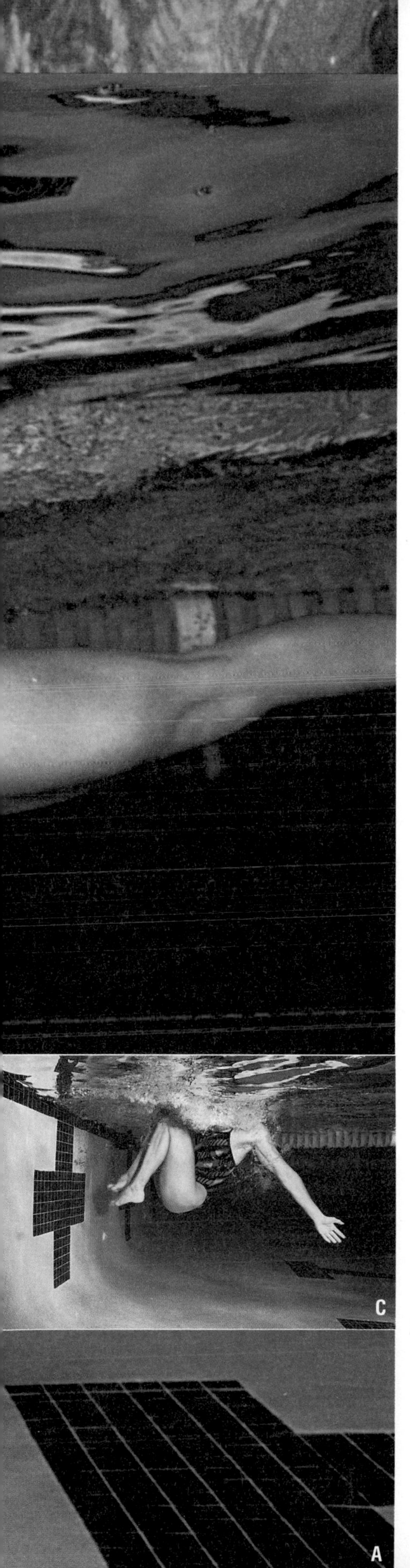


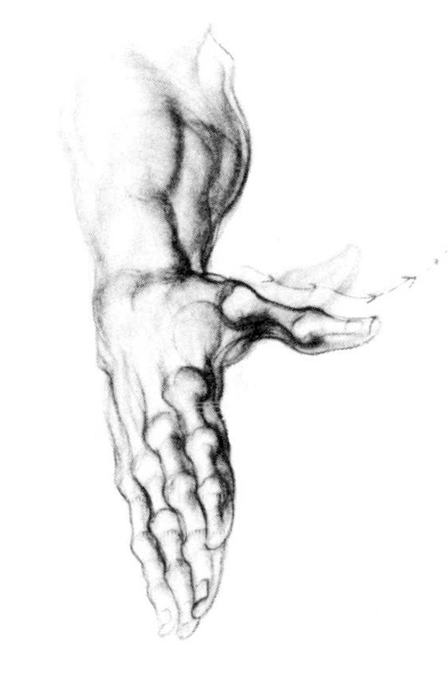

FIG. 7-7, *A-D*

FIG. 7-8, *A-C*

**I**n the breaststroke, push off slightly downward (for a longer glide). When you slow down, take a complete underwater breaststroke pull to the thighs, glide again, and then kick upward as your hands recover close to the body (Fig. 7-8, *A-C*). This brings you to the surface to resume stroking. The underwater pull for the breaststroke turn differs from the usual pull because you pull all the way past the hips and recover the hands close to the body. The entire breaststroke turn and underwater pull are illustrated in Figure 7-9, A-G.

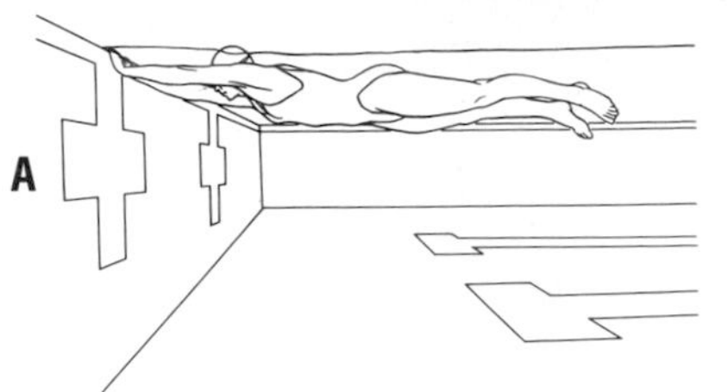

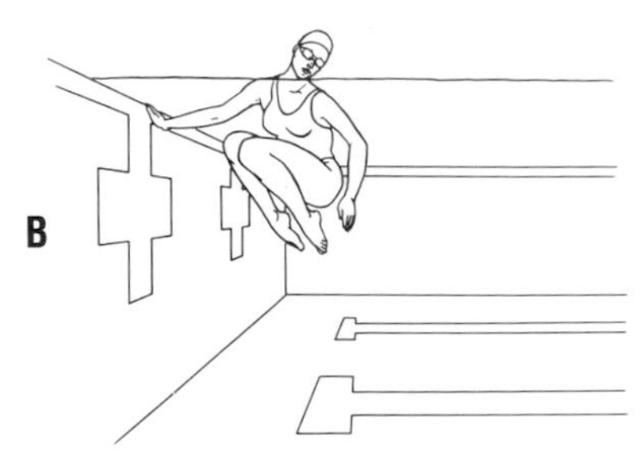

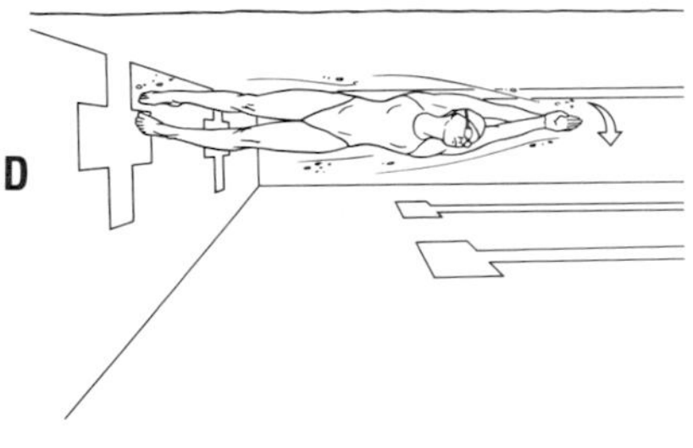

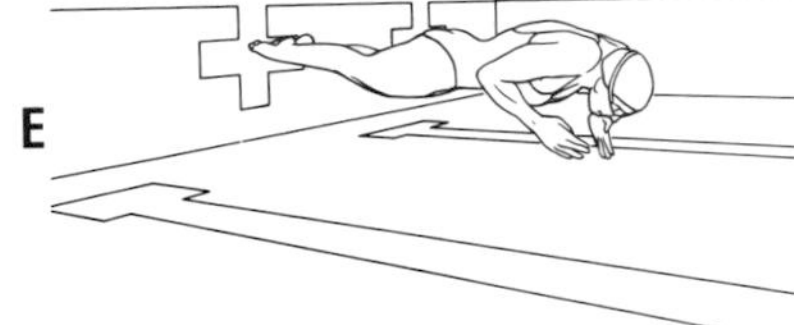

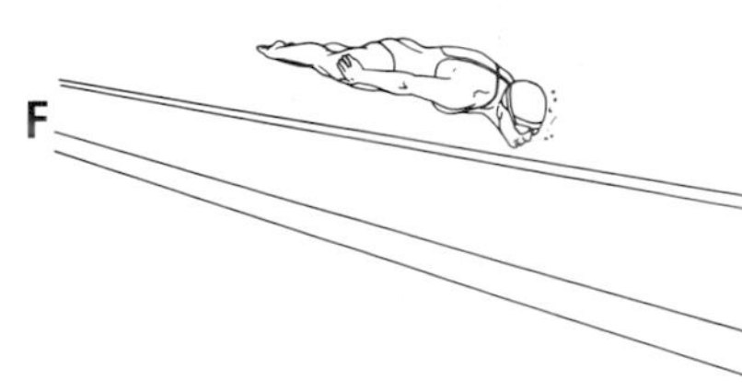

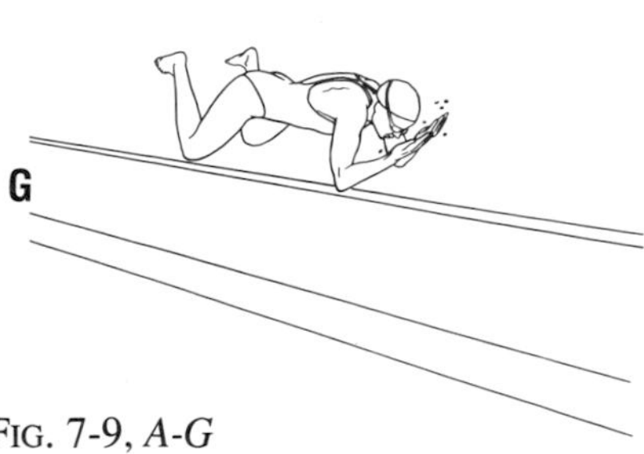

FIG. 7-9, *A-G*

FIG. 7-10, *A-D*

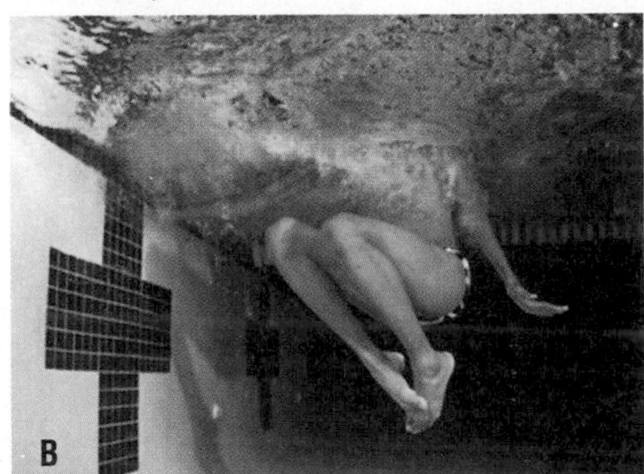

**T**he turn for the butterfly is like the turn for the breaststroke (Fig. 7-10, *A-D*). After the turn, glide a short distance, then dolphin kick to the surface and start stroking. Figure 7-11, *A-E*, illustrates the butterfly turn sequence.

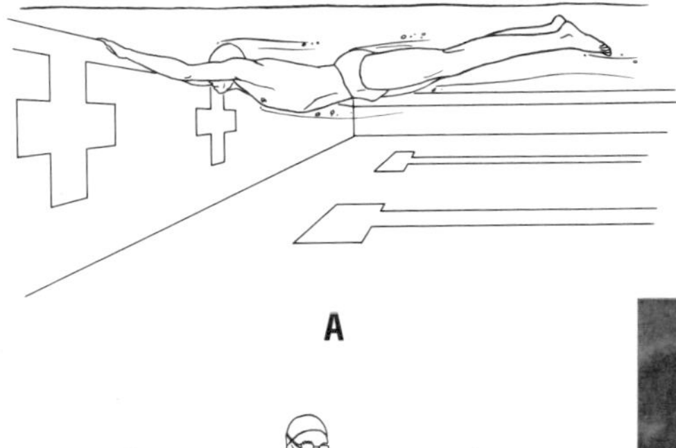


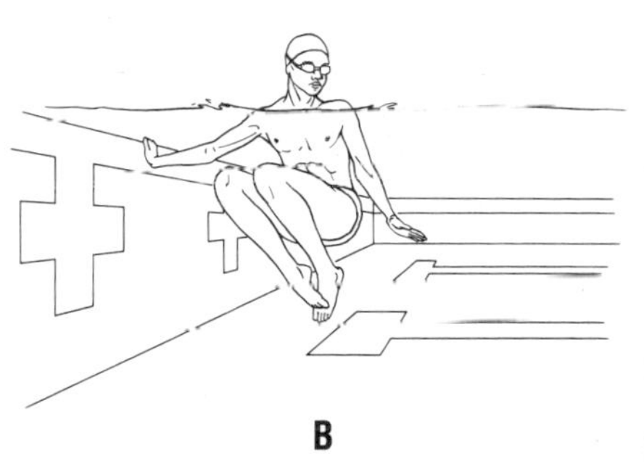


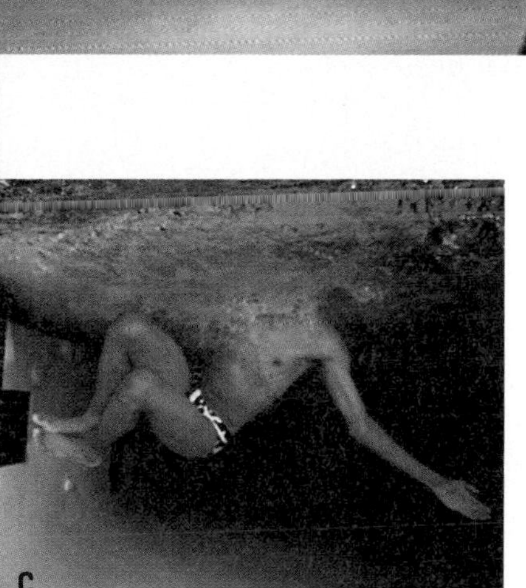

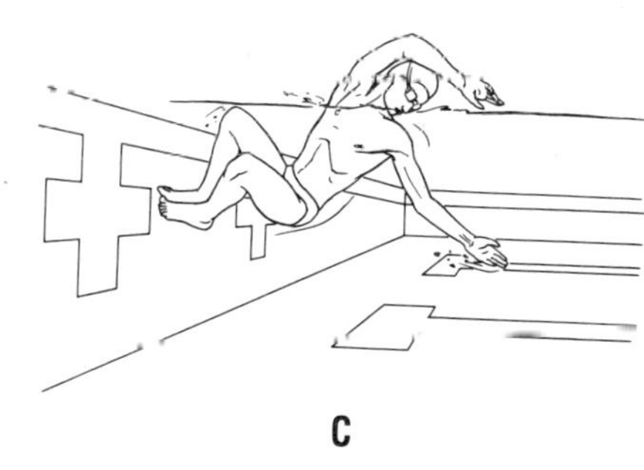


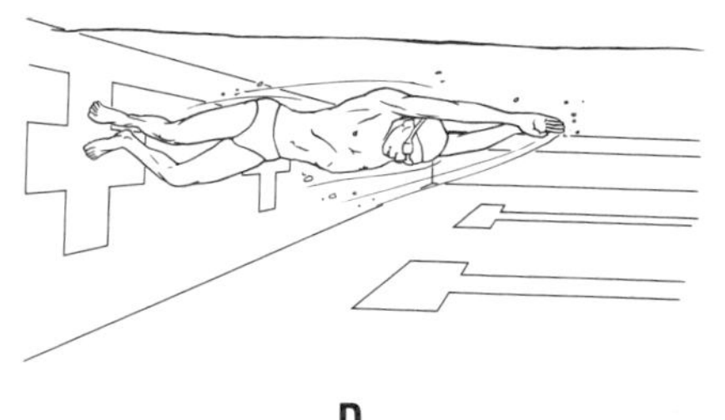


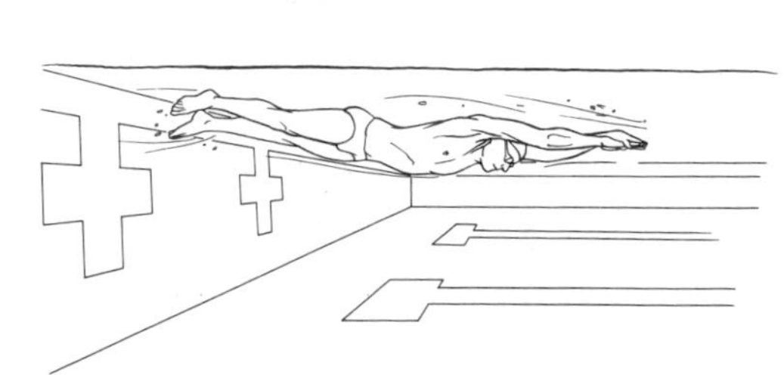


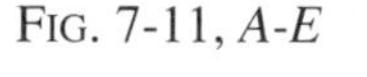
FIG. 7-11, *A-E*

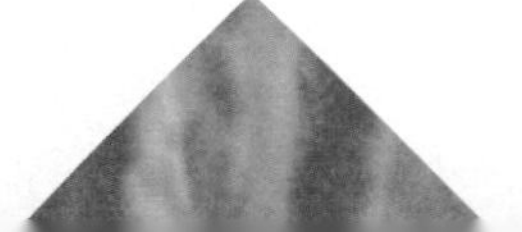

# backstroke FLIP TURN

**R**ules for the competitive backstroke turn were modified in 1991 to let a swimmer touch the wall with any part of the body. Previously, a hand touch was required. During the turn, the shoulders may turn past vertical as long as the motion is part of a continuous turning action. You must return to a position on the back before the feet leave the wall.

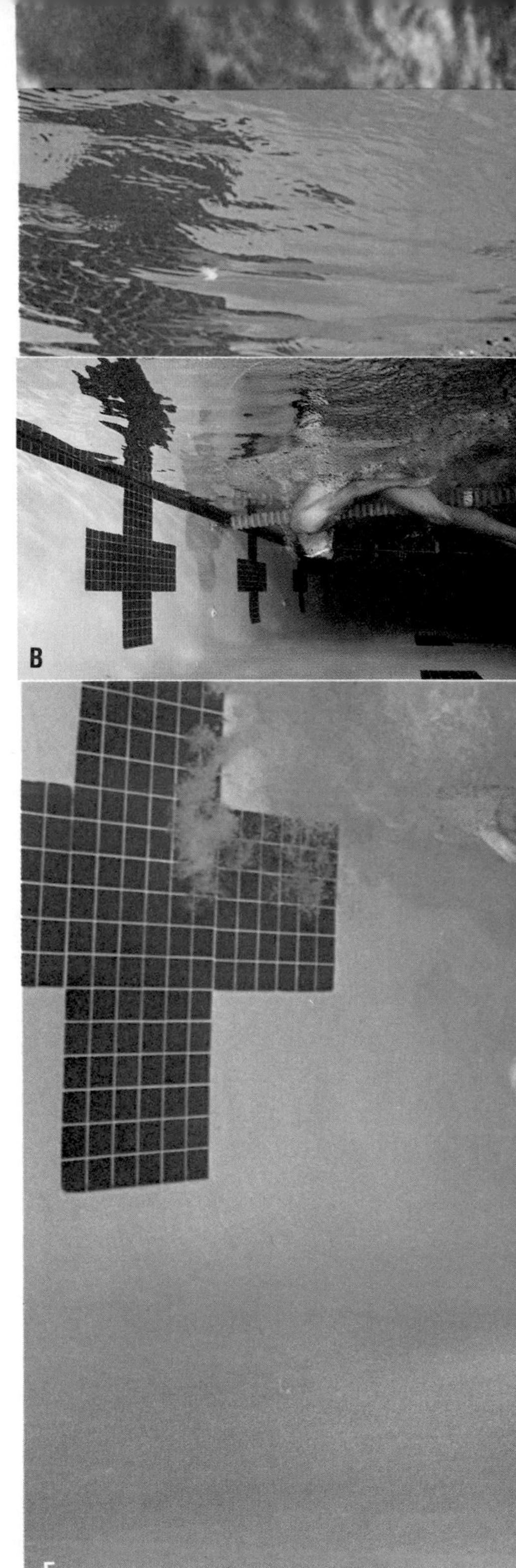

FIG. 7-12, *A-E*

**A**fter you pass the backstroke flags, accelerate toward the wall. Start the flip one stroke from the wall by turning your head and looking toward your pulling arm as it does the catch (Fig 7-12, *A*). As you pull, rotate onto your stomach, drive your head downward, and stop your pulling hand at your hips. At the same time, your other arm recovers across your body, enters the water in the same position as in the front crawl, and pulls to the hips. Drive your head down and start the somersault while tucking your knees tightly to your chest (Fig. 7-12, *B* and *C*). During the somersault, turn both palms toward your body and sweep them toward your head to complete the flip. Keep your legs tucked until your feet contact the wall, toes pointed upward (Fig. 7-12, *D*). While still on your back, push straight off forcefully and go into a streamlined position as you leave the wall (Fig. 7-12, *E*). Properly done, this turn may improve your swim time by as much as 0.5 second per turn. The entire turn is illustrated in Figure 7-13, *A-F*.

**Y**our motion in the turn must be continuous. Any hesitation, dolphin kicks, or extra strokes after turning onto your stomach may disqualify you in a competition.

FIG. 7-13, *A-F*

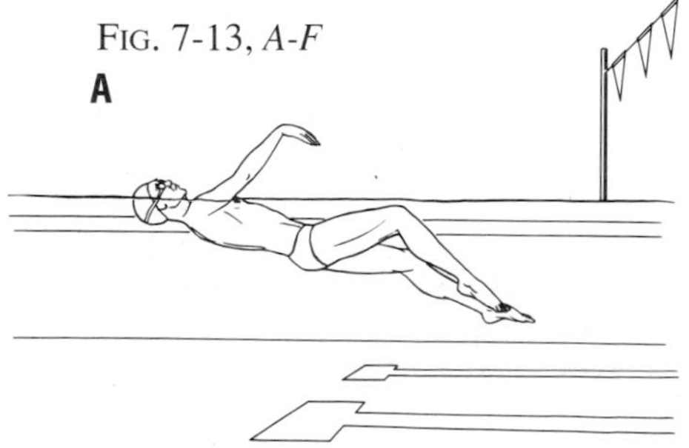

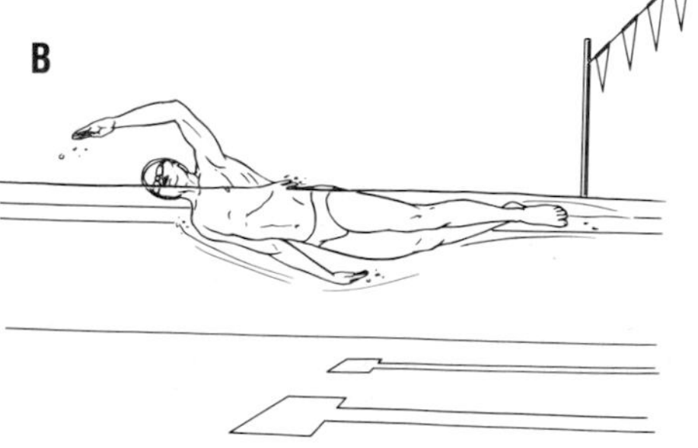

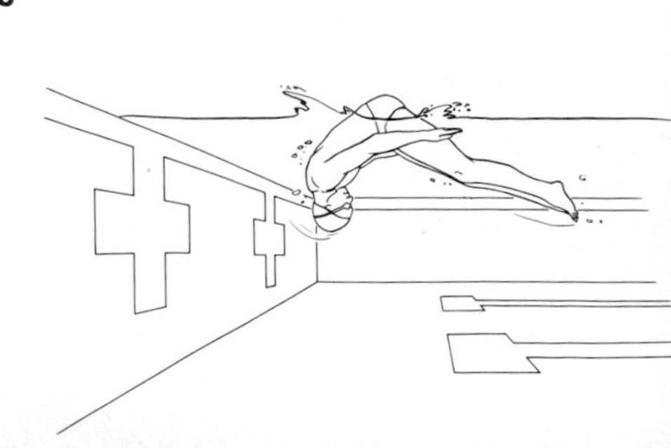

C

D

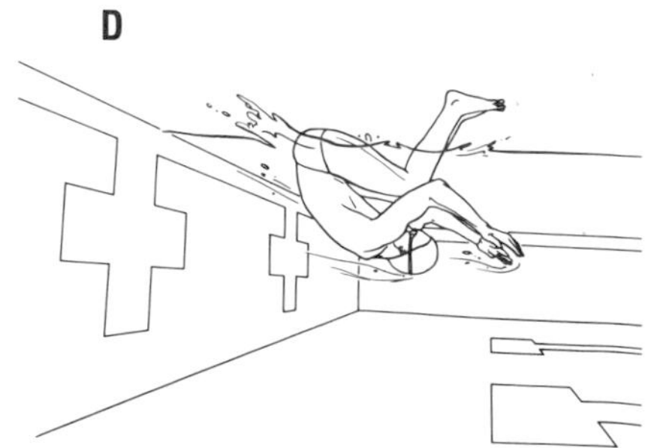


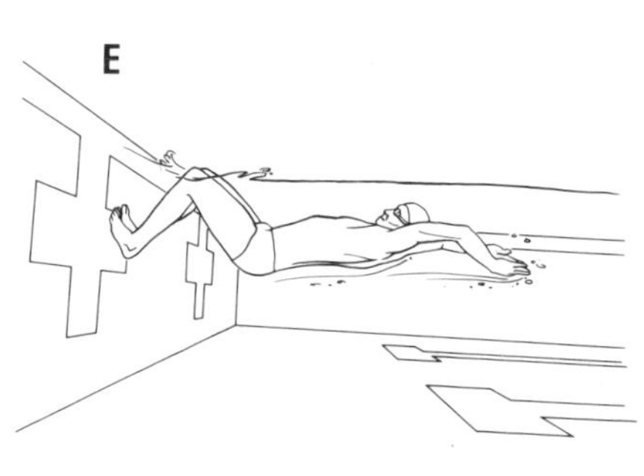


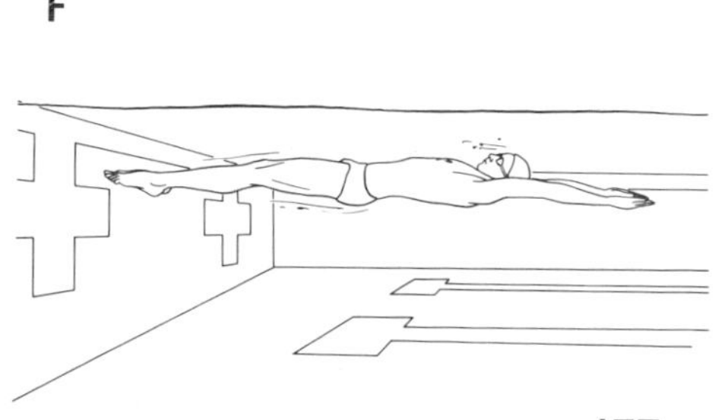

## Summary

You do not have to learn all the skills in this chapter now. As you develop as a swimmer and your goals change, however, these skills will gain value for you. If your goal is fitness swimming, for example, learning more efficient turns helps you make better use of your time in the pool and makes your strokes smoother. If you plan to compete, good starts and turns are essential.

Everyone who swims, whether for leisure or competition, develops a personal starting and turning style. For help learning or improving your skills, ask a coach at your local swim team for some pointers. Remember the safety guidelines at the beginning of this chapter for learning or practicing these skills.

8

# diving

CHAPTER

## Key Terms

**Approach:** The walk toward the end of a diving board before the hurdle.

**Body alignment:** The position of the body in preparation for an entry.

**Entry:** The part of a dive in which the body passes through the surface of the water.

**Flight:** The movement of the body through the air in a dive.

**Fulcrum:** The part of a diving apparatus under the center of a diving board that lets the board bend and spring.

**Hurdle:** The jump to the end of a diving board after the approach.

**Hurdle leg:** The leg lifted in the hurdle.

**Lift:** Used in this chapter to refer to the force of a diving board propelling a diver into the air (not the principle of lift in hydrodynamics).

**Pike position:** A basic diving position with the body bent at the hips and the legs straight.

**Press:** A diver's downward push on a diving board before the upward recoil.

**Progression:** An ordered set of steps, from the simplest to the most complex, for learning a skill.

**Push leg:** The leg that pushes into the hurdle.

**Straight position:** A basic diving position of the body with the body straight or arched slightly backward and the legs straight and together.

**Takeoff:** The propulsive part of a dive in which a diver's feet leave the deck or the end of a diving board.

**Tuck position:** A basic diving position with the body pulled into a tight ball with knees drawn up to the chest and heels drawn to the buttocks.

# Objectives

***After reading this chapter, you should be able to—***

1. List five basic safety guidelines for any dive.
2. Describe how one should be physically ready to learn to dive.
3. Explain how following logical progressions helps overcome diving fears.
4. Name the three parts of a simple dive.
5. Explain why body alignment is important.
6. Explain how diving is affected by the following physical principles:
   - Form drag
   - Action and reaction
   - The effects of gravity on the length (in time) of a dive
   - The effects of body position on the speed of rotation
7. Describe the parts of a diving board used in competition.
8. Define the key terms at left.

***After reading this chapter and completing appropriate course activities, you should be able to—***

1. Demonstrate four basic diving progressions: kneeling position, compact position, stride position, and standing dive.
2. Demonstrate a standing jump from a diving board.
3. Demonstrate a one-step approach and hurdle.
4. Demonstrate a full approach and hurdle.
5. Demonstrate a forward jump, tuck position, from the deck and from a diving board.
6. Demonstrate a standing forward dive in tuck and pike positions.
7. Demonstrate a forward dive, tuck and pike positions, with a full approach and hurdle.

DIVING IS A WONDERFULLY exhilarating activity for most people. On the simplest level, diving gives you an effective way to enter the water. More complicated dives include springing high into the air for a series of breathless, swift, and graceful maneuvers. Dives may include bending, twisting, and somersaulting motions before the body becomes streamlined for a vertical entry into the water.

LEARNING TO DIVE OFFERS YOU MANY BENEFITS. You gain the practical benefit of being able to enter the water quickly. Diving also helps develop muscle tone, flexibility, coordination, balance, and visual and kinesthetic awareness. You will also gain greater self-confidence, courage, determination, and motivation.

YOU MAY WANT TO DIVE JUST FOR FUN, or you may be planning to enter competition. For either goal, this chapter is useful. It presents progressions for learning to dive from the deck and from a diving board. A ***progression*** is an ordered set of steps, from the simplest to the most complex, for learning a skill. The progressions in this chapter will help you reduce the fears or doubts you may have about diving and will help make your diving safe. *Be sure to get instruction from a qualified instructor or coach before trying any dive.*

**Visual and Kinesthetic Awareness**

*Visual and kinesthetic awareness are very important in learning diving skills.* ***Visual awareness*** *is the ability to stay focused on a reference point to determine your body's position in space, such as during your flight from a diving board.* ***Kinesthetic awareness*** *is the ability to perceive what your body is doing at any given moment, such as being aware of the position of your arms and legs while you are rotating. Visual and kinesthetic awareness help you stay in control when doing complex dives. You can improve your skills by keeping your eyes open and focused on a fixed reference point. Another person splashing the surface of the water in front of the diving board can help you focus on the water's surface. This helps you be aware of your body's position in relation to the water and to achieve good body alignment for your entry.*

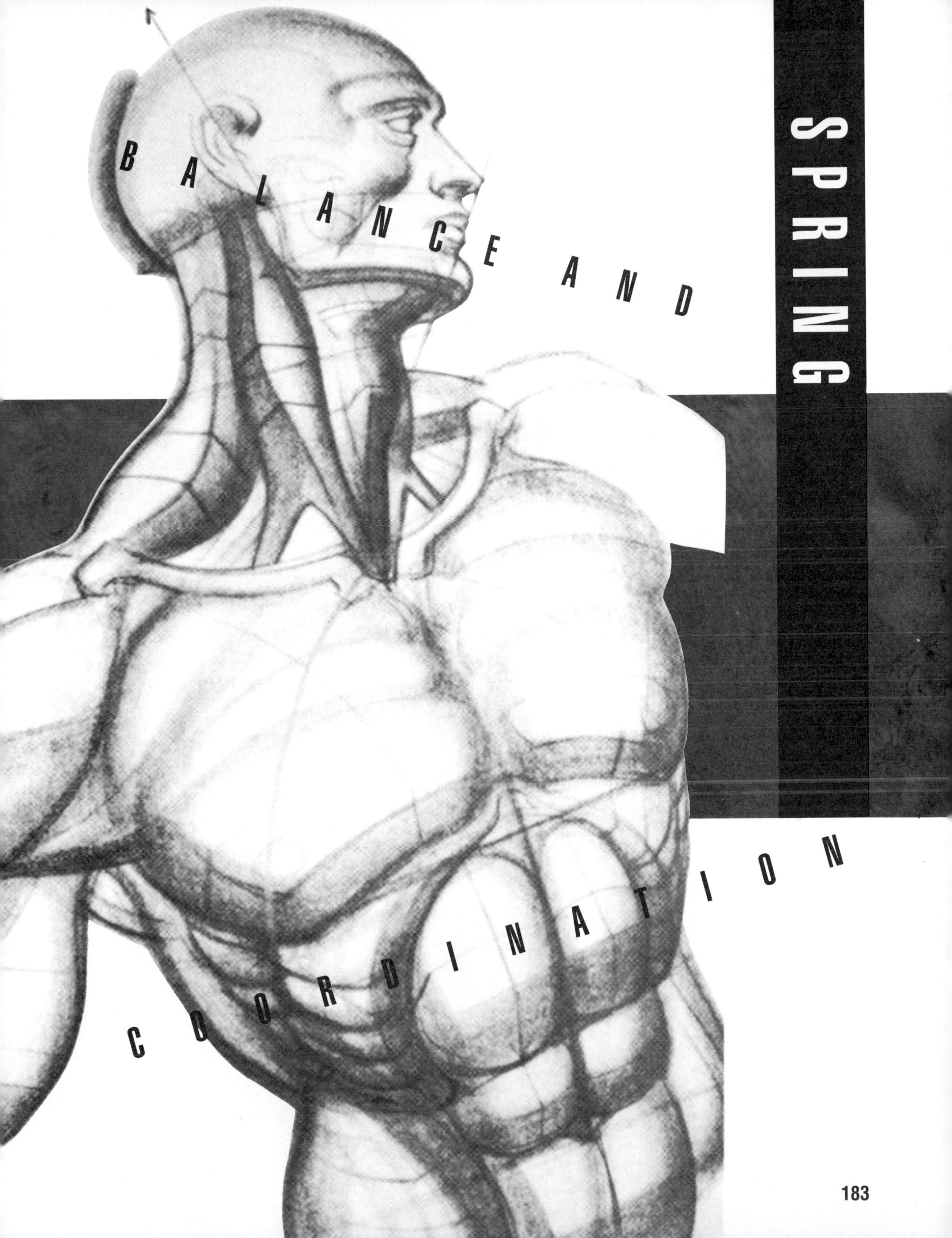

# SPRING

## BALANCE AND COORDINATION

# PRECAUTIONS

Chapter 3 lists rules for safe diving; read that chapter carefully before starting to dive. Also follow these basic guidelines when you dive:

1. Make sure the water is deep enough for diving. No matter how shallow you intend your dive to be, *remember that diving from the deck into water shallower that 9 feet could cause a head or spinal injury or even death.* The American Red Cross recommends that competitive racing starts be taught under supervision and in water at least 9 feet deep. During competition, racing starts should be performed only with proper supervision and in water depths that are in conformance with the rules and regulations of governing bodies such as United States Swimming, the National Collegiate Athletic Association, and the National Federation of State High School Associations. Diving into above-ground pools is never safe.
2. When you dive from a deck or diving board, make sure there is enough room to maneuver and that the water is free of obstructions. Since some people need more room to maneuver than others, be sure you have enough room for yourself. Always dive directly forward from a deck or diving board. When you dive from a deck, the area of entry should be free from obstructions (such as lane lines and kickboards) for at least 4 feet on both sides. For dives from a 1-meter diving board, you need 10 feet of clearance on both sides.
3. Make sure you are physically capable of doing a dive and psychologically ready to try it.
4. In a headfirst dive, extend your arms with your elbows locked alongside your head. Keep your hands together with thumbs touching (or interlocked) and palms facing toward the water. Keeping your arms, wrists, and fingers in line with your head helps you control the angle of entry. This reduces the impact of the water on the top of the head and helps protect you from injury. Keep your body tensed and straight from the hands to the pointed toes (Fig. 8-1).
5. For springboard diving, use equipment that meets the standards set for competition. (See Chapter 3.)

FIG. 8-1

# diver READINESS

## Physical Readiness

To learn to dive, you must first have some basic swimming skills. You must be able to change from a vertical to a horizontal position in the water, change directions, and swim back to the side of the pool. To dive from a diving board, you must be able to swim to the surface, become horizontal in the water, and swim to the side of the pool (Fig. 8-2). These skills are discussed in Chapter 5.

Strength also may be a consideration. You must be able to keep your arms overhead during the ***entry*** (when your body passes through the surface of the water). You can test your ability to do this by submerging and pushing forcefully off the side wall of the pool in a streamlined position (arms alongside the head, as described previously for a headfirst dive) and glide. If you cannot keep your arms aligned, postpone learning to dive until you increase your upper body strength.

Fig. 8-2

## Psychological Readiness

Someone about to fall forward into the water headfirst for the first time may feel fear or apprehension. Although you should always be cautious when you dive, the progressions taught in this chapter can help you minimize any fears. This method helps you reach success at each level. If you take the time to master the skills of each step before moving to the next, you will enjoy the experience more and feel more ready to try the next skill. The following are the most common fears people feel when learning to dive.

### *Fear of Depth*

You may be afraid that you will not be able to swim back to the surface. Someone who is reluctant to dive deep might "belly flop" by lifting the head before entering the water. If you feel hesitant in depths, try to become more comfortable by swimming more often in deep water, if you are qualified to do so. Surface diving and underwater swimming also will increase your self-confidence. (For these skills, see Chapter 5.)

### *Fear of Injury*

Fear of being injured may cause a person to avoid diving entirely. It is true you may feel a little pain if you land incorrectly in the water while trying a dive, but if you follow the safety precautions, actual injury is extremely unlikely. Yet some people may feel fear because they saw someone injured in a dive or may have been hurt themselves. Again, learning the skills for diving in a safe, step-by-step manner prevents injury and helps you overcome the fear of injury.

### *Fear of Height*

The view of the distance to the surface from a diving board or the pool deck may cause anxiety or make some people want to avoid diving altogether. The progressions used in this chapter will help you overcome such fears. Start your diving from as close to the surface of the water as possible and move to a new height only when you feel ready and have the skill to do so.

Any of these fears can affect a beginning or even an advanced diver. If you feel hesitant at any step in a progression, keep practicing the previous step until you feel confident to proceed. Never try a new skill if you are very fearful. If you cannot concentrate on the skill, you are more likely to be injured while trying it.

**Sparging Systems**

*Although diving is a noncontact sport, divers do collide with the water without any protective padding. Surprising as this may sound, if a diver lands horizontally on the water from a height of 10 meters, the force of the impact is measured in thousands of pounds. Such an impact, aside from being quite painful, can cause severe injury, including ruptured organs and even detached retinas.*

*The air sparging system, or "bubble machine," was invented to reduce pain and risk of injury when a diver is learning new dives. Located on the pool bottom, the air sparger shoots air at high velocity into the pool, creating a 50-50 mixture of air bubbles in water. The bubbles form a "mound" of water above the normal surface level of the water to cushion the diver's entry. This protection allows the diver to concentrate on the technique of the dive, rather than on the landing. The beginning diver builds skill and confidence in a more relaxed fashion, thus reducing the risk of injury.*

*Bubble machines have three design factors that help reduce the force of impact:*

1. *The mixture of air and water. Simply by adding 50 percent air to the water, the force of the body's impact upon the water is correspondingly reduced by half.*
2. *Compressibility (squeezability). One cannot compress water very much, but air is very compressible. When a diver lands on the foaming water, he or she is actually squeezing the air out of the water with the force of the impact. The air cushions the entry, just as the holes in a foam rubber pillow, also filled with air, cushion your head when you lie down on it.*
3. *The mound effect. The bubbles create a mound of water for the diver to push aside on impact. This is like jumping on a pile of loose sand on the beach, as opposed to jumping on flat, solid sand.*

*Photo by: Eamonn McCabe*

*Sparging systems can reduce the force of impact of a diver's body on the water by as much as 80 percent. This means that landing flat from 10 meters on bubbles would have almost the same impact as landing flat from 2 meters on "solid" water.*

*Even though the sparging machine can reduce the force of impact, proper alignment is still important. If a diver's body is not "tight" on entry, the force of impact can knock the wind out of the diver and even cause severe tissue injury.*

*Sparging machines are not a substitute for proper skills and are not to be used as a crutch. They are to be used only to help a diver gain the confidence and skill needed to perform the dive into "solid" water.*

*Many new uses have been found for sparging systems, aside from reducing the risk of injuries to competitive divers. Surf simulation (wave pools), treadmill swimming, white water canoeing, and handicap float swims are just a few of the uses recently discovered. When safety precautions are properly taken, as with any activity in or around the water, bubble machines can provide hours of recreational activity for people of any age or circumstance.*

# beginning DIVING

## Components of a Simple Dive

A simple dive has three parts: the stationary starting position, the moment of propulsion called the ***takeoff,*** and the entry into the water. You can use different starting positions, as you'll see below. The takeoff for a simple dive is quite easy, usually a slight push with one or both feet. A good entry involves entering the water at the correct point and keeping the body aligned as it enters the water.

To be sure you dive into the water at the correct point of entry, focus on a target (either an imaginary point on the surface or a real or imagined target on the bottom of the pool) until your hands enter the water. You may close your eyes at that point and open them again after you have entered the water. For any dive, it is important to keep your concentration. Focusing your attention on one place is a good way to do this when you are learning to dive.

Keeping proper ***body alignment*** is crucial for a safe and graceful dive. Head position is very important because it affects the position of the body in general. Moving the head may cause the body to arch or bend. The beginner who lifts the head too quickly may do a painful belly flop.

Muscular control also is important for proper body alignment and the body tension needed for a safe, effective dive. Try to stay in a streamlined position in ***flight*** (the passage of the body through the air)(Fig. 8-3). This helps you keep control and helps make your dives more graceful. Good alignment when entering the water reduces drag and the risk of straining muscles or joints.

Fig. 8-3

### *Physical Principles Involved*

Form drag is an important principle in diving. Try to keep form drag to a minimum in the entry. Lifting the head before a headfirst entry, for example, increases your form drag. Not keeping other body parts aligned (such as not straightening the body at the hips) also can cause a part of the body to be stung by the impact with the water. Being out of alignment causes a big splash, and the dive is not as attractive.

Two other physical principles at work in any dive are the law of action and reaction, when the feet push against the deck in the takeoff, and buoyancy, which helps you return to the surface after the dive.

### The Step Dive

The step dive is useful for practicing correct head and arm position, body alignment, and muscle tension. You can do the step dive from a chair or bench. Put the chair or bench securely in the water to stand on. The water should be at least shoulder deep. When you are on the step, the water level should be at your hips. Extend your arms over your head, bend your knees slightly, and lean forward until you touch the surface of the water (Fig. 8-4). Then push forward into the water with your legs so you are in the prone glide position.

Fig. 8-4

## Progression for a Simple Dive

The steps for learning a simple dive from the pool deck will give you self-confidence and a feeling of success. Remember to move through them at your own pace. Some steps might need lots of practice. If you have good coordination and kinesthetic awareness, you may be able to move more quickly through them. This progression may also be used to learn to dive from a dock.

### *Kneeling Position*

Kneel on one knee while gripping the pool edge with the toes of the other foot (Fig. 8-5). The foot of the kneeling leg should be in a position to help push from the deck. Extend your arms over your head as described on page 185. Focus on a target either on the bottom about 4 feet out from the side or on the surface of the water 1 to 2 feet from the side. The objective is to dive deep. Focusing on a target helps you enter the water at the right place and at the correct angle, avoiding a belly flop. Lean forward, try to touch the water, and when you start to lose your balance, push with your legs. As you enter the water, straighten your body and extend both legs. Practice this skill until you feel comfortable with it and can do it without error.

Fig. 8-5

### *Compact Position*

You do this dive in much the same manner as the dive from the kneeling position. Put one foot forward and one back, with the toes of the leading foot gripping the edge of the deck. Start in the kneeling position. Then lift up so both knees are off the deck and flexed so that you stay close to the water. Extend your arms above your head. Focus on a target the same distance from the deck as in the dive from a kneeling position (Fig. 8-6). Bend forward and try to touch the surface of the water with your hands. When you start to lose your balance, push off toward the water. Bring your legs together as you enter the water.

Fig. 8-6

### *Stride Position*

After several successful dives from the compact position, you should be ready for a dive from the stride position. Stand upright with one leg forward and one leg back. The toes of the forward foot should grip the edge of the pool. Extend your arms above your head. Focus on a target on the bottom of the pool 5 to 6 feet out from the side or on the surface 3 to 4 feet out. Bend your legs only slightly as you bend at the waist toward the water. Try to touch the surface of the water and, as you lose your balance, lift your back leg until it is in line with your torso (Fig. 8-7). The forward leg should stay as straight as possible.

FIG. 8-7

### *Standing Dive*

The final dive from the deck is the standing dive. Stand with your feet about shoulder-width apart with the toes of both feet gripping the edge of the deck. Extend your arms above your head. Focus on a target at the same distance as in a dive from the stride position. Bend at the knees and angle your hands down toward the target (Fig. 8-8, *A*). Push off the deck, lift the hips, and extend your legs so they are in line with your torso (Fig. 8-8, *B*). As you gain confidence, you may move your feet closer together.

### BEGINNER PROGRESSION FROM DIVING BOARD

When you are skilled in diving from the deck, you are ready to learn to dive from a diving board. You can use the same progression as you used to learn to dive from the deck. The surface of the diving board may be rough and scrape your knee in the kneeling position, so you may want to put a pad or wet towel over the board. If the diving board has a movable ***fulcrum,*** move it all the way forward to make the diving board more stable. Once you have learned the same progression to the standing dive, all from a diving board, you are ready to start learning springboard diving skills.

FIG. 8-8, *A-B*

# springboard DIVING

FIG. 8-9, *A-E*

## COMPONENTS OF A SPRINGBOARD DIVE

A springboard dive adds several features to the elements of a simple dive. First, there is a moving start, involving an approach and hurdle. Second, there is the interaction between the diver and the diving board, involving the press and the lift. Third, the diver can execute the dive in many different ways. The propulsive action of the diving board allows time to add twists and somersaults to the **trajectory** (the curved path of the body through the air). Finally, depending on the dive, the entry may be feet first or headfirst.

Diving from a diving board requires more kinesthetic awareness than diving from a deck. Continuing to use a progression of skills helps develop your abilities and confidence as a diver. Before starting on a diving board, be sure that you are able to do a standing dive from the deck with confidence.

As mentioned earlier, you should learn springboard diving only under the supervision of an instructor or coach. The information that follows is intended for your use in Red Cross swimming courses using a 1-meter diving board. If you are interested in competitive diving, seek instruction from a competent diving instructor or coach. Appendix A lists organizations involved with diving.

The ***approach*** is the walk toward the end of a diving board before the hurdle (Fig. 8-9, *A*). It consists of at least three steps, taken slowly and with good posture. The final step before the hurdle is generally a little longer than the others. The ***hurdle*** is the jump to the end of a diving board after the approach (Fig. 8-9, *B* and *C*). These skills determine the diver's trajectory, height, and distance in flight.

There are two parts to the interaction between the diver and the diving board. The ***press*** is the diver's downward push on the diving board (Fig. 8-9, *D*), and the ***lift*** is the force of the diving board pushing the diver into the air (Fig. 8-9, *E*).

## *Physical Principles Involved*

Of the many physical principles that affect a springboard dive, gravity and the law of levers (which affects rotation) are most important. First, the force of gravity affects the diver's upward and downward motion. Lift from the diving board propels the diver upward and slightly forward, and then gravity slows the upward motion, brings the diver to a stationary position in the air for an instant, and pulls him or her down into the water.

Most important here is that the time the diver has in the air for somersaults and turns depends only on the *upward* lift from the diving board. Adding lateral speed, such as running in the approach, does not increase a diver's time in the air. In fact, expending energy running forward may decrease the height of the hurdle and thus reduce the time in the air. Even with a takeoff that seems vertical, there is enough forward motion to keep a diver clear of the diving board throughout the dive if the hurdle is executed properly.

The second principle involves the rotation of a diver in the air. If the diver exerts the same force for all types of somersaults, the spin will be fastest in the tuck position, slightly slower in the pike position, and slowest in the straight position. This is an effect of the law of levers. (See Chapter 4.) Changing body position changes the speed of the rotation. A beginning diver can most easily learn somersaults in the tuck position.

The three basic positions for executing a dive are the tuck, pike, and straight positions. In the ***tuck position,*** the body is bent at the hips and knees. You keep your body in a tight ball by grabbing both legs midway between the ankles and knees and pulling the knees to the chest. Draw your heels up to the buttocks (Fig. 8-10, *A*). In the ***pike position,*** the body is bent at the hips while the legs are kept straight (Fig. 8-10, *B*). In the ***straight position,*** the body is straight or arched slightly backward with the legs straight and together (Fig. 8-10, *C*).

FIG. 8-10, *A-C*

DRY LAND PRACTICE

### *Approach and Hurdle*

The approach and hurdle are important skills for a springboard dive. You should practice them repeatedly on land before trying them on a diving board. Be sure your feet and the deck are dry when you practice.

Put two strips of tape on the deck about 2 feet apart and parallel to each other to mark the distance needed for the hurdle. The first strip is where your toes should be after the last step before the hurdle. The second strip indicates the tip of the diving board.

The hurdle is done by raising the ***hurdle leg*** (the leg that is lifted) into a position like that shown in Figure 8-11. The thigh should be at a 90-degree angle to the body and the leg below the knee parallel to or angled slightly back toward the ***push leg*** (the leg used to push you into the hurdle). Since almost everyone has a dominant side of the body, most divers have a preferred hurdle leg. Because of this, you should at first alternate the legs for the hurdle leg. Once you know which leg you prefer to raise, keep using that leg for your hurdle leg.

The first skill to learn is the one-step approach and hurdle. This lets you concentrate on the hurdle itself. Start with your feet together about 1 foot away from the first strip on the deck. Swing your arms back in preparation for the hurdle. As you step forward with your push leg to the first strip (Fig. 8-12, *A*), begin to swing your arms backward. Lift the hurdle leg,

FIG. 8-11

swing your arms forward and upward into a position above your head, and jump upward and forward with the push leg (Fig. 8-12, *B*). The push leg should stay straight during the jump to the second strip (the end of the "diving board"). The distance covered by the jump depends on a diver's size and strength, but it is usually 1 to 2 feet for adults and less for children.

Midway in the hurdle, start to straighten the hurdle leg so that it is in line with the push leg (Fig. 8-12, *C*). Just before you land in front of the second strip of tape, start to swing your arms backward and downward. You should land on the balls of your feet. (Landing flat-footed on a real diving board will restrict its action and give you less lift into the air.) As your feet contact the deck, flex slightly at the hips and knees and swing your arms forward and upward in front of and above your head (Fig. 8-12, *D*). In the approach and hurdle, focus on the second strip of tape.

Keep your head as erect as possible; you should be able to see the second strip of tape during the hurdle.

Once you have mastered the one-step approach and hurdle, proceed to the full approach and hurdle in your dry land practice. A full approach involves three or more steps, with the final step being slightly longer. In a three-step approach, step first with your push leg and start to swing your arms backward as you start the final step of the approach. (If you use four steps, start with your hurdle leg.) Remember to focus on the second strip of tape and keep your head erect, as in the one step approach and hurdle. The arms should be straight during the approach, hurdle, and lift.

To estimate the starting point for your full approach, place your heels on the strip that simulates the end of the diving board, facing away from the "water." Do your full approach and hurdle away from the strip of tape. Mark the landing place with a third strip of tape. Now turn around and use this as the starting point for your approach. Practice the full approach and hurdle several times on deck before progressing to the diving board.

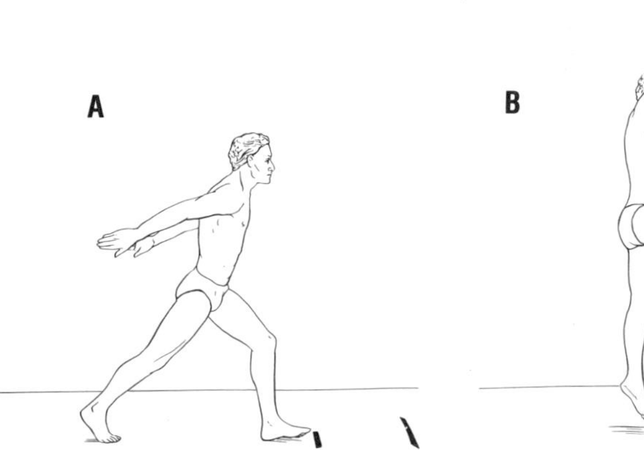


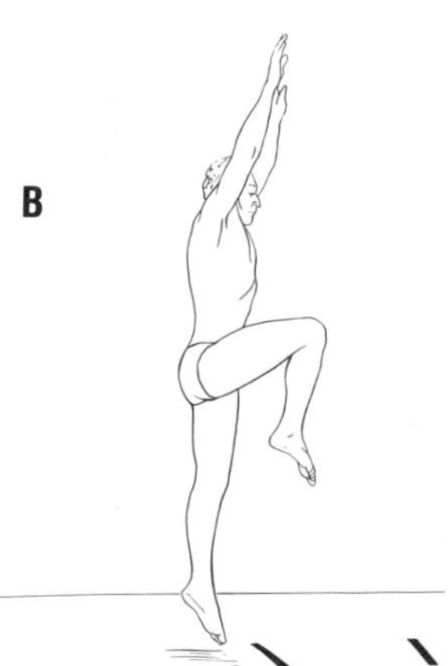


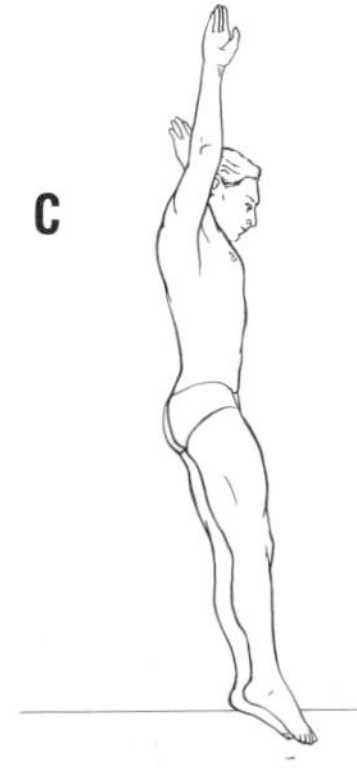

FIG. 8-12, *A-D*

## *Position for Headfirst Entry*

Body position for the entry from a diving board is even more important than from the deck. You must keep good body alignment and rigidity and enter the water vertically. You can practice proper body alignment in a standing position before trying headfirst dives from the diving board in the following way:

1. Hand position: Place one hand on top of the other and grip the bottom hand with the fingers of the top hand. Interlock your thumbs. Flex both wrists so the palm of the bottom hand hits flat on the surface (Fig. 8-13, *A*). This helps you keep proper arm position.
2. Arm position: Raise your arms overhead with your hands in line with shoulders and hips. Lock your elbows. Press your arms tight against your head (Fig. 8-13, *B*).
3. Head position: Keep your head erect and tilted back slightly. Tilting the head back or forward too far may affect body alignment and rigidity and cause injury (Fig. 8-13, *B*).
4. Upper body position: Pull in your stomach and project your rib cage forward (Fig. 8-13, *C*).
5. Hip position: Tilt the top of your pelvis (hips) backward to help reduce sway in the lower back. Such sway can affect body rigidity and lead to injury (Fig. 8-13, *C*).
6. Leg and foot positions: Lock your knees, and keep your legs straight and toes pointed (Fig. 8-13, *C*).

FIG. 8-13, *A-C*

### Diving Board Skills

If you followed the progression described earlier from deck to springboard dives, you have already learned to do a standing dive from a diving board. The following progressions help you learn other skills for springboard dives.

## *Takeoffs*

The following maneuvers help you use the diving board to gain more height for your dives. Practice the approach and hurdle on dry land several times before progressing to the diving board. When you begin on the diving board, always start with the fulcrum as far forward as possible for better stability. Once you are comfortable with these dives, you can adjust the fulcrum.

Standing jump. The standing jump uses arm action to gain greater height for your flight.

1. Stand at the tip of the diving board with your toes at the edge. Keep your arms straight and over your head.
2. Swing your arms backward and downward while you flex at the knees and hips (Fig. 8-14, *A*). Then swing your arms forward and upward while you extend, and jump off the diving board and into the water (Fig. 8-14, *B*). Focusing on a point in the middle of the pool helps keep your head in the proper position.
3. Enter feetfirst with head erect, hands at your sides, and legs straight (Fig. 8-14, *C*).

One-step approach and hurdle. Do the one-step approach and hurdle on the diving board the same way you practiced it on dry land. At first put a strip of tape across the diving board about 2 feet from the tip to help you see where your last step should fall.

When practicing the one-step approach and hurdle, jump to the end of the diving board and spring upward, forward, and into the water. *Do not try to bounce again on the diving board after the hurdle*. Beginning divers have a hard time keeping their balance after a jump. Bouncing into the air and trying to land on the diving board can cause an injury.

Full approach and hurdle. The final step is to include the approach before the hurdle. Most important, determine your starting point first. Do this the same way as on dry land. Make sure the fulcrum is all the way forward for maximum stability, at least for the first few practice jumps into the water.

## *Forward Jump, Tuck Position*

The forward jump tuck lets you experience the feeling of the tuck position during flight. (The term position is sometimes omitted from the names of jumps and dives.) This skill also helps you gain body control. Start with a jump from the deck and progress to greater heights to become more comfortable with the tuck position. A gradual progression also helps ensure your success with a jump tuck from the 1 meter diving board.

Sitting tuck. Use this simple dry land exercise to get used to this position. Sit on the deck and pull your knees up to your chest. Grab both legs midway between the ankles and knees. Pull your knees tight to your chest. You can also practice this skill lying on your back.

Fig. 8-14, *A-C*

JUMP TUCK FROM DECK. After practicing the tuck position sitting or lying on the deck, try the jump tuck from the side of the pool in the following way:

1. Stand at the edge of the pool over water at least 9 feet deep. Grip the edge of the pool with your toes. Hold your arms above your head in line with your upper body.
2. Swing your arms backward and downward while you flex the hips and knees.
3. Then swing your arms forward and upward to a position above your head and in front of your shoulders as you jump as high as possible off the edge of the deck.
4. While in flight, pull your legs up to your chest and grab them briefly (Fig. 8-15).
5. Release your legs and straighten them toward the water. Enter feetfirst with head erect, hands at your sides, and legs straight.

FIG. 8-15

STANDING JUMP TUCK FROM DIVING BOARD. The standing jump tuck from a diving board is done in the same manner as from the deck. Practice it until you are comfortable with this skill before moving on.

JUMP TUCK WITH ONE-STEP APPROACH AND HURDLE. The next step is to combine the one-step approach and hurdle with the jump tuck. This gives you greater height for doing the jump tuck. While in flight, practice the tuck position the same as in the standing jump tuck.

A

B

C

JUMP TUCK WITH FULL APPROACH AND HURDLE. The final step is to do a full approach and hurdle with the jump tuck. Be sure you have mastered the one-step approach and jump tuck before progressing to this step. Do the jump tuck with full approach and hurdle in the same manner as with the one-step approach but now take three or more steps in the approach. You can attain the greatest height in your trajectory with the full approach.

### Forward Dive Fall-In

The forward dive fall-in lets you work on correct body alignment and rigidity for the entry without being concerned with the approach, hurdle, or flight. Be sure you have practiced correct body position first on dry land, as described earlier.

1. Stand with your toes at the tip of the diving board.
2. Hold your arms straight to the side at a 90-degree angle to the upper body (like the letter T).
3. Bend at the waist so your upper body is at a 90-degree angle to your legs (pike position) and focus on a target on the surface of the water about 4 feet from the tip of the diving board (Fig. 8-16, *A*).
4. Rise up onto your toes and fall forward toward the water, keeping focused on the target.
5. Move your arms laterally to the entry position as you fall toward the water (Fig. 8-16, *B*).
6. Extend your body from a pike position to a straight position for the entry (Fig. 8-16, *C*).

*Practice this skill thoroughly before moving on to the next dive.*

FIG. 8-16, *A-C*

FIG. 8-17, *A-C*

## *Forward Dive, Tuck Position*

Once you have learned proper entry technique, you are ready to try a forward dive tuck. The tuck position helps you gain control of your body in flight. It also helps you develop your timing for the entry. You have already practiced the jump tuck from the deck and diving board, so you should be familiar with the mechanics of the tuck position.

STANDING FORWARD DIVE, TUCK POSITION

1. Stand at the tip of the diving board with your arms overhead.
2. Swing your arms backward and downward and then forward and upward, as in the standing jump tuck.
3. As you spring into the air, focus on the entry point. This will help you keep your head in the proper position at the start of the dive (Fig. 8-17, *A*).
4. Push your hips up and, at the same time, let your head go down. Keep focusing on your entry point.
5. Pull your knees up to your chest and grab your legs for a proper tuck position. Your body will rotate forward (Fig. 8-17, *B*).
6. Keep focusing on your entry point so you can tell when to come out of the tuck position to make a vertical entry.
7. As you come out of the tuck, swing your arms out to the side (laterally) to prepare for entry. Swinging the arms out in front can cause your legs to go past vertical.
8. Align your body for the entry (Fig. 8-17, *C*).

FIG. 8-18, *A-C*

You can control your rotation in the tuck in a number of ways. If you drop your head too much before takeoff or push your hips over your head, rotation is increased. Practice will help you learn to rotate the right amount. If it feels as if the dive is going past vertical, come out of the tuck position and reach for the entry. If it feels as if the dive is short of vertical, stay in the tuck position longer.

ONE-STEP APPROACH, FORWARD DIVE, TUCK POSITION. The next step is to combine the one-step approach with the forward dive tuck. Do the one-step approach in the same way as before. This step gives more height than in the standing dive. Your timing for entry may be slightly different, but otherwise this dive is like the standing dive.

FULL APPROACH AND HURDLE, FORWARD DIVE, TUCK POSITION. The final step in this progression is to do a full approach and hurdle with a forward dive tuck. Do not take a full spring the first few times you try this. Take a slight spring at first and then progress to a full spring. This will help you become comfortable with the greater height from the spring and the different timing for coming out of the tuck for the entry.

### *Forward Dive, Pike Position*

You do the forward dive in the pike position by pushing your hips up while reaching for the toes (Fig. 8-18, *A-C*). Keep your legs straight and bend only at the hips. After touching the toes, extend the arms laterally in preparation for the entry. Swinging the arms directly forward causes the legs to lift. Practice the forward dive pike using the same steps as the forward dive tuck:

1. Standing forward dive in the pike position.
2. One-step approach and hurdle.
3. Full approach and hurdle.

## Summary

With proper instruction, diving can be safe and enjoyable. This chapter describes some of the principles involved for learning basic diving skills. Learning these skills in step-by-step progressions is an effective and safe way to develop diving abilities. If you are interested in competitive diving, you can join competitive programs available at many public and private schools, at parks and recreation programs, and through United States Diving.

9

CHAPTER

# disabilities

## AND OTHER CONDITIONS

### Key Terms

**Cardiovascular endurance:** The ability of the heart, lungs, and circulatory system to sustain vigorous activity.

**Disability:** The loss, absence, or impairment of physical or mental fitness that is observable and measurable.

**Down syndrome:** A genetic condition that usually causes delays in physical and intellectual development.

**Hearing impairment:** Partial or total loss of hearing.

**Kinesthetic awareness:** The perception of what the body is doing at any given moment.

**Mainstreaming:** The process of including people with disabilities in the same programs and activities as the nondisabled.

**Motor function:** The brain's ability to direct purposeful physical activities.

**Physiological:** Relating to the processes and functions of the human body.

**Psychological:** Referring to the way the mind works and the attitudes, behaviors, and beliefs reflecting a person's state of mind.

**Rehabilitation:** Restoring a person to normal or near normal physical, mental, and social capability.

**Sensory functions:** Hearing, seeing, touching, tasting, and smelling.

**Spatial orientation:** The understanding of one's location in space and position with reference to other objects.

**Tactile impairment:** Partial or total loss of the sense of touch.

**Vision impairment:** Partial or total loss of sight.

# OBJECTIVES

***After reading this chapter, you should be able to—***

1. List the benefits of aquatics and give examples of these benefits for people with disabilities or other conditions.
2. List the differences in sensory, mental, and motor functions that might affect how people perform in the water.
3. List the aquatic safety precautions for people with disabilities or other conditions.

4. List some characteristics of an aquatics facility that make it accessible to all participants.
5. Describe a continuum of aquatics programming opportunities for people with disabilities.
6. Discuss the advantages and disadvantages of participation in mainstream and nonmainstream programming.
7. Discuss the range of aquatic activities available to people with disabilities.
8. Define the key terms at left.

FIG. 9-1

DEVEL

THE U.S. DEPARTMENT of Health and Human Services estimates over 36 million people in the United States have disabilities. Many other people have conditions such as asthma, seizures, or a heart ailment that may limit their ability to join in recreational activities. Such conditions should not keep people from engaging in aquatics programs. In addition, senior citizens may find that aquatics meets their needs for leisure and fitness (Fig. 9-1).

THIS CHAPTER DISCUSSES THE BENEFITS of aquatics for people with disabilities or other conditions, gives an overview of various disabilities, lists safety considerations, discusses how facilities should be equipped, and surveys program choices. Appendix A lists organizations that promote participation in aquatic activities, including fitness, competition, and leisure activities.

DEPENDING ON YOUR ABILITIES AND INTERESTS, you may want to read this chapter along with certain other chapters. Chapters 5 and 6 are useful for those just learning to swim. Chapter 10 is for those interested in improving their general fitness. Chapters 11 and 12 are for those interested in competition. Whatever your physical condition, *it is important that you check with a health care provider before starting an aquatics program, especially if you have not exercised in a while*. Also, if there is a concern about limitations caused by a physical condition, you may want to consult with a health care provider before entering a program.

MAX

OP YOUR
IMUM POTENTIAL
ABILITY

## Attitudes and Norms

People vary in many ways, some slight or not even observable, some of them more significant. The loss, absence, or impairment of physical or mental fitness that is observable and measurable is called a ***disability.*** It is important that people with disabilities, like anyone else, be able to develop their maximum potential through all possible means.

In some cases, this means society must address its cultural stereotypes. The Americans With Disabilities Act (PL 101-336) has led to an increasing awareness that people with disabilities or other conditions are entitled to the benefits of any programs offered in our communities. Many disabled people have shown that they can excel in all walks of life, including sports and recreation, once they have the opportunity. Unfortunately, some people still are ignorant and fearful of what is different or unknown.

The American Red Cross started a program called Convalescent Swimming for returning disabled veterans during World War II. Red Cross involvement in programs for the disabled continues today. The American Red Cross encourages people with disabilities or other conditions to participate in all its aquatics programs. These programs seek not to label the person or restrict the activities but to meet everyone's individual needs and to focus on their ability, not disability. All people are encouraged to join in these programs based on their own performance standards. A program's focus on similarities in people's needs and behaviors, rather than differences, has a positive effect for everyone. The goal should always be for the person with a disability to be included in regular, mainstream aquatics activities *before* being placed in a nonmainstream program.

## Benefits of Participation in Aquatics

Regardless of one's age or physical condition, swimming has great value. Swimming and aquatic exercise have proved useful in rehabilitation. Aquatics also gives many opportunities to meet the desire for challenge, success, recognition, accomplishment, and social activity. Overall, aquatics offers ***physiological, psychological,*** and social benefits.

Fig. 9-2

### Physiological Benefits

Swimming enhances one's overall physical fitness. Swimming improves and maintains ***cardiovascular endurance*** (the ability of the heart, lungs, and circulatory system to sustain vigorous activity), muscular strength and endurance, and flexibility. It can also help with weight management. (The fitness benefits of swimming and aquatic exercise are discussed in detail in Chapter 10.)

Aquatics also helps to improve ***motor function*** (the brain's ability to direct purposeful physical activities). Motor function includes the following components:

- Speed—The ability to act or move quickly
- Agility—The ability to change direction with controlled body movements
- Perceptual motor function—The ability to integrate what you are perceiving with what you are doing; to develop balance, coordination, and visual and auditory discrimination, and to improve ***spatial orientation*** (the understanding of your location in space and position with reference to other objects)

Although anyone who participates regularly in aquatics gains physiological benefits, these benefits may be particularly important to a person with a disability or other condition. Water may be the only environment where some people can move freely and improve their physical fitness (Fig. 9-2).

## Psychological Benefits

Everyone has a need for psychological growth and for improving one's sense of well-being and one's confidence. The psychological benefits of aquatics for people with disabilities or other conditions include—

- Experiencing success. The opportunity to do something well and to feel successful is very important. In a society traditionally structured for nondisabled people, success is often denied people with disabilities. However, aquatic activities can give everyone the opportunity to reach their goals successfully (Fig. 9-3).

Fig. 9-3

- Enhancing self-image. Being successful makes people feel better about themselves. When others, especially your peers, see you as successful, your self-image improves. This increased self-esteem can lessen the emotional impact of the disability.
- Having fun. Most people enjoy swimming. People with disabilities or other conditions are no exception. With aquatics anyone can release their frustration safely and have a good time. One can have great fun slapping, pushing, splashing, and kicking the water (Fig. 9-4).

Fig. 9-4

- Independent mobility. The ability to move more freely in water can be a tremendous psychological boost, especially for those without many other chances to move around. Many movements that are hard or even impossible on land can be done in water. People with disabilities or other conditions can do many things in the water that minimize differences from the nondisabled on land.

## Social Benefits

**O**ne's sense of one's limitations is affected by the reactions of others. In the past, negative reactions often made small disabilities feel like great barriers. Society is trying to change these conditions by helping people enter the mainstream of society through different activities. Aquatics has many social benefits, such as:

Fig. 9-5

- Peer-group interaction. Aquatics can provide opportunities for acceptance by peers and for learning acceptable social behavior such as sharing and waiting one's turn.
- Normalization or inclusion. Categories and labels for disabilities often focus on the impairment rather than the person. All people should have opportunities to function in the mainstream of society. Aquatics is no exception. People with disabilities or other conditions should participate fully in aquatics programs with nondisabled peers. Swimming in groups also helps one make friends (Fig. 9-5).
- Safety. As one gains more aquatic skills, personal and family safety in, on, or near the water improves. This benefit is a primary goal of the Red Cross aquatics program.

## Needs of People with Disabilities

No two people are alike. People differ in many ways, some of which may affect participation in aquatics. The following sections describe such differences.

### Sensory Function

The ***sensory functions*** are hearing, seeing, touching, tasting, and smelling. While differences in taste and smell seldom matter for aquatics, differences in hearing, sight, and touch can affect one's safety in the water. These differences also affect how people learn, how they perform in and around water, and what teaching techniques are effective for them.

#### *Hearing Impairment*

Many people who have a ***hearing impairment*** (partial or total loss of hearing) were born with it. Hearing problems can also result from childhood disease or advancing age. Some people with hearing impairment may have trouble with balance and/or coordination. This can affect the adjustment to the water.

A person with hearing impairment must focus more on communication when learning to swim. Since they cannot wear hearing aids in the water, people with moderate hearing loss have the same need for clear communication as someone with profound loss. Thus, communication is done visually, by demonstration, gesture, lip reading, and signing (Fig. 9-6). People with hearing impairment must keep their eyes open while swimming. In a properly maintained pool, the chemicals in the water should not irritate their eyes.

Fig. 9-6

#### *Vision Impairment*

***Vision impairment*** (a partial or total loss of sight) may be present from birth or caused by infection, injury, or advancing age. It may also be caused by conditions such as diabetes.

For people with vision impairment, learning to swim requires the use of speech, touch, and sounds and signals such as whistles. Such people should keep their ears uncovered in the water and learn strokes in which the ears stay above the water. Other techniques include placing their hands on the limbs of another swimmer when strokes are demonstrated and measuring distances in steps or strokes.

People with partial vision should use as much functional vision as possible. They can wear glasses while swimming (Fig. 9-7). Wearing an old pair is best, since pool chemicals can corrode frames. An elastic strap or a swimming cap will keep them in place. Diving should not be permitted when glasses are worn. Individuals with contact lenses should wear goggles or a face mask and should avoid diving, surface diving, and swimming under water.

Fig. 9-7

Someone who is totally blind may need a seeing partner. When moving on land, the blind person grasps the partner's elbow and follows the partner's body movement, along with the lead of the elbow, to help learn and to feel secure.

### *Tactile Impairment*

***Tactile impairment*** is the partial or total loss of the sense of touch. Someone with a spinal injury might not feel anything in areas of the body below the injury. A person with **spina bifida** also may lack sensation in the lower part of the body.

Lack of sensation should not keep someone out of aquatics. Since people with tactile impairment would not feel scratches, abrasions, burns, or the rubbing that causes blisters, they must take care to avoid scratching or scraping the skin in the pool. Healing of such an injury is often slow. They must also take care to avoid temperature extremes, wear protective foot covering, check frequently for red skin (which may indicate a pressure problem), and check the shower temperature.

***Kinesthetic awareness*** is the perception of what the body is doing at any given moment. If this function is impaired, the person may not sense his or her body's position in relation to space and other objects (Fig. 9-8). The person may have problems with balance in the water and with learning to float and recover.

FIG. 9-8

MENTAL FUNCTION

Mental function includes intelligence and the capacity to reason and process information. The degree of such an impairment determines how successful the person may be in a regular aquatics program. Most people with impairment in mental function can participate successfully in regular aquatics programs.

### *Impairment in Intelligence*

The most common form of intellectual impairment is **cognitive disability.** Most cognitive disability is present at birth. Such people are below average in intellectual functioning and slow in intellectual development and academic progress. However, there is great variation of abilities within this population. Most experience success in regular aquatics programs, while others may need a more specialized setting.

Developmental delay is common in people with cognitive disability. Learning and development may take place at a slower rate, such that the person's developmental age and mental age lag behind chronological age. In motor skills, however, people with cognitive disability are clearly more like than unlike their nondisabled peers.

***Down syndrome*** is a congenital disorder that usually causes delays in physical and intellectual development. People with Down syndrome vary widely in mental abilities, behavior, and physical development. Many people with Down syndrome can be mainstreamed into regular aquatics programs.

A small number of people with Down syndrome may also have **atlantoaxial instability.** This is a weakness in the ligaments between the first two vertebrae. A swimmer with this condition must not dive, and a health care professional should be consulted about other possible limitations. The National Down Syndrome Congress recommends cervical X rays to determine whether this condition exists.

### *Impairment in Information Processing*

There are several forms of this impairment. The most common cause is a **learning disability.** Autism and behavioral or emotional disturbances are other causes. Many people with this impairment do well in regular aquatics programs. If this impairment affects the person's ability to follow directions, follow safety procedures, behave well in the group, or function with relative independence, a specialized program should be considered.

People with **autism** (a mental disorder characterized by extreme withdrawal, absorption in fantasy, and inability to relate to people) may have severely limited communication skills. Very few people with autism can interact well enough to participate successfully in regular aquatics programs.

**Behavior or emotional disturbances** vary widely. Some behavior differences cannot be seen in most settings. Others may inhibit an individual's functional behavior, so that the person requires custodial care. What is most important is how well the person deals with reality. The more a person's perception differs from actual reality, the less he or she will behave in socially acceptable ways.

A person with a behavior or emotional disturbance who can relate positively to the aquatic experience and control his or her behavior in the group can participate successfully in a regular aquatics program. If the behavior is not appropriate, particularly in terms of safety, specialized aquatics programming should be considered. A calm class environment, clear expectations about behavior, and consistency in enforcing safety procedures and pool rules help provide a positive aquatic experience.

## Motor Function

Motor function refers to the brain's ability to direct purposeful physical activities. The brain and nervous system control the muscular and skeletal systems. Impairment in any of these systems can result in decreased physical capability. If the person cannot use a body part because of impaired or lost function, motor activity is limited. **Orthopedic impairments** are disorders of bones, joints, tendons, blood vessels, and nerves that impede locomotor function. Such impairment can be caused by trauma (such as amputation, spinal lesions, or peripheral nerve injury), a **congenital** condition (such as spina bifida), or an infection (such as poliomyelitis and tuberculosis). Impairment may also be caused by dislocated hips, osteomyelitis, osteoarthritis, and **Perthes disease**.

### *Absence of Motor Function*

Complete loss of use of a body part can result from congenital or traumatic **amputation.** A prosthesis such as an artificial limb may be used for land activities. Often the person can function quite normally on land, and the absence of a limb may not even be noticeable. However, a prosthesis must usually be removed before the person enters the water. The person

may need a larger locker or a special place to keep the prosthesis while swimming. A private place to dress is desirable. Someone with a single leg often can still get from the locker room to the pool by another method such as seat scooting on the deck. Most people with amputations participate successfully in regular aquatics programs.

Complete loss of the use of a body part can also result from spinal cord injury, stroke, and/or damage to nerves controlling those body parts. Whatever the cause, nerve impulses from the brain do not reach the muscles to move the body part. **Paralysis** (loss of sensation, voluntary motion, or both) may affect the legs (as in **paraplegia**), one side of the body (as in **hemiplegia**), or both arms and legs (as in **quadriplegia**).

A person with paralysis may also have other bodily dysfunction. People with a lack of bowel and bladder control usually are on a bowel training program or wear a collection bag. People who have had a stroke may have varying degrees of paralysis and sometimes **aphasia** (inability to speak or to form intelligible speech). Aphasic people often understand what is said to them but cannot respond well by speaking. Special considerations for people with paralysis include:

- Weight-bearing activities should be limited.
- If sensation is reduced, especially in the hands and feet, the person should be careful to avoid cuts or abrasions caused by scraping.
- Poor circulation increases tendency toward chilling and fatigue, which should be avoided.
- Individuals with lack of bowel and/or bladder control should empty collection bags before swimming and be sure they are secured to the body. If the person does not have a collection bag, a cloth diaper and tight-fitting rubber pants should be worn.

Fig. 9-9

People lacking the function of a body part can participate successfully in regular aquatics programs (Fig. 9-9). They may need assistance in the locker room, moving to the pool, and entering the water. Paralysis of multiple body parts may limit motor function so severely that a specialized aquatics program is needed until the person adjusts to the water and becomes mobile in the water.

### *Impairment of Motor Function*

Motor function can also be temporarily impaired because of illness or trauma, a permanent but stable condition, or a progressively degenerative condition. Other temporary conditions that impair motor function include recovery from orthopedic surgery, broken bones, and muscle strains and sprains. For such people, aquatics can play an important part in rehabilitation.

***Rehabilitation*** (restoration of a person to normal or near normal physical, mental, and social capability) is also important for someone with permanent motor impairment such as **cerebral palsy.** Cerebral palsy is a central nervous system dysfunction in which the person has limited or no control of the muscles. The degree of impairment varies greatly from mild to severe. The five general groups of cerebral palsy are spastic paralysis, athetosis, ataxia, rigidity, and tremor. A person may have more than one type. Cerebral palsy is caused by damage to the brain before, during, or after birth. The extent to which the effects of cerebral palsy are visible depends on the degree of damage. A person with cerebral palsy might have any of these characteristics:

- Limited range of movement in affected joint areas
- Limited control over voluntary movement of affected limbs or joints
- Random and/or involuntary movements
- Absence of normal muscle tone or an overabundance of muscle tone
- Abnormal muscle reflex patterns
- Impaired speech
- Possible seizures

These characteristics may lead to limited ability to move around. People with cerebral palsy may walk unaided, walk with crutches, wear braces, use a manual wheelchair, or use an electric wheelchair. They may speak well or use a conversation board or mechanical communication device. Some people mildly affected with cerebral palsy can participate quite successfully in regular aquatics programs. Swimming is very good for increasing and maintaining range of motion in joints and muscle flexibility. With a greater impairment, specialized aquatics instruction may be needed.

Degenerative conditions may affect the person's participation in aquatics. **Multiple sclerosis** and various forms of **muscular dystrophy** lead to decreased motor function over time. Most people can join regular aquatics programs in early phases of these diseases. As the condition progresses, the following changes are likely:

- Decreased control over voluntary motor activity
- Weakened muscles
- Increased susceptibility to other illnesses
- Impaired balance
- Increased difficulty with locomotion
- Decreased thresholds for fatigue
- Impairment of other body functions
- Development of sensory symptoms such as numbness, tingling, and sensations of pain

People who swam before the onset or progression of the disease can stay functional in the water long after motor function on land is severely impaired. With help in the locker room and in getting to, from, into, and out of the pool, they may stay with their peers and family members in a regular program as long as they wish. Someone who joins a program after the disease is progressing or who is experiencing problems in breathing, maintaining head control, recovering balance, or staying in a safe position in the water may need specialized instruction and assistance.

## Other Physical Conditions

Other physical conditions may require extra attention when the person joins an aquatics program. These conditions should not prevent the person from participating in aquatics. In fact, people who have any of the following conditions can benefit greatly from aquatic exercise. (For more information on swimming as a lifetime fitness activity, see Chapter 10.)

### Aging

About 30 million people in the United States are 65 and older. With aging comes an increase in chronic disease, especially cardiovascular disease. For many people, however, much of the reduced function that occurs with aging is related to physical inactivity. Exercise is a key element for good health and independent living for the elderly.

Elders who want to learn to swim or resume swimming again but have not gotten much exercise recently should talk to a health care provider before starting any exercise program. They should also begin gradually. The primary goal is usually to reach and maintain a level of fitness, improve one's physical condition, or delay the onset of **chronic** disease. Most aquatics programs for the elderly are very similar to other programs. The water should be slightly warmer, at least 83 degrees F (28 degrees C), and the aquatic activity should be less intense than that for a younger group. For those with a chronic disease, the intensity may have to be reduced even more.

### Arthritis

The major goal of an aquatics program for arthritics is to decrease pain and increase the range of motion in the affected joints (Fig. 9-10). Aerobic exercise of moderate intensity is effective and also improves cardiovascular endurance. People with arthritis are generally more comfortable in warmer water (86-95 degrees F or 30-35 degrees C), although water at the high end of this range may be too warm for an aerobic workout. Aquatic activities should not worsen the pain. If pain does result and does not subside within 2 hours after the workout, the person should shorten future workouts or modify the painful activity.

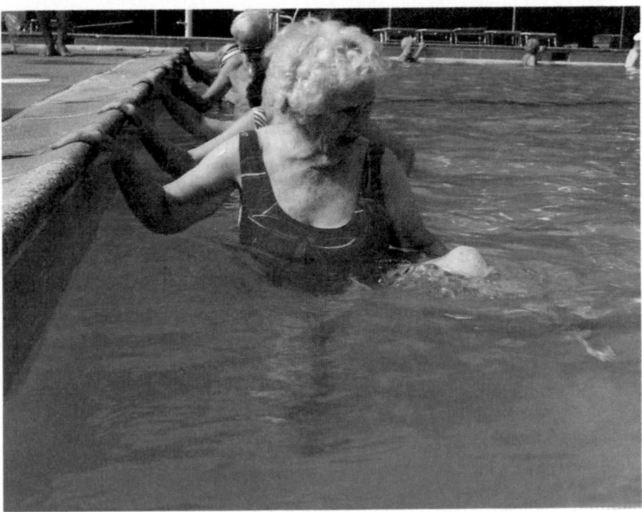

Fig. 9-10

### Asthma or Allergies

Someone with **asthma** and/or allergies can enjoy aquatics. Indeed, the breath control learned with aquatic skills often helps relieve the symptoms of asthma and allergies. Those who are allergic to pool chemicals should seek out a pool with a different chemical composition. A person using an asthma medication inhaler should keep the inhaler at pool side. If respiratory distress occurs, breathing can be improved by moving the person to a calm, quiet environment; keeping them warm; allowing them to rest; and helping them focus their attention on something other than breathing.

### Cardiac and Blood Conditions

A person with a blood disorder (such as sickle cell anemia) or a cardiac condition can join in aquatic activities that are paced to their level of endurance with minimal physical stress. Comfort is important. When the person gets cold or tired, experiences discomfort, or otherwise becomes stressed, activity should be terminated for the day. Overexertion is to be avoided.

Aerobic exercise is good for people recovering from some cardiovascular or respiratory conditions. Walking and swimming are the most popular activities for cardiac rehabilitation, but aquatic exercise has recently become more popular because it is easily tolerated and has a low risk of injury. (For more information on aquatic exercise, see Chapter 10 and Appendix B.)

In most cases, the body's response to exercise in the water is like that on land, provided that the water is a proper temperature. Cold water slows the heart rate and is a stress on the cardiovascular system. Water that is too warm may cause heat stress.

Cardiac patients should exercise at a lower intensity, depending on their physical abilities, but aquatic exercise is safe for most cardiac patients. An exception is the post-operative patient requiring continuous monitoring for variations in heart rate. Patients should follow guidelines set by their health care providers.

### Cystic Fibrosis

**Cystic fibrosis** is an inherited disorder of the glands that causes abnormalities in respiration, perspiration, and digestion, as well as hyperactivity of the **autonomic nervous system.** A person with cystic fibrosis can join an aquatics program during the early stages of the disease. Breathing exercises learned in aquatics can enhance air exchange in the lungs and help maintain health and fitness. The person may need to cough and spit phlegm often but can use the pool gutter/drain for this. When the person becomes tired or cold, the activity should stop for the day. As the disease progresses, aquatic activity will become too physically stressful for the body and will eventually have to stop. Physical comfort and the person's desire to continue are the key factors in deciding how long to stay in a program.

### Diabetes

Diabetics should never exercise alone because of the risk of a diabetic emergency. Increased activity may upset one's insulin balance. Dizziness, drowsiness, and confusion can be serious problems in the water and may lead to a dangerous situation. A diabetic emergency can also result in unconsciousness.

### Fragile Bones

People with **osteogenesis imperfecta** (fragile bones) find swimming an excellent form of exercise, since swimming helps build muscle mass, stimulate bone growth, and maintain flexibility. However, they must be careful to avoid physical trauma, which could occur from such things as manipulating a body part, swimming in turbulent water, or colliding with another person. They should always wear a life jacket for safety and use strokes that are not strenuous, such as the elementary backstroke. They should not dive or jump into the water.

### Obesity

People who are overweight should exercise at a moderate level for the first few weeks. After that, they may extend the workout because the duration of the exercise is more important for weight management than intensity. Since this group is extremely buoyant, it is important that the limbs move with sufficient speed to make the exercise beneficial.

Fig. 9-11

The overweight person is at some risk for coronary heart disease and may have other risk factors such as high blood pressure, high blood sugar, and high cholesterol. Aerobic exercise provides benefits that counteract all of these risk factors. Changes in body composition occur slowly unless the diet is modified as well. Weight management programs that combine diet with exercise produce better results than diet or exercise alone (Fig. 9-11). The key to successful weight management is to follow the program consistently. Obese people may find it easier to stay with an aquatic exercise program because the environment is cool, comfortable, and relaxing, as well as beneficial.

### Seizures

Seizures may be a symptom of other medical conditions. In general, a person who has seizures that are medically controlled can join an aquatics program, as long as it is supervised. If a seizure occurs while the person is in the water, the person should not return to the water that day. A seizure that occurs in the water is like a near drowning and should be treated as such. (For more information, see Chapter 13.) Usually a person with active seizures should not join an aquatics program until the seizures are under control.

**S**wimmers with conditions that can cause seizures usually do not need a special program, but more careful observation may be needed. Since the condition cannot be seen, one should notify the instructor or lifeguard of any condition that could lead to a seizure or loss of consciousness.

## Safety

**P**ool hazards exist in any aquatics program but are a greater risk for some people with disabilities or other conditions. The person's vision, balance, sense of direction, concept of space, perception of space and distance, and muscular control should all be considered. For instance, a wet pool deck that a nondisabled person can safely cross can be a real hazard to someone with limited mobility.

**B**oth the participant and the instructor of the program should be aware of the following special considerations:

- People with impaired mobility, balance, or coordination may need help moving on wet decks and ramps. A person using crutches or a walker or who has a prosthesis also may need help.
- If an individual uses a wheelchair, it should be used between the locker room and pool. Showering should be omitted and the chair should be covered with towels after the swim. Brakes must be locked when the person is entering and leaving the chair. Children, too, should use their wheelchairs, as it is unsafe to carry anyone, even small children, on wet, slippery decks.
- People with limited control of their legs should not enter the water feetfirst from a diving board or from a height; twisting and injury to muscles is possible. Headfirst entries from the deck and board should be learned.
- Safety precautions for specific medical conditions should be followed carefully. When in doubt, check the doctor's recommendation.
- To ensure safety for the visually impaired, decks should be kept free of clutter, doors should be kept either completely closed or wide open rather than ajar, possible hazards should be explained verbally, life lines should be used to mark depth variance, and people with visual disabilities should be instructed to alert the instructor or lifeguard when they need help.

**S**afety education is a vital part of every aquatics program. Safety skills can be learned in an enjoyable way by all who use the swim area. People with disabilities or other conditions should learn reaching, throwing, and wading assists. Everyone should learn how to wear a life jacket. (Chapter 2 more fully discusses water safety, and Chapter 13 discusses rescue techniques.) Everyone should learn personal safety skills, and basic water safety courses should be taken whenever possible.

## Facilities

**R**elatively few swimming facilities in the United States were built exclusively for people with disabilities. However, with little or no adaptation, swimming facilities can be used by most people with disabilities (Fig. 9-12). The Education for Handicapped Children Act (PL 94-142) has helped ensure accessible education facilities. Many community pools are attached to schools and recreation departments and, under this law, must be accessible to people with disabilities. The Americans With Disabilities Act requires that people with disabilities have access to all community recreation programs.

**P**eople with disabilities and those who assist in their care should consider several factors when choosing a facility. The specific disability determines which factors to consider.

Fig. 9-12

### Building Structure

- Parking for people with motor impairment near the entrance to the facility
- Absence of stairs between entry and locker rooms
- Easily understood hallway access for people with vision impairment
- Directional signs for people with impaired hearing
- Doorways wide enough for wheelchairs (32-inch minimum width)

### Locker Rooms

- Accessible bathroom facilities for people with impaired mobility
- Directional signs for people with impaired hearing
- Private dressing rooms for people who wear a prosthesis or urinary device or who have other privacy needs
- Uncomplicated traffic pattern to pool area to ease access for people with visual impairment
- Hand-held or low-level shower heads for people who shower seated in a chair or on the floor
- A shower chair for use by people with impaired balance or mobility
- Shower temperatures set to prevent scalding
- Grab bars in toilets and in shower areas for people with impaired mobility
- A dressing table or area of floor specially covered and designated for people who need to dress or be helped to dress lying down
- Hair dryers mounted at various heights

### Pool

- Decks free of clutter
- Clearly understandable safety signs and depth markings; signs with pictures as well as words, a tape recording of pool rules, and a textured contour line along a wall; clear indication of depth, exits, and location of emergency equipment
- Life lines marking changes of depth
- Ramp and/or walk-in steps (may be portable)
- Handholds at or slightly above water level; if it is hard to hold on to the edge of the pool, a rope or railing can be added
- Devices to assist a person with a disability in and out of the water; several types of lifts are available for pool use, most of which are portable and can be removed from the deck when not in use

## Programming

People with disabilities or other conditions have many different opportunities to participate in aquatics programs. On one end of the continuum are regular programs in which people with disabilities are included in the same lessons and activities as the nondisabled (Fig. 9-13). This is called ***mainstreaming.*** On the other extreme is one-to-one instruction in an adapted aquatics program provided by a Water Safety Instructor specially trained to teach people with disabilities. Between these extremes are a variety of possibilities.

The selection of the right program is an important decision. People with disabilities or other conditions should participate in whatever program best meets their needs. They should also be able to move from program to program when their needs change. Everyone should have access to Red Cross aquatics programs. However, program administrators also have a responsibility to others in the class or program. At times, it is necessary to set up special programs for people with disabilities or other conditions so that everyone can benefit from the classes they take.

People with disabilities or other conditions have the following rights and responsibilities when they are applying for an aquatics program:

- The right to general information about the aquatics program, so they can determine if it suits their needs
- The right to apply for entry into the program
- The right to a specific explanation if the instructor believes the program is not suitable for the person
- The responsibility to give the instructor any pertinent information concerning their condition
- The responsibility to comply with an instructor's request for a pretest or trial lesson if needed
- The responsibility to provide one's own assistance, if needed, for dressing and for pool entry and exit

People with disabilities or other conditions also must choose between mainstream programming and special programming. For those who can join a mainstream program, aquatics is a rich, rewarding experience. However, not all people can or will ever be ready for mainstream programs. The decision must be made on an individual basis, considering both the needs of the person and the benefits and structure of the program. Both mainstream and nonmainstream programs have advantages as well as disadvantages, as shown at right.

Fig. 9-13

## Mainstreaming

### Advantages

- Increased opportunity for participation
- Possibility for family or social group to participate together
- Stronger self-concept as a result of success
- Development of skills transferable to any aquatic environment
- Opportunity to enjoy peer and/or community contact

### Disadvantages

- Lack of instructors trained in mainstreaming
- Lack of accessible facilities
- Program might not adapt to meet individual needs
- Larger class sizes might not give enough support
- Possible lack of peer sensitivity

## Nonmainstreaming

### Advantages

- Instruction given by specially trained instructors
- Class size is small
- Peers may be more sensitive and considerate
- Adapted programs are often held in specially designed facilities, making accessibility easier

### Disadvantages

- Environment is not average mix of people
- Interaction with larger groups of people is not usually possible
- Opportunities might not be available for families to participate together
- Participants might not learn to participate in nonadapted facilities

**Special Olympian**

*To say that swimming is the most important thing in the life of Sam Reid, Jr., is not an overstatement; it is a fact. Sam, a 22-year-old from North Carolina, has been a competitive swimmer since 1983. He swam the 200-meter individual medley at the 1990 United States Olympic Festival, the premier event for U.S. amateur athletics. He has participated in local, state, and international competitions, winning gold medals in a variety of events.*

*It's an extraordinary achievement for any athlete, but for Sam, a Special Olympics athlete, these victories are the culmination of his consistent training, daily practice, steadfast determination, and personal courage.*

*Special Olympics is a year-round program of sports training and competition for individuals with cognitive disability. Swimming is one of the 22 Olympic-type sports offered through Special Olympics. Participation has enabled Sam to develop athletic skills, physical fitness, self-esteem, confidence, and long-lasting friendships with coaches and other swimmers.*

*Because of his outstanding achievements in swimming, Sam Reid, Jr., was selected as the Special Olympics Aquatics Athlete of the Year. Others who participate in Special Olympics might not have medals like Sam's, but the benefits of their involvement are just as golden.*

## Expanding Opportunities in Aquatics

### Competition

People with disabilities or other conditions have opportunities in two types of competitive programs. The first is with nondisabled peers. Regular swim teams and swim clubs should be open to any person who makes the qualifying standards, despite any impairment. A disability is not a barrier to successful competition against nondisabled peers. (See Chapter 12 for a discussion of organizations that sponsor competitive events.)

Competition is also available through organizations geared to those with specific disabilities. These organizations are listed in Appendix A.

### Leisure

Leisure activity is important for everyone. Recreational activities include skin diving, SCUBA (Fig. 9-14), boating, adventure recreation, water sports, and water park activities. All these are opportunities to develop additional aquatic skills. People with disabilities or other conditions who are interested in any of these activities should do the following:

- Determine what swim skills are needed to begin the activity and learn those skills first.
- Get a medical recommendation before starting a new, active leisure pursuit, especially those involving adventure or risk.
- Take any needed lessons from a qualified or certified instructor.
- Advise the instructor, program director, or lifeguard of any limitations. This knowledge will help them provide a safe environment.
- Participate with a nondisabled buddy. This can make learning more fun and ensures a person is there to help if needed.

People with disabilities are river rafting, arctic kayaking, solo sailing, exploring the ocean bottom, sliding down flumes, photographing coral reefs, channel swimming, sit and slalom water skiing (Fig. 9-15), and generally doing everything that nondisabled people are doing. Appendix A lists additional instructional and participation resources.

Fig. 9-15

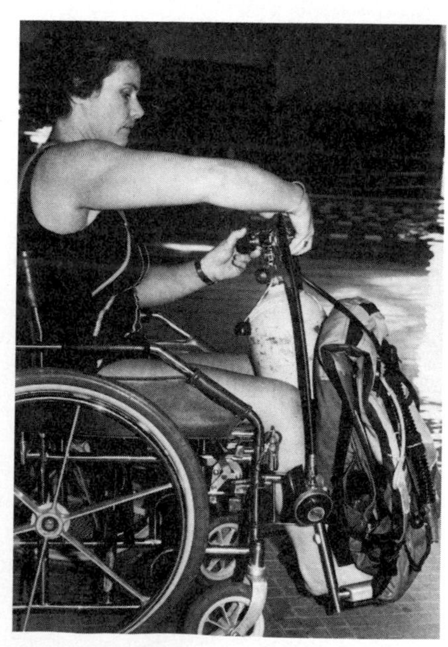

Fig. 9-14

## Summary

**P**eople with disabilities or other conditions can participate successfully in aquatic activities. Whether their goal is fitness, competition, or leisure, aquatics programs are a way to meet their needs.

# CHAPTER 10 lifetime fitness

## Key Terms

**Aerobic exercise:** Sustained, rhythmic, physical exercise that requires additional effort by the heart and lungs to meet the increased demand by the skeletal muscles for oxygen.

**Aquatic exercise:** Water activity generally done in a vertical position with the face out of the water.

**Cardiovascular system:** The heart and blood vessels, which bring oxygen and nutrients to the body through the circulation of blood.

**Fitness swimming:** A swimming program in which the workouts have a specified level of intensity and are sustained for a set period of time.

**Flexibility:** The range of motion in a joint or group of joints.

**Intensity:** How hard you work out when you exercise.

**Metabolic rate:** The amount of energy produced by the body in a given period of time.

**Overload:** A fitness principle based on working somewhat harder than normal so that the muscles and cardiovascular system must adapt.

**Progression:** In an exercise program, gradually increasing frequency, intensity, and/or time so that an overload is produced.

**Target heart rate range:** The ideal heart rate range for an individual to maintain during exercise for greatest cardiovascular benefit.

**Training effect:** An improvement in functional capacity of a system (cardiovascular, respiratory, muscular) that results from an overload of that system.

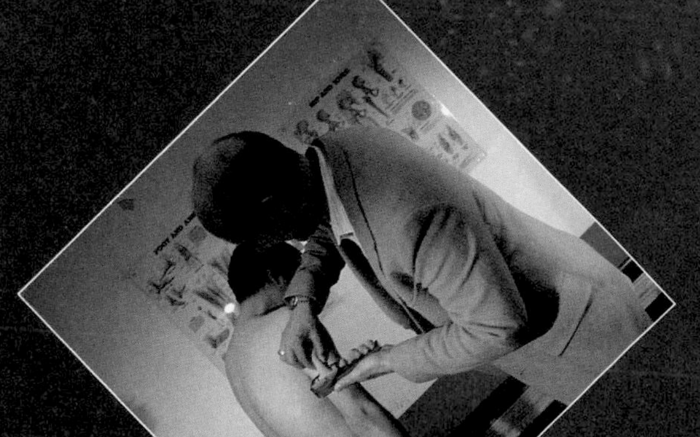

# Objectives

***After reading this chapter, you should be able to—***

1. Describe the health benefits that add up to the training effect.
2. Explain the advantages of swimming over other forms of aerobic exercise.
3. Explain the F.I.T. principle and its components.
4. Explain the importance of keeping the heart rate in a specific range during exercise.
5. Explain the meaning of perceived exertion.
6. List the five components of a workout.
7. Describe principles of safety and etiquette in fitness swimming.
8. Name the three phases of a fitness program.
9. Name the four factors that affect an aquatic exercise workout.
10. Describe safety precautions for muscular development sets.
11. Define the key terms at left.

***After reading this chapter and completing appropriate class activities, you should be able to—***

1. Calculate your target heart rate range for aerobic conditioning.

**B**ECAUSE OF MODERN TECHNOLOGY, most of us use less physical effort in our daily living than did previous generations. In most work activities, people do not exert themselves enough to maintain good physical health and fitness. People with inactive lifestyles are more prone to various serious health problems, including **cardiovascular disease** (disease of the heart and blood vessels), obesity, **hypertension** (high blood pressure), diabetes (from inadequate **insulin** in the body), and muscle and joint problems (Fig. 10-1, *A* and *B*). Far fewer people would die from cardiovascular disease if they exercised more. Now more than ever people need physical activity in their daily lives. One encouraging note: even if you have not exercised much in the past, starting an exercise program now will help you live a longer, healthier life.

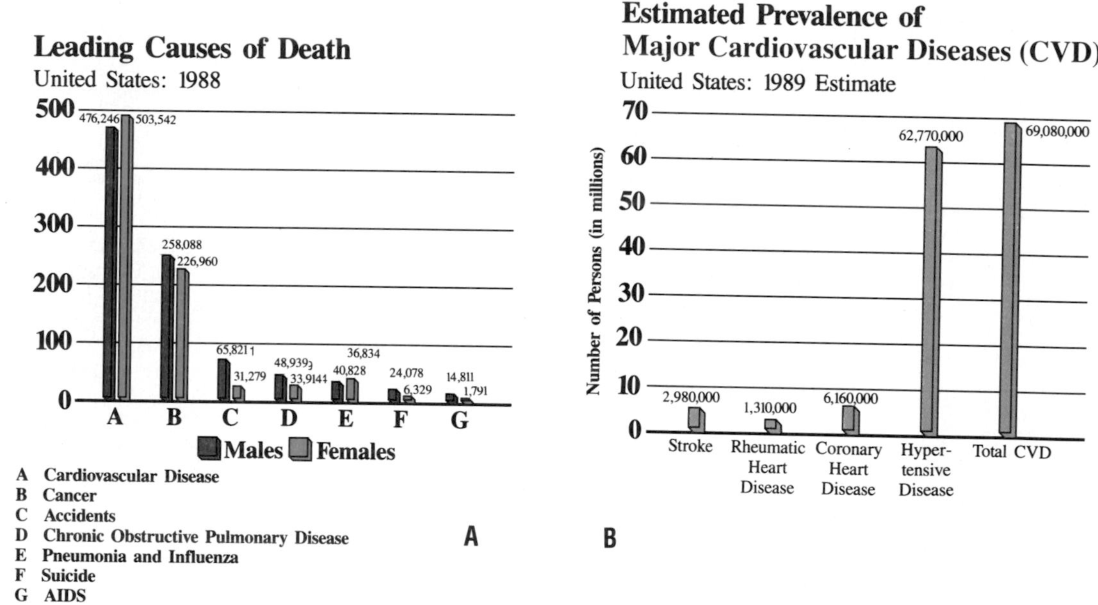


FIG. 10-1, *A-B*

PHYSICAL FITNESS IS A VITAL COMPONENT of good health. It was once defined as the capacity to carry out everyday activities without excessive fatigue and still have enough energy in reserve for emergencies. However, our present everyday activities are far less strenuous than in the past. Physical fitness is no longer viewed as just the absence of disease. Fitness is a means to reach optimal health.

Fig. 10-2

Fig. 10-3

THIS CHAPTER DISCUSSES TWO BASIC TYPES of aquatic fitness programs: fitness swimming and aquatic exercise. ***Fitness swimming*** is a swimming program in which the workouts have a specified level of intensity and are sustained for a set period of time (Fig. 10-2). Fitness swimming is an excellent way to improve overall physical fitness and especially the health of the ***cardiovascular system*** (the heart and blood vessels, which bring oxygen and nutrients to the body through the circulation of blood).

***AQUATIC EXERCISE*** IS WATER ACTIVITY generally done in a vertical position with the face out of the water (Fig. 10-3). In aquatic exercise, you walk, jog, and dance in shallow water or run in deep water, sometimes using a flotation device (Fig. 10-4). You may also push or pull your limbs against the resistance of the water, such as standing in neck-deep water and flexing your elbow to bring your fist toward your shoulder (known as a biceps curl). Some aquatic exercise programs focus on cardiovascular fitness; others emphasize muscular strength and flexibility.

**AS WITH ANY PHYSICAL ACTIVITY OR FITNESS PROGRAM,** *see your health care provider before you begin your program.* This is especially true if you have not exercised for a long time.

TRAINING AS IT IS USED IN THIS TEXT refers to a physical improvement program designed to prepare a person for competition in a sport. It is characterized by exercise of higher intensity than that used to improve fitness. A person who undertakes a training program should already have a good level of fitness before the training begins.

THIS CHAPTER FOCUSES ON DEVELOPING FITNESS through fitness swimming or aquatic exercise. If you are just beginning a fitness program, or if you want to include aquatics in your fitness program, this chapter is for you. If you want to use swim training for greater levels of fitness or for competition, Chapter 11 provides guidance for a more strenuous approach to aquatic workouts.

Fig. 10-4

## Benefits of Aerobic Exercise

***Aerobic exercise*** is sustained, rhythmic, physical exercise that requires additional effort by the heart and lungs to meet the increased demand by the skeletal muscles for oxygen. Such exercise, when it is frequent enough, changes the body in ways that improve your health. The benefits of aerobic exercise are known as the ***training effect.*** The body improves in the following ways:

- Cardiovascular endurance
- Muscular strength and endurance
- Flexibility
- Weight management

Research by Kenneth Cooper, M.D., was instrumental in developing the modern understanding of aerobic exercise.

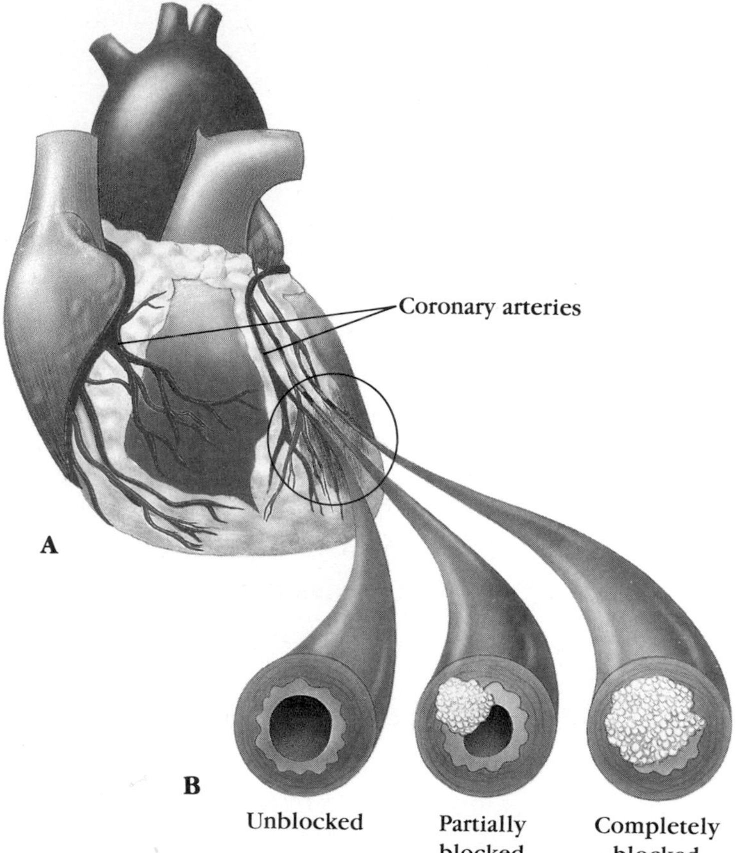


Fig. 10-5, ***A-B*** *A*, The coronary arteries supply the heart muscle with blood. *B*, Buildup of materials on the inner walls of these arteries reduces blood flow to the heart muscle and may cause a heart attack.

### Cardiovascular Endurance

The cardiovascular, or circulatory, system supplies oxygen and nutrients to the body through the blood. Cardiovascular diseases cause more than half of the deaths in the United States. The most common type is **coronary artery disease.** This results from the narrowing and hardening of the coronary arteries, which carry needed oxygen-rich blood to the heart (Fig. 10-5). Risk factors that contribute to coronary artery disease include smoking, high blood pressure, obesity, high **cholesterol** in the blood, diabetes, and lack of exercise.

With the right exercise, cardiovascular efficiency (also known as **aerobic capacity**) improves. The heart becomes stronger and can pump more blood with each beat. Circulation improves, and the blood vessels stay healthy. Other benefits include:

- Lower heart rate at rest and in moderate exercise
- Shorter recovery time (the time it takes for the heart to resume its regular rate after exercise)
- Improved blood circulation to heart muscle
- Increased capacity of the blood to carry oxygen
- Increased ability of muscles to use oxygen
- Decreased **lactic acid,** a by-product of exercise that may cause muscle soreness and fatigue
- Lower resting blood pressure (especially in people with high blood pressure)
- Lower cholesterol levels

### Muscular Strength and Endurance

Muscular performance involves both strength and endurance. **Muscular strength** is the ability of muscle to exert force. Strength leads to endurance, power, and resistance to fatigue. Muscular strength protects against joint injury and helps the body keep good posture.

Weakness in some muscles causes an imbalance that can impair normal movement and cause pain. For instance, weak abdominal muscles combined with poor flexibility in the lower back and hamstring muscles (at the back of the thigh) can lead to lower back pain. Lower back pain is a major problem in the United States, costing millions of dollars a year in lost productivity. Muscular imbalances cause up to 80 percent of all lower back problems. Thus, muscular strength is an important factor for staying healthy, and aquatic activity is a popular, effective way to develop this strength (Fig. 10-6).

**Muscular endurance** is the ability of muscle to contract repeatedly with the same force over an extended period of time. Greater muscular strength often improves muscular endurance. For many people, muscular endurance, which helps to resist fatigue, is more important than strength for athletic activity.

Muscular strength and endurance generally decrease as one gets older or becomes less active. This may reduce one's ability to do everyday chores and enjoy recreation. For this reason, the American College of Sports Medicine recommends that muscular development exercises be performed two to three times per week.

Aerobic exercise also has the following benefits, especially when strength and flexibility exercises are included:

- Improved range of motion and function
- Increased strength and endurance
- Increased strength of tendons and ligaments
- Improved muscle tone
- Improved posture
- Reduction of lower back pain and other disorders caused by inactivity

FIG. 10-6

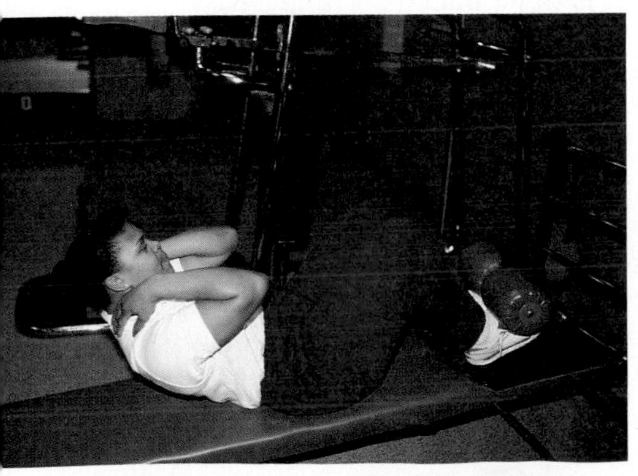

**Measuring Body Composition**

*You can have your body composition tested to see the effect of your diet and training program on your muscle and fat composition. The test breaks down your body weight into the total lean weight and the total fat weight. When you exercise and watch what you eat, your muscle strength and capacity increase and your percentage of body fat declines. The body composition test lets you monitor these changes.*

*There are many ways to measure body composition. Anthropometric tests measure the circumference of different body parts and then calculate body composition. Skinfold tests use a caliper to measure fat under the skin at different places, then make similar calculations (Fig. 1). Bioimpedance tests measure electric currents through the body (Fig. 2). Since the current is slowed down more by fat than by muscle, the speed of the current can be used to calculate body composition.*

*The most accurate technique is underwater weighing, also known as hydrostatic weighing (Fig. 3). This technique is based on a law discovered by Archimedes, a mathematician and inventor who lived in ancient Greece. According to legend, Archimedes was looking for a way to determine the purity of the gold in King Hiero's crown when he discovered the physical principle of buoyancy. This is the basis for hydrostatic weighing. (For more details on buoyancy, see Chapter 4.)*

*Because fat is less dense than water, and because bone and muscle are denser than water, a person with a higher percentage of bone and muscle for the same total body weight will weigh more in water than a person with a higher percentage of body fat because he or she has a higher body density (lower percentage of body fat). This principle allows for hydrostatic weighing and accurate determination of body fat percentage.*

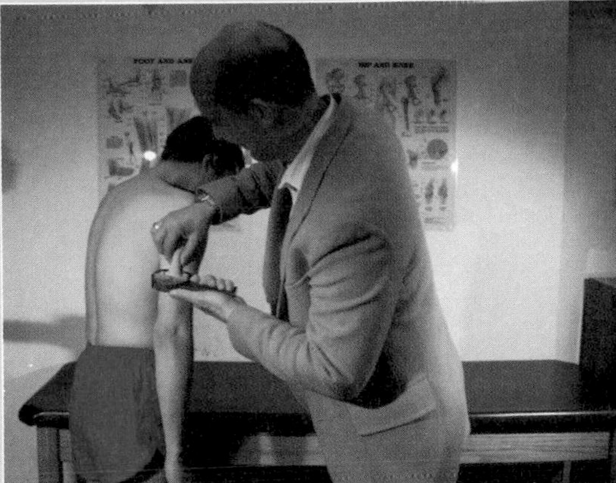

FIG. 1

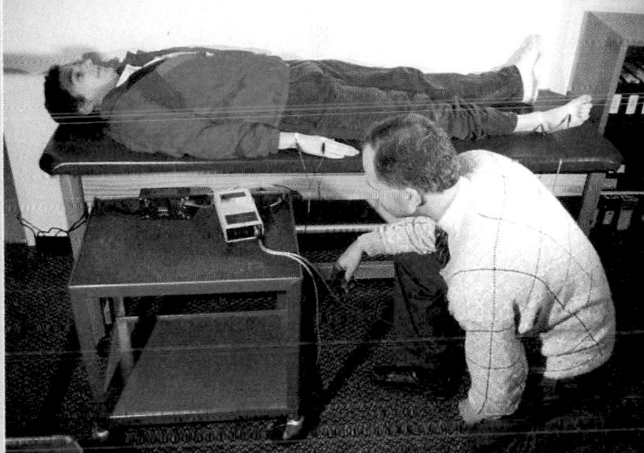

FIG. 2

FIG. 3

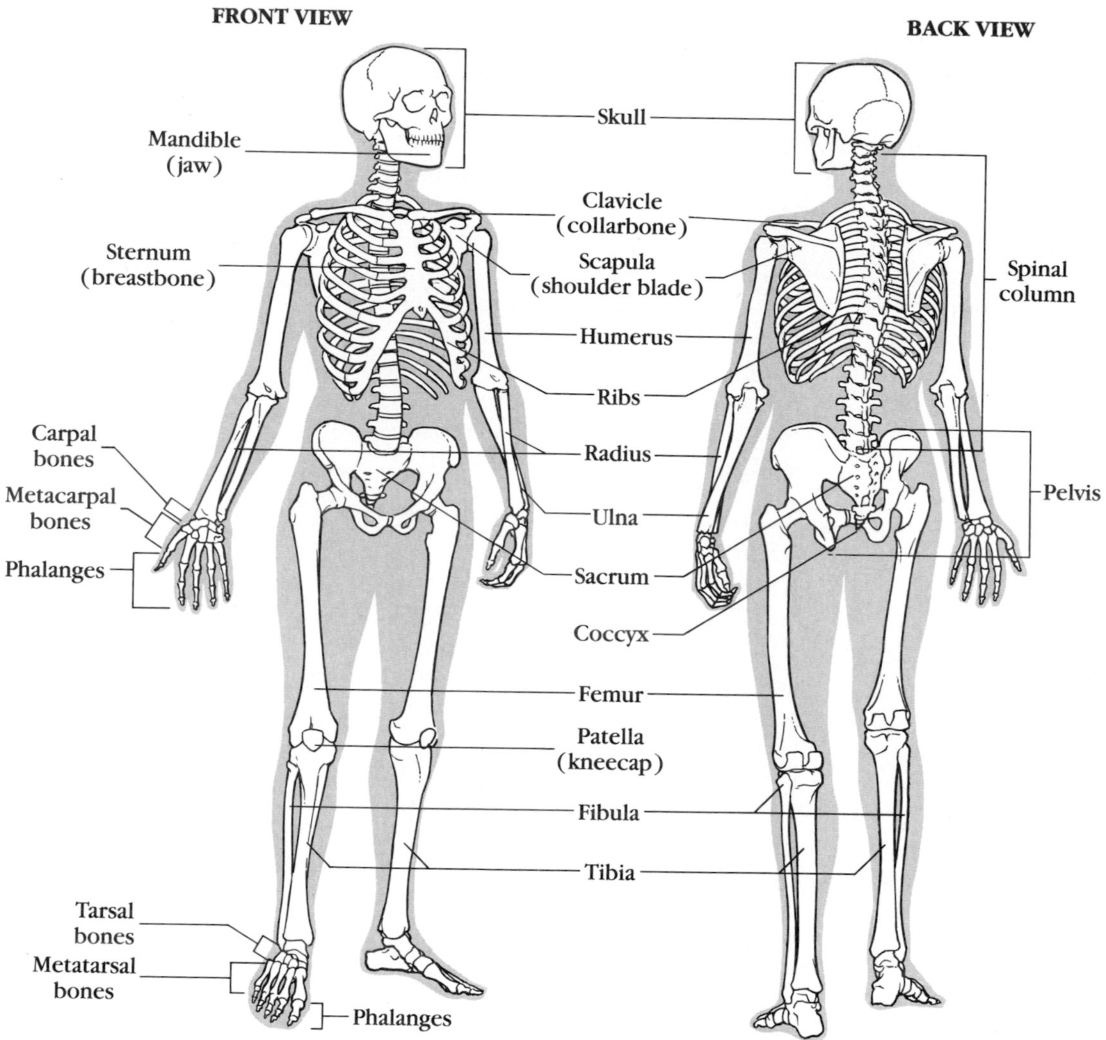


FIG. 10-7, *A-B* *A,* The bones of the skeleton give the body its shape and protect vital organs.

## FLEXIBILITY

***Flexibility*** is the range of motion in a joint or group of joints. Flexibility can vary from joint to joint in the same person. Thus, if you have flexibility in some joints, it does not mean that you have overall flexibility in your body. Good flexibility helps prevent injuries to the bones, muscles, tendons, and ligaments (Fig. 10-7). **Ligaments** are the strong elastic tissues that hold bones in place at joints (Fig. 10-8). **Tendons** attach muscles to bones. Flexibility is partly determined by heredity but can be improved by stretching. Stretching is an important part of the warm-up for any exercise. If your workout includes a muscular development set, be sure at the end of the session to stretch the muscles on which you were focusing. (Exercises for stretching are included in Appendix B.)

## WEIGHT MANAGEMENT

Up to half of the adults in the United States are thought to be **overfat.** That means the percentage of fat in their bodies is higher than recommended. This is not the same as being overweight. A person is **overweight** if the weight is more than the average based on sex, height, and frame size. These standards are published in tables with a weight range for males and females of different heights and frame sizes. However, these tables do not account for body composition. Because muscle is heavier than fat, someone with large muscles may be classified as overweight while having a normal percentage of body fat. Thus, it is more important to consider actual body fat than just weight. For information on how to have your body fat measured, ask your doctor or other health care specialist.

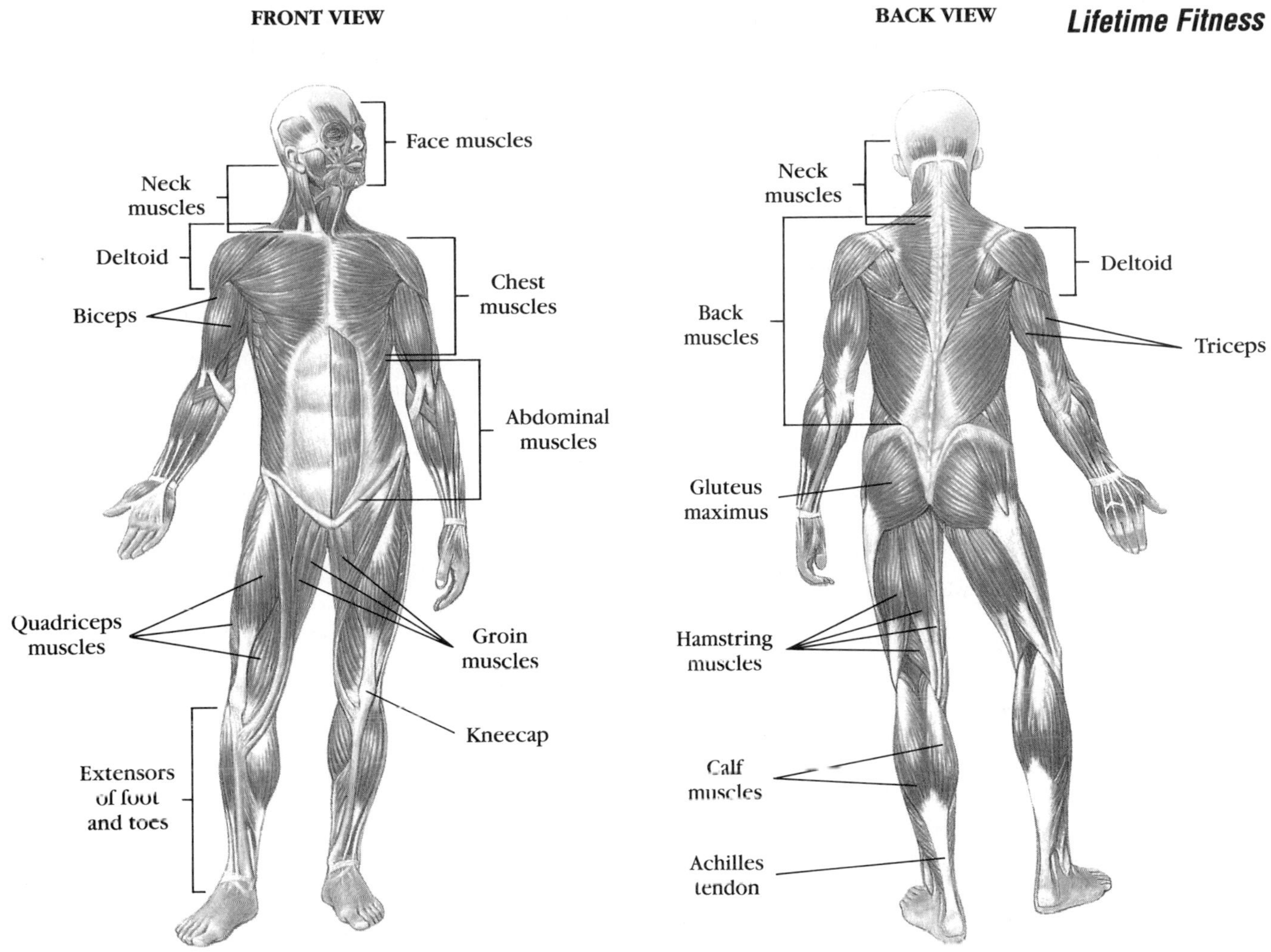

**FRONT VIEW**

Face muscles
Neck muscles
Deltoid
Biceps
Chest muscles
Abdominal muscles
Quadriceps muscles
Groin muscles
Kneecap
Extensors of foot and toes

**BACK VIEW**

Neck muscles
Deltoid
Back muscles
Triceps
Gluteus maximus
Hamstring muscles
Calf muscles
Achilles tendon

FIG. 10-7 *cont'd* *B,* Skeletal muscles, muscles that attach to bones, constitute the majority of the body's muscles.

**O**verfat individuals are at greater risk for many chronic health problems, such as diabetes, high blood pressure, coronary artery disease, stroke, and some types of cancer. They may also have low self-esteem. A person is considered **obese** if body fat exceeds 20 percent of total body weight for males or 30 percent for females. Obese people are $2^1/_2$ times more likely to die of cardiovascular disease than people with normal body fat. For these reasons, proper body weight and percentage of body fat have become a national health priority.

**R**egular exercise is important for successful long-term weight control. Exercise increases the **basal metabolic rate** (the amount of calories the body burns at rest). Moderately intense exercise also depresses your appetite and improves your mood. A person who exercises can eat more than an inactive person and still not gain weight.

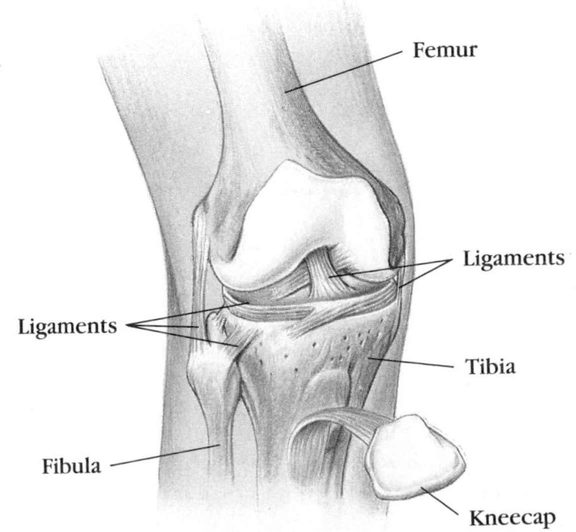


FIG. 10-8 A typical joint consists of two or more bones held together by ligaments.

Aerobic exercise helps you control body weight in the following ways:

- Increases the rate at which your body burns calories
- Decreases body fat
- Maintains lean muscle tissue when losing weight or dieting
- Increases your body's ability to use fat as fuel

### Specific Benefits of Exercising in Water

Whether you engage in aquatic exercise or fitness swimming, exercise in water has unique benefits. Buoyancy lessens the impact on the joints and thus the risk of injury. Because water helps cool the body during exercise, workouts in cool water are refreshing, a benefit for those prone to heat stress. On the other hand, exercise in warm water increases blood circulation and promotes healing of injured tissues. Warm water eases muscle spasms, relaxes tight muscles, and increases joint motion.

Aquatic exercise is a popular form of aerobic exercise. Water resistance also helps improve muscular strength and endurance. Moving in and through the water helps maintain and improve flexibility. Because water resistance can be controlled or adjusted by the participant's speed or motions, workouts can be designed to meet the needs of everyone regardless of their fitness level.

## Adjusting Exercise Levels

Your body is affected by any exertion. Pulse and breathing rates speed up, you may start to sweat, and you begin to burn calories. Physical fitness can come from exerting your body in certain ways. To reach or maintain a certain level of fitness, your exercise must put a stress on the cardiovascular system at the right level, without too much or too little work, and it must be of sufficient duration. To become more fit, you must work harder than normal so that the muscles and cardiovascular system are forced to adapt. This is called ***overload.*** You must also exercise regularly to maintain the same level of fitness.

### The F.I.T. Principle

To reach and stay at a good level of fitness, you set up and follow an exercise program. A good program depends on the frequency (F), intensity (I), and duration, or time (T), of your workouts. This is called the F.I.T. principle.

*Frequency* is how often you do the exercise. You should exercise 3 to 5 days a week. Exercising more than 5 days does not lead to better results. Your frequency depends on your own goals. For example, to lose fat, it is better to exercise 5 days a week rather than 3.

***Intensity*** is how hard you work out when you exercise. This is the most difficult of the three factors to assess. Results are best if the intensity of the workout stays at a specific level. If you exercise outside this level, cardiovascular improvement is slower. Very-low-intensity exercise has some benefits, but the benefits to the cardiovascular system are not proportional to the effort you make. High-intensity exercise is difficult to sustain, so your workouts are shorter and the resulting benefit to the cardiovascular system is limited.

The *time* you spend exercising also affects the benefits. You should spend at least 15 minutes at the recommended level of intensity, not counting the warm-up or cool-down.

A typical aerobic workout lasts 20 to 30 minutes. Going beyond 60 minutes does not lead to benefits that are proportional to the extra time spent, but more exercise time can help when you are training for specific activities.

### Target Heart Rate Range

The simplest way to know if you are exercising at the proper intensity is to measure your heart rate, since this measures physiological stress. The more intense the exercise, the higher the heart rate. The ideal heart rate range for an individual to maintain during exercise for greatest cardiovascular benefit is called the ***target heart rate range*** (Fig. 10-9). You can calculate it in several ways. The best way is to

**Target Heart Rate Zones**
**Beats per Minute / Beats per 10 Seconds**

| % of Maximum | 20 | 30 | 40 | 50 | 60 | 70 | 80 | 90 |
|---|---|---|---|---|---|---|---|---|
| 10 | 83/14 | 84/14 | 83/14 | 83/14 | 81/13 | 80/13 | 79/13 | 78/13 |
| 20 | 98/16 | 98/16 | 94/16 | 98/16 | 90/15 | 88/15 | 86/14 | 84/14 |
| 30 | 110/18 | 107/18 | 104/17 | 101/17 | 98/16 | 96/15 | 92/15 | 89/15 |
| 40 | 123/20 | 119/20 | 115/19 | 111/19 | 107/18 | 103/17 | 99/17 | 93/16 |
| 50 | 136/23 | 131/22 | 126/21 | 121/20 | 116/19 | 111/19 | 106/18 | 101/17 |
| 60 | 148/25 | 143/24 | 137/23 | 131/22 | 125/21 | 119/20 | 113/19 | 107/18 |
| 70 | 162/27 | 155/26 | 148/25 | 141/23 | 134/22 | 127/21 | 120/20 | 113/19 |
| 80 | 174/29 | 166/28 | 158/26 | 150/25 | 142/24 | 134/22 | 126/21 | 118/20 |
| 90 | 182/31 | 178/30 | 169/28 | 160/27 | 151/25 | 142/24 | 133/22 | 124/21 |

**Age (years)**

FIG. 10-9

calculate a percentage of the **predicted maximum heart rate** (MHR), which depends on your age and resting heart rate (RHR). The best time to take your resting heart rate is when you wake up in the morning. Or you can lie quietly for at least 10 minutes and then count your pulse for a full minute.

In general, a workout should raise your heart rate to between 60 and 85 percent of your predicted maximum heart rate. This is your own target heart rate range. Once you know your resting heart rate, you can calculate your target heart rate range in a few easy steps. First, find your predicted maximum heart rate by subtracting your age from 220 (Step A in Table 10-1). Then subtract your resting heart rate from that number (Step B). Multiply this by 60 percent (the lower limit of the recommended intensity) and add back the resting heart rate (Step C). Also multiply the number in Step B by 85 percent (the upper limit of the recommended intensity) and add back the resting heart rate (Step D). Your target heart rate range (in beats per minute) is between the lower and the upper intensity limits (Step E). You might find it convenient to divide the numbers in Steps C and D by 6 (Steps F and G). This gives you your target heart rate range in beats per 10 seconds (Step H). When you take your pulse during exercise, you can compare your actual heart rate for 10 seconds against your target heart rate range for the same amount of time. Table 10-1 shows how to use the formula to find the target heart rate range for a person age 30 with a resting heart rate of 78. Appendix C contains blank tables so you can compute your own target heart rate range.

TABLE 10-1. Calculating the Target Heart Rate Range for a Person Age 30, With a Resting Heart Rate of 78*

| | | |
|---|---|---|
| A. | 220 − 30 (age) | = 190 (MHR) |
| B. | 190 − 78 (RHR) | = 112 |
| C. | (112 × .60) + 78 | = 145 (60% intensity) |
| D. | (112 × .85) + 78 | = 173 (85% intensity) |
| E. | Target heart rate range | = 145-173 beats per minute |
| F. | 145 ÷ 6 | = 24 |
| G. | 173 ÷ 6 | = 29 |
| H. | Target heart rate range | = 24-29 beats per 10 seconds |

**Note:* This formula is for aerobic exercise on land. For some aquatic activities, the results must be adjusted. (See page 236.)

If you keep your heart rate within your target range when you exercise, you will progress safely toward fitness if you exercise frequently and long enough. The 60 to 85 percent range is appropriate for most people. The cardiovascular health of a sedentary person may begin to improve with an intensity level as low as 50 percent. Very fit athletes might not reach their training goals with less than 85 percent intensity.

FIG. 10-10

You can measure your heart rate during exercise with a **pulse** check (Fig. 10-10). Feel your pulse at the **carotid artery** in the neck or the **radial artery** in the wrist (Fig. 10-11). Your heart rate will drop fast when you pause to do this, so find the pulse quickly. Count the beats for 10 seconds and compare your results to your target heart rate range in beats per 10 seconds. (Or you can multiply by 6 to calculate your target heart rate range in beats per minute.) To check your pulse, start timing on the first beat and count "0." Count "1" on the second beat and so on.

If your heart rate is below the target range, you should increase the intensity of your workout. You can move faster or, in aquatic exercise, make larger arm and leg motions. If your heart rate is above the range, decrease the intensity. Make smaller movements, slow down, or take rest breaks more often. If

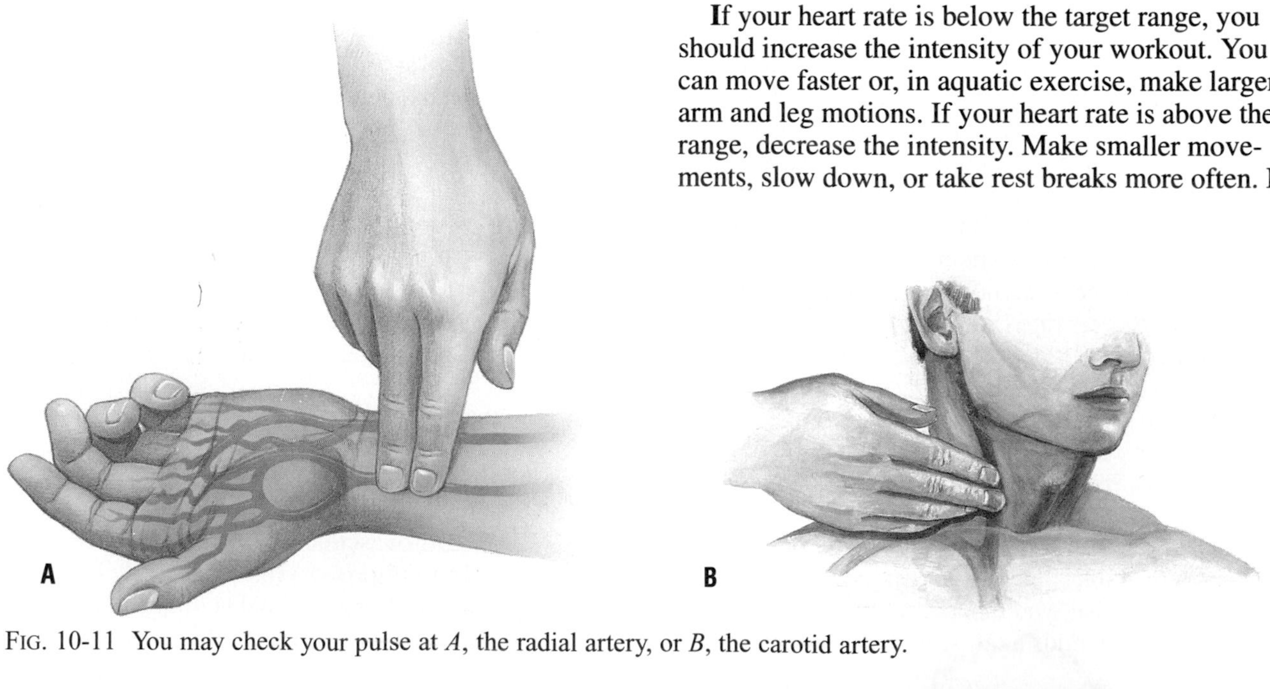

A

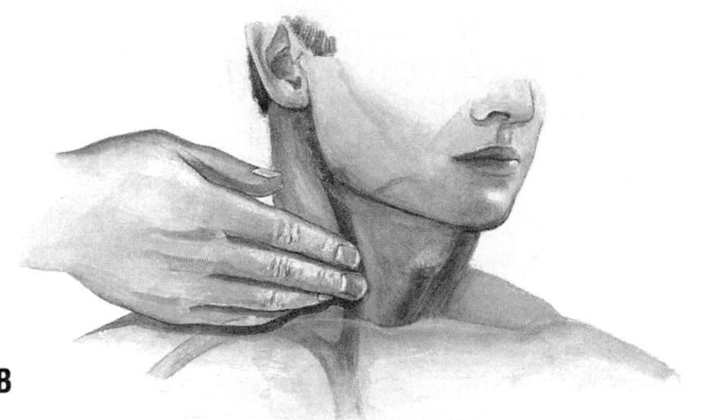


FIG. 10-11 You may check your pulse at *A*, the radial artery, or *B*, the carotid artery.

| Perceived Exertion | % Workload |
|---|---|
| 20 | 100% |
| 19-Very, Very Hard | 90% |
| 18 | |
| 17-Very Hard | 80% |
| 16 | |
| 15 Hard | 70% |
| 14 | |
| 13-Somewhat Hard | 60% |
| 12 | |
| 11-Fairly Light | 50% |
| 10 | |
| 9-Very Light | 40% |
| 8 | |
| 7-Very, Very, Light | |
| 6 | |

FIG. 10-12 Borg's Perceived Exertion Scale.

you are *often* above or below your range but still feel you are at the right intensity, this formula might not work for you. In that case, you might use the method of perceived exertion, which is discussed below.

## RATE OF PERCEIVED EXERTION

Many factors, such as stress, illness, and fatigue, can affect heart rates. In addition, because obtaining accurate exercise heart rates can be extremely difficult, an alternative method of monitoring intensity has been developed. This method is called the **Rate of Perceived Exertion** (RPE). RPE is a valid and reliable method for determining the intensity of a workout and is based on how hard an individual feels he or she is working. Studies have shown that RPE correlates highly with other intensity indicators, such as heart rate and ventilation (Fig. 10-12).

In the initial phase of an exercise program, RPE is often used with the heart rate to monitor intensity. To do this, identify a number on the RPE scale that corresponds with your perceived intensity, then check your heart rate to see how the two numbers relate. Once you understand the relationship between heart rate and RPE, you can rely less on heart rate and more on the way you feel.

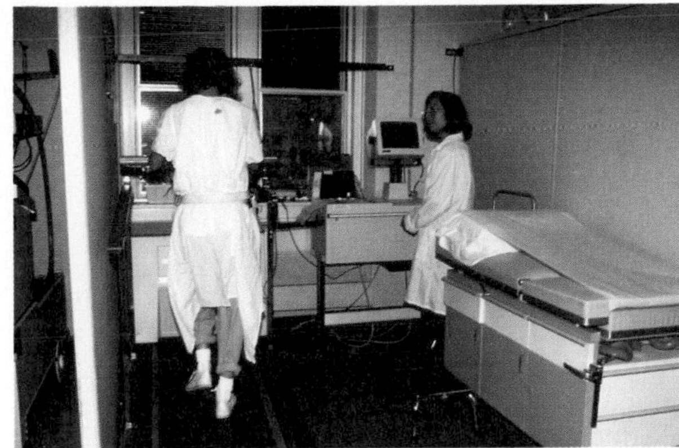

FIG. 10-13

## SAFETY CONSIDERATIONS FOR A FITNESS PROGRAM

For most people, a fitness program is not risky. Some people, however, cannot start a program at 60 percent intensity and continue for 15 minutes. If you have not exercised in a long while, this intensity could even be dangerous. A general health assessment to measure your level of fitness is in order whenever you begin an exercise program.

A health assessment can be as simple as a physical examination or as complex as an exercise stress test (Fig. 10-13). Consult your health care provider. Once you know your initial level of fitness, you can determine the exercise intensity that is safe for beginning your program.

Knowing your swimming skill level also is very important. With lower skill levels, you use more energy, even at slow speeds. Swimming even one length of the pool can be exhausting. Rest as often as you need and use resting strokes, like the sidestroke and the elementary backstroke, when starting your program. Check your heart rate at each break to make sure it is in your target range. Your goal is to increase the time you spend continuously swimming and gradually decrease the rest breaks.

*Always* watch out for exercise warning signals. They may mean you need immediate medical attention. The following signals tell you to stop the workout:

- An abnormal heart action (such as a heart rate that stays high for some time after you stop exercising)
- Pain or pressure in the chest, arm, or throat
- Dizziness, light-headedness, or confusion during or immediately following the workout
- Breathlessness or wheezing

If you feel any of these, tell the instructor or lifeguard. If conditions persist, see your health care provider.

## Components of a Workout

Your workout should be designed to meet your own fitness goals. A safe, effective workout has a warm-up, stretching, the aerobic set (the main part of the workout), and a cool-down. A muscular development set may follow the aerobic activity.

### Warm-Up

The warm-up prepares the body for the increased work. The warm-up raises deep muscle temperatures, increases blood flow, and helps you adjust to the workout environment. Since pool water is often 15 to 20 degrees F (8 to 11 degrees C) cooler than skin temperature, you may want to spend some time warming up at poolside before you enter the water. A good warm-up is important to help prevent injury to muscles and joints. The warm-up should last 5 to 10 minutes or about 15 to 20 percent of the total workout time or distance. The warm-up may consist of slow walking, jogging, or low-intensity swimming (Fig. 10-14). A person with a disability may need a longer, more gradual warm-up.

Fig. 10-14

### Stretching

Stretching makes joints more flexible and improves range of motion (Fig. 10-15). Do your stretching during the warm-up or right after it. Stretching can prevent soreness and help you perform better. It can also reduce your risk of injury.

Proper stretching requires slow, gentle movements, holding the stretch for 10 to 30 seconds. Do not force a joint beyond the normal range of motion. You should feel no pain or discomfort during the stretch. Stretches for swimming are given in Appendix B.

Fig. 10-15

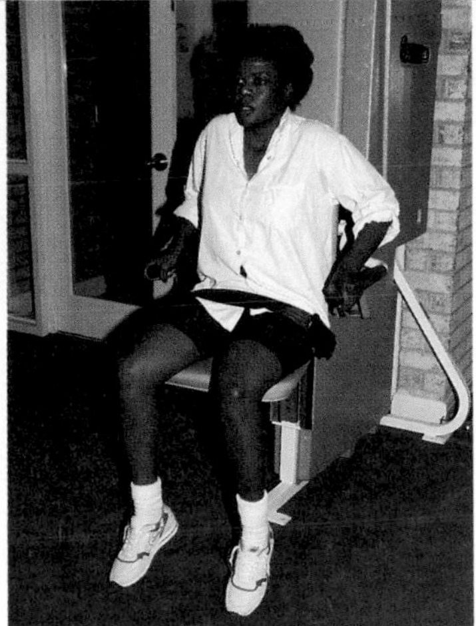
Fig. 10-16

## Aerobic Set

To benefit from an aerobic workout, you must keep your heart rate in your target range for at least 15 minutes. At a lower level of intensity, you will not increase your fitness level as much. The aerobic **set** should make up 50 to 70 percent of the workout time and distance. Much of the following sections on fitness swimming and aquatic exercise apply to the aerobic sets for those exercise programs.

## Muscular Development Set

The American College of Sports Medicine recommends that a fitness program include some exercise for muscular development. Probably the most popular form of exercise for muscular development is resistance training (weight lifting). The muscles are overloaded by using barbells, dumbbells, or a weight machine (Fig 10-16). Strength development for fitness should be general in nature. That is, you should try to overload muscles from each muscle group rather than focus on a few muscle groups. It is best to use one or two exercises for each muscle group.

A person needs to warm up thoroughly and be instructed in the proper way of executing each exercise. The next step is to identify the proper weight for each exercise. It is recommended that a beginner use a weight that can be lifted 12 to 15 times in one set.If you cannot lift the weight at least 12 times without a break in the set, the weight is too heavy for that exercise.

Once you select the amount of weight you will use for each exercise, you may begin your weight lifting program. A standard program for beginners is to lift the selected weight 10 times (repetitions) for 3 sets. The more often you do resistance training, the easier the selected weight will be to lift. As you improve, try each exercise with the next heavier weight to maintain the overload. Strength training should be performed two or three times per week as part of your regular fitness program. For more information on safe weight lifting techniques, consult a coach or a trainer at a health club.

Strength training with aquatic exercise (page 242) is another way for fitness swimmers to improve muscular strength and endurance. In aquatic exercise, because it is hard to calculate the resistance of the water, performing only three sets might not provide the overload needed to increase strength and endurance. The overload for strength improvement may depend solely on increasing the number of sets and the number of repetitions per set. You must rely on your perception of overload to determine if you are working hard enough.

## Cool-Down

The last part of your workout is a cool-down period. This is a tapering off to let the heart rate, blood pressure, and ***metabolic rate*** (the amount of energy produced by the body in a given period of time) go back to their initial levels. A proper cool-down helps return the blood from the working muscles to the brain, lungs, and internal organs. The cool-down helps you recover from fatigue and may prevent muscle soreness later.

Cool-down activities are like warm-up activities. You may change to a resting stroke so you can slow down the workout gradually and keep blood from collecting in the muscles (Fig. 10-17). You may stretch in a stationary position toward the end of the cool down, but not immediately after strenuous activity in the aerobic set or the muscular development set. A typical cool-down lasts 5 to 10 minutes or 10 percent of the total time or distance of the workout.

Fig. 10-17

## Phases of a Fitness Program

Fitness improves when you gradually increase the exertion of your workout. As your body adapts to a workload, the work level should gradually increase. This is referred to as ***progression.*** You can increase the workload by increasing the frequency, intensity, or duration (time) of your workouts (the F.I.T. principle). In general, increase the duration first, then the intensity or frequency. Remember that you cannot become more fit unless you increase the stress of the exercise on your body.

How fast your condition improves depends on how fit you are when you begin your program and other individual factors. For safe and effective exercise, increase the overload gradually in three phases: the initial phase, the improvement phase, and the maintenance phase. You should know that it is possible for one's condition to decline if the workload decreases or stops.

### Initial Phase

This phase should include exercise of a very low intensity. If you have not exercised in a long time, this phase helps increase your workload slowly and comfortably. Move on to the improvement phase when you can comfortably maintain 60-percent intensity for at least 15 minutes. Be patient. You may need up to 10 weeks before going to the improvement phase.

### Improvement Phase

The improvement phase begins when you reach the minimum level to attain cardiovascular fitness, namely, exercising three times per week for at least 15 minutes at a level of at least 60 percent intensity. Your fitness will improve by increasing frequency, intensity, or length of time. For example, exercising five times a week leads to improvements sooner than only three times a week, if all else is the same. You will improve more rapidly in this phase than in the initial phase, but be sure to stay well within your target heart rate range. Remember to increase the duration before you increase intensity or frequency.

### Maintenance Phase

This phase begins when you reach the fitness goals that you set for yourself. Your goal here is to sustain your fitness level rather than increase your workload. You exercise at a comfortable level and set different goals. For example, now that your cardiovascular system is more fit, you might work on learning a new stroke or explore other activities to vary your program. This will help keep your workouts interesting.

### Reversibility of Training

The physical fitness you gain from exercise can be lost. If you stop exercising regularly, your fitness level will decrease and you will gradually return to the shape you were in when you began your exercise program. It is better to maintain your current level of fitness than to let it decline and try to regain it. Having once been physically fit does not make it any easier to get back into shape, except that you may not have to learn specific skills again for doing the workout. Fitness declines quickly but can be maintained with as few as two workouts a week. The key is to develop fitness habits you can keep using for a lifetime.

## Fitness Swimming

You should design your fitness swimming program carefully. This means starting at the right level and following an effective progression in your exercise plan. This section will help you design a program to progress from an inactive lifestyle to your desired fitness level. Depending on your current fitness level, you may move through the initial phase quickly or even skip it. Remember, the success of your program depends on a comfortable, practical plan that you can continue the rest of your life.

Always use a warm-up, stretching, an aerobic set, and a cool-down in each workout. You should also include a muscular development set in two or three workouts each week.

Note that the target heart rate range with swimming should be 10 to 13 beats *below* that for similar exercise on land. (For the person in the example used ear-

FIG. 10-18

lier, the target heart rate range would be 132 to 160 beats per minute or 22 to 27 beats per 10 seconds.) A swimmer's horizontal position and the smaller muscle mass used in swimming prevent the heart rate from increasing as much as in vertical, dry land exercise of the same intensity. Remember to lower your target heart rate range by this much for fitness swimming.

Check your heart rate before, during, and after your workout to ensure you are at the right intensity. Also, check your resting heart rate every few weeks because exercise gradually lowers it. Then recalculate your target heart rate range to make sure your body is still overloaded without exceeding your target range.

### INITIAL PHASE

The following are examples of specific exercises for designing your own program. These assumptions have been made:

1. The pool is 25 yards long (a common length for indoor pools in the United States). If the pool you use is longer or shorter, make adjustments for your workout.
2. You can swim 1 length of the pool using any stroke.
3. You do your workouts on three nonconsecutive days per week.
4. You have done a gradual warm-up, including stretching exercises, before the aerobic set.

Between lengths, rest or walk or jog in the water for 15 to 30 seconds (Fig. 10-18). Try to keep a continuous effort without becoming too tired. To find a safe level to start, swim 1 length and check your heart rate. If it is above your target range, start with Step 1. If your heart rate is well within the target range, start with Step 3. If the water is too deep for walking or jogging, use a life jacket or stay in water no deeper than your shoulders. Remember that using a life jacket does not substitute for knowing how to swim.

In this phase of the program, you need not reach the target heart rate range of 60 percent intensity. If you have not exercised in a long while, you may begin at 50 percent for the progression.

Proceed with each step of your workout until you can do it easily, keeping your heart rate close to the lower limit of the target range. The initial phase can take as long as 10 weeks, so don't try to rush through it at an uncomfortable pace.

**Step 1.** In chest-deep water, walk 5 minutes and exercise your upper body with an underwater arm stroke such as the breaststroke. Check your heart rate after each length. If you can walk 5 minutes without your heart rate rising above the target heart rate range, rest 15 to 30 seconds and do the 5-minute walk two more times. Gradually decrease the rest period until you can walk 15 minutes continuously. Be sure your heart rate does not go past the upper limit of the target range.

**Step 2.** In chest-deep water, walk 1 length using the arm stroke as is in Step 1, then jogging 1 length. Rest 15 to 30 seconds after the jogging length. Continue for 15 minutes. Check your heart rate at each break. Gradually decrease the rest breaks until you can walk or jog 15 minutes continuously. Check your heart rate every 5 minutes in the workout.

**Step 3.** Swim 1 length and then rest by walking or jogging 1 length. Continue for 5 minutes Check your heart rate to be sure your heart rate is not too high. If it is, rest another minute. If your heart rate is within the target range, continue alternating swimming lengths with walking or jogging lengths. Check your heart rate every 5 minutes. Gradually decrease the rest breaks until you can swim or jog continuously for 15 minutes.

**Step 4.** Swim 1 length, rest 15 to 30 seconds, and swim another length. Use a resting stroke on the second length or just swim more slowly. Check your heart rate. Continue this sequence for 15 minutes. Gradually decrease the rest break to 10 seconds.

**Step 5.** When you can swim 15 minutes continuously or with minimum rest as in Step 4, recalculate your target heart rate range at 60 percent and repeat Step 4. When you can swim continuously for 15 minutes at an intensity of 60 percent, you have completed the initial phase. Move on to the improvement phase.

There are several ways to check your progress. One way is to check your resting heart rate every 3 to 4 weeks. As you become more fit, your resting heart rate will drop. As it drops, be sure to recalculate your target range with the new resting heart rate to continue to overload your system properly. Another indication of progress is that your heart rate returns to normal more quickly as your fitness improves.

## Improvement Phase

People have very different improvement phases. If you begin your program with a low level of fitness, you may progress more slowly than someone who is more fit. You have two options here. Level 1 is for someone progressing from the previous phase. Level 2 offers other training methods to add variety to your program. Both options use the assumptions listed for the initial phase.

### *Level 1*

These steps move in 2-week increments. Do not move to a more difficult step until you can do the prior step easily. You might not need the full 2 weeks for some steps.

**Weeks 1-2.** Swim 2 lengths. Rest 15 to 30 seconds. Repeat for 15 minutes. Check your heart rate during the breaks.

**Weeks 3-4.** Swim 3 lengths followed by a slow length or resting stroke. Rest 15 to 30 seconds. Continue for 20 minutes. Through this period, gradually shorten the rest breaks to 10 seconds.

**Weeks 5-6.** Swim 5 lengths followed by a slow length or resting stroke. Rest 15 to 30 seconds. Check your heart rate. Continue for 20 minutes. With each successive workout, gradually decrease the rest breaks to 10 seconds.

**Weeks 7-8.** Swim continuously for 20 minutes. Rest only when needed but not longer than 10 seconds. If possible use resting strokes instead of breaks. Check your heart rate every 10 minutes in the workout.

**Weeks 9-10.** Swim continuously for 20 minutes. With each successive workout, add 1 or 2 lengths until you can swim continuously for 30 minutes.

**Weeks 11-12.** Swim 30 minutes continuously without rest. In the last week of this progression, test your progress by swimming a timed 12-minute swim.

After you reach the 30-minute goal, you can continue to increase the overload by raising the intensity or lengthening the workout. When you do this, be sure to change only one **variable** (frequency, intensity, or time) at a time. Keep your progression gradual.

### *Level 2*

Whatever your level of fitness, you can design your own workout with various training methods. When planning your workout, remember the F.I.T. principle and do not try to progress too fast.

**12-Minute Swimming Test**
Distance (Yards) Swum in 12 Minutes

| Fitness Category | | 13–19 | 20–29 | Age (years) 30–39 | 40–49 | 50–59 | >60* |
|---|---|---|---|---|---|---|---|
| I. Very poor | (men) | <500* | <400 | <350 | <300 | <250 | <250 |
| | (women) | <400 | <300 | <250 | <200 | <150 | <150 |
| II. Poor | (men) | 500–599 | 400–499 | 350–449 | 300–399 | 250–349 | 250–299 |
| | (women) | 400–499 | 300–399 | 250–349 | 200–299 | 150–249 | 150–199 |
| III. Fair | (men) | 600–699 | 500–599 | 450–549 | 400–499 | 350–449 | 300–399 |
| | (women) | 500–599 | 400–499 | 350–449 | 300–399 | 250–349 | 200–299 |
| IV. Good | (men) | 700–799 | 600–699 | 550–649 | 500–599 | 450–549 | 400–499 |
| | (women) | 600–699 | 500–599 | 450–549 | 400–499 | 350–449 | 300–399 |
| V. Excellent | (men) | >800 | >700 | >650 | >600 | >550 | >500 |
| | (women) | >700 | >600 | >550 | >500 | >450 | >400 |

*< Means "less than"; > means "more than."
From Cooper K. H.: *The Aerobics Program for Total Well-Being,* New York: Bantam Books, 1982.

**Cooper 12-Minute Swimming Test**

*The 12-minute swimming test, devised by Kenneth Cooper, M.D., is an easy, inexpensive way for men and women of all ages to test their aerobic capacity (oxygen consumption) and to chart their fitness program.*

*The test encourages the swimmer to cover the greatest distance possible in 12 minutes, using whatever stroke is preferred, resting as necessary, but doing the best he or she can.*

*For instance, a woman between the ages of 30 and 39 is in excellent condition if she can swim 550 yards or more in the 12 minutes allowed for the test. However, a woman of the same age would be considered in very poor condition if she could not swim at least 250 yards in the same amount of time.*

*The easiest way to take the test is to swim in a pool with known dimensions, and it helps to have someone there to record the number of laps and the time, preferably with a sweep second hand.*

*Care must be taken with the 12-minute test however. It is not recommended for anyone over 35 years of age, unless he or she has already developed good aerobic capacity. The best way to determine this, of course, is to see a physician.*

Chapter 11 describes many training techniques you can incorporate into your workout. These help you develop specific aspects of fitness or swimming skills. You can use each alone or combine them.

## Maintenance Phase

Once you reach your fitness goals, you might not wish to increase your workload any more. Consider your original goals and either set new ones or maintain your current fitness level by staying with your present workout. What is most important is that you stay at least at the minimum level of fitness.

If your goal is to train for competition, take a look at the methods described in Chapter 11. Chapter 12 discusses different competitive events and organizations and how to get started.

## Swimming Etiquette

You may feel frustrated in your swimming workout to have to share the pool with other swimmers. Cyclists do not have to share their bikes, and runners can usually find a quiet road, but fitness swimmers rarely get a lane to themselves. Proper swimming etiquette helps ease this problem.

To share a lane you need to be organized and cooperative and to know your swimming level. You must first know your exercise speed. Your workout will be better in a lane where other swimmers are doing a similar type of workout (pulls, kicks, repeat short distances, long continuous swims) at a speed similar to yours. Most pools have lanes for fast, medium, and slow swimmers, but swimmers still vary a great deal in speed within a lane.

Once you find the best lane, use **circle swimming** so that all swimmers can enjoy the workout (Fig. 10-19). Circle swimming is swim-

Fig. 10-19

FIG. 10-20

ming in a counterclockwise pattern around the line on the pool bottom in the lane's center. With the correct etiquette, a faster swimmer overtaking a slower swimmer in the lane signals to pass by tapping the lead swimmer's foot. The lead swimmer should stop at the wall or pull over to let the faster swimmer pass. It is common courtesy to allow the new lead swimmer at least a 5-second lead before following. Although this may seem to disrupt your workout, such short breaks will not affect the intensity.

## AQUATIC EXERCISE

Aquatic exercise is water activity generally done in a vertical position with the face out of the water. Aquatic exercise has grown in part from athletics. Coaches wanted to rehabilitate injured athletes in a way that was safe but also good for cardiovascular conditioning. Water exercise was the perfect activity. Aquatic exercise programs have recently become a new physical fitness avenue for health-conscious people, in addition to being a rehabilitation method.

Aquatic exercise varies in many ways. The water temperature and depth used, the style of aerobic dancing or calisthenics with range of motion activities, and the specific motions used all vary from program to program (Fig. 10-20). People do aquatic exercise to manage their weight, relieve stress, feel better, and generally become more fit. Another advantage of aquatic exercise is that you do not have to know how to swim.

People with disabilities may get a special benefit from aquatic exercise. As discussed in Chapter 9, these individuals can improve their level of fitness, range of motion, and muscular strength and endurance with aquatic activity.

### FACTORS THAT AFFECT YOUR WORKOUT

In aquatic exercise, you maintain the proper intensity by adjusting your body position and by moving in the water. The following factors affect the intensity the most:

- Buoyancy, as it relates to proper water depth and body position
- Resistance the working muscles must overcome, affected by how much surface area the body presents as it moves through the water
- Speed of movement
- Type of movement

#### *Buoyancy and Water Depth*

Buoyancy reduces the pull of gravity on the limbs and trunk. The deeper the water, the more support it gives. Exercise in water that is only ankle-, knee- or waist-deep has little support against the impact of the feet landing when jogging or dancing. In deeper water, the body has more buoyancy, but in neck-deep water it is hard to keep balance and control. Increased buoyancy also reduces the workload, so you may have trouble getting your heart rate into the target range.

Exercise in chest-deep water may be best because the arms stay submerged. Using your arms also helps you keep balance and proper body alignment. The effort of pushing the water improves upper body strength and endurance and helps make the exercise aerobic. Arm work under water improves the muscles that stabilize the trunk. These muscles, particularly the abdominal muscles, gain strength and help reduce stress in the lower back.

Obese people may need to adjust their workouts if their hips and thighs cause the center of buoyancy to be lower. The legs then tend to rise toward the surface, making it hard to keep balance. Obese people may want to exercise in shallower water, but it should still be deep enough to support and protect the body from hard landings.

The way you exercise also affects the intensity of the workout. With bouncing and bounding movements (such as those commonly associated with aerobic dance done out of the water), the heart rate might not reach the target range since the body has a short rest while it drifts back to the bottom. However, movements involving walking, jogging, or aerobic dance in the water can be of value as you progress to workouts of higher intensity. Aquatic exercise helps avoid problems that are associated with the impact of landing.

### Resistance

Exercise intensity is greater when the surface area of the body presented to the water is larger. By choosing which limbs to maneuver in which way(s), you can adjust the resistance your body encounters when it pushes against the water. For example, a biceps curl uses more effort with an open hand than with a fist (Fig. 10-21). Moving a longer body segment, such as the whole arm kept straight from the shoulder, uses more effort than a shorter body segment, such as the forearm during a biceps curl. You may also adjust resistance by using equipment designed for this purpose.

### Speed of Movement

The speed of movement in the exercise also affects the intensity of the workout. Faster movements result in greater resistance and use more effort. In aquatic exercise, this principle applies more to the speed of moving the limb than to the speed of moving the whole body from one point in the pool to another.

### Type of Movement

Some types of movement require more effort than others. When your limbs move through the water in aquatic exercise, the water behind the limb is set in motion and stays in motion. With a curved motion such as in sculling, the limb takes the path of least resistance around the moving water. With an angular motion such as the biceps curl, the limb movement reverses and the limb crashes into the moving wall of water. Thus, angular motions involve more continuous effort (Fig. 10-22).

## Workout Design

An aquatic exercise workout should have the same components as a fitness swimming workout. The warm-up lasts 5 to 10 minutes and consists of walking, slow jogging, and slow aerobic activities, in the water or at poolside if the water is not warm enough. Stretching may be added after the warm-up. If you chill early in the workout, you may be more comfortable stretching after the aerobic set.

The aerobic set should be rhythmic and continuous and use both arms and legs (Fig. 10-23). Monitor your heart rate several times during this set to be sure it stays in the target range.

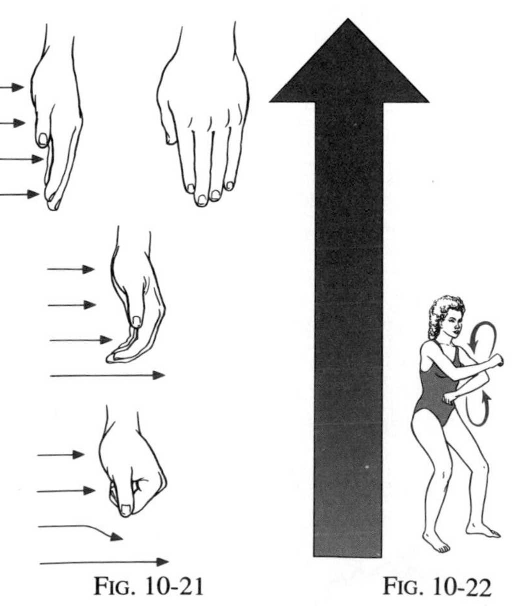

Fig. 10-21

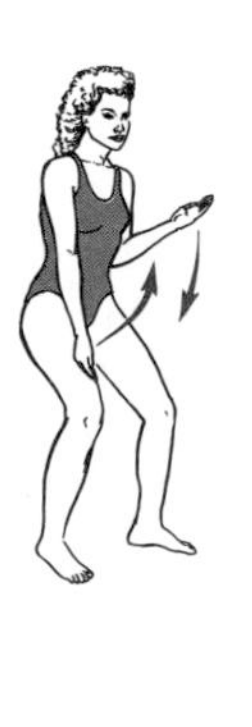

Fig. 10-22

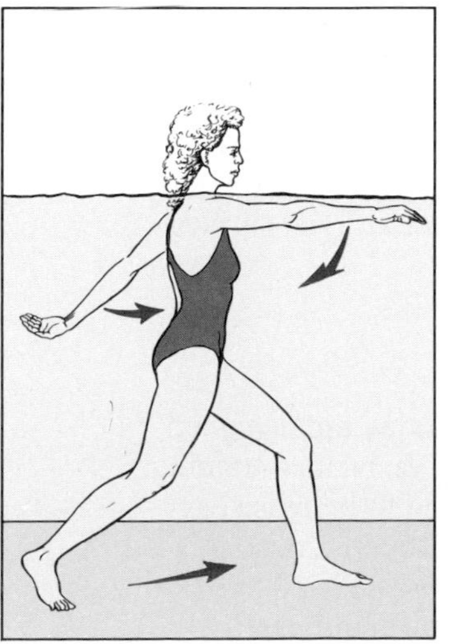

Fig. 10-23

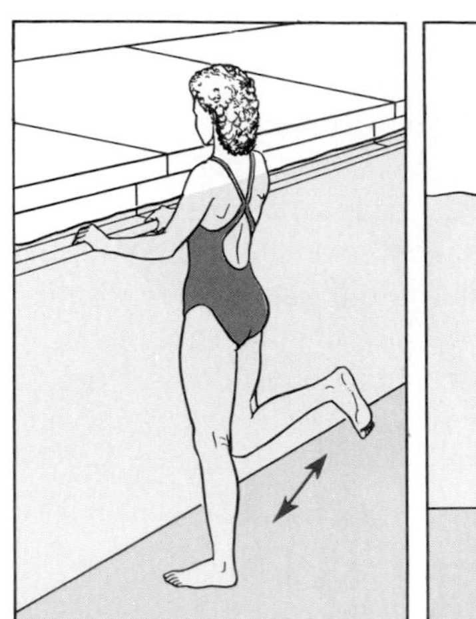
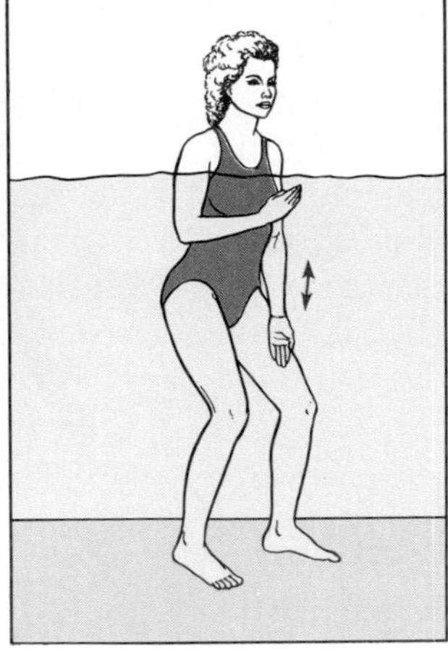

FIG. 10-24

Although target heart rates for swimming are 10 to 13 beats lower than for similar dry land exercise, the issue is less clear for aquatic exercise. Some research shows that heart rates from vertical aquatic exercise are lower than rates on land. Other studies report that heart rates are the same as rates in dry land programs with similar intensity. If you subtract 10 to 13 beats from your target heart rate range when you do aquatic exercise, you may underestimate the intensity needed to reach your goals.

Two or three times each week, your workout should include a muscular development set. This promotes flexibility, range of motion, strength, and muscular endurance (Fig. 10-24).

The cool-down in an aquatic workout should consist of slow, rhythmic activities. A good format for the cool-down is simply to reverse the warm-up activities.

## AQUATIC EXERCISE FOR MUSCULAR DEVELOPMENT

The intensity of resistance training increases directly with the size of the surface area and the speed of movement. It will seem as though you are lifting more weight if your movements are faster and the surface area meeting resistance is larger.

### *Equipment*

Several devices on the market today are designed to provide greater overload during resistance training. Some use the principle of buoyancy to increase exercise intensity. Wearing buoyant cuffs on wrists or ankles means that greater force must be used to move your limbs under water. Other devices increase the surface area of the limbs to provide resistance.

Devices for aquatic resistance training are not recommended for the beginner. For most people, the water alone provides an adequate overload for improvements in strength and muscular endurance. However, the more advanced exerciser may need such equipment to help maintain the proper intensity for his or her workout.

### *Safety Precautions*

Follow these guidelines in your muscular development sets to keep your aquatic exercise safe:

- Use the right equipment. It is important to use equipment specifically designed for aquatic exercise. Improvised equipment may cause injury. Always use equipment you can control. Once a piece of equipment is put in motion, it may continue to move, striking your body. If you do not possess enough strength to stop and reverse the motion or to stabilize your body during the movement, your safety may be jeopardized.

- Keep your body centered. Body alignment is especially important when you are using equipment for resistance training. Choose exercises in which you move toward and away from the center of your body. Movements with limbs fully extended, such as leg or arm circles, may cause injury.

- Stabilize the trunk when you lift. The larger surface area of some devices requires a greater degree of trunk stability for safe lifting technique. Stability throughout the lift is affected by the inertia of the equipment and, to a limited degree, by buoyancy. When you perform lifting motions, your back should be flat, with the abdominal muscles tight, the knees slightly bent, and the feet flat on the pool bottom.

- Isolate and work one muscle group at a time. This focuses your attention and gives the best improvement for individual muscle groups. Be sure to exercise opposing muscle groups equally.

- Work major muscle groups first. If you work the smaller, assisting muscle groups first, they will fatigue early and limit the work you can do with major muscle groups.

- Plan your movements. First imagine where the piece of equipment will be at the end of the movement, then perform the action. Use exercises that involve a full range of motion and be sure to return fully to the starting position. Be sure the equipment stays in the water. Shock to joints and muscles when equipment passes into or out of the water can cause injury.
- Use correct breathing. Do not hold your breath. This increases your blood pressure and may increase your feelings of stress. Instead, adjust your breathing to the rhythm of the exercise. Exhale during the work phase and inhale during the recovery phase.
- Stop any exercise that causes sharp pain. Sharp pain can be a signal of a serious health problem. Seek immediate help for persistent pain in the chest or arm (pain that does not go away within 10 minutes and is not relieved by resting or changing position). Report any recurring pain to your health care provider.

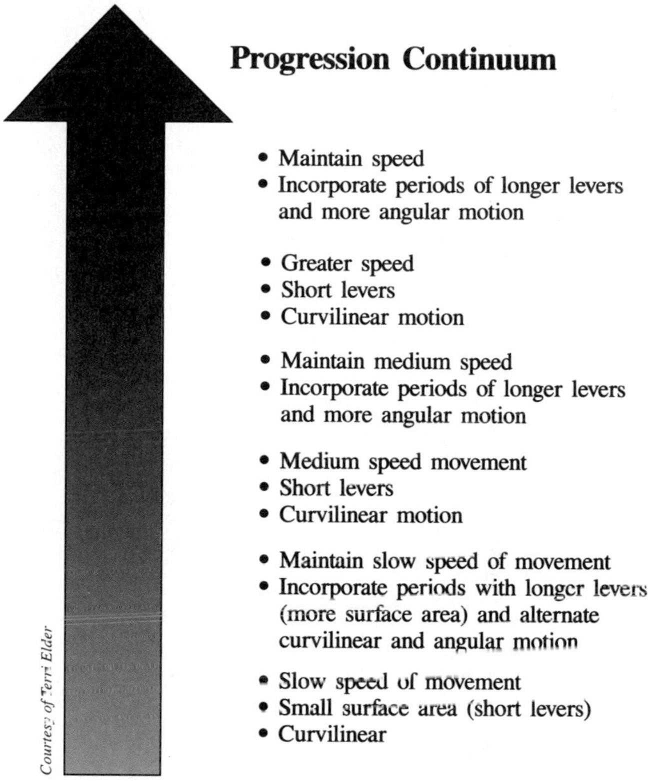

FIG. 10-25

## PROGRESSIONS FOR AQUATIC EXERCISE

You can easily progress in aquatic exercise because you can manipulate three factors (resistance due to surface area, speed of movement, and type of movement) to reach the level of intensity you need. If you are less fit, start with low-level exercises such as walking in chest-deep water or slow jogging in waist-deep water. Use slow, rhythmic movements with small surface areas. (See Appendix B for examples.) If you are generally fit, exercise with larger surface areas, faster speeds, and angular motion to reach the right intensity. Once you learn how to adjust your intensity, you can exercise in the same class with others who are exercising at different intensities.

The key to progressively overloading the system and maintaining target heart rates is to control how surface area, speed, and type of movement interact (Fig. 10-25). You can stay at the same intensity with a smaller surface area (for example, moving from chest-deep water to waist-deep water) if you increase the speed of movement (such as walking or jogging faster). You can also change from angular motion to curved motion without losing intensity as long as you increase the surface area and/or the speed.

## SUMMARY

Regular aerobic exercise is beneficial in many ways. Water is a good vehicle for reaching one's fitness goals with a low risk of injury. You can design a fitness program to meet your personal needs, whether you are a person with a disability or a star athlete.

The success of your aquatic fitness program depends on its design. It should meet your fitness needs and your personal goals. Your program should be supervised, monitored often, and evaluated for its success. If your current program is not meeting your needs, reevaluate it and adjust it to reach your goals more effectively. If the program gives you the results you want, you are more likely to keep using it and enjoy the benefits of greater health. When you enroll in a water fitness exercise program, be sure that the instructors are trained in water exercise programs. Appendix A includes organizations that provide training programs.

# CHAPTER 11 training

## Key Terms

**Aerobic exercise:** Sustained, rhythmic, physical exercise that requires additional effort by the heart and lungs to meet the increased demand by the skeletal muscles for oxygen.

**Anaerobic exercise:** Exercise at an intensity that oxygen is not supplied consistently. Anaerobic exercise involves high-intensity events that last 2 minutes or less.

**Heat:** In competition, a procedure followed when there are more entrants in a swimming event than there are lanes in the pool.

**Overload:** A fitness principle based on working somewhat harder than normal so that the muscles and cardiovascular system must adapt.

**Specificity:** The principle that different exercises lead to different specific benefits for the body.

**Stroke frequency:** The number of complete arm cycles in a set period of time.

**Stroke length:** Distance traveled in one complete cycle of the arms.

**Swim meet:** A competitive event in swimming; may be a contest between teams or between individuals who are not grouped into teams.

**Taper phase:** The 1-week to 3-week period in a training season before a peak performance, in which the person in training decreases distances but raises the intensity almost to racing speed.

# Objectives

***After reading this chapter, you should be able to—***

1. Describe the principles of specificity, overload, and progression as they apply to a training program.
2. Explain the difference between aerobic and anaerobic exercise and the role of each in a training program.
3. Name the phases of a training season and explain the purposes of each.

4. Describe safety precautions and preparations for open water competition.
5. Define the key terms at left.

***After reading this chapter and completing appropriate class activities, you should be able to—***

1. Demonstrate at least five training techniques and explain why you would use them.

SOME PEOPLE DEFINE TRAINING as any organized program of exercise designed to reach a certain level of fitness or performance. Since the preceding chapter focused on helping you meet your fitness goals, this chapter focuses on helping you do more. You will learn how to train to increase the strength or endurance of specific muscle groups, to learn new aquatic skills or improve the ones you have, or to prepare yourself for competition.

TRAINING DIFFERS FROM FITNESS EXERCISE in several ways. The first difference is the intensity of workouts. The goal of fitness exercise is to stay within the target heart rate range, usually at the lower end if you are just starting your fitness program. When training, one is often at the upper end of the target rate range and at times past it. The second difference is in the amount of time spent in muscular development. The American College of Sports Medicine recommends that muscular development exercises be performed two to three times per week, whether your objective is fitness or training. In a training program, improved strength and endurance is a critical goal. Thus, muscular development sets are usually more frequent and more extensive in a training program.

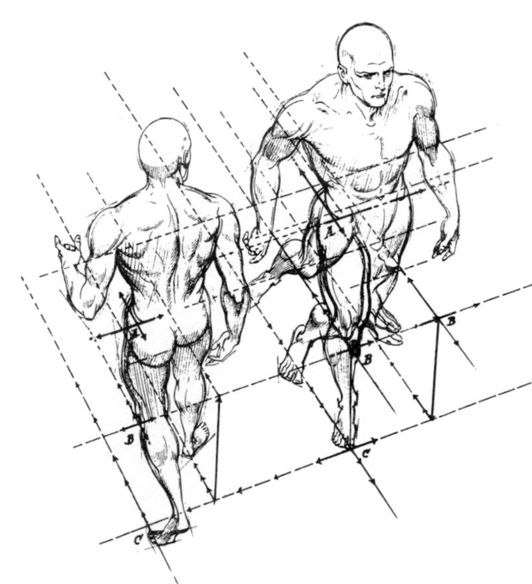

# PRACTICE

# PERFORMANCE

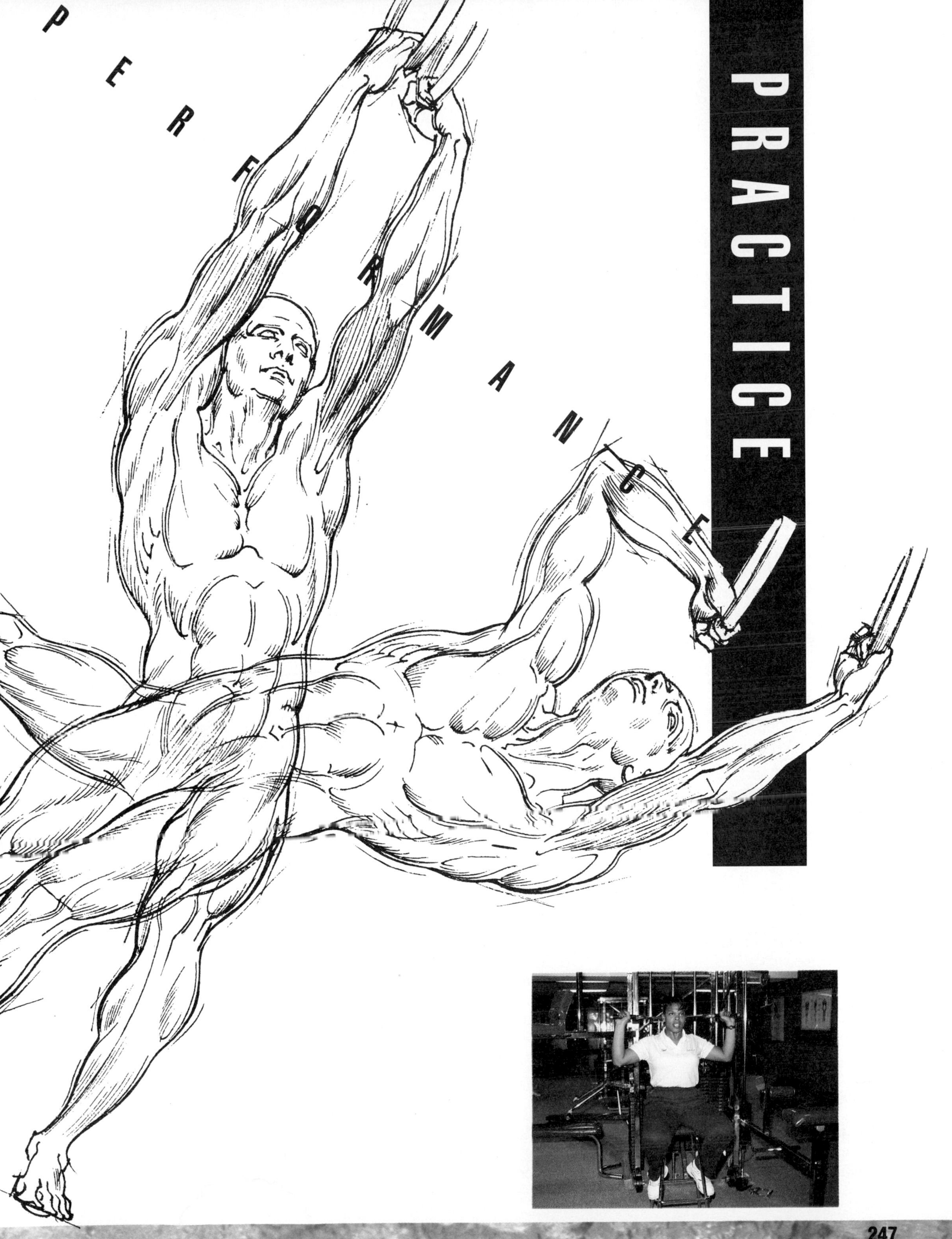

FIG. 11-1

## PRINCIPLES OF TRAINING

Your training program should follow certain principles to help you meet your goals. The next sections give you guidelines for any type of aerobic exercise, including aquatic exercise and fitness swimming.

### SPECIFICITY

The principle of ***specificity*** states that the benefits of exercise relate directly to the activity performed. Put another way, beyond the general benefits of exercise, there is very little transfer of effects from one kind of activity to another. For example, a runner who trains on the track will not have much improvement in swimming performance. Specific arm muscles do most of the work in swimming, while specific leg muscles are used in running. Still, both activities improve one's aerobic capacity.

The principle of specificity is important in two areas, the energy system used and the nerves and muscles exercised in a given activity. The following sections explain the importance for your training program.

### *Energy Systems*

Two major energy systems supply energy to the muscles. The **anaerobic** (without oxygen) **energy system** uses the most rapidly available source of energy—sugars and carbohydrates stored in the body—for muscular activity. The anaerobic energy system is the primary source of energy for ***anaerobic exercise*** (exercise at an intensity that oxygen is not supplied consistently). A person who is fit is usually exercising anaerobically if the heart rate is above the 85 percent level of intensity. For someone who is unfit or underfit, exercise may be anaerobic at an intensity much less than 85 percent. (For more information on target heart rate range as an indicator of intensity, see Chapter 10.)

For longer-lasting exercise, the **aerobic** (oxygen-using) **energy system** gives the muscles energy. This system breaks down carbohydrates, fats, and proteins for energy. The body uses this system for ***aerobic exercise*** (sustained, rhythmic, physical exercise that requires additional effort by the heart and lungs to meet the increased demand by the skeletal muscles for oxygen).

The specific energy system the body uses in an activity depends on how long and intense the activity is. The benefits of training depend on which energy system is being used. Improvements in the aerobic energy system need continuous, low- to moderate-intensity training. Improvements in the anaerobic energy system need high-intensity, short-duration training. For example, if you are training to improve your sprint performance, swimming repeated distances at low intensities is not effective (Fig. 11-1). Types of exercise can be located along a continuum such as below:

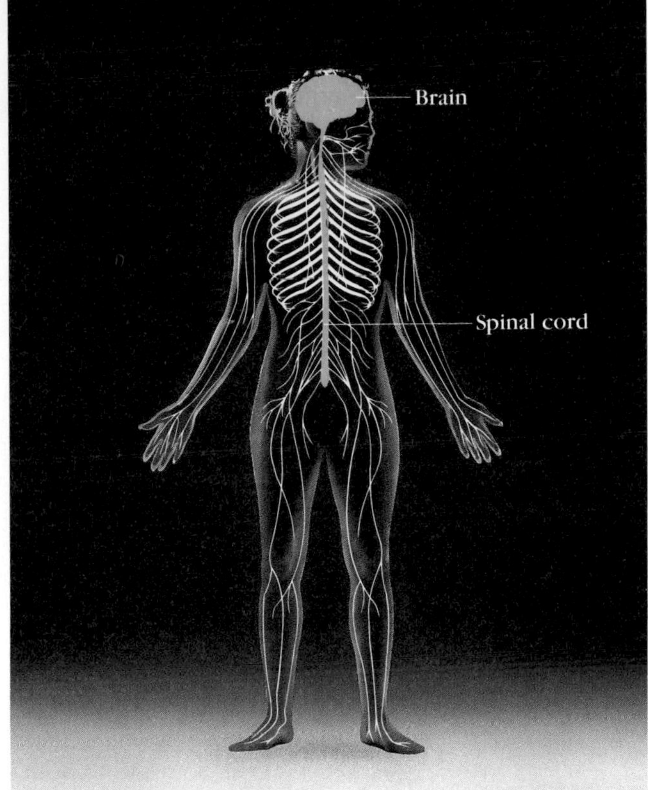


FIG. 11-2 The nervous system.

### *Neuromuscular Changes*

At the level of muscles and nerves, one should focus training on the patterns and speed of movements (Fig. 11-2). For example, if you are training for a backstroke event, you should train with the backstroke rather than the breaststroke. To improve the muscular strength of your upper body, you should exercise those muscle groups; you can do this by isolating them (using pull buoys in some exercises to concentrate on armstroke technique) or by using resistance training focused on the upper body.

Remember, training has the best results when the method conditions the appropriate energy system and uses a similar pattern and similar speed as the desired performance.

| Mostly aerobic (low to moderate intensity, long duration) | Mixture of aerobic and anaerobic exercise | Mostly anaerobic (high intensity, short duration) |
|---|---|---|
| Swimming | Recreational basketball | Sprints of any kind (running, swimming, cycling, etc.) |
| Aerobics or aquatic exercise | Racquetball | Field events in track competition |
| Distance running or walking | Weight training | |
| Distance cycling | Baseball or softball | |
| Cross-country skiing | Football | |
| Rowing | | |
| Water polo | | |
| Workouts on exercise equipment such as bikes and treadmills | | |

## Overload

The principle of ***overload*** states that a body system improves only if the system is regularly worked at loads greater than normal. For example, you can increase muscular strength by lifting weights, but the amount of weight must gradually increase if you want to continue increasing your strength. You can improve muscular endurance, on the other hand, by increasing the number of repetitions rather than the load. For example, you can lift the same amount of weight but use more repetitions.

Chapter 10 explains how you can adjust three factors to overload your whole body or specific muscle groups or systems. These are frequency, intensity, and time—the F.I.T. principle. You also learned that the simplest way to monitor exercise intensity is to keep track of your heart rate, which indicates how hard you are working. The way you *perceive* or *feel* how hard you are working also can be a reliable indicator of exercise intensity. (See "Rate of Perceived Exertion" in Chapter 10.)

## Progression

As your body adapts to any work load, you should gradually increase that level. You cannot improve more unless the load is raised above the original overload. This principle of progression is shown in the phases of a fitness program in Chapter 10. This principle also affects how an athlete designs the training season (see pages 254-256).

## Stroke Length and Stroke Frequency

An obvious training goal for competitive swimmers is to improve speed. To do this, two concepts are involved. ***Stroke length*** is the distance traveled in one complete cycle of the arms: from the time the hand enters the water, through the pull phase, to exit and reentry. To determine stroke length, count the cycles it takes to swim a known distance, then divide that distance by the number of strokes. ***Stroke frequency*** is the number of complete arm cycles in a specified length of time. To determine stroke frequency, count the cycles you swim in a known amount of time, then divide the number of cycles by the number of seconds. For example, a swimmer covers 50 meters in 25 seconds with 25 arm strokes:

$$\text{Stroke Length} = \frac{\text{distance stroked}}{\text{number of cycles}}$$

$$\text{Stroke Length} = \frac{\text{50 meters}}{25}$$

$$\text{Stroke Length} = \text{2.0 meters/cycle}$$

$$\text{Stroke Frequency} = \frac{\text{number of cycles}}{\text{time}}$$

$$\text{Stroke Frequency} = \frac{25}{25}$$

$$\text{Stroke Frequency} = \text{1 cycle/second}$$

Speed is the product of stroke length and stroke frequency:

$$\text{Speed} = \text{stroke length} \times \text{stroke frequency}$$

Using the above example, speed would be:

$$\text{Speed} = \text{2 meters/cycle} \times \text{1 cycle/second}$$
$$\text{Speed} = \text{2 meters/second}$$

To increase your speed, you need a corresponding increase in stroke length and/or stroke frequency. You can increase speed efficiently by improving your stroke to get greater distance from each stroke while not increasing the number of cycles per second. If, on the other hand, the stroke length stays the same and you increase your stroke frequency, you use more energy to reach the same speed. Thus, the ideal is to increase speed while decreasing stroke frequency.

Mike Barrowman holds the world record in the 200-meter breaststroke.

**Mike Barrowman**

*World-class swimmer Mike Barrowman, the 23-year-old University of Michigan graduate from Potomac, Maryland, set a new world record in the 200-meter breaststroke at the 1992 Olympic Games in Barcelona. Breaking records is not new to Barrowman; this was the sixth time he has recorded the world's fastest time in the event.*

*Barrowman's legacy in the 200-meter breaststroke began with the Phillips 66/USS Long Course Nationals in Austin, Texas, in August 1989 when he clocked in at 2:12.90. Since then, he has whittled away at his record-breaking time, first by knocking off .01 second at the 1989 Pan Pacific Championships in Tokyo, then by slicing off another .36 second at the 1990 Goodwill Games in Seattle, Washington. He did it again in January 1991 at the World Championships in Perth, Australia, lowering the record by another .30 second. His fourth record-smashing performance was in August 1991 at the National Championships in Ft. Lauderdale, Florida, where he clipped an astounding .63 second off his Perth record. The new record, set at Barcelona, is 2:10.16, a reduction of .44 second.*

*What are the keys to Barrowman's record-shattering performance? The answer is two-fold. For one thing, no one spends more time in the pool than Barrowman. When he finished in a disappointing fourth place in the 1988 Olympics, he vowed to train harder than ever and has won 16 of 17 races in the 200-meter event since.*

*The other component of his success is the unusual "wave action" technique he learned from his Hungarian coach, Joszef Nagy. Based on the laws of physics, this technique calls for the swimmer's head, arms, back, rear, and legs to lie along a straight line, streamlined. This enables the swimmer to maintain a position of least resistance. The pull is wide and is used only to move the body forward, rather than to lift the body up. The arms are used primarily for sculling. The hands are turned out. During the kick, the shoulders, hips, and knees lie in a straight line. The result is that the swimmer undulates through the water, saving time and energy. With this "wave action" breaststroke, along with dry land exercises developed specifically for this method of swimming, Barrowman has raised the stroke to such perfection that, for him, the only question is how many more world records he will set, only to break them again.*

## TRAINING TECHNIQUES

The following are several training techniques that you can use in your workouts to meet specific fitness and training goals. You can use them alone or in combination. The distances you swim, the time it takes you to swim them, and the duration of rest periods depend on various factors, such as the time you have for training, your training goals, and the observations of your coach or trainer, if you have one. Using different techniques also adds variety to your workouts.

FIG. 11-3

**OVER DISTANCE.** This method involves swimming long distances with moderate exertion with short or no rest periods (Fig. 11-3). The progressions in Chapter 10 are a good example. Over-distance training is used to improve your endurance. Your heart rate stays in the low to middle level of the target range for the whole swim. You can also use this for a warm-up activity.

**FARTLEK.** This method gets its name from the Swedish word that means "speed play" and was popularized by runners. It breaks swims into slow and fast lengths of the pool, using the same stroke. It can make long swims more interesting and is good for developing speed and endurance at the same time.

FIG. 11-4

**INTERVAL SETS.** This is one of the most common swimming training methods. Intervals are a series of repeat swims of the same distance and time interval (Fig. 11-4). They give you a specific rest period between the time spent swimming.

An example of an interval set is "8 × 100 on 1:30." The first number represents the number of times you repeat the distance. The second number (100 in this case) is the distance of each swim in yards or meters, and the 1 minute and 30 seconds is the total amount of time for the swim and rest. If you swim the 100 in 1:15, you have 15 seconds to rest. This short rest period keeps your heart rate within the target range without dropping back to your resting rate. Used primarily in the main set of a workout, interval swimming is the best all-around method to develop both speed and endurance.

**REPETITION.** This technique uses swim sets of the same distance done at close to maximum effort (up to 90 percent of maximum), but with rest periods as long as or longer than your swim time. Repetition sets develop your speed and anaerobic capacity. This training method is used after you have developed a good aerobic base. It is usually used after the aerobic set as a muscular development set.

**SPRINTS.** These are short, fast swims (100 percent effort) to simulate race conditions. The rest between sprints is usually long enough to let the heart return to its resting rate. Like repetition swims, sprints improve your anaerobic capacity.

**STRAIGHT SETS.** With this method you swim at a steady speed throughout the set. Monitoring your time helps you keep an even pace. This method is often used by distance swimmers.

**NEGATIVE SPLIT SETS.** Negative-splitting involves swimming the second half of each swim period faster than the first half. For example, if you swim 200 yards four times, the second 100 should be faster than the first 100 in each repetition.

**DESCENDING SETS.** Often confused with negative splitting, descending sets refers to decreasing the time on successive swims. To swim 200 yards four times in a descending set, each 200 would be faster than the 200 preceding it.

**LADDERS.** Ladders are several swims with regular increases or decreases in distance. For example, you swim a 25, then a 50, and finally a 75.

**PYRAMIDS.** A pyramid is a swim of regular increases and decreases in distance. For example, you swim a 25, then a 50, then a 75, then a 50, and finally a 25. A variation of both pyramids and ladders is to increase the number of times you repeat the distance as the distances get shorter, for example, 1 x 500, 2 x 400, 3 x 300, 4 x 200, and 5 x 100.

**BROKEN SWIMS.** Broken swims are timed swims that are faster than your racing speed and are interrupted by short periods of rest (for example, 10 seconds). Such a swim is followed by a long rest. On completing the entire swim, you subtract the total time of rest from the final time to determine your swimming time. Broken swims are a highly motivating method of training because they simulate stress conditions of competition while yielding a swimming time that may be faster than your racing time for an actual event. Broken swims are often combined with other variations, such as negative splits and descending swims.

FIG. 11-5, *A-C* Dry land training options: *A,* stretch cords, *B,* swim bench, and *C,* weight training.

## DRY LAND TRAINING

**D**ry land training is the use of training techniques done out of the water to improve swimming skills. These techniques fall into two areas, flexibility and strength training. Done properly, resistance training builds both strength and flexibility (Fig. 11-5, *A-C*). A half hour of resistance training 3 days a week, combined with 15 minutes of stretching, can produce favorable results. While most coaches prefer dry land training before a swimming workout, you can do it before or after your swim, depending on your schedule. (For more information on resistance training, including safety precautions, see Chapter 10.)

## THE TRAINING SEASON

In general, there are two competitive swimming seasons. The short course season for 25-yard pools usually runs from September to May; the long course season for 50-meter pools, from June to August.

For either season, your training should follow three phases to culminate at your goal, the competitive event. These phases are individually set, based on your goals. The phase of training determines the type of workouts. The following is a description of each training phase of the swimming season, along with suggested workouts to help you train effectively.

### EARLY SEASON PHASE

About 6 to 8 weeks long, this phase focuses on general conditioning to build a foundation for the whole season. Long, easy swims using various strokes help build endurance. Swim at a slower rate and make needed changes to your stroke technique, flip turns, and breathing pattern. Supplementing your swimming with dry land exercise helps to improve strength, flexibility, and cardiovascular conditioning.

### MID-SEASON PHASE

In this phase, which is about 8 to 12 weeks long, start to tailor your training to your specific goals. Your workouts increase in distance, and you pay more attention to fine tuning your strokes (Fig. 11-6). Quality is the emphasis of the workout. Use dry land training at maintenance level during this time.

### TAPER PHASE

The ***taper phase*** is the last and shortest part of your training, usually lasting 1 to 3 weeks. As the date you have set for your peak performance draws near, decrease the distances you swim but raise the intensity almost to your racing speed. Do this by resting more between sets and by using broken swims and descending sets. Practice your starts and turns to improve your technique. The specifics of the taper phase depend on the individual and the length and time of training in the earlier phases. For example, sprinters usually taper for 2 to 3 weeks, while distance swimmers taper for about 5 to 10 days.

FIG. 11-6 Tethered swimming is one method of fine tuning your stroke techniques.

INTERNATIONAL SWIMMING HALL OF FAME
INTERNATIONAL SWIMMING
HALL OF FAME AQUATIC COMPLEX
POOL HOURS 10:00 - 4:00
TIME IS 346
PACE CLOCK 1655
AMERICAN AIRLINES
OFFICIAL AIRLINE OF ISHOF
Alamo Rent A Car

## Sample Training Workouts

The following workouts are divided into the three phases. They include samples of over distance, fartlek, interval, and sprints.

**Early Season**

| | |
|---|---|
| Warm-up | 4 × 200 swim/pull/kick/swim |
| Main set | 800 maintain even pace at 100's |
| | 1,650 broken swim with 15 seconds rest after each interval |
| | 1 × 500 |
| | 1 × 400 |
| | 1 × 300 |
| | 1 × 200 |
| | 1 × 100 |
| | 1 × 75 |
| | 1 × 50 |
| | 1 × 25 |
| Cool-down | 200 easy swim |

**Mid-Season**

| | |
|---|---|
| Warm-up | 8 × 100 alternating between swimming and kicking |
| Main set | 5 × 200 broken swims on 4:00 with 10 seconds rest at each break |
| | 1 × 100 |
| | 2 × 50 |
| | 5 × 300, swim first 200, kick last 100; rest 15 seconds between swims |
| Cool-down | 12 × 50 on 1:00 |

**Taper Phase**

| | |
|---|---|
| Warm-up | 300 easy swim |
| | 6 × 50 descending set on 2:00 |
| Main set | 4 × 100 broken swims on 3:00 with 20 seconds rest at each break |
| | 2 × 50 |
| Cool-down | 200 easy swim |
| | starts and turns |

## Tips for Your First Meet

So you've decided to test your skills by entering a ***swim meet.*** To find out about local meets, contact your local pool or swim team or get in touch with one of the organizations discussed in Chapter 12. They can help you find a local organization that sponsors meets. You can usually get a meet information sheet with lists of events, deadlines, and other information.

Look over information about the meet carefully. Complete the entry form, and don't forget any entry fees or deadlines. If you are in a club or on a team, your coach may send in all the registrations together. Choose which events you feel comfortable to enter, and check that they are spaced far enough apart for you to rest in between. Make a list of your events and when they occur in the meet. You will feel enough anxiety without having to remember where you're supposed to be and when. During the meet, if you need more rest or are not ready for an event, you can change your mind even after you've entered. Just let the officials know you won't be participating.

At your first meet, you might feel unsure of yourself. Almost everyone feels the jitters, so don't be surprised if you feel a few "butterflies in your stomach" or if you can't sleep the night before. Use the checklist at right to help you remember what to bring.

## Items to Bring to a Swim Meet

- Swimming suits. Since it's no fun sitting around in a wet suit, bring more than one. Change into a dry suit after warm-ups and your events.
- Swim cap (if you wear one). An extra one is handy in case yours rips.
- Goggles. A spare pair or strap is a good idea.
- Towels. Bring at least two, the larger the better.
- Warm clothes. To keep from getting chilled between events, wear a sweat suit, tee-shirt, and socks and shoes. If outdoors, bring a hat, sunglasses, or an umbrella to protect you from the sun.
- Toiletries. After the meet, you want to clean up, so don't forget the shampoo, soap, and lotions. For safety, use plastic bottles only. If the meet is outdoors, don't forget the sunscreen lotion.
- Lock. Keep your belongings safe in a locker.

Other items you may want to have along are pencil and paper to keep your own notes and records, a stopwatch, a beach chair, cooler, snack food, pain relief medication, cash, and a camera.

You have spent a lot of time training your body for competition, but it's also important to prepare your mind. Think positive. Meets are a way to evaluate your training and performance so you may be able to set new goals for the next season. Moreover, you can help your body perform by "rehearsing" the event mentally again and again. To build self-confidence, think about the things you do well.

When you get to the pool, check in with the meet organizers to let them know you're there and to verify the events you have entered. This information should be listed on the heat sheet, usually posted in a window, on a bulletin board, or on a table. Look for a crowd of swimmers.

Some events are divided into ***heats***. This is done when there are more competitors than there are lanes in the pool. At such times, entrants are organized into several groupings (e.g., eight competitors at a time if the pool has eight lanes). Depending on the organization of the meet, the winner may be the person who swims the fastest time in his or her heat, or the fastest swimmers from several heats match each other in a final heat.

Now it is time to warm up. Find a lane with people swimming about the same speed as you. Do not dive into the warm-up pool; ease into the pool from the edge or jump feetfirst. Pay attention to others in the lane. As you swim a few laps, loosen up. Practice the strokes you'll be swimming. The warm-up should raise your pulse rate. As you warm up, orient yourself to the pool. Get used to the targets on the wall and find out if the wall is slippery. If you are swimming the backstroke, check to see if the flags are the same number of strokes from the wall. If you are not used to the starting blocks, get up on one to judge the distance to the water. You might be more comfortable starting from the deck or in the water.

During the race, swim at a constant pace. Use your first few strokes to establish your pace and stroke rhythm. Stay mentally alert during the race by focusing on whatever actions—such as turns—you had to work hard on to get right. Try to get someone to time your **splits** (segments of a race) during the race. This will help you analyze your race performance. You can use the data you collect now as a standard for setting your next goal.

After the race, stay in the water until your body cools down and your pulse returns to normal. You can do some easy laps, bob, scull, or float. Review your race. If your time was not as good as you hoped, remember you will have another chance. The important thing is to have fun while you improve your health.

## Training for Open Water Competition

Triathlons and cross-training techniques have led more and more people to open water competitions (Fig. 11-7). Open water swimmers need to consider the psychological and physical differences of open water. A swimmer may feel fear of being disoriented, of hazards in open water (rocks, sandbars, bites and stings from marine life), or of being overpowered by the water. The fear itself is probably more dangerous than the actual situation. Staying calm, knowing your limits, and using the techniques discussed below will help you cope with tense moments.

Anytime you swim in open water you may be at risk for **hypothermia.** This life-threatening situation happens when the body loses so much heat that the core temperature drops below normal. Be alert to the possibility of hypothermia if the water temperature is below 70 degrees F (21 degrees C). Temperatures below 60 degrees F (15 degrees C) pose an immediate threat of hypothermia. Constant shivering is an important warning signal. An even more critical signal is loss of judgment, which can quickly worsen the effects of the cold.

Following certain precautions helps prevent hypothermia. First, practice in cold water. Repeated exposure to cold water acclimates the body. Second, insulate yourself. Most heat is lost through the head. Wearing multiple swim caps or a neoprene swim cap helps hold the heat in. You can also purchase a body suit or vest to insulate your body (Fig. 11-8, *A-C*).

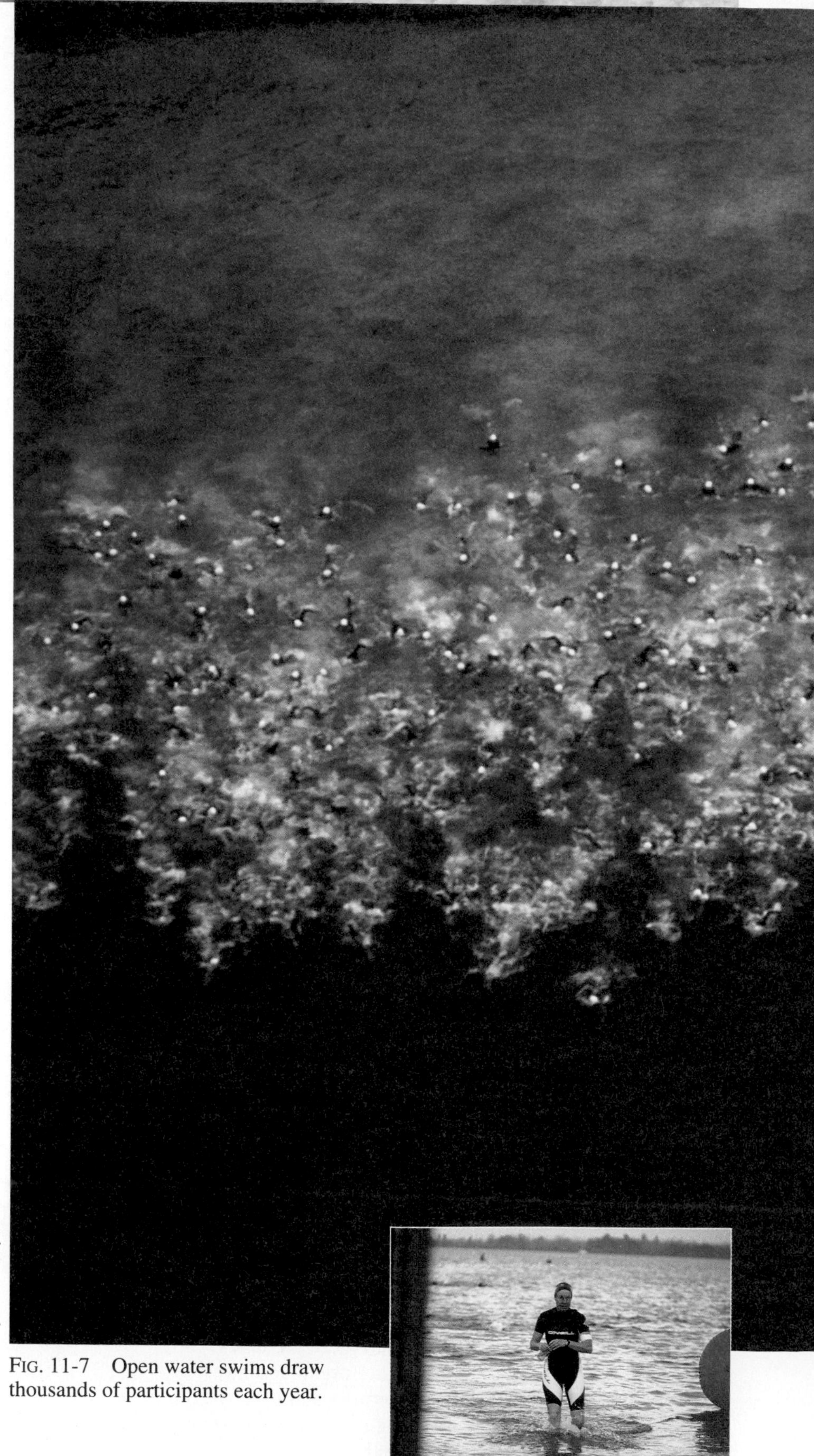

*Allsport USA/Vandystat*

Fig. 11-7 Open water swims draw thousands of participants each year.

A

Fig. 11-8, *A-C* Wet suits are available in a variety of styles.

B
C

### Cross-Training—Triathlon

*In the past, cross-training was defined as the principle that a power-producing effect results from exercising one body part while keeping another stationary. The inactive part becomes noticeably stronger. For instance, if one forearm is immobilized in a cast, regularly squeezing a small rubber ball with the other hand will increase the strength of the immobilized forearm.*

*The benefits of such a program are clear. The stress on the bones, muscles, and tendons used primarily in one sport is markedly reduced because the person uses different muscle groups in the other sport(s). In addition to strengthening the different muscle groups, the cross-trainer diminishes the risk of injury as well. An added benefit of cross-training, of course, is the fun involved in multiple sports.*

*For today's fitness expert, however, cross-training means combining several fitness components to maintain optimal health. This includes stretching to warm up and cool down the musculoskeletal system, reducing the risk of injury; resistance and/or weight training to increase strength; and aerobic endurance activities to improve cardiovascular fitness. Also included is a diet rich in nutrients to meet daily requirements.*

*Sports enthusiasts bring an additional meaning to the definition of cross-training. Cross-training is a method of exercising so that the effects of training in one sport enhance the effects in another. Simply put, it combines two or more aerobic endurance sports into one training program.*

*Triathlons are increasingly popular cross-training competitions. In general, a triathlon could be a race combining any three sports done consecutively, such as kayaking, cycling, and running. However, the most frequent configuration is swimming, bicycling, and running, in that order. Triathlons began in the 1970s. Many races sprang up across the country as fund-raising events or extensions of biathlons combining biking and running or biking and swimming.*

*The best known triathlon is the Ironman Triathlon World Championship held in Kona, Hawaii. It is a 2.4-mile swim, a 112-mile bike ride, and a 26.2-mile run. Worldwide, it is considered the premier endurance event. Each contestant completes each event individually.*

*However, a triathlon can also be a relay competition. Three teammates compete, each doing one leg of the race. It can also be organized as a stage-event triathlon, in which each sport has a set start and finish time, possibly on different days.*

*Competing in the three events of any triathlon is an example of what can be achieved through cross-training: total body fitness. This requires full development of motor skills, muscular strength, and cardiovascular fitness. It also involves all the ingredients of maintaining optimal health.*

## Training in the Pool

Training for open water is much like training for a long-distance swim. Train in the longest pool available or swim around the perimeter of the pool. The fewer turns you take, the more carryover you will have for your event.

Practice taking your goggles off and putting them on in the deep end without the support of the pool bottom or sides. Also practice the proper methods for releasing a cramp in deep water. (See Chapter 2.) If you can practice this in the pool, do so. It's safer to plan ahead.

## Training in Open Water

For better or for worse, the best way to train for open water swimming is by doing it. Never swim alone; swim with a partner or ask the lifeguard to keep an eye on you. Be aware of certain characteristics of open water. Open water is never as calm as the roughest, most crowded pool. To combat roughness, recover your elbows higher and roll your shoulders more to keep from catching them on the waves.

Getting off course can be a problem in open water. How do you swim in a straight line? By looking. You lift your head after you breathe and before putting your face back in the water. Practice this in the pool before venturing out into open water. Alternating breathing (breathing on each side) or having a friend paddle alongside in a boat also will help you swim in a straight line.

775
764

Allsport USA/Vandystat

## The Event Itself

The start of any open water event is usually chaotic (Fig. 11-9). Races with a lot of swimmers often use staggered starts, so you will be asked to position yourself. Be honest and smart. If you are unsure of your time, start among swimmers of moderate ability. If you are too far forward for your ability, you will be in the way as better swimmers climb over and go around you. Staying to the side of the pack means you may swim slightly farther to get on course, but you will avoid the jumble of swimmers in a mass start. In most events, you have to wear a provided swimming cap. For safety, many meets use color-coded caps based on age or ability. If you are unsure of your ability, request a cap color to alert the lifeguards. If you drop out of an open water event, you must immediately notify the course officials so that everyone is accounted for at the end of the race.

## Summary

Training takes more time, effort, and planning than fitness swimming or aquatic exercise, but the rewards are greater. Health benefits include cardiovascular endurance, muscular strength, flexibility, and weight management. The guidelines here can help you develop a training program to meet your needs. For a fitness program, see Chapter 10. Chapter 12 gives information about opportunities for competition.

Fig. 11-9

12

# CHAPTER

# competitive ACTIVITIES

## Key Terms

**Figures:** In synchronized swimming, movements in the water composed of basic positions and transitions from one position to another.

**Freestyle:** A competitive event that allows any stroke, although the front crawl is generally used.

**Freestyle relay:** A common competitive event in which each member of a four-member team swims any stroke one quarter of the total distance.

**Individual medley:** An event in which the competitor swims one quarter of the total distance using a different competitive stroke in a prescribed order (butterfly, backstroke, breaststroke, freestyle).

**Masters:** A classification in some organizations for swimmers 19 years old and older and divers 21 years old and older.

**Medley relay:** A competitive event in which each member of a four-member team swims one quarter of the total distance and then is relieved by a teammate. The first uses a backstroke start and swims the backstroke, the second swims the breaststroke, the third swims the butterfly, and the fourth swims freestyle.

**Synchronized swimming:** A rhythmical water activity performed in patterns in time with music.

**Triathlon:** A sporting event made up of three different activities, usually swimming, biking, and running, in that order.

# Objectives

***After reading this chapter, you should be able to—***

1. Describe opportunities for competition in each of these sports:
   a. Swimming
   b. Diving
   c. Triathlon
   d. Synchronized swimming
   e. Water polo

2. Describe the benefits of competition for participants.
3. Define the key terms at left.

FIG. 12-1

NOW THAT YOU ARE SWIMMING, you may be interested in other ways to enjoy aquatics. The world of competitive activities has many possibilities for you to explore, regardless of your age.

THE FITNESS BENEFITS OF SWIMMING are described in detail in Chapter 10 and the principles of training in Chapter 11. Both types of benefits are increased even more in competitive aquatics. The discipline of following a program for a whole season strengthens the "training effect" for anyone who swims to keep fit (see Chapter 10). Competition also lets you gauge your progress by the variety of events in which you compete or the number of meets you enter. You might even win some medals.

IMPROVING YOUR FITNESS and achieving personal goals helps you feel better about yourself. Whether you compete against friends or strangers or merely try for a personal best time, seeing your progress adds to your sense of achievement. Of course it's also a great feeling to finish ahead of a person or a team that has beaten you in the past! You will even feel better about yourself when you are recognized as a fair and friendly competitor or when you know you have achieved certain goals, regardless of how you finish in a competition.

FINALLY, TEAM COMPETITION gives social benefits (Fig. 12-1). You might already swim with friends regularly, but training and competing with a club or team leads to friendships with strong bonds. You also have the chance to meet—and come to respect—a broad range of competitors whom you might not know otherwise. You come to admire others for their endurance, skill, or form, and you will receive compliments yourself. All these benefits increase your motivation to keep practicing and to "try, try again" in competition.

COMPETITION IS ALSO OPEN TO PEOPLE with disabilities. Depending on the skill level, a person with a disability may compete against the nondisabled or in events held specifically for people with disabilities. (For organizations that sponsor such events, see Appendix A.)

COMPETITIVE SWIMMING IS AN INTERNATIONAL SPORT and a lifetime recreational activity for everyone. Whole families are often involved for many years. Diving, water polo, and synchronized swimming also are

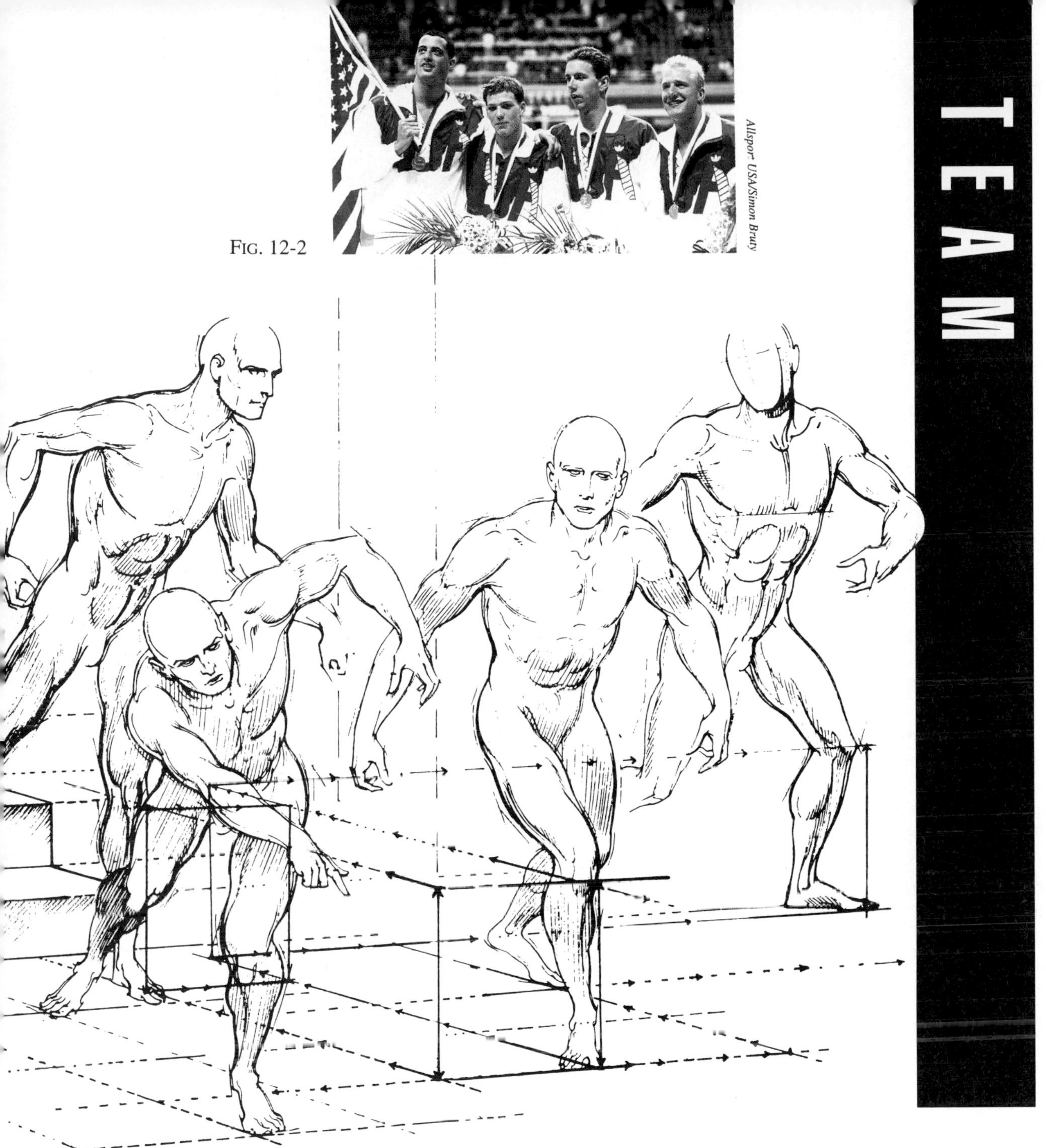

Allsport USA/Simon Bruty

Fig. 12-2

important in the world of aquatics. These three sports have enthusiastic participants from novices to Olympic competitors (Fig. 12-2).

THE ***TRIATHLON*** HAS ONLY RECENTLY DEVELOPED as a competitive sport, but many new participants join each year. The event is made up of three different activities, usually swimming, biking, and running, in that order. Triathlons often start with an open water swim.

**R**EGARDLESS OF HOW DEEPLY YOU ARE INTERESTED or involved in competitive activities, this chapter might whet your appetite to join in or at least to become a more educated spectator.

## Competitive Swimming

You can engage in competitive swimming in various settings, usually related to your age, school affiliation, or ability. Several organizations promote and conduct swimming events. One or more of the organizations described below offer programs that meet your needs. Some organizations are more prominent in certain geographical regions than others.

### United States Swimming

United States Swimming, Inc. (USS), is the national governing body for amateur competitive swimming in the United States. USS was founded in 1980, based on the passage in 1978 of the Amateur Sports Act, which specified that all Olympic sports would be administered independently. Before this act, USS was the Competitive Swimming Committee of the Amateur Athletic Union (AAU). As the national governing body, USS conducts and administers competitive swimming in the United States. USS makes rules, implements policies and procedures, conducts national championships, gives out safety and sports medicine information, and selects athletes to represent the United States in international competition. USS is organized on three levels:

- International. The international federation for amateur aquatic sports is the Federation Internationale de Natation Amateur (FINA). USS is affiliated with FINA through United States Aquatic Sports (USAS), which regulates the four aquatic sports of swimming, synchronized swimming, diving, and water polo.
- National. USS is a Group A member of the United States Olympic Committee (USOC) and has voting representation in the USOC House of Delegates.
- Local. Within the United States, USS is divided into 59 Local Swimming Committees (LSCs), each one administering USS activities in a specific geographical area. Each LSC has its own bylaws for local operations. There are currently 2,400 swim clubs with 20,000 nonathlete members (parents, officials, administrators, coaches), 170,000 year-round athlete members, and 25,000 seasonal athletes (4 months/year).

Fig. 12-3

USS has the following classifications for competitions:

- Senior—for all registered swimmers
- Junior—for all registered swimmers 18 years of age and younger
- Age Group/Junior Olympic—for all registered swimmers grouped by the following ages:
  - — 10 and under
  - — 11-12
  - — 13-14
  - — either 15-16 and 17-18 or 15-18

  An 8-and-under age group competition may be conducted.
- Post Age Group—for all registered swimmers older than 18 years of age whom an LSC elects to include in its age group program
- ***Masters***—for all swimmers 19 years of age and older who register with United States Masters Swimming (see page 270)
- Long Distance—for all registered swimmers

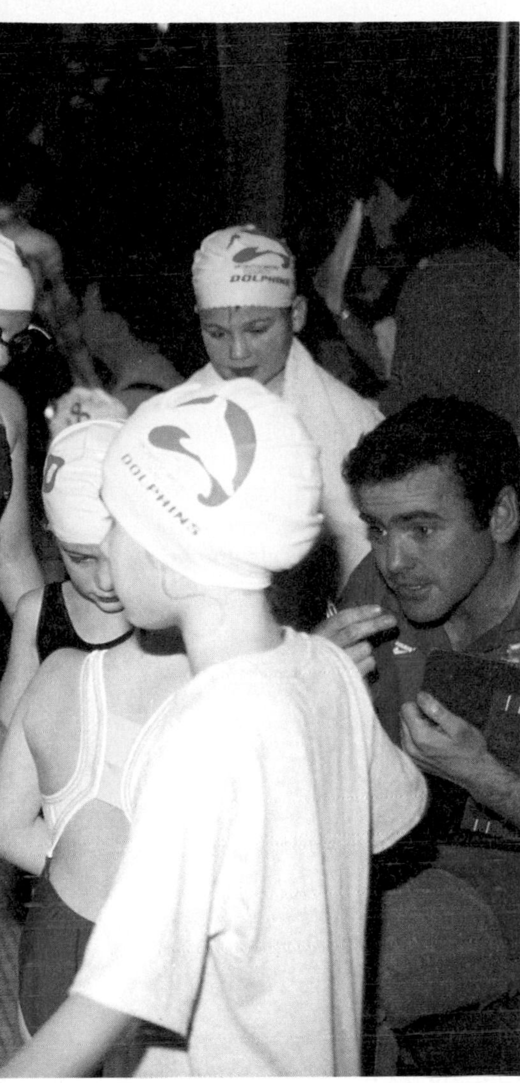

In USS, as in other organizations that promote competitive swimming, athletes learn about perseverance and determination, goal setting and achievement, dedication, loyalty, and commitment. Each swimmer is a valuable part of the team, and swimmers learn cooperation with teammates and adults. Above all, they learn that competitive swimming is fun (Fig. 12-3).

Coaching and officiating opportunities, paid and volunteer, are available at all levels of USS. Contact your LSC or USS for details.

The national headquarters of United States Swimming is located at the Olympic Training Center, 1750 E. Boulder Street, Colorado Springs, CO 80909, (719) 578-4578.

**Events in a Swim Meet**

*The following table gives typical swimming events grouped by age for swimmers up to age 18. The actual events held in a meet depend on the sponsoring organization.*

| Age | Distance* | Stroke |
|---|---|---|
| 10 and under | 50 | Freestyle |
| | 100 | Freestyle |
| | 100 | Individual medley |
| | 50 | Backstroke |
| | 50 | Breaststroke |
| | 50 | Butterfly |
| | 200 | Freestyle relay |
| | 200 | Medley relay |
| 11-12 | 50 | Freestyle |
| | 100 | Freestyle |
| | 200 | Individual medley |
| | 50 | Backstroke |
| | 50 | Breaststroke |
| | 50 | Butterfly |
| | 200 | Freestyle relay |
| | 200 | Medley relay |
| 13-14 | 50 | Freestyle |
| | 100 | Freestyle |
| | 200 | Freestyle |
| | 200 | Individual medley |
| | 100 | Backstroke |
| | 100 | Breaststroke |
| | 100 | Butterfly |
| | 400 | Freestyle relay |
| | 400 | Medley relay |
| 15-16 | 50 | Freestyle |
| | 100 | Freestyle |
| | 200 | Freestyle |
| | 200 | Individual medley |
| | 100 | Backstroke |
| | 100 | Breaststroke |
| | 100 | Butterfly |
| | 400 | Freestyle relay |
| | 400 | Medley relay |
| 17-18 | 50 | Freestyle |
| | 100 | Freestyle |
| | 200 | Freestyle |
| | 200 | Individual medley |
| | 400 | Individual medley |
| | 100 | Backstroke |
| | 100 | Breaststroke |
| | 100 | Butterfly |
| | 400 | Freestyle relay |
| | 400 | Medley relay |

*May be yards or meters.

**International Center for Aquatic Research**

*United States Swimming, the national governing body for the sport of swimming, is committed to enhancing performance at all levels of competition. Thus, an extensive Sports Medicine and Science Program was established to deliver programs to (1) enhance technical instruction and (2) help athletes determine effective training techniques that lead to faster swimming.*

*The centerpiece of this program is United States Swimming's International Center for Aquatic Research at the U.S. Olympic Training Center in Colorado Springs. This $3 million facility represents U.S. Swimming's investment in and commitment to the development of swimmers. With its state-of-the-art medical, scientific, and technological equipment, the Center uses the rapid collection and analysis of information to help identify and nurture the talents of athletes.*

*The Center includes laboratories that conduct research on specific factors affecting performance. As a whole, the Center has programs in three areas: (1) research in the area of human performance, (2) service for testing and evaluating athletes, and (3) education for coaches, athletes, and sports practitioners on how to apply principles of science and medicine to enhance performance.*

## United States Masters Swimming

United States Masters Swimming (USMS) is an umbrella organization with responsibility and authority over the Masters Swimming Program in the United States. Through its 55 local Masters Swimming Committees and more than 450 local Masters swim clubs, USMS offers competitive swimming to 28,000 swimmers 19 years of age and older.

Competitions are organized by age groups of 5-year (and one 6-year) spans (19-24, 25-29, 30-34, etc., to 95 and over). Events include 50, 100, 200, 500, 1,000, and 1,650 ***freestyle*** (400, 800, and 1,500 in meters); 50, 100, and 200 backstroke, breaststroke, and butterfly; and 100, 200, and 400 ***individual medley*** (an event in which each quarter of the total distance is swum using a different stroke in a prescribed order—butterfly, backstroke, breaststroke, freestyle). There are also ***freestyle*** and ***medley relays*** for men, women, and mixed teams. In a medley relay, each member of a four-member team swims one quarter of the total distance and then is relieved by a teammate. The first uses a backstroke start and swims the backstroke, the second swims the breaststroke, the third swims the butterfly, and the fourth swims freestyle. Open water swims are held in many locations in the summer, ranging from 1 to 10 miles.

Masters Swimming's credo is fun, fitness, and competition (Fig. 12-4). Masters swimmers enjoy the

*Courtesy of Karl Maley*

Fig. 12-4

Courtesy of Karl Maley

FIG. 12-5

benefits of swimming with an organized group, participating in structured workouts, and developing friendships with other adult swimmers. Members participate in a wide range of activities from noncompetitive lap swimming to international competition. Socializing at meets is another reason that Masters Swimming is popular.

Coaching and officiating opportunities, paid and volunteer, are available at all levels of USMS. Contact your local Masters Swimming club or USMS for details.

The national headquarters of United States Masters Swimming is located at 2 Peter Avenue, Rutland, MA 01543, (508) 886-6631.

### YMCA COMPETITIVE SWIMMING AND MASTERS SWIMMING

YMCA Competitive Swimming trains individuals of all ages to compete in YMCA programs that may lead to **cluster,** field, and national championships. More than 800 YMCAs offer age group competitive swimming to more than 50,000 boys and girls (Fig. 12-5). YMCA age group competition is organized at four levels:

- Interassociation meets
- Cluster, league, and district championships
- State or field championships
- National championships

Competition is organized in four age groups: 10 and under, 12 and under, 14 and under, and senior.

YMCA Masters Swimming is an age-grouped competitive program for adults, starting at age 20. Groups are divided by 5-year spans: 20-24, 25-29, 30-34, and so on, with no top age limit. Some YMCAs also sponsor competitive teams in springboard diving and synchronized swimming. YMCAs may register with U.S. Masters Swimming and represent the YMCA in regional and national competition.

The national headquarters of YMCA Competitive Swimming and Masters Swimming is located at the YMCA of the U.S.A., Oakbrook Square, 6083-A Oakbrook Parkway, Norcross/Atlanta, GA 30093, (404) 662-5172.

### NATIONAL COLLEGIATE ATHLETIC ASSOCIATION

The National Collegiate Athletic Association (NCAA) is the organization for U.S. colleges and universities to speak and act on athletic matters at the national level. The NCAA is also the national athletics accrediting agency for collegiate competition.

Founded in 1905 when 13 schools formed the Intercollegiate Athletic Association of the United States, the NCAA has grown to over 1,000 member institutions. The NCAA enacts legislation on

FIG. 12-6 University of Texas women's swim team, 1991 NCAA Division I champions.

Courtesy of University of Texas Women's Athletics

nationwide issues, represents intercollegiate athletics before state and federal governments, compiles and distributes statistics, writes and interprets rules in 12 sports, conducts research on athletics problems, and promotes and participates in international sports planning and competition (in part through membership in the U.S. Olympic Committee).

The NCAA sponsors the following national championships:

- Division I Men's Swimming and Diving Championships
- Division I Women's Swimming and Diving Championships
- Division II Men's Swimming and Diving Championships
- Division II Women's Swimming and Diving Championships
- Division III Men's Swimming and Diving Championships
- Division III Women's Swimming and Diving Championships

There are over 16,000 participants in intercollegiate swimming and diving, with over 1,300 in the division championships (Fig. 12-6).

The national headquarters of the National Collegiate Athletic Association is located at 6201 College Boulevard, Overland Park, KS 66211-2422, (913) 339-1906.

## THE NATIONAL JUNIOR COLLEGE ATHLETIC ASSOCIATION

The National Junior College Athletic Association (NJCAA) was founded in 1937 to promote and supervise a national program of junior college sports and activities consistent with the educational objectives of junior colleges. The NJCAA interprets rules, sets standards for eligibility, promotes academics through the Academic All-American and Distinguished Academic All-American programs, publishes a monthly magazine, provides weekly polls, and distributes sport guides.

The NJCAA first sponsored track and field events, which drew participants only from California schools. Today, there are approximately 550 member institutions throughout the United States, ranging in enrollment size from 500 to 25,000 students. The NJCAA sponsors 28 national championships, 15 for men and 13 for women. At the Men's and Women's National Swimming and Diving Championships each year, the NJCAA presents All-American Awards, Swimmer/Diver of the Year Award, and Swimming/Diving Coach of the Year Award. Nearly 350 athletes, representing 35 teams, participate in aquatics.

The national headquarters of the National Junior College Athletic Association is located at 1825 Austin Bluffs Parkway, P.O. Box 7305, Colorado Springs, CO 80933-7305, (719) 590-9788.

## The National Federation of State High School Associations

The National Federation of State High School Associations consists of the High School Athletic Associations of the 50 states and the District of Columbia. Also affiliated are 10 Canadian Provinces, the Bermuda School Sports Federation, the Guam Interscholastic Activities Association, the Philippine Secondary School Athletic Association, the St. Croix Interscholastic Athletic Association, and the St. Thomas-St. John Interscholastic Athletic Association.

The federation began in Illinois in 1920 and is a service and regulatory organization for its members. It provides central record keeping, publishes rule books and a journal, and conducts conferences. It oversees over 30 interscholastic sports and lists swimming and diving among the 10 most popular sports. Over 8,000 high schools have registered swimming and diving teams with over 170,000 swimmers (Fig. 12-7). Its goal is to promote the educational value of interscholastic sports.

The headquarters of the National Federation of State High School Associations is located at 11724 Plaza Circle, P.O. Box 20626, Kansas City, MO 64195, (816) 464-5400.

## Local Options

When you are ready to try competitive swimming, finding a local team to join is usually easy. The lifeguard at your local pool can often give you information. Local swim clubs and public recreation departments often sponsor teams or rent space to teams. Many locations have outdoor pools with seasonal teams that welcome beginning competitors. Leagues group swimmers by skill level and often provide instruction. Many national caliber swimmers started as "summer" swimmers. As their love of the sport grew, they sought out more challenging teams.

Fig. 12-7

**Summer Swim Leagues**

*Are swim leagues popular? Just ask one of over 20,000 children 18 and under in the Washington, D.C., metropolitan area who swim in a league. They join a league for many reasons. Team swimming teaches discipline, builds character, and strengthens friendships. Belonging to a team is also a lot of fun. Most teams have their own cheers, banners, and team logos on suits and swimming caps. Some children paint their team's initials on their bodies with sun block, and a few have haircuts sporting their team emblem. They often hold pep rallies between practices and before meets. To encourage accomplishment and growth, meets are held between teams of equal ability.*

*Adults are also deeply involved in these leagues. Some parents wear team colors and monitor their children's performance with stopwatches. Others volunteer their time to coordinate league activities or to coach, although some teams have paid coaches. In northern Virginia, one league has been functioning for over 30 years.*

*Washington is perhaps a little different from some other urban areas. Because of the city's fabled heat, swimming is one of the few sports pursued in the summer. The area also has a great number of community pools, but no one knows whether the popularity of swimming has led to the increase in facilities or vice versa. Whether a league is sponsored by an association, a country club, or a municipal recreation department, everyone agrees that the water's fine. Many other cities also have strong programs of swim leagues for youths.*

## Competitive Diving

Competitive diving has grown rapidly in the past few years. Dives once considered difficult even on the 3-meter board are now done regularly on the 1-meter board. This progress results in part from technological advances in the way diving boards and stands are manufactured. Training has also improved with the use of trampolines and dry land diving facilities with overhead spotting belts, individualized weight training and flexibility programs, and improved coaching.

The unification of rules through the concerted efforts of United States Diving, the NCAA, and FINA has standardized requirements and equipment. As a result, training has also been standardized.

Competitive springboard diving is really a form of aerial acrobatics. The water eases the shock of landing, just as the net catches trapeze acrobats. Springboard diving can be as spectacular as it is challenging. It thrills the spectator as well as the performer.

Competitive diving combines the power of a gymnast with the grace of a dancer. Its challenge is overcoming forces of nature, spinning and twisting gracefully in the air before disappearing into the water. A well-balanced dive seems powerful and easy at the same time. When it is expertly timed and controlled, the springboard dive is a thrilling acrobatic feat.

Striving to become a good diver can also help you grow as a person. You will develop qualities such as self-discipline, confidence, poise, and persistence (Fig. 12-8).

Fig. 12-8

The challenges of competitive diving foster a sense of adventure, achievement, and self-esteem.

## United States Diving

United States Diving, Inc., is the national governing body of diving. United States Diving is a member of United States Aquatic Sports, Inc., the U.S. member of FINA. Current membership in United States Diving includes 10,000 registered athletes (about 5,500 women and 4,500 men) and 1,500 nonathlete members. United States Diving is organized into four programs:

- Junior Olympic—provides a developmental diving and physical fitness program for the youth of the United States and teaches fundamentals of diving and benefits of participation in competitions.
- Senior—further develops and identifies U.S. divers of national and international caliber to compete in National Championships, Olympic Games, World Championships, Pan American Games, and other national and international competition.
- International—exposes superior divers to the demands of international competition to better prepare them for world class competition and to offer a better understanding of other life-styles and cultures.
- Masters—provides a continuing physical fitness program for diving enthusiasts 21 years of age and older who no longer compete in the Senior program.

The goal of United States Diving is to help each athlete gain the physical, mental, emotional, and social benefits of its programs. All divers have the opportunity to realize the poise, maturity, grace, and strength inherent in diving and to reach their personal goals (Fig. 12-9). For some, satisfaction comes from knowing they have done their best; for others, it is international recognition. Coaching and officiating opportunities are available at all levels of United States Diving.

Fig. 12-9

The national headquarters of United States Diving is located at the Pan American Plaza, 201 S. Capitol Avenue, Suite 430, Indianapolis, IN 46225, (317) 237-5252.

The following organizations also promote diving:

- The YMCA
- The NCAA
- The National Federation of State High School Associations

These are described in the earlier section on competitive swimming.

**Components of a Competitive Dive**

*Competitive dives have grown in variety and intricacy over the past several decades. New combinations of skills are still being proposed to be used in competition. All dives, however, involve some combination of the following elements, although not all combinations are approved for competition—or even possible. (For more information on the terms below, see Chapter 8.)*

***Apparatus:*** *A dive may be made from a 1-meter or 3-meter springboard or from a platform that is 1, 3, 5, 7½, or 10 meters high.*

***Takeoff:*** *A diver may leave the apparatus facing forward (using an approach and hurdle from a springboard or a standing jump from a platform) or facing backward (using a backward press).*

***Somersaults:*** *Regardless of the takeoff, somersaults may be forward (with a rotation in the direction the diver is facing) or reverse (with the opposite rotation).*

***Body position:*** *The body may be in tuck, pike, or straight position.*

***Twists:*** *A twist is a rotation along the midline of the body, which is held straight during the twist. Twisting may be combined with somersaults in some dives.*

***Entry:*** *The entry may be headfirst or feet-first.*

*Depending on the combination of elements, each dive is assigned a degree of difficulty. Judges' evaluations are based on the approach, the elevation (whether the dive reaches an appropriate height), the execution, and the entry. A diver's score in competition is based on both the degree of difficulty of the dive and the judges' scores.*

FIG. 12-10

## TRIATHLON

Since the first known swim-bike-run triathlon was held in San Diego in 1974, the sport has grown tremendously. There are now an estimated 200,000 to 300,000 active triathletes in the United States. This sport has encouraged cross-training and led to technological improvements in clothing and equipment. Other sports have more recently been assembled into triathlons, including cross-country skiing, speed skating, and canoeing. Some events last several days.

Participants from age 15 to over 70 compete in 5-year age groups at regional, zone, and national levels. Some triathlons are team efforts. For beginners, completing the course is seen as a tremendous personal achievement (Fig. 12-10). Fitness enthusiasts engage in the sport to gain the benefits of cross-training. Some career triathletes compete as much as 25 times a year.

Part of the appeal of the triathlon is its variety. Doing three types of aerobic exercise can be much more challenging and rewarding than the same amount of exercise in one form. Because different sports use different muscle groups, training for and competing in a triathlon lead to greater overall fitness. Moreover, proficiency in one sport can make up for some weaknesses in another.

Most triathlons with a swimming component are held in open water (ocean, bay, tidal river, or lake). Salt water gives more buoyancy, but ocean waves and currents in bays or rivers can be a problem. Fresh water is easier on the taste buds but gives less buoyancy, and some muddy or grassy lake bottoms can be unpleasant.

## TRIATHLON FEDERATION/USA

Triathlon Federation/USA (Tri-Fed/USA), founded in 1982, is the national governing body for the sport of triathlon in the United States. It represents 27,500 registered athletes. The sport is also represented internationally by the International Triathlon Union. Advocates of the sport are working to have the triathlon included as an Olympic event. Tri-Fed/USA recognizes four categories of distance:

- Sprint. These events vary greatly, depending on local organizers, and are often called training triathlons. The national championship event is a 0.5-mile swim, 13.5-mile bike race, and 3-mile run.
- International. This category, also called "short course," uses the distances proposed for an Olympic event: 1.5-kilometer swim, 40-kilometer bike race, and 10-kilometer run.
- Long. With a 1.2-mile swim, 56-mile bike race, and 13.1-mile run, this category is half the ultra distance.
- Ultra. This category includes the world-famous Ironman race, first held in Hawaii, comprising a 2.4-mile swim, a 112-mile bike race, and a full 26.2-mile marathon.

About 2,000 triathlons are held in the United States each year. Three quarters are in the International distance category.

The national headquarters of Triathlon Federation/USA is located at 3595 E. Fountain Boulevard, Suite F-1, P.O. Box 15820, Colorado Springs, CO 80935-5820, (719) 597-9090.

## Synchronized Swimming

***Synchronized swimming*** is both a sport and an art form. This rhythmical water activity is performed in definite patterns in time with music. Duets, trios, and teams also perform in synchronization with each other (Fig. 12-11). Competition in synchro, as it is sometimes called, requires both figure and routine events. Routines are judged on technical merit and artistic expression. The combination of scores for figures and routines determines final placement.

Fig. 12-11

The term *synchronized swimming* was first used in a water show at the 1933 Chicago World's Fair. Before this, swimmers used floating patterns and transitions with minimal swimming in performances that were called water ballets.

The synchronized swimmer learns skills like those of the gymnast and dancer. The sport requires tremendous strength and endurance to give the appearance of graceful, effortless movement through the water. A synchronized swimming routine lasts 3½ to 5 minutes. The swimmer needs the same cardiorespiratory endurance as a middle-distance swimmer. The artistic quality of movement gives the sport great spectator appeal. Like dancers, synchronized swimmers move in specific directions to specific beats with a personal manner of presentation (Fig. 12-12).

Fig. 12-12

### Facilities and Equipment

A large, deep pool is best, but many aspects of synchro can be taught and enjoyed in any pool. A minimum depth of 8 feet is needed for good vertical descent. Clear water, a light-colored pool bottom, and good lighting enhance viewing.

The musical accompaniment may use any type of equipment at poolside. Underwater speakers are critical, and portable underwater speakers can be used in facilities without permanent equipment.

The swimmer's equipment includes a comfortable suit and nose clip. This clip squeezes the nostrils together to prevent water from entering the nose and sinuses.

### Strokes and Figures

The swimmer can modify the basic strokes in endless creative ways to enhance the routine's composition and appeal. Many strong swimmers are attracted to synchronized swimming because of the creative possibilities that require great strength and excellent swimming skills.

The synchro swimmer uses versions of the front crawl, elementary backstroke, sidestroke, back crawl, and breaststroke to move from place to place within the routine. To modify the strokes, various parts of the recovery can be held, accented, or modified to fit the music's mood and tempo. **Hybrid strokes** use parts of different strokes. The routine typically covers all areas of the pool.

The swimmer often adapts strokes in the following ways:

- The face is kept above the water. Facial expressions are an appealing part of the routine.
- Arms are carried higher during recoveries.
- The kick is deeper to avoid splashing.
- Only the head and arms are above the water.
- Each phase of the arm stroke is carefully planned and synchronized to the music and the other swimmers.

***Figures*** are movements in the water composed of basic positions, their variations, and transitions from one position to another. Basic positions include prone, supine, and vertical layouts (a position in which the body is straight); the pike; and the tuck.

Sculling is a basic skill developed more highly in synchronized swimming. U.S. Synchronized Swimming describes eight basic sculling positions:

- Back layout position, arms at sides, direction of head
- Back layout position, arms at sides, direction of feet
- Back layout position, arms overhead, direction of head
- Back layout position, arms overhead, direction of feet
- Front layout position, arms at sides, direction of head
- Front layout position, arms at sides, direction of feet
- Front layout position, arms overhead, direction of head
- Front layout position, arms overhead, direction of feet

These movements provide support and balance for the body and are used for propulsion in figures and strokes.

The rotary, or eggbeater, kick is used in synchro swimming because it helps the swimmer keep a high vertical position. It leaves the swimmer's hands free to create various movements. This kick is described in Chapter 5.

You can get started in synchronized swimming in a beginner's program at a community pool or recreation center. Such a program often concludes with a demonstration performance.

## United States Synchronized Swimming

United States Synchronized Swimming, Inc. (USSS), is the national governing body of synchronized swimming. USSS was founded in 1979 to promote and support all competitive and noncompetitive levels of the sport. It also selects and trains athletes to represent the United States in international competition. The 5,000 registered members, who range in age from 6 to 80, belong to its 200 registered clubs. Masters swimming for USSS includes participants who are 20 years old and older, while for international Masters competition, participants are 25 years old and older, based on rules set by FINA. There are clinics, camps, and training programs for every level of swimming ability. There is also a training and certification program for coaches.

Three synchro events are recognized internationally: solo (one swimmer), duet (two swimmers), and team (up to eight swimmers). The Olympics include solo and duet events. However, in 1996, the team event will replace the solo and duet events. There are also compulsory figure competitions.

USSS competitions also include the trio event (three swimmers) for junior national, age group, U.S. open, and collegiate events. USSS sponsors six championships each year:

- U.S. National Synchronized Swimming Championships (elite)
- U.S. Junior National Synchronized Swimming Championships
- U.S. Age Group Synchronized Swimming Championships
- U.S. Open Synchronized Swimming Championships
- U.S. Collegiate Synchronized Swimming Championships
- U.S. Masters Synchronized Swimming Championships

In addition, three national teams of 10 members each are selected annually.

Synchronized swimming combines skill, stamina, and teamwork with the flair of music and drama. Coaches, psychologists, physiologists, nutritionists, dance specialists, and former champions all contribute their expertise. This sport is increasingly popular with both spectators and participants. Noncompetitors can participate as coaches, volunteers, and judges.

The national headquarters of United States Synchronized Swimming is located at Pan American Plaza, 201 S. Capitol Avenue, Suite 510, Indianapolis, IN 46225, (317) 237-5700.

FIG. 12-13

## WATER POLO

The century-old sport of water polo is a team sport similar in ways to both soccer and basketball. It is played as recreation and at competitive levels up to the Olympics. Even beginners who make their own rules can enjoy themselves and the activity.

Water polo evolved from its "anything goes" reputation of the early years to the skilled, fast-moving sport of today. The old-style game let players take both the ball and each other under water. Makeshift water polo contests were held in Great Britain as far back as the 1860s. The game was first played in open water with boats or rafts as goals. Goal frames were introduced in 1887, and water polo came to the United States in 1888 from England.

Water polo was a demonstration sport in the 1900 Paris Olympics and was officially added to the 1908 London games. Of the 14 teams in the 1920 Olympics, the Hungarians dominated when they introduced ball passing in the air. Underwater play was still permitted and continued to result in many injuries. The underwater action was less exciting for spectators, and the sport fell out of favor in the United States. Many rule changes and injuries later, surface play returned in the late 1940s.

The sport's popularity continues to grow, as ball handling skills and speed-swimming elements make it exciting to watch and challenging to play. According to United States Water Polo, Inc., the governing body for water polo, the number of registered players has grown by 25 percent in the last 5 years. Water polo is still most common on the East and West Coasts but is growing more popular in the Midwest. Water polo is popular with coaches of swim teams. The sport is used for conditioning early in a season and to provide variety to training later in a season.

A water polo team has seven players who play both offensive and defensive roles, much as in basketball. Players generally specialize in particular roles. Shooters generally do the scoring. Drivers are the quickest swimmers and move continually to receive or block passes. Holemen take position in front of the goal and are key members of the offense. They are often under the most physical attack. The goalie is the only player allowed to use two hands or a closed fist and to step on or jump from the bottom.

The ball is passed from player to player and thrown into the goal past the defending goalkeeper to score one point (Fig. 12-13). Players, except for the goalie, cannot touch the bottom or sides of the pool and must tread water, swim, or kick throughout the game. Players may dribble the ball ahead of them as they swim, using the waves made by their arms and chest to move the ball. Players use a strong rotary kick to rise high in the water to make or receive a pass or block a shot.

Games are 34 minutes long, divided into four 7-minute periods with three 2-minute breaks. Two referees and two goal judges enforce the rules. Major violations include seriously kicking or holding an opposing player and can result in 45-second penalties for the offending player. Minor fouls include deliberate face splashing, play interference, or using a clenched fist or two hands to play the ball. Most offensive fouls are penalized with loss of ball possession.

## EQUIPMENT

Rectangular goals are set at water level at the ends of a 30 by 20 meter pool. Regulation games are played in a minimum depth of 2 meters. The nonslip rubber ball is slightly smaller than a volleyball and weighs 15 ounces. For identification, players wear blue and white numbered caps, and goalies wear a red cap with number 1. The close-fitting cloth caps must have plastic cups built in to protect the ears. Strong players can hurl the ball over 40 miles an hour, and players without protection could receive ear injuries.

If you are an athlete who enjoys swimming, teamwork, and strategy, water polo may be your sport.

## UNITED STATES WATER POLO

United States Water Polo, Inc. (USWP), is the national governing body for water polo in the United States. There are nearly 11,000 members in 500 clubs nationwide. Local clubs compete in matches and may progress to regional and zone competition. Qualifying teams from seven geographic zones compete in national championships. National championships for women began in 1963. Teams compete in indoor and outdoor tournaments at the junior and senior levels. Age group competition is organized as 13 and under, 15 and under, and 17 and under, although many teams mix ages widely. Coed teams and leagues are sanctioned but do not have national competitions. USWP publishes a magazine with useful articles and match results.

The national headquarters of United States Water Polo is located at 201 S. Capitol Avenue, Suite 520, Indianapolis, IN 46225, (317) 237-5599.

## Summary

**C**ompetitive swimming and diving organizations hold many competitive and recreational activities for all family members. Organizations that sponsor competition for individuals with disabilities are listed in Appendix A. Mental, physical, and social well-being all develop through structured training sessions, meets, and interaction with teammates, coaches, meet officials, and families. The organizations named here can give you more information about how you can participate.

13

# rescue techniq

CHAPTER

## Key Terms

**Abdominal thrusts (Heimlich maneuver):** A technique for unblocking an obstructed airway by giving forceful pushes to the abdomen.

**Active drowning victim:** A person exhibiting universal behavior that includes struggling at the surface for 20 to 60 seconds before submerging.

**Drowning:** Death by suffocation when submerged in water.

**Emergency medical services (EMS) personnel:** Trained and equipped community-based personnel dispatched through a local emergency number to provide emergency care for ill or injured people.

**Emergency medical services (EMS) system:** A network of community resources and medical personnel that provides emergency care to victims of injury or sudden illness.

**Heat cramps:** Painful muscle spasms, usually in an arm or leg.

**Heat exhaustion:** A form of shock, often resulting from strenuous work or exercise in a hot environment.

**Heat stroke:** A life-threatening condition that develops when the body's cooling mechanisms are overwhelmed and body systems begin to fail.

**Hypothermia:** A life-threatening condition in which the body is unable to maintain warmth and the entire body cools.

**In-line stabilization:** A technique used to minimize movement of a victim's head and neck while providing care.

**Passive drowning victim:** An unconscious victim face-down, submerged or near the surface.

**Rescue breathing:** A technique of breathing for a non-breathing victim.

ues

# Objectives

*After reading this chapter, you should be able to—*

1. List characteristics of a drowning victim.
2. List at least eight pieces of safety equipment used in reaching or throwing assists.
3. Describe rescue techniques that someone in a boat might perform.
4. Describe techniques for ice rescue.
5. Describe the signals of heat exhaustion, heat stroke, and hypothermia and the care for each.
6. List two spinal injury rescue techniques.
7. Define the key terms at left.

*After reading this chapter and completing appropriate course activities, you should be able to—*

1. Use reaching and throwing rescue techniques to assist a near-drowning victim, using an arm, leg, pole, or shepherd's crook for reaching and at least three devices for throwing.
2. Demonstrate two specific techniques for stabilizing a victim with a suspected spinal injury.

KNOW

WATER PROVIDES PEOPLE WITH SOME OF THE most popular leisure activities, but water activities can be dangerous. The large number of drownings each year, such as the 4,600 in 1989, emphasizes this. ***Drowning*** is death by suffocation when submerged in water. Most people do not realize that many who drown never intended to go in the water in the first place.

EVERYONE SHOULD LEARN HOW TO SWIM WELL ENOUGH TO avoid the risk of drowning and should know enough about basic rescue methods to help someone else in an emergency. Everyone should also know about the emergency medical services (EMS) system and how to activate it. The American Red Cross Community Water Safety course gives instruction in water safety for everyone, including nonswimmers.

THIS CHAPTER DESCRIBES DIFFERENT RESCUE TECHNIQUES for drowning emergencies, including out-of-water assists and in-water assists. It also discusses rescue breathing, choking, seizures, and spinal injuries. Finally, it discusses how to rescue a swimmer if you are in a boat and how to perform an ice rescue. It also describes treatment for hypothermia and heat-related illness.

# BASIC ASSIST RESCUE METHODS

FIG. 13-1

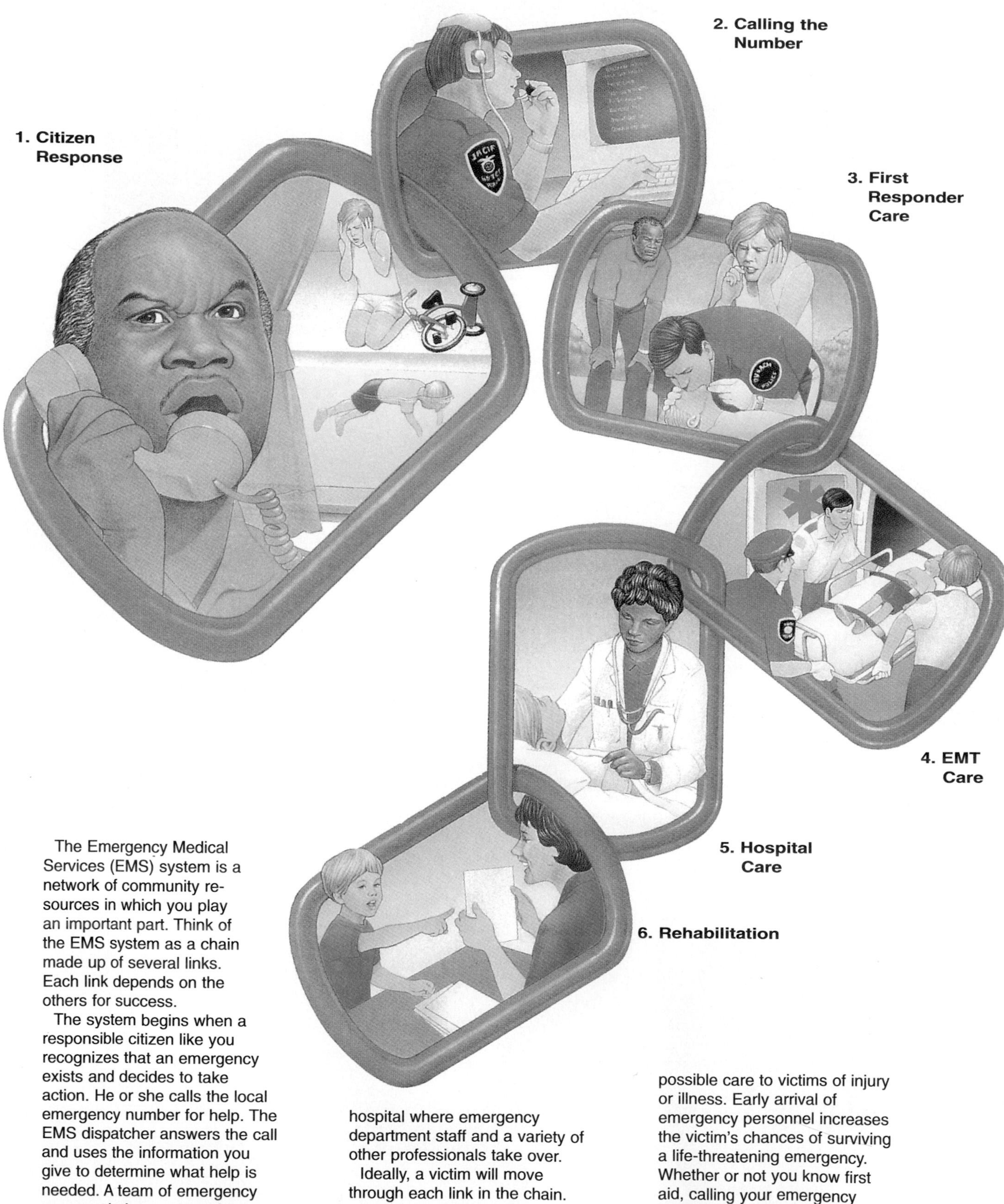


The Emergency Medical Services (EMS) system is a network of community resources in which you play an important part. Think of the EMS system as a chain made up of several links. Each link depends on the others for success.

The system begins when a responsible citizen like you recognizes that an emergency exists and decides to take action. He or she calls the local emergency number for help. The EMS dispatcher answers the call and uses the information you give to determine what help is needed. A team of emergency personnel gives care at the scene and transports the victim to the hospital where emergency department staff and a variety of other professionals take over.

Ideally, a victim will move through each link in the chain. All the links should work together to provide the best possible care to victims of injury or illness. Early arrival of emergency personnel increases the victim's chances of surviving a life-threatening emergency. Whether or not you know first aid, calling your emergency number is the most important action you can take.

## Helping Others

There may be a time when someone else is in trouble in the water. While there are some basic skills you can learn to aid a person in the water, always remember to stay safe. If there is any chance that you cannot easily assist the person in trouble, call for professional assistance.

### Emergency Medical Services (EMS)

The ***Emergency Medical Services (EMS) system*** is a network of professionals linked together to give the best care for victims in all emergencies, both in and out of the water. The system begins when you or another citizen sees an emergency occurring and takes action. When you call 9-1-1 or the emergency number in your community, the **EMS dispatcher** takes your information and summons trained professionals to the scene. These may include police or fire personnel, other rescuers, and an ambulance and **emergency medical technicians (EMTs)** (Fig. 13-1).

These professionals will take over the care of the victim, including transporting the person to a hospital or other facility for the best medical care. Your role in this system is to recognize the emergency, decide to act, and call EMS for help.

### Recognizing An Emergency

An emergency can happen to anyone in or around the water, regardless of how good a swimmer the person is or what he or she is doing at the time. A strong swimmer can get into trouble in the water because of sudden illness. A nonswimmer playing in shallow water can be swept into deep water by a sudden wave. The key to recognizing an emergency is staying alert and knowing the signals that indicate an emergency is happening.

Use all your senses when observing others in and around the water. You may *see* that a swimmer is acting oddly, or you may *hear* a scream or sudden splash. You may *smell* an unusual odor, such as a strong chlorine odor that could indicate a problem. Watch for anything that seems unusual.

Being able to recognize a person who is having trouble in the water may help save that person's life. Most drowning people cannot or do not call for help. They spend their energy just trying to keep their heads above water. They might slip under water quickly and never resurface. There are two kinds of water emergency situations, a swimmer in distress and a drowning person. Each kind of emergency poses a different danger and can be recognized by different behaviors.

A swimmer in distress may be too tired to get to shore or to the side of the pool but is able to stay afloat and breathe and may be calling for help. The person may be floating, treading water, or clinging to a line for support. Someone who is trying to swim but making little or no forward progress may be in distress (Fig. 13-2). If not helped, a person in distress may lose the ability to float and become a drowning victim.

Fig. 13-2

FIG. 13-3

FIG. 13-4

An ***active drowning victim*** is vertical in the water but unable to move forward or tread water. His or her arms are at the side pressing down in an instinctive attempt to keep the head above the water to breathe (Fig. 13-3). All energy is going into the struggle to breathe, and the person cannot call for help. A ***passive drowning victim*** is not moving and will be floating facedown on the bottom or near the surface of the water (Fig. 13-4). Table 13-1 compares characteristics of drowning persons.

The following conditions and situations are serious and require you to call EMS:

- Possible drowning
- Injury to the head or spine
- Difficulty breathing
- Persistent chest or abdominal pain or pressure
- No pulse
- Unconsciousness
- Severe bleeding, vomiting, or passing blood
- Seizure, severe headache, or slurred speech
- Poisoning
- Possible broken bones
- Multiple injuries

TABLE 13-1 Characteristics of Distressed Swimmers and Drowning Victims Compared to Swimmers

| Behaviors | Swimmer | Distressed Swimmer | Active Drowning Victim | Passive Drowning Victim |
|---|---|---|---|---|
| Breathing | Rhythmic breathing | Can continue breathing and call for help | Struggles to breathe; cannot call out for help | Not breathing |
| Arm and Leg Action | Relatively coordinated movement | Floating, sculling, or treading water; can wave for help | Arms to sides, pressing down; no supporting kick | None |
| Body Position | Horizontal | Horizontal, vertical, or diagonal, depending on means of support | Vertical | Face down submerged near surface |
| Locomotion | Recognizable progress | Little or no forward progress; less and less able to support self | None; has only 20-60 seconds before submerging | None |

## DECIDING TO ACT

Once you recognize that there is an emergency, you need to decide to act–and how to act. This is not always as simple as it sounds. Often people are slow to act in an emergency because they're not sure exactly what to do or they think someone else will do whatever's needed. What if no one else is there or is taking action? If you decide to act, you may save the person's life.

To prepare yourself for this moment of decision, think now about emergency situations and what you might do. Five common concerns sometimes keep people from acting. The following are ways to overcome these concerns and prepare yourself to take action:

1. Don't hesitate to act because there are other people at the scene. Maybe you are the only one who knows rescue techniques or first aid. Don't be embarrassed to step forward. Others may want to help but do not know what to do. You can give them directions, such as to call 9-1-1.
2. Don't hesitate to act because the victim is a stranger, or older or younger than you, or different from you in some other way. The person may be acting strangely because of a sudden illness or medication. Don't focus on what makes the person different from you–concentrate instead on another person needing your help. Some day, you may need help from someone.
3. Don't hesitate to act because of the injury or illness itself. It may be unpleasant, and the sight of blood or vomit can be upsetting. Turn away if you need to, and take deep breaths and try to control your feelings. Do what you can. Make sure someone has called EMS, and comfort the victim as best you can. Give first aid if you are able.
4. Don't hesitate to act because you fear catching any disease from the victim. It is extremely unlikely that you would catch a disease by rescuing someone or giving first aid. Usually, you are giving first aid to a friend or family member and don't have to worry about a serious contagious disease. Even with strangers, the risk is low, and you can take precautions to make the risks even lower. Try to prevent direct contact with the person's body fluids. For example, when stopping bleeding put on disposable gloves. Put a clean cloth over the wound before applying pressure, or have the person apply the direct pressure with his or her own hand. Wash thoroughly afterwards.
5. Don't hesitate to act because of a fear of doing something wrong. Remember that once you've called EMS, professional help is on the way and you're giving first aid usually only for a few minutes. Before acting, first consider whether you have the skills needed to make the rescue or give the first aid. If you do only what you have been trained to do, you do not have to worry about making anything worse. The worst thing, after all, is to do nothing. You should not worry about being sued if anything goes wrong, because "Good Samaritan" laws protect people who give first aid willingly and voluntarily, as they have been trained to do.

Once you have decided to act, proceed safely. Make sure the scene is safe–don't go rushing into a dangerous situation where you too may become a victim. If the person is in the water, decide first whether he or she needs help getting out, and then act based on your training. If the person is out of the water, quickly try to determine what help the person needs and check for any dangers to you or others helping. Look for any other victims. Look for bystanders who can help you give first aid or call for help.

## Calling for Help

If the victim is in the water, your first goal is to stay safe yourself. Rushing into the water to help a victim may lead to you becoming a victim too. Once you ensure your safety, your goal is to help get the person out of the water. If the person is unconscious, send someone else to call EMS personnel while you start the rescue. If the person is conscious, you can first act to get the person out of the water and then determine whether EMS is needed.

If the victim is not in the water, as soon as you determine that there is an emergency, call EMS immediately. If you are in doubt about whether the victim needs professional help, don't hesitate–call EMS personnel. Always call for any of the emergency situations listed earlier.

Make the call to EMS personnel yourself, or ask someone else at the scene to call (Fig. 13-5). If possible, send two people to make the call. Tell the caller(s) to report back to you and tell you what the dispatcher said.

Be sure the caller(s) stay on the phone after giving all of the information to the dispatcher, in case there are any questions. Make sure that the dispatcher has all the correct information to get the right help to the scene quickly. Be prepared to tell the dispatcher the following:

- The location of the emergency (exact address, city or town, nearby intersections or landmarks, name of the facility)
- The telephone number of the telephone being used
- The caller's name
- What happened
- The number of victims
- The help being given so far

Remember, do not hang up first because the dispatcher may need more information.

Fig. 13-5

## Out-Of-Water Assists

You can help a person in trouble in the water by using reaching and throwing assists. Wherever possible, start the rescue by talking to the person. Let him or her know help is coming. If it is too noisy or if the person is too far away to hear you, use gestures. Tell the person what you want him or her to do to help with the rescue, such as grasping a line, rescue buoy, or any other flotation device. Ask the person to move toward you by kicking or stroking. Some people have reached safety by themselves with the calm and encouraging assistance of someone calling to them.

### Reaching Assists

If the person is close enough, you can use a reaching assist to help him or her out of the water. Firmly brace yourself on a pool deck or pier and reach out to the victim with any object that will extend your reach, such as a pole (Fig. 13-6), an oar or paddle, a tree branch, a shirt, a belt, or a towel. Community pools and recreational areas, as well as hotel and motel pools, often have reaching equipment beside the water, such as a **shepherd's crook** (an aluminum or fiberglass pole with a large hook on one end) (Fig. 13-7). When the victim grasps the object, slowly and carefully pull him or her to safety. Keep your body low and lean back as you do this.

If the victim cannot grasp the shepherd's crook, use the hook to encircle the victim's body. Keep yourself firmly braced, put the hook around the victim's chest under the armpits, and carefully pull him or her to safety. Be careful not to injure the victim with the point of the hook while you do this. For a victim on the bottom of a pool, try to reach him or her with the hook. Try to encircle the victim's body and pull the victim to the surface. Then bring the victim to the edge and turn him or her faceup.

If you have no object for reaching, lie flat on the pool deck or pier and reach with your arm. If you are already in the water, hold onto the pool ladder, overflow trough, piling, or other secure object with one hand and extend your free hand or one of your legs to the victim (Fig. 13-8, *A* and *B*). Do not release your grasp at the edge or swim out into the water.

### Throwing Assists

An effective way to use equipment to rescue someone beyond your reach is to throw to the victim a floating object with a line attached. The person can grasp the object so that you can pull him or her to safety. Objects you can throw include a heaving line, ring buoy, throw bag, rescue tube, or homemade device (Fig. 13-9). You can use any floating object at hand, such as a picnic jug or innertube. Safety equipment for throwing may be in plain view in swimming

Fig. 13-6

Fig. 13-7

A

B

FIG. 13-8

FIG. 13-9

areas in community pools, hotel and motel pools, and public waterfronts. Recreation and aquatic supply stores sell this equipment for residential pools. You can use certain types of equipment for throwing assists.

You can make your own **heaving jug** to throw to a victim. Put a half-inch of water in a gallon plastic container, seal it, and attach 50 to 75 feet of floating line to the handle. Throw it by holding the handle and using a swinging motion. The weight of the water in the jug helps direct the throw (Fig. 13-10).

**A heaving line** should float. It should be white, yellow, or some other highly visible color. A buoyant, weighted object on the end will make throwing easier and more accurate. Hang about half of the coiled line on the open palm of your nonthrowing arm, and throw the other half underhand to the victim.

**A ring buoy** is made of buoyant cork, **kapok**, cellular foam, or plastic-covered material and weighs about 2 pounds. It should have a towline or lightweight line with something at the end to keep the line from

FIG. 13-10

FIG. 13-11

slipping out from under your foot as you throw it. The buoy and coiled line should be kept on a safety post where anyone can quickly grasp it to throw to someone in trouble. Hold the underside of the ring with your fingers, and throw it underhand (Fig. 13-11).

The **throw bag** is a small but useful device. It is a nylon bag containing 50 to 75 feet of coiled floating line. A foam disk in the bag gives it shape and keeps it from sinking. Throw bags are often used in canoes and other boats. Throw the throw bag with an underhand swing (Fig. 13-12).

The **rescue tube** is a vinyl, foam-filled floating support about 45 to 54 inches long (Fig. 13-13). It is the most effective equipment in lifeguarding. It is popular because it is easy to use and can support three to five people, depending on its size. Attached to the rescue tube is a tow line and shoulder strap with a total length of 6 to 12 feet.

To perform a throwing assist, follow these guidelines:

1. Get into a stride position (with the leg opposite that of your throwing arm in front of the other leg). This position lets you keep your balance when you throw the equipment.
2. Bend your knees.
3. Step on your end of the line with your forward foot.
4. Try to throw the device just beyond the victim but within reach.
5. Throw the device so that any wind or current will bring it back to the victim.
6. When the victim has grasped the device, slowly pull him or her to safety. Lean back away from the victim as you pull.

If the throwing assist does not work and the water is shallow enough for wading, try a wading assist with equipment.

## IN-WATER ASSISTS

### WADING ASSIST WITH EQUIPMENT

If the water is shallow enough that you can stand with your head out of the water, wade into the water

FIG. 13-12

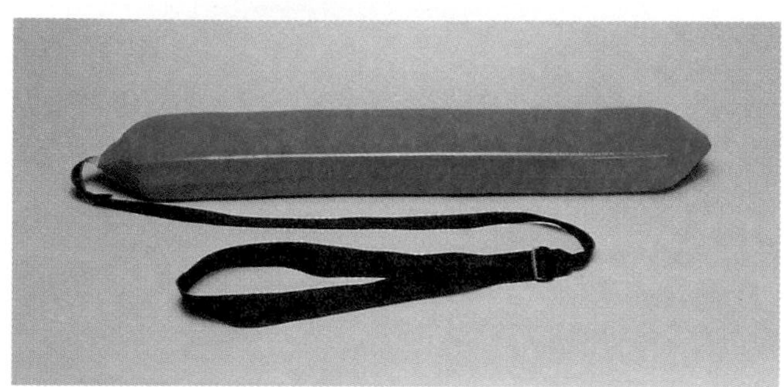
Fig. 13-13

to assist the person. Take a buoyant object and extend it to the victim. Use a rescue tube, a ring buoy, a buoyant cushion, a kickboard, or a life jacket. You may also reach with a ring buoy, tree branch, pole, air mattress, plastic cooler, or paddle (Fig. 13-14, *A* and *B*). If a current or soft bottom makes wading dangerous, do not enter the water.

**O**nce the victim grasps the object, either pull the victim to safety or (if it is a buoyant object) let it go and tell the victim to kick toward safety using it for

Fig. 13-14

support. Always keep the object between you and the victim to help prevent the victim from grasping you.

A victim who has been lying motionless and face-down in the water for several seconds is probably unconscious. If the water is not over you head, wade into the water carefully with some kind of flotation equipment and turn the person face up. Bring him or her to the side of the pool or to the shoreline, and then remove the victim from the water.

### Walking Assist

If the victim is in shallow water where he or she can stand, he or she may be able to walk with some support. Use the walking assist.

1. Place one of the victim's arms around your neck and across your shoulder.
2. Grasp the wrist of the arm that is across your shoulder, and wrap your free arm around the victim's back or waist.
3. Maintain a firm grasp, and help the victim walk out of the water (Fig. 13-15).

Fig. 13-15

Fig. 13-16

### Beach Drag

You may use the beach drag with a victim in shallow water on a sloping shore or beach. This method works well with a heavy or unconscious victim.

1. Stand behind the victim, and grasp him or her under the armpits, supporting the victim's head, when possible, with your forearms.
2. While walking backward slowly, drag the victim toward the shore (Fig. 13-16).
3. Remove the victim completely from the water or at least to a point where the head and shoulders are out of the water.

You may use a two-person drag if another person is present to help you (Fig. 13-17).

Fig. 13-17

### Helping Someone Who Has Fallen through Ice

If a person falls through ice, never go out onto the ice yourself to attempt a rescue. This is a very dangerous situation, and you are likely to become a victim yourself. Instead, follow these guidelines:

1. Send someone to call EMS immediately. Trained rescuers may be needed to get the person out of the ice, and even if you succeed in rescuing the person, he or she will probably need medical care.
2. From a secure place on land, try a reaching or throwing assist. Use anything at hand that the person can grasp for support: a tree branch, a pole, a life jacket, a weighted rope, and so on (Fig. 13-18). Act quickly because within 1 minute, the victim's hands will be too numb to grasp the object.
3. If you can do it safely, pull the victim to shore. If you cannot, talk to the victim and make sure he or she is secure as possible with the object until help arrives.

Fig. 13-18

## SPECIFIC EMERGENCIES

In previous chapters, you learned how important it is to recognize an emergency when it occurs and to take action. In addition to rescuing a person from the water, you should also be prepared for other kinds of emergencies in and around the water that may require first aid (Fig. 13-19).

People may need first aid because of injuries or sudden illness. The emergency may be caused by something that happened in the water, such as a person hitting his or her head against an object. The emergency may have occurred by itself, for example, when a person has a seizure in the water. In either case, you need to act quickly to save the person's life or prevent further problems or disability.

Before you give first aid, you need the person's consent if the victim is conscious. When you first reach the person, advise the person of your level of training and say what you want to do. Ask the person if that is OK. With unattended children or an adult who is unconscious or unable to respond, you can assume you have the person's consent and give first aid.

In any emergency situation, remember to call 9-1-1 or the local emergency number as soon as you see there is an emergency, or ask someone else to call. Remember also to make sure the scene is safe before going to the victim–don't risk your safety or that of others at the scene. Once you decide it is safe to go to the victim, your goal then is to provide first aid for the short time until help arrives.

This section does not cover all types of first aid for all kinds of injuries and illnesses. For a complete first aid course, ask your local American Red Cross chapter about available first aid and CPR courses. In this

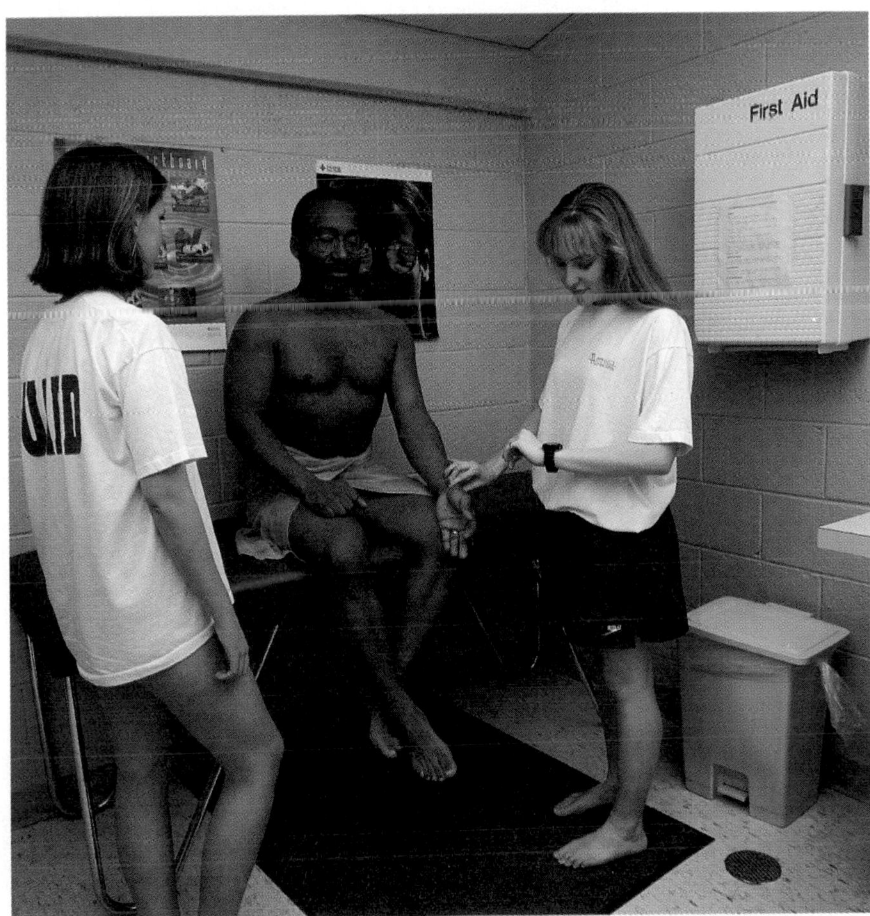


FIG. 13-19

section, you will learn basic first aid for a few problems that happen in and around the water. These are–

- Absence of breathing.
- Choking.
- Heat emergencies.
- Hypothermia.
- Bites and stings.
- Splinters and fishhooks.
- Seizures.
- Spinal injuries.

## Rescue Breathing

***Rescue breathing*** is a way to help a nonbreathing person get air. Air is breathed into the person to supply the oxygen needed to survive. Rescue breathing is given to a victim who is not breathing but whose heart is still beating.

Rescue breathing for a victim in the water is extremely difficult. When you rescue a victim and find he or she is not breathing, get the person out of the water as quickly as possible and have someone call EMS.

To determine whether the person is breathing, position the person on his or her back on a flat surface. Use the technique called the **head-tilt/chin-lift** to open the **airway** (Fig. 13-20). This maneuver moves the tongue away from the back of the throat. With one hand on the forehead, tilt the head back. Using the other hand, lift the chin.

Next, put your ear close to the person's mouth and nose while you watch to see if the chest is rising and falling (Fig. 13-21). If you cannot see, hear, or feel any signs of breathing, the person is not breathing. Have someone call ***emergency medical services (EMS) personnel***. Begin rescue breathing by making a seal with your mouth, pinching the victim's nose, and blowing two slow breaths. Watch as the chest gently rises and falls. Check for a pulse (Fig. 13-22). If the pulse is present but the person is still not breathing, continue rescue breathing. Appendix F on pages 334 and 335 describes the steps for rescue breathing and possible air blockage in more detail.

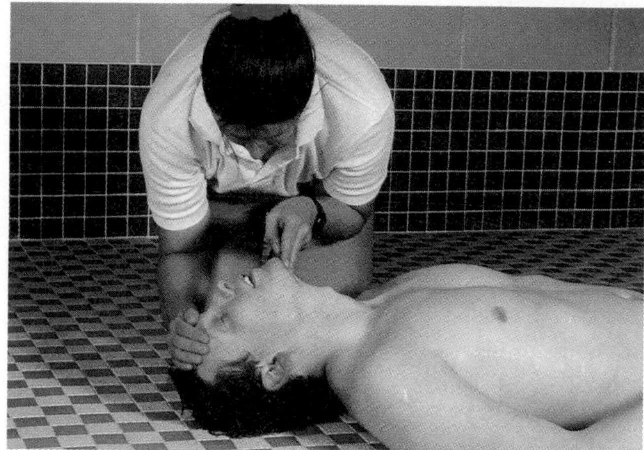

Fig. 13-20

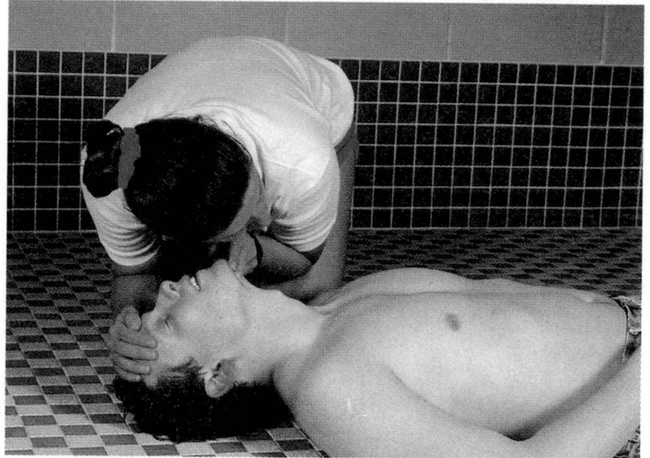

Fig. 13-21

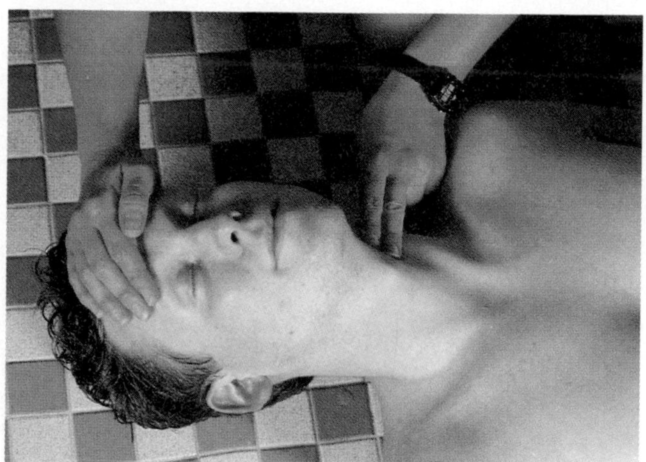

Fig. 13-22

### Air Blockage

Emergencies in and around water can result in a person's air passage being blocked. This can happen when someone is chewing gum while swimming, goes into the water with food in the mouth, or becomes a drowning victim. When a person's air passage (airway) is blocked, your goal is to open the airway as quickly as possible (Fig. 13-23). Check the mouth for any obvious obstruction, such as food or fluid. If the airway is obviously obstructed, give ***abdominal thrusts (Heimlich maneuver)*** for children or adults to clear the airway. If the airway appears clear but the person is not breathing, attempt rescue breathing.

### Heat Emergencies

It is best to try to prevent heat emergencies from occurring in the first place. You should know how to care for someone with either heat cramps, heat exhaustion, or heat stroke.

***Heat cramps*** are painful muscle spasms, usually occurring in the arms and legs. Have the victim rest in a cool place. Give cool water to drink. Usually, rest and fluid are all the victim needs to recover. The victim should *not* take salt tablets or salt water. They can make the situation worse.

A person may be experiencing ***heat exhaustion*** if the skin is cool, moist, pale, or red and he or she has a headache or feels nauseated, faint, dizzy, or exhausted. The person should move to a cool environment, rest, and drink cold water (Fig. 13-24). Give a half glass of water every 15 minutes. Loosen tight clothes, and remove any clothes soaked with sweat. Put cool, wet cloths on the skin. If the victim's condition does not improve within 30 minutes or if the victim vomits, refuses water, or becomes less alert or unconscious, call for medical help immediately. These may signal that the victim is developing heat stroke.

***Heat stroke*** is a life-threatening condition. The body cannot cool itself, and body systems start to fail. It usually occurs when people ignore the signals of heat exhaustion. Sweating stops, and the victim has hot, red, dry skin and a very high body temperature (often as high as 106 degrees F, 41 degrees C). Breathing may be rapid and shallow. The victim may vomit and may lose consciousness. Heat stroke is a life-threatening emergency. Call EMS personnel immediately and give this first aid:

1. Remove the victim from the sun or hot environment.
2. Cool the victim. Apply cool, wet cloths, such as towels or sheets, to the victim's body if you have not already done so. If you have ice packs or cold packs available, put them on the victim's wrists, ankles, neck, and armpits. Do *not* apply rubbing alcohol, which can worsen the condition.

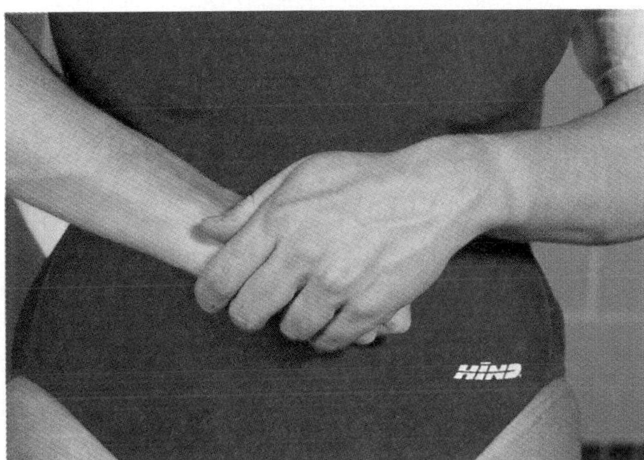

Fig. 13-23

Fig. 13-24

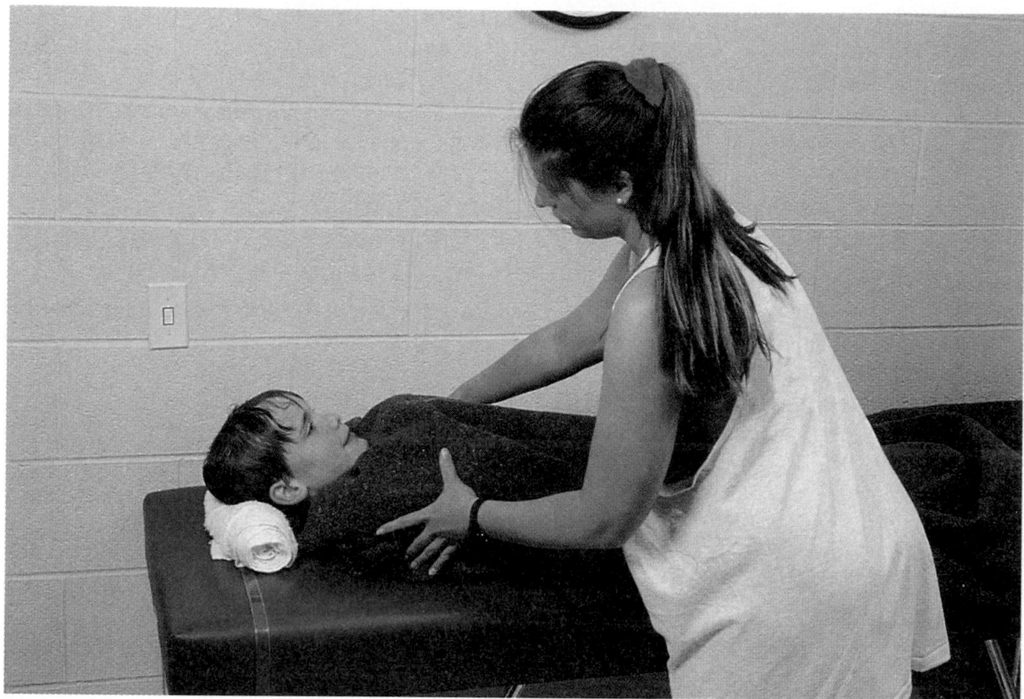

Fig. 13-25

## Hypothermia

People near water in cool weather should know the hazards and take care to stay safe. Falling into cold water may easily lead to hypothermia, as described in Chapter 2. Anyone in cold water or in wet clothes for a long time may develop hypothermia.

Bluish lips and shivering may be the first signals of hypothermia. Other signals include a feeling of weakness, confusion, a slow or irregular pulse, numbness, slurred speech, and semiconsciousness or unconsciousness. Being exposed to cold water is a severe physical shock. Call for emergency help immediately and give this first aid:

1. Handle the victim very gently, and monitor breathing.
2. Remove wet clothes, dry the victim, and move him or her to a warm environment. Do *not* warm the victim too quickly, such as by immersing him or her in warm water. Rapid warming may cause heart problems. Remember that hypothermia can be life threatening.
3. Wrap the victim in blankets or put on dry clothes (Fig. 13-25).
4. If the victim is alert, give warm liquids to drink. Do *not* give the victim alcohol or caffeine.

## Bites and Stings

Activities in and around the water may bring you or others in your group into contact with insects, snakes, or aquatic life that may sting or bite. If you go to open water areas, you may come in contact with spiders, scorpions, or ticks. The sections below describe first aid for these more common problems.

### *Insect Stings*

Although insect stings are painful, they are rarely fatal. Fewer than 100 deaths are reported each year. Some people, however, have a severe allergic reaction to an insect sting that can become a life-threatening emergency.

To care for an insect sting, first examine the site to see if the stinger is in the skin. If it is, scrape the stinger away from the skin with your fingernail or a plastic card such as a credit card (Fig. 13-26). Do not

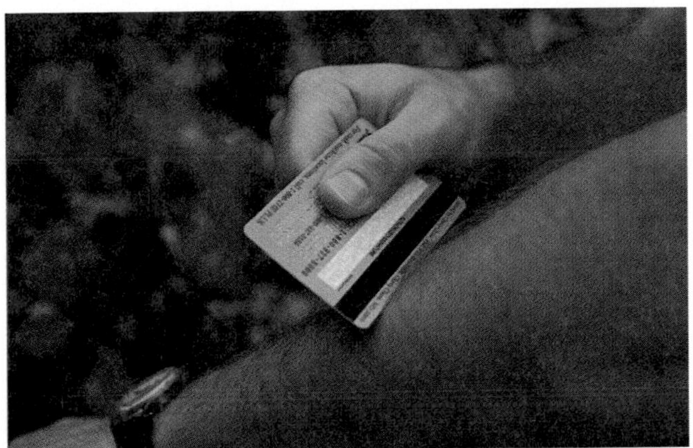

FIG. 13-26

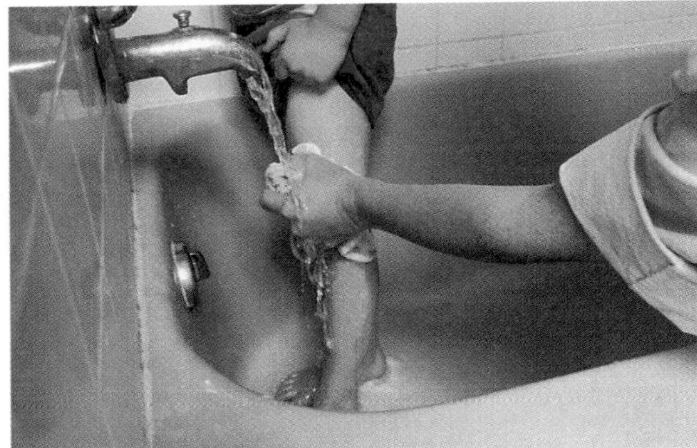

FIG. 13-27

remove the stinger with tweezers, since putting pressure on the stinger can cause more poison to be injected.

Wash the site with soap and water (Fig. 13-27). Cover to keep it clean. Apply a cold pack to the area to reduce pain and swelling. Watch for any signs of allergic reaction. The skin or body area may swell and turn red. The person may experience hives, itching, rash, weakness, nausea, vomiting, dizziness, and breathing difficulty including coughing and wheezing. The throat and tongue may swell making breathing difficult or impossible.

If you see any of these signs of an allergic reaction after an insect bite or sting, watch the person carefully. If the person has any breathing difficulty or says that his or her throat is closing, call EMS at once. Help the person into the most comfortable position for breathing. Stay with and reassure the person. People who know they are allergic to certain insect stings may carry a kit with them in case of an allergic reaction. The kit has a medication that can be injected into the body to counteract the allergic reaction. Assist the person with the kit if needed.

### *Marine Life*

In salt water, stingrays, some sea anemones and sea urchins, some types of fish, and certain jellyfish give painful stings that may cause problems such as allergic reaction (Figs. 13-28 to 13-31). If the sting is from a Portuguese man-of-war, jellyfish, or sea anemone, soak the injured part in vinegar as soon as possible. You can use baking soda or alcohol as an alternative. Do not rub the wound or apply ammonia or fresh water. If the sting is from a sting ray, sea urchin, or spiny fish, flush the wound with tap water or ocean water. Keep the injured part from moving and soak it in nonscalding hot water for about 30 minutes. Watch the person in case an allergic reaction occurs, and call EMS personnel immediately.

If you are frequently in the same waterfront, find out what other marine life may be present and what to do if a bite or sting occurs.

Denise Tackett/Tom Stack & Associates

FIG. 13-28 Sting ray.

Gerald and Buff Corsi/Tom Stack & Associates

FIG. 13-29 Sea anemone.

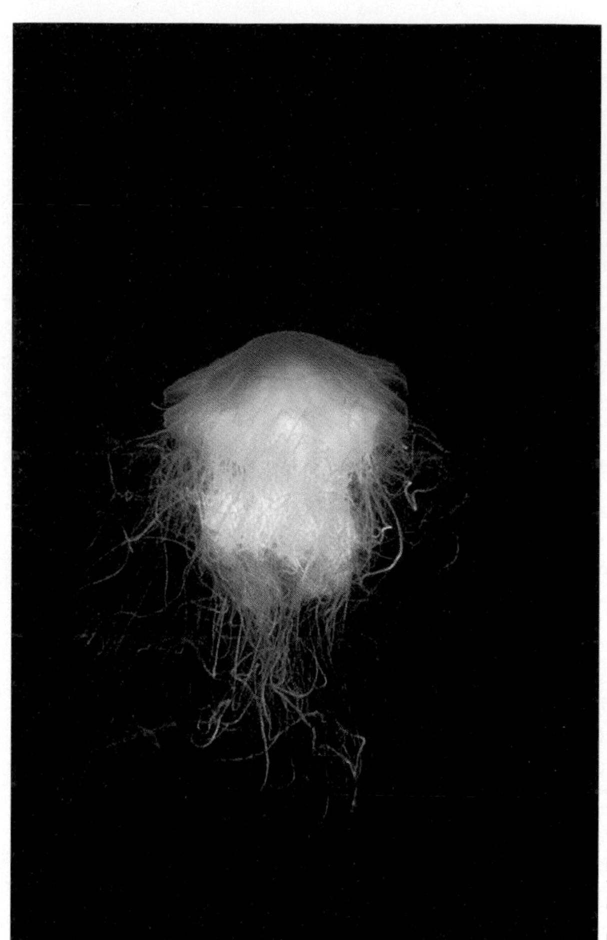

Tom Stack/Tom Stack & Associates

FIG. 13-31 Jellyfish.

Wendy Shattil, Robert Rozinki/Tom Stack & Associates

FIG. 13-30 Portuguese man-of-war.

## *Snakes*

Snakebites kill very few people in the United States. Rattlesnakes account for most snakebites and nearly all deaths from snakebites, and rattlesnakes are rarely seen immediately around water. Water moccasins and copperheads, however, are sometimes encountered in certain fresh-water areas. Usually if you leave them alone, they will move away and leave you alone. Figures 13-32 to 13-35 show the four kinds of poisonous snakes found in the United States.

Most snakebite deaths occur because the victim has an allergic reaction, is in poor health, or is slow to receive medical care.

To give first aid to someone bitten by a snake, wash the wound and immobilize the injured area, keeping it lower than the heart, if possible. Call EMS personnel. Do *not* apply ice to a snakebite. Do *not* apply a tourniquet. Do *not* use electric shock. If for any reason the victim has to be taken to a medical facility, the victim should be carried to a vehicle or should walk very slowly. If you are going into an area more than 30 minutes away from medical care and you know the area has poisonous snakes, you should have a snakebite kit in your first aid supplies and know how to use it.

John Shaw/Tom Stack & Associates

FIG. 13-32 Rattlesnake.

John Cancalosi/Tom Stack & Associates

FIG. 13-34 Water moccasin.

David M Dennis/Tom Stack & Associates

FIG. 13-33 Coral snake.

David M Dennis/Tom Stack & Associates

FIG. 13-35 Copperhead.

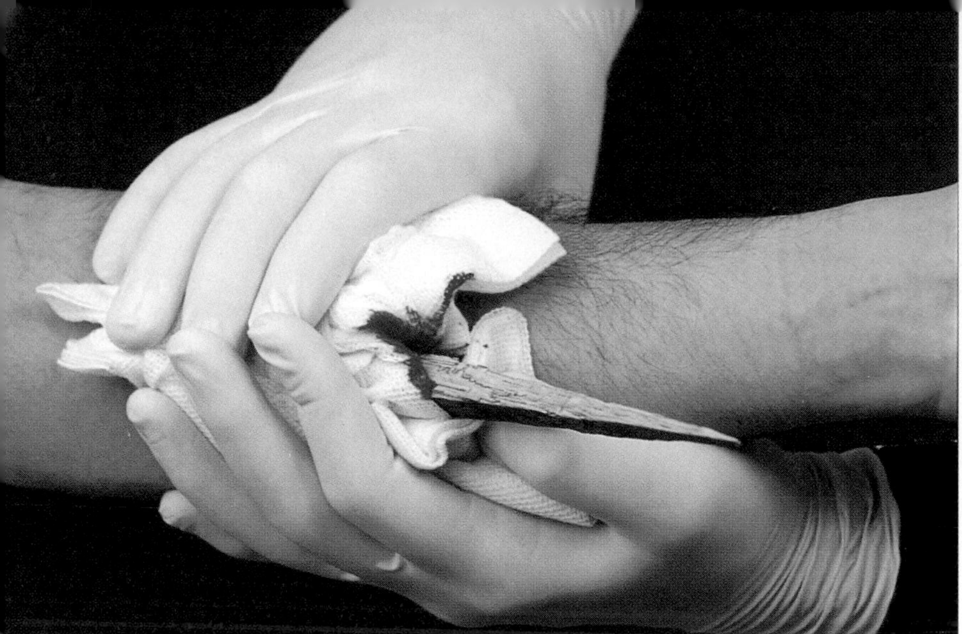

Fig. 13-36

## Splinters, Fishhooks, and Other Objects in a Wound

Activities around the water may lead to a person getting splinters or other objects in a wound, requiring first aid. If any object, such as a fishhook, a piece of wood, glass, or metal, is stuck in the wound, *do not* remove it. Place dressings or clean cloth around the object to keep it from moving. Then bandage the dressings in place around the object (Fig. 13-36). With serious injury, wait for EMS personnel. With less serious injuries, such as a splinter in the hand or foot, the object can be removed.

A splinter in the skin can be removed with tweezers (Fig. 13-37). After removing the splinter, wash the area. Then cover it to keep it clean. If the splinter is in the eye, do not attempt to remove it. Call EMS personnel; the victim needs medical help.

If a fishhook is deeply embedded in a person's skin, do not try to remove it. Treat it like an object stuck in a wound and secure it with dressings and bandages. The person should see a doctor. If the fishhook is not embedded but has cut the skin, clean the wound, stop the bleeding with direct pressure on the cut, and cover it with a sterile dressing (Fig. 13-38). The victim should check with his or her doctor to see if a tetanus booster shot is needed.

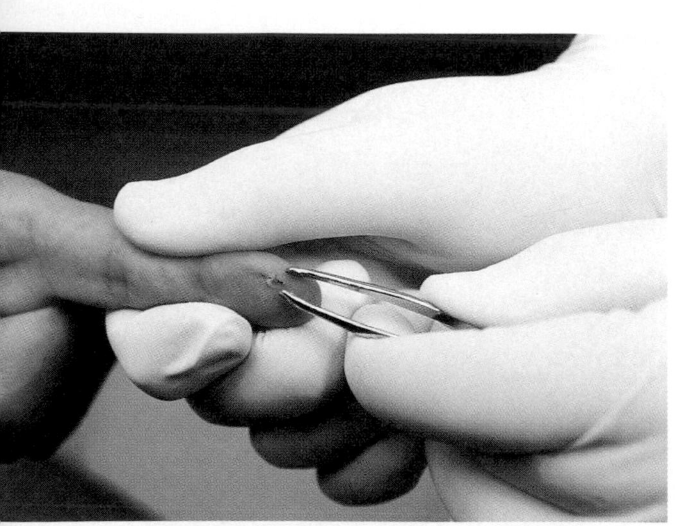

Fig. 13-37

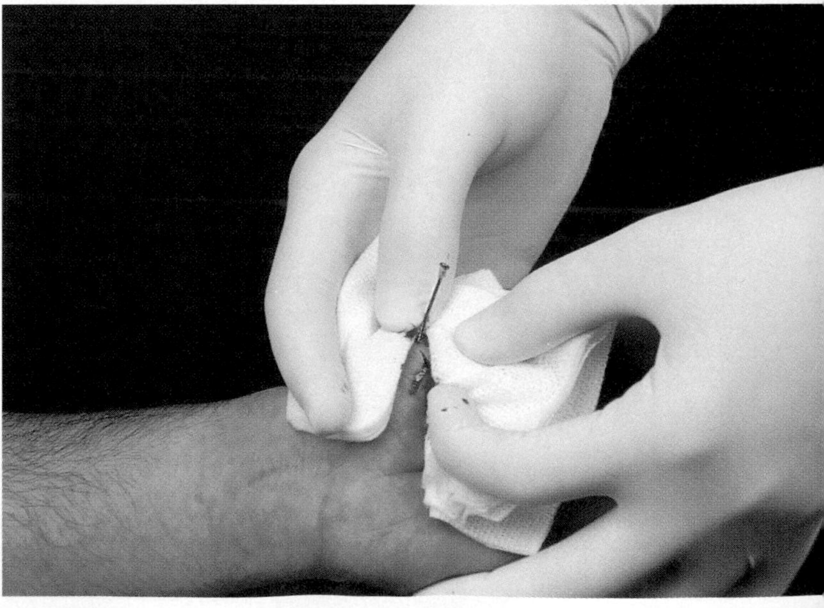

Fig. 13-38

### Seizures

Seizures, sometimes called convulsions, are a temporary loss of consciousness, sometimes accompanied by uncontrolled muscle contractions. Seizures are caused by different kinds of illness or injury. Sometimes the person knows he or she had seizures before, but in other cases the person may never have had a seizure. Seizures present a special problem in and around the water because the person may suddenly become unconscious and slip under water.

There are different types of seizures. Someone having a less serious seizure may suddenly stare off into space for a few seconds and then become fully alert again without muscular contractions. A more serious seizure may have the following characteristics:

- A peculiar sensation preceding the seizure lasting a few seconds. He or she may hear, see, smell, or taste something peculiar or not there, may feel pain, or may have a sensation warning him or her to move to safety.
- A sudden rigidity of the person's body, sometimes after a high-pitched cry.
- Loss of consciousness.
- Uncontrolled muscular movement, during which the victim may lose bladder and bowel control. The victim may also salivate, hold his or her breath, and clench the jaw. The heart rate increases.
- After the seizure, a state of drowsiness and confusion. Then the victim gradually regains consciousness and may complain of a headache.

First aid for someone having a seizure includes the following:

- Protect the victim from injury. If on land, clear the area of any hard or sharp objects and loosen any tight clothing.
- Do not try to restrain a victim having muscular contractions.
- Do not put anything in the victim's mouth.
- If on land, turn the victim on the side if needed to let saliva or vomit drain out.
- Have someone call EMS personnel.
- Stay with the victim until the EMS personnel arrive. Monitor the victim's breathing. If the victim stops breathing, start rescue breathing.
- Help the victim rest and feel comfortable. Be reassuring and supportive. Protect the victim's privacy by keeping onlookers at a distance.

A seizure in the water requires quick action. Often the victim goes under water quickly without warning or a call for help. A seizure victim may breathe water into the lungs, which can cause life-threatening problems.

If someone has a seizure in the water, support the victim to keep the head and face above water so that he or she can breathe. Have someone call EMS personnel. Remove the victim from the water as quickly as possible, and check breathing and pulse. Place the victim on his or her side to let any fluids drain from the mouth (Fig. 13-39). Now care for the victim as you would care for a person having a seizure out of the water.

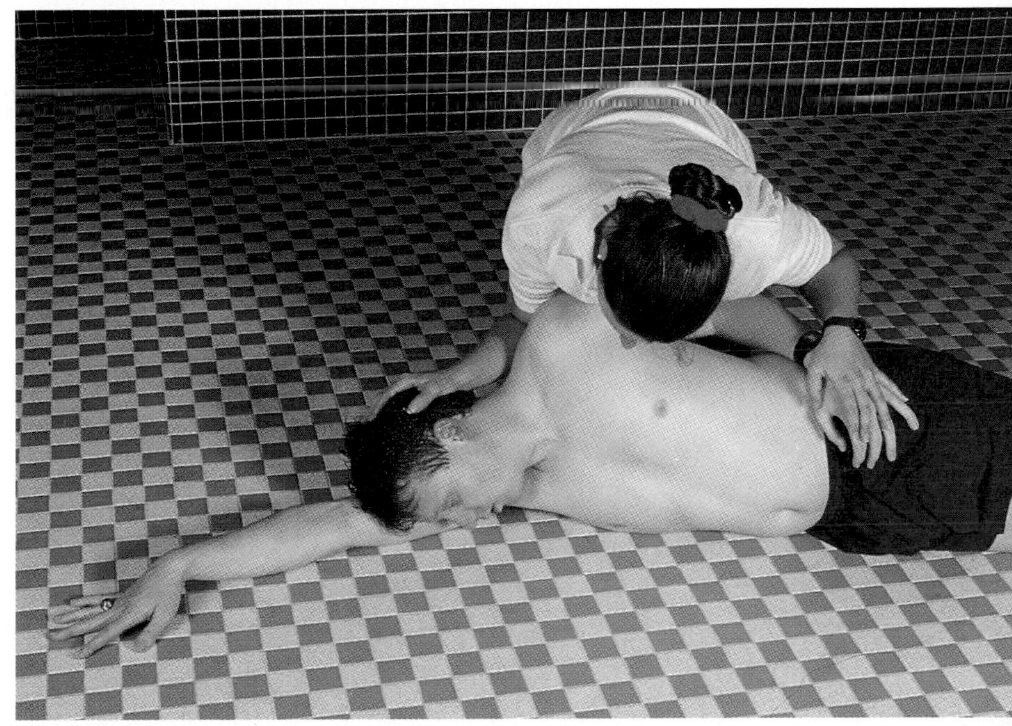

Fig. 13-39

## Spinal Injury

In earlier chapters, you learned that headfirst entries into shallow water and other unsafe activities can cause spinal injuries. Now you will learn how to recognize a potential spinal injury in the water and what to do to prevent further injury.

Usually you find that a spinal injury is caused by hitting the bottom or an object in the water. Your major concern is to keep the person's face out of the water to let him or her breathe and to prevent the person's head and back from moving further. Movement can cause more injury and increase the risk of the person being paralyzed. Your goal is to keep the spine from moving until help arrives. To do this, it helps to understand the spine and know how to recognize a possible spinal injury.

The spine is a strong, flexible column of bones called vertebrae. It supports the head and trunk and protects the spinal cord. The spinal cord is a bundle of nerves that run through the vertebrae and go out to all parts of the body (Fig. 13-40, *A* and *B*). Any injury to the spine can damage these nerves and cause paralysis or death. An injury can happen anywhere along the back or neck up to the head, but neck injuries most commonly result from headfirst entries into the water.

If you are unsure whether a person has a spinal injury, think about what the person was doing and what happened to cause the injury. The following are situations in which spinal cord injury is possible:

- Any fall from a height greater than the victim's height
- Any person found unconscious for an unknown reason
- Any serious head injury
- Any injury from a diving board, water slide, or diving from a height (such as a bank or a cliff)
- Diving into shallow water

If the person is conscious, ask how he or she is feeling. The following signals may also indicate a spinal injury:

- Pain along the spine at the site of the injury
- Loss of movement in the hands and feet, arms and legs, or below the injury site
- Loss of sensation or tingling in the arms, legs, hands, or feet
- Disorientation
- Back or neck shape looks wrong
- Bruise over the spine
- Impaired breathing
- Obvious head injury
- Fluid or blood in the ears

If you think the person may have spinal injury, give care assuming the spine *is* injured. If the victim is in the water, your goal is to prevent any further movement of the head or neck and move the person to safety. Always check first whether a lifeguard or other trained professional is present before touching or moving a person who may have a spinal injury. This section describes what you can do by yourself or with the assistance of bystanders to care for a victim of spinal injury.

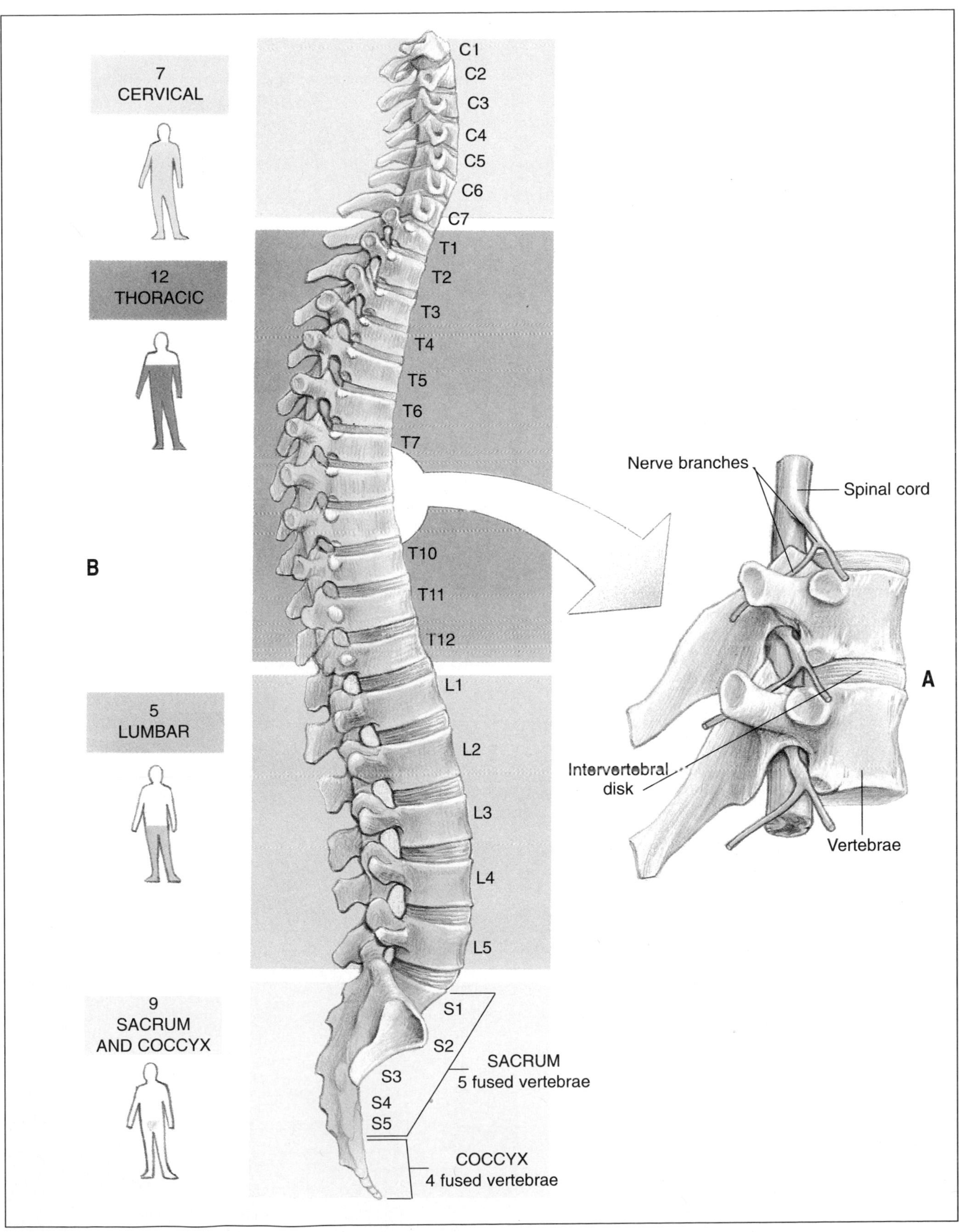
7
CERVICAL
12
THORACIC
5
LUMBAR
9
SACRUM
AND COCCYX
B
C1
C2
C3
C4
C5
C6
C7
T1
T2
T3
T4
T5
T6
T7
T10
T11
T12
L1
L2
L3
L4
L5
S1
S2
S3
S4
S5
SACRUM
5 fused vertebrae
COCCYX
4 fused vertebrae
Nerve branches
Spinal cord
A
Intervertebral
disk
Vertebrae

FIG. 13-40

*General Guidelines for Care*

You can stabilize a victim's spine in several ways while the person is still in the water. These methods are described in the next sections. Follow these general guidelines for a victim with suspected spinal injury in shallow water:

- Be sure someone has called 9-1-1 or the local emergency number. If other people are available, ask someone else in your group or a bystander to help you.
- Minimize movement of the victim's head, neck, and back. First, try to keep the victim's head in line with the body. This technique is called ***in-line stabilization***. Do this without pulling on the head. Use your hands, arms, or body, depending on which technique you use. The two methods described in the next section can be used.
- Position the victim face up at the surface of the water. This may require you to bring a submerged victim to the surface and to a face-up position. Keep the victim's face out of the water to let the victim breathe.
- Check for consciousness and breathing once you have stabilized the victim's spine. A victim who can talk or is gasping for air is conscious and breathing.
- Support the victim with his or her head and spine immobilized until help arrives.

*Specific Techniques*

The following sections describe two methods for stabilizing the victim's spine in the water. These methods will enable you to provide care for the victim whether he or she is face up or face down.

**HIP/SHOULDER SUPPORT.** This method helps limit movement to the spine. Use it for a victim who is face up. Support the victim at the hips and shoulders to keep the face out of the water.

1. Approach the victim from the side, and lower yourself to chest depth.
2. Slide one arm under the victim's shoulders and the other under the hip bones. Support the victim's body horizontally, keeping the face clear of the water (Fig. 13-41, *A* and *B*).
3. Do not lift the victim but support him or her in the water until help arrives.

A

B

FIG. 13-41

**HEAD SPLINT.** This method provides better stabilization than the hip/shoulder support. Use it for a victim face down at or near the surface in the water. This victim must be turned face up to breathe.

1. Approach the victim from the side.
2. Gently move the victim's arm up alongside the head. Do this by grasping the victim's arms midway between the shoulder and elbow. Grasp the victim's right arm with your right hand. Grasp the victim's left arm with your left hand.
3. Squeeze the victim's arms against his or her head. This helps keep the head in line with the body (Fig. 13-42, *A*).
4. With your body at about shoulder depth in the water, glide the victim slowly forward.
5. Continue moving slowly, and rotate the victim toward you until he or she is face up. This is done by pushing the victim's arm that is closest to you under water, while pulling the victim's other arm across the surface (Fig. 13-42, *B*).
6. Position the victim's head in the crook of your arm with the head in line with the body (Fig. 13-42, *C*).
7. Maintain this position in the water until help arrives.

A

B

FIG. 13-42

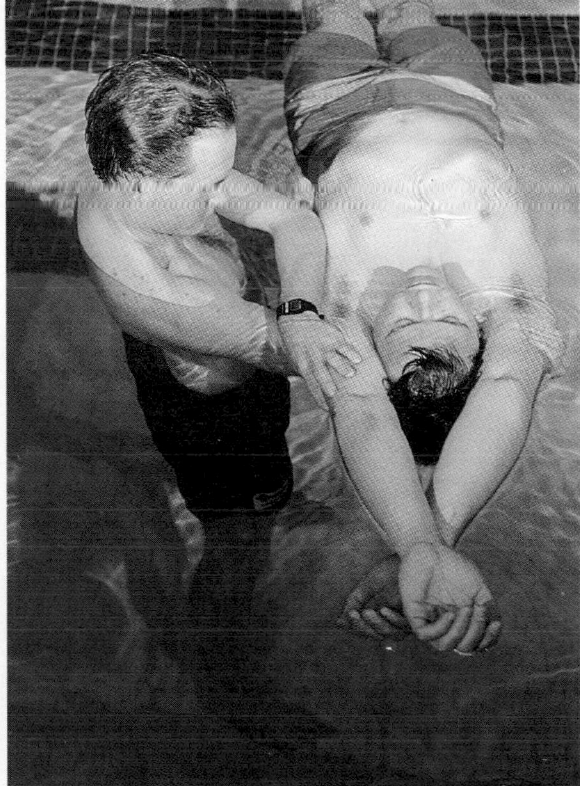

C

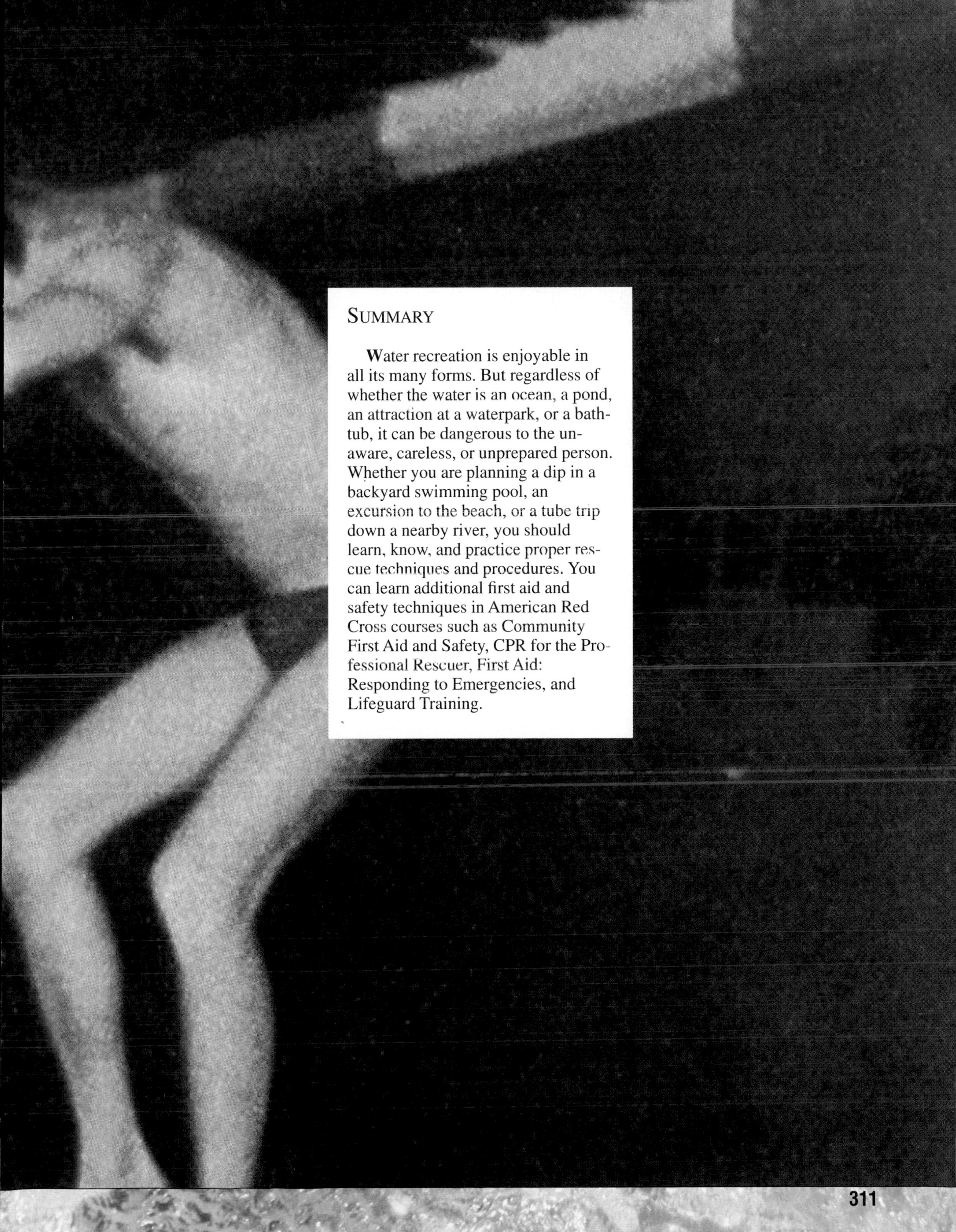

## Summary

**W**ater recreation is enjoyable in all its many forms. But regardless of whether the water is an ocean, a pond, an attraction at a waterpark, or a bathtub, it can be dangerous to the unaware, careless, or unprepared person. Whether you are planning a dip in a backyard swimming pool, an excursion to the beach, or a tube trip down a nearby river, you should learn, know, and practice proper rescue techniques and procedures. You can learn additional first aid and safety techniques in American Red Cross courses such as Community First Aid and Safety, CPR for the Professional Rescuer, First Aid: Responding to Emergencies, and Lifeguard Training.

# organizations that promote aquatics

## Organizations That Promote Aquatics for the General Population

**American Alliance for Health, Physical Education, Recreation and Dance (AAHPERD)**
1900 Association Drive
Reston, VA 22091
(703) 476-3400

**American Camping Association**
**Bradford Woods**
5000 State Road 67 N
Martinsville, IN 46151-7902
(317) 342-8456

**American Canoe Association**
8580 Cinderbed Road, Suite 1
P.O. Box 1190
Newington, VA 22122-1190
(703) 737-8300

**American Red Cross**
**Health and Safety Services Department**
8111 Gatehouse Road
Falls Church, VA 22042
(703) 206-7180

**American Swimming Coaches Association**
301 SE 20th Street
Ft. Lauderdale, FL 33316
(305) 462-6267

**Aquatic Exercise Association**
P.O. Box 1609
Nokomis, FL 34274
(813) 486-8600

**Boy Scouts of America**
1352 Walnut Hill Lane
Irving, TX 75038-3096
(214) 580-2000

**The Canadian Red Cross Society**
1800 Alta Vista Drive
Ottawa, Ontario
Canada, K1G 4J5
(613) 739-3000

**The Commodore Longfellow Society**
2531 Stonington Road
Atlanta, GA 30338

**Federation Internationale de Natation Amateur (FINA)**
Avenue de Beaumont 9
Lausanne 1012
Switzerland

**Girl Scouts of America**
420 Fifth Avenue
New York, New York 10018
(212) 852-5720

**International Swimming Hall of Fame**
1 Hall of Fame Drive
Fort Lauderdale, FL 33316
(305) 462-6536

**National Collegiate Athletic Association**
6201 College Boulevard
Overland Park, KS 66211-2422
(913) 339-1906

**National Federation of State High School Associations**
P.O.Box 20626
11724 NW Plaza Circle
Kansas City, MO 64153
(816) 464-5400

**National Intramural and Recreation Sports Association (NIRSA)**
850 SW 15th Street
Corvallis, OR 97333
(503) 737-2088

**National Junior College Athletic Association**
P.O. Box 7305
Colorado Springs, CO 80933-7305
(719) 590-9788

**National Recreation and Park Association (NRPA)**
650 West Higgins Road
Hoffman Estates, IL 60195
(708) 843-7529

**National Safety Council**
1121 Spring Lake Drive #558
Itasca, IL 60143
(630) 285-1121

**National Spa and Pool Institute (NSPI)**
2111 Eisenhower Avenue
Alexandria, VA 22314
(703) 838-0083

**National Swimming Pool Foundation**
10803 Gulfdale, Suite 300
San Antonio, TX 78216
(210) 525-1227

**The Royal Life Saving Society Australia**
P.O. Box 1567
North Sidney, NSW 2059
02-957-4799
FX 02-929-5726

**The Royal Life Saving Society Canada**
287 McArthur Avenue
Ottawa, Ontario
Canada K1L 6P3
(613) 746-5694

**The Royal Life Saving Society UK**
Mountbatten House
Studley
Warwickshire
B80 7NN
0527 853943

**Triathlon Federation/USA**
3595 East Fountain Boulevard, Suite F-1
P.O. Box 15820
Colorado Springs, CO 80935-5820
(719) 597-9090

**United States Coast Guard (USCG)**
Commandant (G-NAB)
2100 Second Street, S.W.
Washington, DC 20593-0001
(202) 267-1060

**United States Coast Guard Auxilliary**
3131 North Abingdon Street
Arlington, VA 22207
(703) 538-4466

**United States Diving, Inc.**
Pan American Plaza
201 South Capitol Avenue, Suite 430
Indianapolis, IN 46225
(317) 237-5252

**United States Masters Swimming**
261 High Range Road
Londonderry, NH 03053-2616
(603) 537-0203

**United States Power Squadron**
P.O. Box 6568
Richmond, VA 23230
(804) 355-6588

**United States Rowing Association**
Pan American Plaza
201 South Capitol Avenue, Suite 400
Indianapolis, IN 46225
(317) 237-5656

**United States Sailing Association**
Box 209
15 Maritime Dr. 02871
Newport, RI 02840
(401) 683-0800

**United States Swimming, Inc.**
One Olympic Plaza
Colorado Springs, CO 80909
(719) 578-4578

**United States Synchronized Swimming, Inc.**
Pan American Plaza
201 South Capitol Avenue, Suite 510
Indianapolis, IN 46225
(317) 237-5700

**United States Water Polo, Inc.**
1685 W. Uintah
Colorado Springs, Co 80904
(719) 634-0699

**World Water Park Association**
P.O. Box 14826
Lenexa, Kansas 66285-4826
(913) 599-0300

**YMCA of the U.S.A.**
101 North Wacker Drive
Chicago, IL 60606
1-800-872-9622

**YWCA of the U.S.A.**
726 Broadway
New York, NY 10003
(212) 614-2700

## Organizations That Promote Aquatics and Other Activities for People With Disabilities

**American Athletic Association for the Deaf**
10604 East 95 Street Terrace
Kansas City, MO 64134

**American Water Ski Association Disabled Ski Committee**
681 Baily Woods Road
Dacula, GA 30211

**American Wheelchair Sailing Association**
512 30th Street
Newport Beach, CA 92663

**C.W. Hog**
**(Cooperative Wilderness Handicapped Outdoor Group)**
Idaho State University
P.O. Box 8118
Pocatello, ID 83209

**Dwarf Amateur Athletic Association**
9187 Breeze Court
Springfield, VA 22152

**National Handicapped Sports**
451 Hungerford Drive, Suite 100
Rockville, MD 20850
(301) 217-0960

**National Ocean Access Project**
410 Severn Avenue, Suite 306
Annapolis, MD 21403
(410) 280-0464

**National Wheelchair Athletic Association**
3595 East Fountain Boulevard, Suite L-1
Colorado Springs, CO 80910
(719) 574-1150

**Shared Outdoor Adventure Recreation (SOAR)**
P.O. Box 14583
Portland, OR 97214
(503) 238-1613

**Special Olympics**
1350 New York Avenue, N.W., Suite 500
Washington, DC 20005-4709
(202) 628-3630

**Special Populations Learning Outdoor Recreation and Education (S'PLORE)**
27 West 3300 S.
Salt Lake City, UT 84115
(801) 484-4128

**United States Amputee Athletic Association**
P.O.Box 560686
Charlotte, NC 28256

**United States Association for Blind Athletes**
33 North Institute Street
Colorado Springs, CO 80903
(719) 630-0422

**United States Cerebral Palsy Athletic Association**
34518 Warren Road, Suite 264
Westland, MI 48185
(313) 425-8961

**United States Olympic Commitee on Sports for the Disabled**
1750 East Boulder Street
Colorado Springs, CO 80909
(719) 390-8900

**United States Wheelchair Swimming**
229 Miller Street
Middleboro, MA 02346
(508) 946-1964

**Vinland National Center**
3675 Ihduhapi Road
P.O. Box 308
Loretto, MN 55357
(612) 479-3555

**Voyageur Outward Bound School**
10900 Cedar Lake Road
Minnetonka, MN 55343
(612) 542-9255

**Wilderness Inquiry**
1313 5th Street, S.E., Box 84
Minneapolis, MN 55414
(612) 379-3858

# aquatic exercises

## Warm-up and Cool-Down

You should gradually ease your body into and out of your water workout through stretching and light conditioning exercises. Before the workout, stretching elongates the muscles, reduces tension, and promotes freer movement, helping to relax your mind and body. Ligaments and **connective tissues** are "loosened up," preparing the body for more vigorous work. Stretching before the workout also helps prevent injuries such as muscle strains and helps prevent muscle stiffness and soreness the next day. The latest research shows that it is better to reserve the longer, fuller, "developmental" stretches for the end of the workout. Since the muscles are "warmed up" by that time, that is the best time to increase your overall flexibility.

Throughout the workout, you should perform **static stretches**—slow, relaxed, sustained stretches held for a number of seconds. For the most beneficial results, the muscles must be stretched beyond their normal length, but gently and easily. Begin slowly, letting the tension in the muscles gradually decrease as you hold the stretch. Do not stretch to the point of pain. Pay attention to your body. If it hurts, you are doing something wrong. Ease up on the position slowly until you find a degree of tension that is comfortable.

Hold each stretch for 10 to 30 seconds unless otherwise specified. If you are new to stretching or if your muscles are very tight, don't hold the stretch longer than 15 seconds. Relax the muscles as you stretch.

Do not hold your breath while you are stretching. Breathe slowly, rhythmically, and with control. If you cannot breathe naturally while you are holding a stretch, you are not relaxed. Ease the tension until you can resume your natural breathing pattern.

Stretching helps you become more aware of your whole self. As you stretch, focus on various parts of your body, getting in touch with them, tuning them up. When done correctly, stretching is peaceful and relaxing.

Light conditioning exercises are the prelude to the more strenuous aerobic set of the workout. They promote circulation by pumping the blood from the heart to the muscles. Your heart rate begins to rise, and so does your body's deep muscle temperature. These exercises also help your body to adjust to the water temperature. This part of the warm-up is easily accomplished by walking in the pool or swimming any stroke slowly at first, then gradually accelerating and alternating slower with faster work, until you begin to perspire. Other choices for a warm-up include the bobbing and/or treading skills discussed in Chapter 5.

At the end of the aerobic set of the workout, the heart rate needs to return to its resting level gradually. A sudden stop of aerobic activity can cause blood to pool in the muscles, depriving the heart and brain of oxygen. This can lead to lightheadedness and/or nausea. You can cool down easily by repeating something similar to the warm-up segment, varying it as you like for as long as it takes your pulse to return to its pre-exercise rate, usually 3 to 5 minutes.

## The Stretches

This section includes different stretches that concentrate on all the major muscle groups of the body. Dry land stretches are included for those who prefer to do their stretching before they enter the water. Use the ones that work best for you as the basics of your routine; try the others for variety or to relieve boredom.

FIG. B-1

## STRETCHES TO RELIEVE LOWER BACK TENSION

Because many swimming activities force the back to **hyperextend** or arch, it is important to stretch the muscles of the lower back before and after any workout.

FIG. B-2

STRETCH 1. Lie on your back with bent knees, feet flat on the floor. Pull your abdominal muscles in and tighten your buttocks. This flattens your lower back against the floor. Hold for 5 to 8 seconds. Relax. Repeat 2 or 3 times. This exercise strengthens the **buttocks** and **abdominal muscles** and is popularly known as the "pelvic tilt." Once you learn it, this exercise can be done anytime while sitting or standing to help improve posture (Fig. B-1).

FIG. B-3

STRETCH 2. Take the same position as in Stretch 1. Relax. With soles of the feet touching, simply let the natural pull of gravity stretch the **groin** area. Hold for 30 seconds. To loosen up the hips as well, rock the legs back and forth no more than an inch in each direction 10 to 12 times. Be sure the effort originates from the hips rather than the knees (Fig. B-2).

FIG. B-4

STRETCH 3. Take the same position as in Stretch 1. Interlace your fingers behind your head and keep your shoulders and upper back flat on the floor. Relax. From this position, cross the right leg over the left knee and use the right leg to pull the left knee gently down to the right, toward the floor. Do not force your knee to the floor. You don't have to touch the floor with your knee. Stretch within your limits. Breathe naturally. Relax, keeping the elbows, shoulders, back of the head, and lower back flat on the floor. Repeat with the other leg. This exercise stretches the lower back, side, and top of the hip (Fig. B-3).

FIG. B-5

STRETCH 4. Take the same position as in Stretch 1. Straighten your legs, then pull your right knee up gently and hug it toward your chest. This relaxes the lower back. Now stretch the outside of the right hip by pulling your right knee across your body toward your left shoulder. Repeat with the other side.

STRETCH 5. Take the same position as in Stretch 1. Pull both knees to your chest. Relax. To increase the stretch, curl your head up toward your knees, tucking your chin into your chest. This relaxes the lower back.

FIG. B-6

STRETCH 6. Take the same position as in Stretch 1. With hands interlaced behind your head, gently use your arms to pull your head forward until you feel the tension in the back of the neck. Hold for 5 to 10 seconds. Repeat 2 or 3 times. Now, to stretch the muscles on the side of the neck, return to starting position. Slowly pull your head toward your right knee. Hold for 5 seconds. Let the tension subside. Return to starting position. Repeat 2 or 3 times. Repeat with other side.

STRETCH 7. Take the same position as in Stretch 1. Look at the ceiling. With head and shoulders relaxed, turn your chin toward your shoulder for an easy stretch on the side of the neck. Hold for 5 seconds. Then repeat on opposite side, keeping your head resting on the floor.

STRETCH 8. Take the same position as in Stretch 1. With fingers interlaced behind your head, pinch your shoulder blades together to tighten the muscles of the upper back. Your chest will rise slightly. Hold this tension for 5 or 6 seconds, then relax. Then pull your head forward as in Stretch 6. This releases tension and allows for freer movement of the neck.

These last three stretches are excellent for reducing tension in the neck and upper spine. They are relaxing and promote greater flexibility of the head and neck.

STRETCH 9. When you become more confident of your stretching technique, you can do the pelvic tilt and pinch your shoulder blades together at the same time, remembering to flatten the lower back and tighten the buttocks and abdominal muscles. Hold this position for about 5 seconds. Then relax and pull your head forward, to stretch your neck and upper back, as in Stretch 6. Repeat 2 or 3 times.

STRETCH 10. Take the same position as in Stretch 1. Straighten the legs, flatten the lower back, and pull the abdominals in. Extend your arms straight back behind your head and reach as far as you can comfortably, arms in one direction, legs reaching for the other. Hold for at least 5 seconds. Relax. Repeat 2 or 3 times. This exercise is great for your arms, shoulders, rib cage, abdominals, spine, and ankles (Fig. B-4).

STRETCH 11. Lie with the legs straight as in Stretch 10. Stretch diagonally. Extend the right arm overhead as you stretch the left leg in the opposite direction, pointing your toe. Hold for at least 5 seconds. Relax. Repeat with other side (Fig. B-5).

STRETCH 12. Use the straight leg position as in Stretch 10. With your head, neck, and shoulders relaxed and resting on the floor, extend the right arm straight out to the right from the shoulder. Now bend the right knee and draw it up toward your chest. With hand resting on the side of your thigh, gently pull your right leg across the left leg and then down toward the floor until you feel the tension in your lower back and side of the hip. Keeping the feet and ankles relaxed, breathe easily. Do not force the stretch. You do not have to touch the floor to feel the tension. This is not a flexibility contest. Repeat with the other side. This is a good cool-down stretch to relax the back after your workout (Fig. B-6).

## STANDING UPPER BODY STRETCHES

The following exercises can be done in or out of the water. If performed in the water, they should be done in water at least waist-deep, with feet flat on the pool bottom. For the following series, unless otherwise noted, stand with legs about shoulder-width apart, knees slightly bent. This establishes firm support for stretches that use lateral or side-to-side movements. Press shoulders down slightly and keep abdominals in and buttocks tight.

STRETCH 13. Slowly look up and down. Then, head erect, slowly turn the head to the right and to the left. Next, tilt the head down to the left as if the ear were reaching for the shoulder. To increase the stretch, place the left hand on top of the head and pull gently. Now tilt the head to the right and stretch the other side. This exercise stretches the neck and shoulders.

STRETCH 14. Place the right hand on the hip for support. Extend your left arm up and over your head. Gently bend from the waist to the right side, extending your arm toward your right hip. Hold for 10 to 15 seconds or until you feel the tension in the waist, front of the hip, upper arm, and spine. Relax. Repeat with the other side. To increase the stretch, let go of the hip and clasp the hands together, gently pulling one arm down toward the ground. Do not force it. Hold the stretch, then relax. Do not bounce or jerk back to the upright position. Return with control.

STRETCH 15. Place both hands about shoulder-width apart on a fence or ledge. In the pool, hold onto a ladder or the pool gutter. Your feet are directly under your hips, and you are looking straight ahead. Let your head hang down between your shoulders, and let

Fig. B-7

Fig. B-8

your upper body be pulled down by gravity until you feel the tension, then relax. This stretches the upper body and back.

Stretch 16. Begin with arms extended above the head, fingers interlocked (one hand on top of the other) (Fig. B-7). Stretch the arms up and back slightly from the shoulder joint to stretch the shoulders, rib area, and muscles on the back of the arm. Hold the stretch for 8 seconds as you breathe naturally.

Stretch 17. Extend the arms overhead. Bend the right elbow at an angle of about 45 degrees. Your elbow should be pointing straight up, and you should be able to pat yourself on the back with your right hand. Grasp the elbow with the left hand and apply gentle pressure, feeling a stretch in the triceps and the top of the shoulder. Hold for 15 seconds, breathing easily. Relax. Repeat with the left arm (Fig. B-8).

Stretch 18. For the shoulders and the middle of the upper back, extend your arms straight out in front of you. With the right elbow slightly bent, slowly pull your right arm across the front of your chest, toward the opposite shoulder. Hold for 10 seconds. Relax. Repeat with the other arm (Fig. B-9).

Stretch 19. To stretch the upper back, clasp hands behind the head. Touch elbows in front, squeezing your head with gentle but firm pressure. To stretch the **pectoral muscles**, return to starting position and try to pinch your shoulder blades together in back. Repeat several times.

Stretch 20. You can do a series of standing stretches for the arms, shoulders, and chest in or out of the water using a towel. Just be sure you have an extra in case you drop the towel in the water. Grasp the towel at both ends. With arms straight, lift the towel comfortably, without straining, up and over your head and down behind your back. You can isolate any area during this stretch by holding the towel still at any point where you feel particularly tight. You can increase the stretch by moving your hands closer together. If you have difficulty moving up, over, or behind the head, your hands are too close together.

Fig. B-9

Fig. B-10

## Standing Lower Body Stretches

Stretch 21. Stand and face the pool wall or some other support, a few feet away. Lean forward and rest forearms on the wall. Step forward with your right leg, keeping that knee slightly bent while you extend the left leg straight behind you. Keep the left heel flat on the ground. Try not to hunch over. With toes pointing straight ahead, slowly move your hips forward and down, feeling a stretch in the **calf muscle** and the **Achilles tendon** of the left leg. Hold for 20 to 30 seconds. Repeat with the other side (Fig. B-10).

Stretch 22. Take the same position as in Stretch 21. Slightly bend your left leg. Lower your hips down and forward, keeping your back flat and toes pointed straight ahead. Keep your heel down. Hold for 20 to 30 seconds. Repeat with the other side. This stretches the calf and the Achilles tendon.

Stretch 23. Face the pool wall. Grasp the pool wall or gutter with both hands. Place both feet on the wall 18 to 20 inches below the hands, toes pointed up. The knees are slightly bent. Keeping your heels on the wall and with feet flexed, slowly begin to straighten your legs. Hold for 20 to 30 seconds. Repeat with the other side. This stretches the **hamstrings** and the lower back.

Stretch 24. Grasp the pool wall or gutter with both hands. With one foot pointed straight ahead toward the wall, place the other foot flat on the wall, no higher than hip level. Slowly begin to straighten the leg. Hold for 20 seconds. Repeat with the other leg. You should feel the pull in the hamstrings (Fig. B-11).

Stretch 25. Stand up straight, knees slightly flexed. Holding on to your support with your left hand, reach behind and grasp the top of your left foot with your right hand, holding on to your foot in the most comfortable spot. Pull your foot slowly up as far as you can toward your buttocks, pressing your knee straight down to the ground. Do not let your knee rotate out to the side. Feel the stretch in the muscles in the front of the thigh, the **quadriceps**. Repeat with the other side.

Fig. B-11

Fig. B-13

Stretch 26. Lean against the pool wall, back flat against the wall. With toes pointed straight ahead, raise one knee toward the chest. Grasp your leg behind your knee and slowly pull the knee into your trunk. This stretches the lower back, hips, buttocks, and upper hamstrings. Hold for 25 seconds. Repeat with the other leg.

The next series of stretches for the legs are classic "runner's stretches" and should be done on the pool deck.

Stretch 27. Stand with feet about shoulder-width apart. Keep your shoulders down, abdominals in, and buttocks tight. Step forward with your right foot. With toes pointing straight ahead, place your hands on your thighs for support and lean forward slightly. Don't hunch over. This stretches the calf muscle (Fig. B-12).

Fig. B-12

Stretch 27A. Now lunge forward and place your hands on the floor for support. Your weight is shifted onto the ball of your forward foot. The back leg is straight. Circle the hips gently 3 or 4 times for full range of motion in the hips, hamstrings, and groin. Don't force or bounce the stretch. Hold this comfortably for 20 seconds (Fig. B-13).

Stretch 27B. Now drop the back knee and lift your body up. Rest your hands on the tops of your thighs for support. Lean forward carefully just a few inches to stretch the **hip flexors**. Hold for 20 seconds (Fig. B-14).

Fig. B-14

Fig. B-15

Stretch 27C. Place the left hand on the ground for support, then reach around with your right hand and grasp the top of the left foot. Slowly move the front of the hips forward and pull your left foot toward your buttocks until you feel slight tension in the front of the thigh. Hold for 20 seconds. This stretches the quadriceps (Fig. B-15).

Stretch 27D. Release the foot and lean back as you straighten your right leg. Point the toe, then flex the foot. Be sure to use your arms and hands for balance and support as you get a comfortable stretch in the calf and hamstring. Now release the tension in the right leg as you bend your knee and bring it underneath you so that you are on all fours. Support yourself with your arms as you plant your feet firmly on the ground. Now slowly roll up to bring yourself to a standing position. Let your abdominal and quadriceps muscles, rather than your lower back, do the work of lifting you up (Fig. B-16). Now repeat Stretch 27 through Stretch 27D with the other side.

Stretch 28. With hands on your hips and toes pointing straight ahead, take a wide step to the right and lunge, feeling the tension in the inner thigh. Hold for 20 seconds. Flex the left foot to increase the stretch. Lunge in the other direction and repeat the stretch on the other side.

Stretch 29. Return to standing position and, with knees and ankles together, place your hands on your thighs for support as you circle your knees clockwise to stretch the ligaments and tendons in the ankle and knee areas. Do this for 6 to 8 repetitions, then reverse to a counterclockwise direction.

Fig. B-16

## Cardiovascular Workouts

Here are some examples of cardiovascular workouts you can perform in chest-deep water. You can begin by slowly warming up and then gradually increasing your efforts to move into the lower end of your target heart rate range. You should incorporate some of the upper body resistance routines covered in this section to help balance yourself in the water, to increase your aerobic capacity, and to take advantage of the water's resistance to strengthen and tone the upper body. One of the advantages of aquatic exercise is that you can get your cardiovascular workout and your resistance training done simultaneously, saving time. Make sure you monitor your heart rate every 5 to 10 minutes, using the methods described in Chapter 10, and be sure to work out for a minimum of 15 minutes three times a week. If the pool bottom is rough, you may want to wear socks or the special aquatic shoes described in Appendix D during your workout to protect your feet.

### Walking and Jogging

Stand erect in chest-deep water. Walk or jog back and forth across the pool.

*Variation 1.* For more resistance, hold a kickboard in front of you with straight arms. The kickboard should be perpendicular to the water. (For a list of equipment that can be used to help increase the overload in all aquatic exercise, see Appendix D.)

*Variation 2.* Run in place and lift your knees as high as possible without bouncing. Swing your arms naturally as you would if you were jogging on dry land.

*Variation 3.* Repeat Variation 2, but this time do a straddle jog by lifting the knees to the side instead of to the front of the body.

*Variation 4.* Walk across the pool lifting your legs straight out in front of your body. Land on your toes, but be sure to place the heel of your foot on the pool bottom to keep your calf muscle from tightening up.

*Variation 5.* Skip in place.

*Variation 6.* Coordinate the different arm stroke movements described in Chapter 6 with your legs as you walk or jog.

*Variation 7.* For a more advanced workout, get into very deep water and jog back and forth without touching the pool bottom. If you are not very buoyant, use a life jacket.

*Variation 8.* Begin with your legs in stride position, right leg in front (as in a lunge). Your legs are bent, feet are flat on the pool bottom. Reverse the lunge, so that your left leg is in front. Your arms should move in opposition to your legs to help maintain your balance and reach your target heart range. Repeat the cycle again and again.

### Jumping

Jumping Jacks. Stand in chest-deep water with arms at your sides. Keeping arms and legs slightly bent and toes pointed straight ahead, jump energetically and land with the legs straddled, arms out to the side. The arms rise only to the surface of the water, legs are as far apart as possible. Pull your arms and legs together with force. With fluid movement, repeat the cycle.

*Variation.* Instead of returning the legs to the starting position with feet together, cross the arms and legs in front of you.

Scissors Jump. Stand up straight in chest-deep water. Keep your legs straight. Jump up while scissoring your legs. Use your arms to make sculling motions, such as a figure-eight, palms pressing down to protect you on the landing. Jump again and scissor in the other direction.

*Variation.* With arms slightly bent, synchronize your arm and leg movements, crossing your arms in front and then behind your back.

Double Leg Lifts. Keeping your back straight, lift both knees together toward the surface. Don't lean forward. Land lightly by pressing down hard with the arms.

### Hopping

Stand up straight in chest-deep water. Keeping the knees together and slightly bent, balance yourself on the ball of one foot as you hop forward. With arms under water, use some of the sculling motions or arm strokes discussed in Chapters 5 and 6 to aid in balance and to help elevate your heart rate. The idea is not to

Fig. B-17

try to hop up and out of the water. If you do, the short rest you get while your are sinking back down to the pool bottom will lower your pulse. You must move forward, using strong, rounded, whole arm movements for your heart rate to reach and stay in the target range.

*Variation 1.* Stand up straight in chest-deep water with legs straight. Swing one leg out to the side to no more than a 45-degree angle while you hop twice on the other leg. Keep your arms curved in front of your body to scull with downward force as you hop. Return the leg to starting position and, with fluid motion, repeat with the other leg in the opposite direction.

*Variation 2.* Stand erect in chest-deep water with your hands relaxed at your sides. Shift your weight onto one foot as you flex your knees slightly, and lift your free leg backward and slightly to the side. Press down hard with your opposite hand to meet your foot. Now shift your weight to the other foot and repeat the movement on the other side.

*Variation 3.* Stand up straight in chest-deep water with feet shoulder-width apart. The following movements are to be done in one continuous motion. Shift your weight onto the ball of your left foot and lift your right leg so that it is flexed 90 degrees at the hip and 90 degrees at the knee. Hop on your left leg. Hop again as you return to the starting position briefly. Hop again as you immediately kick your right leg straight out to no more than hip level. Repeat these movements with the left leg. This is essentially an aquatic "can-can," but remember that you are not trying to kick your leg up and out of the water. Your arms should be pressing the water down to aid in balance and to keep you from bouncing. You are using your whole body *in the water* to work the resistance of the water, to tone and firm the muscles, and to get a good aerobic workout. Depending on your level of fitness, you can vary this routine by changing the angles at which you kick your leg out or by lifting your leg to the side instead of to the front (Fig. B-17).

## Resistance Exercises for Strengthening and Toning

The following exercises are designed to take advantage of water's buoyancy and resistance to strengthen and tone the body's major muscle groups. You must remember to assume the following lifting position as you work to support the lower back because you are literally lifting, pushing, or pulling the water. For the following exercises, stand up straight in chest-deep water, feet shoulder-width apart, knees slightly bent, abdominals tight, and hips tucked under. As you become more advanced, you can use some of the equipment described in Appendix D to increase the overload, but this is not recommended if you are a beginner.

### Upper Body Routines

Routine 1. Stand up straight facing the pool wall in chest-deep water. Your legs are slightly bent, and your feet are at least 1 foot from the wall. With arms at your sides, bend the elbows to grasp the side of the pool and pull yourself to the wall. Now push yourself away from the wall. Push and pull vigorously. This strengthens and tones the chest, shoulders, and arms.

Routine 2. Stand erect in chest-deep water with feet shoulder-width apart. With elbows slightly bent, extend your arms out to the sides at shoulder height. Circle your arms forward. Keep your fingers and wrists firm to increase the resistance. Then reverse the movement.

*Variation 1.* Make larger and then smaller circles.

*Variation 2.* Flex your palms up and down as you change direction. This is good for shoulders and upper arms.

ROUTINE 3. Stand up straight in chest-deep water with your arms out to the sides and elbows slightly bent. Your feet are shoulder-width apart. With fingers together, palms facing down, pull the arms down to the side. Return to starting position vigorously with palms facing up. This is good for the shoulders and upper back.

ROUTINE 4. Stand erect in chest-deep water with feet shoulder-width apart. Arms are out to the side at shoulder height, elbows are slightly bent. With palms facing forward, pull the arms together in front of your chest. Turn the palms out and push the arms back to the starting position with just as much energy. This tones the chest muscles and the front of the shoulders.

ROUTINE 5. Stand up straight in chest-deep water with feet shoulder-width apart. Extend the arms out to the sides at shoulder height. Palms are facing forward. With elbows bent, pull your arms toward your chest and touch your chest. Return to starting position forcefully but this time rotate your hands so that your palms are facing outward as you push your arms away from your chest. This exercise strengthens and tones the **biceps** and **triceps.**

ROUTINE 6. Stand up straight in chest-deep water with feet shoulder-width apart. With elbows tucked tight into your sides, palms up, fingers together, pull the water up hard to work the biceps. Now push down hard to work the triceps. As a variation, do the exercise with palms down.

ROUTINE 7. Stand erect in chest-deep water with arms out to the sides at shoulder height, elbows slightly bent, palms facing out. Make small pushes forward. Then, with palms facing back, make small pushes backward. With palms facing down, repeat the movement downward. With palms facing up, push the arms upward. This is a good exercise for the chest and upper arms. Increasing the speed of your movements will increase the resistance.

ROUTINE 8. Stand up straight in waist- to chest-deep water facing the pool wall. With hands shoulder-width apart, grasp the pool wall or gutter with both hands and straighten the arms to push yourself up and out of the water. Return to starting position. This exercise uses the pool wall for resistance, and it strengthens and tones shoulders and triceps.

ROUTINE 9. Stand up straight in waist- to chest-deep water with your back against the pool wall. Reach behind you and grasp the pool wall or gutter with your hands close to your body. Straighten the elbows, lifting your body out of the water. This is not an easy exercise. To make it easier, you can start in the corner of the pool for better leverage. Pushing off from the pool bottom helps. This exercise also uses the pool wall for resistance, and it strengthens and tones the forearms, shoulders, and triceps.

ROUTINE 10. Stand erect in chest-deep water with arms straight out in front of you. Open and close the hands as fast as possible with fingers spread wide. This strengthens the muscles of the fingers and hands.

## MIDDLE BODY ROUTINES

For the next exercise, stand with your back against the wall. Reach behind you and grasp the pool gutter with both hands, letting the gutter support your shoulders and upper arms. If this support position causes pain, however, stop and choose an alternative exercise from this section to work the abdominal muscles.

ROUTINE 11. Keeping your legs together, bend your knees upward toward your chest and then extend your legs straight out again (Fig. B-18).

FIG. B-18

*Variation.* Keeping the abdominals tight and the legs straight, perform exaggerated flutter kicks, trying to touch the bottom of the pool with your feet. This works the quadriceps and the abdominals.

FIG. B-19

ROUTINE 12. Maintain the same support position as in Routine 11. Draw the knees up to the chest and roll the thighs first to the right and then to the left. This works the hips and the inner and outer thighs. It is good to perform this exercise after a middle body routine because it helps relax the lower back muscles, which tend to become tense during middle body work.

ROUTINE 13. For alternative abdominal work, stand and face the pool wall. Float on your back and rest your lower legs on the side of the pool. Clasp your hands behind your head. Tuck your chin into your chest and pull yourself forward slightly, tightening your abdominal muscles to do the work. Return to starting position (Fig. B-19).

ROUTINE 14. Float in a prone position and place one hand on the pool wall or gutter and the other hand directly underneath it for support. With fluid motion, pull your knees into your chest and straighten them out to the right. Then pull them into your chest again and straighten them out to the left. This works the **external oblique** muscles and the lower abdominals.

## LOWER BODY ROUTINES

ROUTINE 15. Stand up straight with your lower back pressed against the wall in waist- or chest-deep water. Lift your right leg so that it is flexed 90 degrees at the hip and 90 degrees at the knee. Extend the leg so that it is nearly straight but not locked. This works the quadriceps. Repeat with the left leg.

ROUTINE 16. With shoulders, hips, and knees aligned and your foot relaxed, try to bring the heel of the right foot back and up to reach the buttocks. Alternate with the left foot. Try not to arch your back. This strengthens and tones the hamstrings.

If the last two routines are performed vigorously, they could be part of your cardiovascular workout, so you would be getting your lower body resistance work done at the same time.

ROUTINE 17. Stand erect in chest-deep water. With toes pointed, lift the right leg out to the side at an angle of no more than 45 degrees. Return to starting position forcefully and repeat with the other leg. Remember that the movement originates from the hip. It strengthens and tones the inner and outer thighs.

ROUTINE 18. With the right foot relaxed, lift the right leg forward no higher than your hip. Without turning your body, move the leg to the side and return it vigorously to the starting position. Again, the movement is from the hip. This is also for the inner and outer thighs. Repeat with the left leg.

ROUTINE 19. Lift the right leg until your thigh is parallel to the pool bottom, knee bent at a 45-degree angle. Without turning your body, move the knee to the side and back again vigorously to work the inner and outer thigh muscles. Keep your foot directly under your knee to avoid knee strain. Repeat with the other leg.

ROUTINE 20. With knees slightly flexed and feet together, lift your right leg back just enough to feel the tension in the buttocks. Do not arch the back. Repeat with the left side.

ROUTINE 21. Lift the right knee to the chest and, with fluid motion, lower the right leg and lift the right heel up slightly to the back, tightening the buttocks as you do so. Do not arch the back. Repeat with the left leg.

ROUTINE 22. Keeping your right leg straight, gently pull it away from the midline of the body and make a figure-eight pattern with your foot. Reverse the direction. This movement is from the hip and works the upper legs and buttocks. Repeat with the left leg.

# appendix C

# tables for calculating target heart rate range

TABLE 1. Calculating the Target Heart Rate Range for Aerobic Exercise on Land

| | | | | | |
|---|---|---|---|---|---|
| A. | 220 | − | ______ (age) | = | ______ (MHR*) |
| B. | ______ (MHR) | − | ______ (RHR†) | = | ______ |
| C. | (______ (Line B) | × .60) + | ______ (RHR) | = | ______ (60% intensity) |
| D. | (______ (Line B) | × .85) + | ______ (RHR) | = | ______ (85% intensity) |
| E. | Target heart rate range in beats per minute | | | = | ______ (Line C) to ______ (Line D) |
| F. | ______ (Line C) | ÷ | 6 | = | ______ (60% intensity) |
| G. | ______ (Line D) | ÷ | 6 | = | ______ (85% intensity) |
| H. | Target heart rate range in beats per 10 seconds | | | = | ______ (Line F) to ______ (Line G) |

*Predicted Maximum Heart Rate.
†Resting Heart Rate.

TABLE 2. Calculating the Target Heart Rate Range for Swimming

| | | | | | |
|---|---|---|---|---|---|
| A. | 220 | − | ________ (age) | = | ________ (MHR*) |
| B. | ________ (MHR) | − | ________ (RHR†) | = | ________ |
| C. | (________ (Line B) × .60) + | | ________ (RHR) | − 10 to 13 beats = | ________ (60% intensity) |
| D. | (________ (Line B) × .85) + | | ________ (RHR) | − 10 to 13 beats = | ________ (85% intensity) |
| E. | Target heart rate range for swimming in beats per minute | | | = | ________ (Line C) to ________ (Line D) |
| F. | ________ (Line C) | ÷ | 6 | = | ________ (60% intensity) |
| G. | ________ (Line D) | ÷ | 6 | = | ________ (85% intensity) |
| H. | Target heart rate range for swimming in beats per 10 seconds | | | = | ________ (Line F) to ________ (Line G) |

*Predicted Maximum Heart Rate.
†Resting Heart Rate.

# appendix D

# equipment

Swimming and aquatic exercise require very little special equipment. Other than a pool, all you really need is a swimsuit. As with many sports, however, high-tech equipment is being developed for swimming and aquatic exercise. You can buy a "swimman" to listen to your favorite audio cassette or FM station or a stopwatch to help you count laps or to give you an instant split recall. The only thing that might limit you is your pocketbook. The more traditional equipment, such as hand paddles, fins, and kickboards, can be found at almost any pool. These and other devices can help you learn skills faster, improve your technique, and provide some basic equipment. If not, you can always bring your own. Much of the equipment discussed can be purchased at any well-equipped sporting goods store.

## Swimsuit and Cap

Most fitness swimmers prefer Lycra swimsuits because they dry quickly between workouts. Females usually prefer one-piece suits, although two-piece suits may be worn. Males usually choose brief-style trunks, which produce less drag than boxer-style trunks. Swimsuits should be rinsed with fresh water.

## Goggles

Goggles increase underwater visibility and protect the eyes from swimming pool chemicals. Goggles are made in a variety of sizes, shapes, and colors. Most have an adjustable nose piece and head strap. Goggles should fit comfortably over the eye socket. Check the fit by pressing the eyepiece to see if it develops a suction around the eye. Then adjust the strap and/or nose-piece to hold the goggles in place. The pressure of the water should help keep the goggles in place without an excessively tight strap. When swimming outdoors, you may choose to use goggles with colored lenses to reduce glare.

## Kickboard

The kickboard is one of the most commonly used pieces of equipment in swimming. This simple device supports the upper body and allows for easy breathing when you practice your kicks. This way, you can learn a new kick or practice a familiar one. The kickboard also provides some resistance, so it can be used to increase the workload during either the aerobic segment of your workout or during the strengthening and toning portion.

A kickboard can also be used for support during stroke drills. This allows you to isolate one arm at a time. Rotate the board so that the long edge faces you, providing a greater base of support for balance when you use it to learn new strokes.

## Pull Buoy and Leg Float

A pull buoy is usually made up of two cylinders of styrofoam joined together with a nylon cord or strap. Held between the thighs or lower legs so that you cannot kick, a pull buoy provides buoyancy for the legs so that the arms can be isolated. With this support, you can learn new strokes, improve your arm action, and build upper-body strength. A pull buoy can be used with or without paddles.

Leg floats are made of foam in the shape of a figure eight. The narrow middle section is squeezed between the thighs or the lower legs. It is used just like a pull buoy.

## Hand Paddles and Webbed Gloves

Hand paddles are devices worn on the hands (and sometimes the arms) during portions of a fitness or training workout. Paddles help strengthen the shoulders, chest, and arms by increasing form drag. They come in a variety of shapes and sizes. Choose paddles that extend up to an inch around your hand in a shape that feels comfortable as you swim.

Hand paddles can also improve your awareness of your hand moving through the water. If they twist or pull away from your palm, you're probably doing something wrong, such as dropping the elbow or twisting the hand. You can use hand paddles alone or combine them with a pull buoy or other devices to concentrate on your arm stroke. They should be used sparingly, since the increased resistance can cause strain on the shoulder muscles. Stop using them if shoulder pain develops.

Webbed gloves also rely on increased form drag to help make upper-body strength training more efficient. These may be used during the aerobic portion or the strengthening and toning segments of your workout.

## Weights and Weight Belts

Wrist and ankle weights also can be used to increase the intensity of the aerobic or muscular development segment of your workout. However, because they increase the impact of the body on the bottom of the pool, there is greater risk of injury using weights than there is when using equipment designed to increase the water's resistance only.

Weight belts are used to help those who are very buoyant maintain a balanced position in chest-deep water when they are doing aquatic exercise.

## Fins

Fins are useful for both the beginner and the accomplished swimmer. They provide increased propulsion while improving strength in the leg muscles and promoting greater ankle flexibility. The less skilled swimmer builds confidence, moves through the water faster, and increases awareness of body position in the water. Swimmers of all skill levels might find fins very helpful in training and in the learning of new skills. You can use them while swimming, or with a kickboard to emphasize leg work.

Fins come in a variety of styles. Flexible blades are easier to use than the stiffer ones. Be sure to choose fins that are comfortable and will not rub against your ankle or heel. If fins are too small, they could cause cramps in your foot. If they are too large, they could cause blisters, although wearing socks or the aqua shoes mentioned below should help prevent this. It is a good idea to try fins out before purchasing them.

## Barbells, Swim Bars, and Swim Belts

Barbells take advantage of the laws of buoyancy to increase the water's resistance and therefore increase upper-body strength and endurance. Instead of weights, styrofoam or plastic is attached to both ends of the bar to inhibit movement through the water. They may be used during strengthening and toning exercises performed in the water.

A swim bar is a longer version of a barbell, but it is held with both hands and primarily helps you keep your balance during water walking or jogging. It can also be used instead of holding onto the wall when you work on your abdomen and lower body, or like a kickboard to support you when you practice your kicks.

A swim belt is worn around the waist to keep you stable and afloat while you walk or jog in the water without touching the pool bottom. A life jacket serves the same purpose. However, non-swimmers should not rely on these devices for support in deep water.

### Steps or Bench

Step or bench training is among the more recent innovations for varying a water workout. Taking advantage of the pool stairs or a weighted bench, you step up and down rhythmically for an intense, yet low-impact aerobic workout that focuses on the lower body. You must work against the resistance of the water on the step up as well as the step down. You can improve the muscular strength of your upper body at the same time if you use wrist or ankle weights or any of the buoyant hand, arm, or ankle equipment mentioned previously.

### Drag Devices

Drag boards or "pull boards" force you to work harder against the added resistance they provide. A drag board looks like a kickboard, except that it has two holes where you put your feet so the board is around your ankles. As you swim, the drag board becomes vertical, increasing drag. The drag board may be used in conjunction with the pull buoy.

The drag suit has large outer pockets that fill with water as you swim, and this increases drag. The drag suit should allow for normal body position in the water, and you should be able to swim any stroke.

A training tube is placed around the ankles in a figure eight. It can help you work on arm strokes, and the inflation can be changed to vary the buoyancy and drag. The training tube may also be used as a substitute for a kickboard.

The stretching tether, usually constructed with surgical tubing, is a device for providing resistance other than drag. One end of the tether is secured to the swimmer's waist with a belt while the other end is looped around a starting block. The swimmer first swims a lap against the resistance of the elasticized tether. The greater the distance attempted, the harder it becomes to get anywhere. Then, during the second lap, the swimmer sprints faster than is normally possible because he or she is aided by the pull of the tether.

### Dry Land Resistance Equipment for Swimmers

Any resistance equipment used to increase muscular strength should concentrate on exercises that help improve swimming speed and endurance. When using dry land equipment, keep in mind the principle of specificity of training discussed in Chapter 11.

During dry land training, you work with the device against gravity, gradually increasing the resistance, i.e., the weight, and the number of times you move the added weight in order to build muscle strength and endurance. More traditional dry land resistance devices (stationary weight machines like Nautilus and Universal; free weights, such as barbells and dumbbells; and stretch cords and/or pulleys) may be used if the routines involve the muscles used in swimming and if the movements are as similar to those of swimming as possible.

The mini-gym and **isokinetic** swim bench were designed specifically with swimmers in mind, and they permit swimmers to duplicate a full range of swimming motions. What is also unique about these devices is that they are isokinetic. This means that the resistance automatically adjusts to the force applied by your muscles, so that as your muscles tire, and your effort weakens, the resistance also decreases, lessening the chance of injury. The swim bench has the added feature of measuring the force of your pull as you simulate swimming movements.

### Pace Clock

One of the most useful pieces of equipment for the fitness swimmer is the pace clock. A pace clock is simply a large stopwatch used on the pool deck to assist in timing predetermined distances, interval sets, or even an entire workout. In addition, the pace clock makes it easy to do quick pulse checks throughout a workout.

Pace clocks are either digital or have sweep hands. Many pools have a pace clock at one or both ends of the pool. If a pace clock is not available, a water-resistant watch works almost as well.

### Aqua Shoes

These are flexible shoes constructed with nylon uppers and rubber or neoprene nonslip soles. They help prevent injury in people who lack sensation in the lower extremities. They may be worn in the water and if they have some arch support are excellent for aquatic exercise, especially if the bottom of the pool has a rough surface.

# appendix E

# the emergency medical services system

This appendix explains what an EMS system is, how a victim of injury or sudden illness "enters" the system, and what should happen when EMS personnel arrive at the scene of the emergency. At the end of this appendix is a chart of instructions for making an emergency telephone call.

## What Is An Emergency Medical Services (EMS) System?

To save a life in a life-threatening situation, two things must happen. Emergency care must be started immediately by a trained bystander, and this care must be continued and enhanced by EMS personnel when they arrive. If no one with first aid training is nearby to begin emergency care immediately, or if the community's EMS system cannot quickly provide the right kind of help, a victim's chances of survival may be greatly reduced.

## Components of an EMS System

Providing the victim with the right care at the right time is not an easy task. Although most communities have some way of sending medical help to victims of sudden illness or accidents, this help might not include everything that the victim needs and might not arrive in time to give the victim the best chance of surviving. Your community's ability to get the right help to the victim as quickly as possible requires both planning and resources. EMS systems that do this effectively usually have the following parts:

1. Trained citizens. Trained citizens can give first aid and alert the EMS system that a medical emergency has happened.
2. Trained personnel. To provide the best help quickly, an EMS system has specially trained personnel. These may include emergency medical technicians (EMTs), emergency medical technician-paramedics (paramedics), first responders (police, fire fighters), emergency dispatchers, and hospital emergency department physicians and nurses trained in emergency medicine.
3. Special equipment. Different situations and medical needs require specialized medical, rescue, and transportation equipment.
4. Communications systems. How well the EMS system works depends on how quickly citizens can alert the system that an emergency has happened and how quickly the dispatcher can get the appropriate emergency personnel to the scene. Communications systems are also important because EMS personnel often need to communicate with the hospital emergency department as they care for the victim at the scene of the emergency and on the way to the hospital.
5. Management and evaluation. An EMS system needs a management structure that includes administration and coordination of all parts of the system, medical supervision and direction, and ongoing evaluation and research.

## The Responsibilities of the Rescuer in the EMS System

For the victim of a medical emergency to receive care from the EMS system, the victim must "enter the system." This means that the EMS system must be told about the emergency, and care should be given until EMS personnel arrive. These important first steps are generally performed by a citizen rescuer.

There are three things that you must do to make sure that a victim enters the EMS system with the best chance of survival:

1. Recognize that a medical emergency has happened.
2. Give first aid.
3. Phone the EMS system for help.

## How an EMS System Responds to a Call for Help

In many communities, a dispatcher answers your call. The dispatcher is very important in making sure that the victim gets the right care immediately. In some systems, this person has special training to get specific information from the caller and to know which personnel and equipment to send to the scene. Some dispatchers can also give first aid instructions to the caller over the phone when it is necessary.

### *Basic Life Support and Advanced Life Support*

The information you provide to the EMS dispatcher is important. It will help determine the type of care that the dispatcher sends to the scene of an emergency: The dispatcher may send either an ambulance capable of continuing basic life support or an ambulance capable of delivering advanced life support. The care sent will depend on the needs of the victim and the services available in your community.

### *First Responder*

When a dispatcher receives a call for emergency medical help, the dispatcher selects the type of care that is needed and sends the appropriate personnel. This may include police, fire, rescue, and ambulance personnel, depending on the type of emergency and the resources available at the time of the call.

In many communities, police and fire fighters may arrive at the scene before the ambulance because they are often located closer to the scene of the emergency. If you have been caring for a victim, the first responder may take over or ask you to assist. On the other hand, the first responder may tell you to continue care while he or she attends to other problems at the scene. It is important that you do not stop caring for a victim until the first responder takes over. You should expect the first responder to ask you for information about the victim. Information that you have gained from your primary and secondary surveys of the victim may be valuable to first responders, EMTs, paramedics, and to the hospital staff who will care for the victim later.

### *When the Ambulance Arrives*

When the ambulance arrives, the EMTs or paramedics take over responsibility for care of the victim and provide additional medical care. Their goal is to begin to stabilize the victim's condition (correct life-threatening problems) at the scene. Once this has been done, the EMS personnel prepare the victim for transport to the appropriate hospital emergency department, and they continue caring for the victim on the way. When the ambulance arrives at the hospital, the EMS personnel transfer responsibility for care of the victim to the emergency room staff.

# Instructions for Emergency Telephone Calls

## Emergency Telephone Numbers

EMS ____________ Fire ____________ Police ____________

Poison Control Center ____________________________

## Other Important Telephone Numbers

Doctor ____________ Telephone number ____________

Facility manager ____________ Telephone number ____________

Head lifeguard ____________ Telephone number ____________

Weather Bureau telephone number ____________

Name and address of medical facility with 24-hour emergency cardiac care:

____________________________

## Information for Emergency Call

(Be prepared to give this information to the EMS dispatcher.)

1. Location

   Street Address ____________________________

   City or Town ____________________________

   Directions (cross streets, roads, landmarks, etc.) ____________________________

   ____________________________

2. Telephone number from which the call is being made
3. Caller's name
4. What happened?
5. How many people injured?
6. Condition of victim(s)
7. Help (first aid) being given

*Note:* Do not hang up first. Let the EMS dispatcher hang up first.

# appendix F

## lifesaving essentials for adults and children

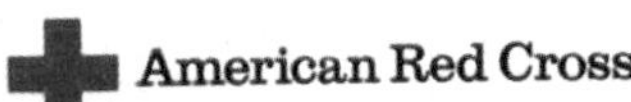

# Adult Lifesaving Steps

## CHECK

- Check the scene for safety
- Check the victim for consciousness, breathing, pulse, and bleeding

## CALL

- Dial 9-1-1 or local emergency number

## CARE

- Care for conditions you find

### If conscious but choking...

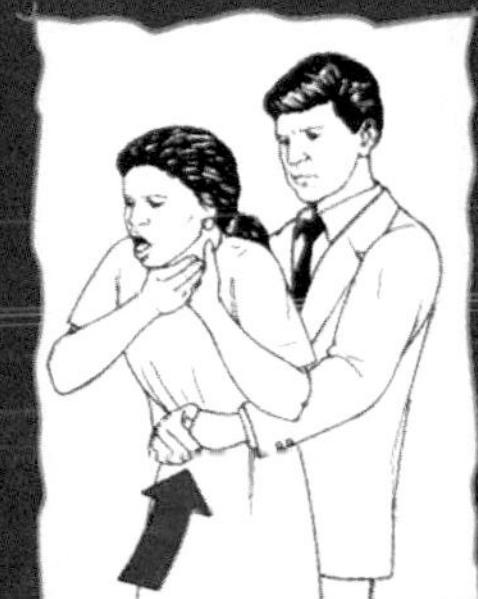

Give abdominal thrusts until object comes out

### If not breathing...

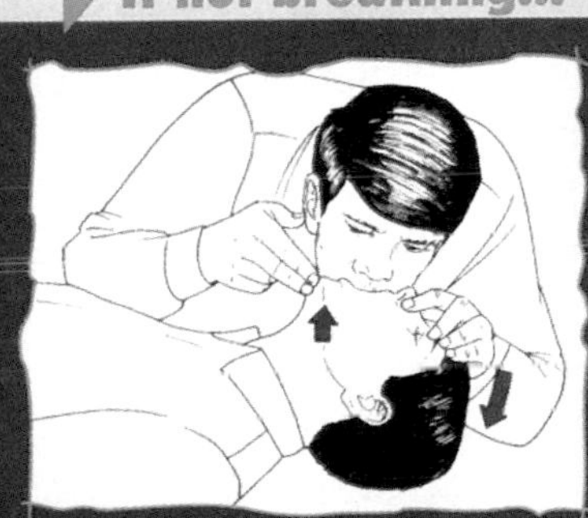

Give 1 slow breath about every 5 seconds

### If air won't go in...

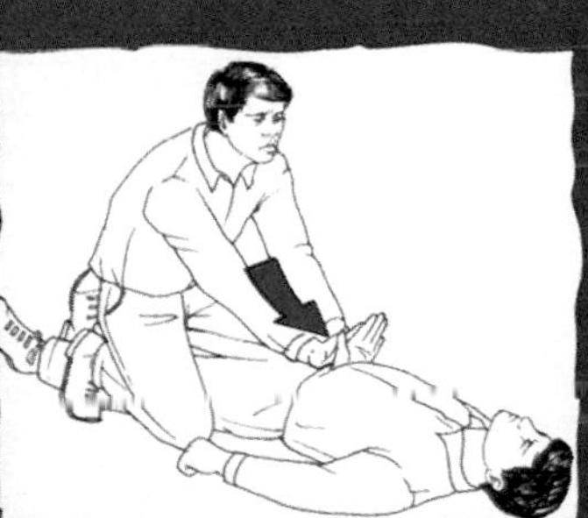

STEP 1

Give up to 5 abdominal thrusts

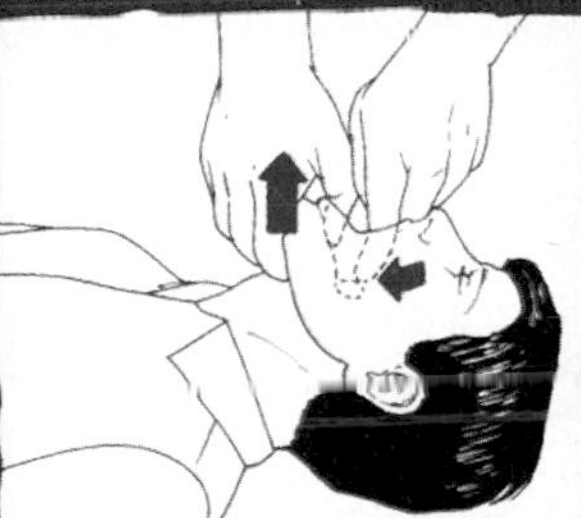

STEP 2

Clear any object from mouth

STEP 3

Reattempt breaths

**Repeat steps 1, 2, & 3 until breaths go in or help arrives**

### If not breathing and no pulse...

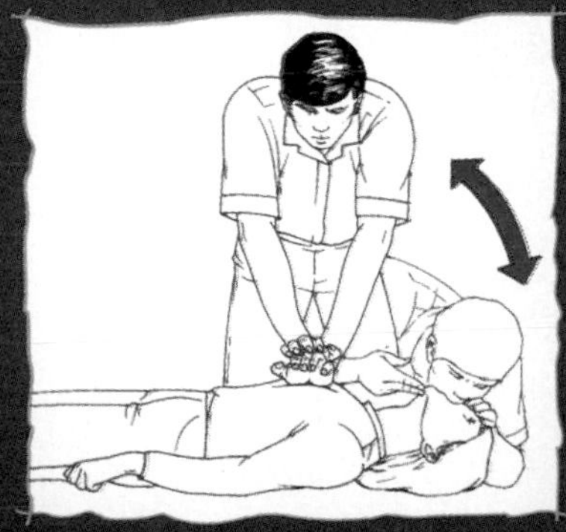

Give CPR—repeat sets of 15 compressions and 2 breaths

### If bleeding...

Apply pressure, elevate, and bandage

**Local Emergency Telephone Number:** __________

Everyone should know what to do in an emergency. Call your local American Red Cross __________ for information on CPR and first aid courses.

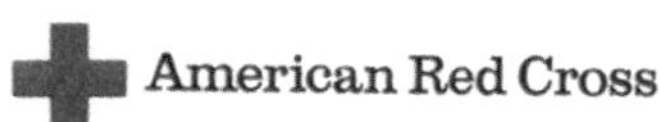


# Infant & Child Lifesaving Steps

**CHECK**
- Check the scene for safety
- Check the victim for consciousness, breathing, pulse, and bleeding

**CALL**
- Dial 9-1-1 or local emergency number

**CARE**
- Care for conditions you find

## INFANTS (birth to 1)

### If conscious but choking...

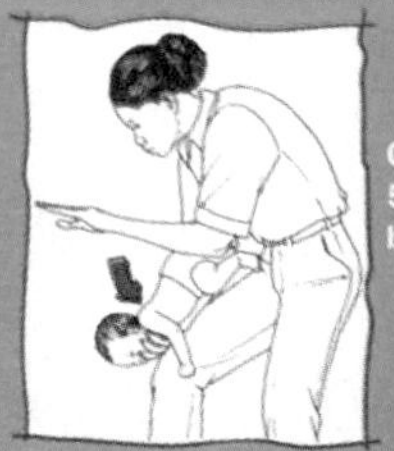

Give 5 back blows ...

And 5 chest thrusts

Repeat blows and thrusts until object comes out

### If not breathing...

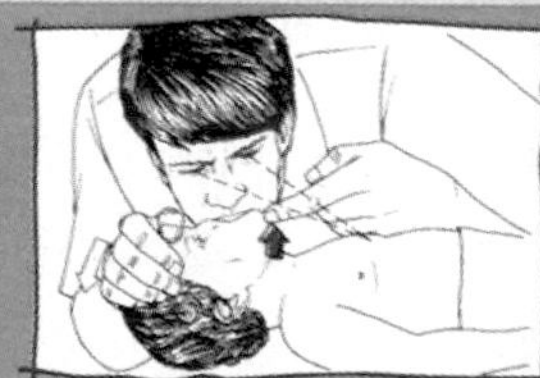

Give 1 slow breath about every 3 seconds

### If air won't go in...

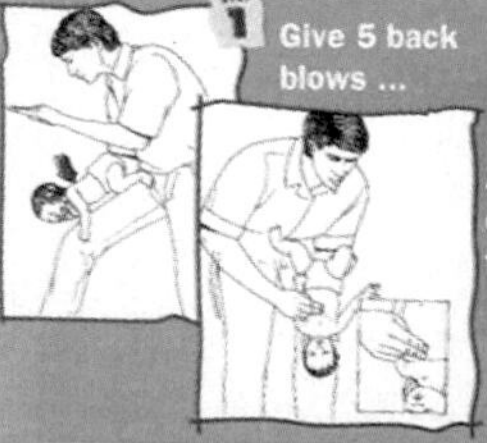

Step 1: Give 5 back blows ... And 5 chest thrusts

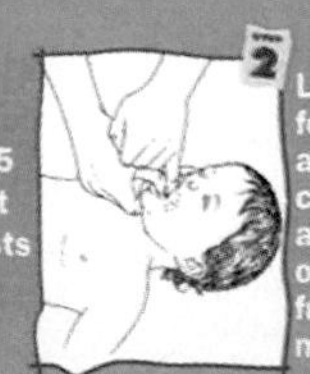

Step 2: Look for and clear any object from mouth

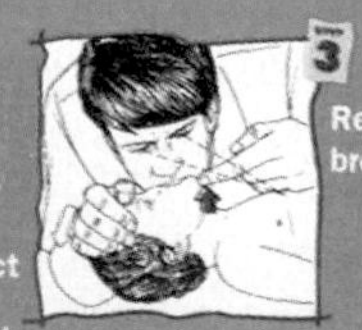

Step 3: Reattempt breaths

### If not breathing and no pulse...

Give CPR—repeat sets of 5 compressions and 1 breath

## CHILDREN (1-8)

### If conscious but choking...

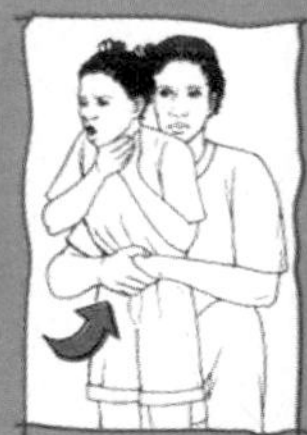

Give abdominal thrusts until object comes out

### If not breathing...

Give 1 slow breath about every 3 seconds

### If air won't go in...

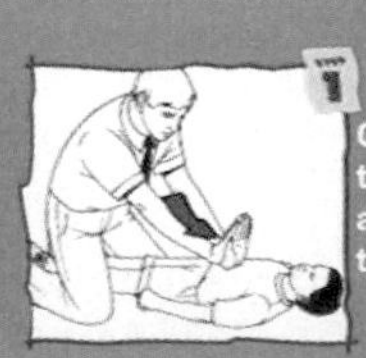

Step 1: Give up to 5 abdominal thrusts

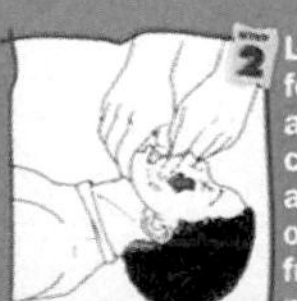

Step 2: Look for and clear any object from mouth

Step 3: Reattempt breaths

Repeat steps 1, 2, & 3 until breaths go in or help arrives

### If not breathing and no pulse...

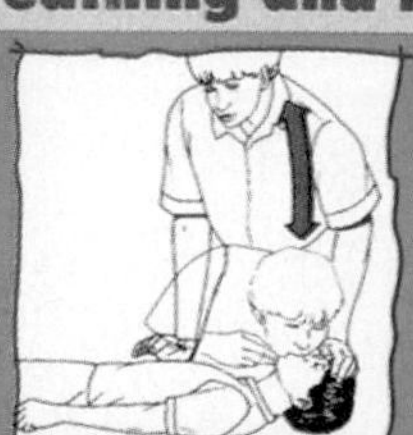

Give CPR—repeat sets of 5 compressions and 1 breath

## If bleeding...

Apply pressure, elevate, and bandage

**Local Emergency Telephone Number:** ____________________

Everyone should know what to do in an emergency. Call your local American Red Cross ____________________ for information on CPR and first aid courses.



Stock No. 652038
July, 1993
ISBN: 0-8016-7751-3
For ordering information, please call 1-800-633-6699

# GLOSSARY

## PRONUNCIATION GUIDE

*The accented syllable in a word is shown in capital letters.*

river = RIV er

*An unmarked vowel that ends a syllable or constitutes a syllable has a long sound.*

silent = SI lent

*A long vowel in a syllable ending in a consonant is marked ¯.*

snowflake = SNO flāk

*An unmarked vowel in a syllable that ends with a consonant has a short sound.*

sister = SIS ter

*A short vowel that constitutes a syllable or ends a syllable is marked ˘.*

decimal = DES ĭ mal

*The sound of the letter **u** in an unaccented syllable is spelled* **ah.**

ahead = ah HED

**ABDOMINAL MUSCLES:** A pair of muscles that extend vertically along the whole abdomen.

**ABOVE-GROUND POOL:** A portable pool that has water 36 to 48 inches deep at the wall. The wall is positioned on the ground and may be disassembled and stored.

**ACHILLES (AH KIL E–Z) TENDON (TEN DON):** Tendon that connects the calf muscle to the heel.

**ADIPOSE (AD ĭ PO–Z) TISSUE:** Body tissue that stores fat.

**AEROBIC (Ĕ RO BIK) (OXYGEN-USING) ENERGY SYSTEM:** The energy system in the body that breaks down carbohydrates, fats, and proteins for energy.

**AEROBIC CAPACITY:** The largest volume of oxygen a person can absorb in a minute. Exercise that requires more oxygen is anaerobic.

**AEROBIC EXERCISE:** Sustained, rhythmic, physical exercise that requires additional effort by the heart and lungs to meet the increased demand by the skeletal muscles for oxygen.

**AMPUTATION:** Removal of a limb from the body.

**ANAEROBIC (AN Ĕ RO BIK) (WITHOUT OXYGEN) ENERGY SYSTEM:** The energy system in the body that uses the most rapidly available source of energy–sugars and carbohydrates stored in the body–for muscular activity.

**ANAEROBIC EXERCISE:** Exercise at an intensity that oxygen is not supplied consistently. Anaerobic exercise involves high-intensity events that last 2 minutes or less.

**APHASIA (ah FA zhah):** A defect in language function characterized by an inability to speak or to form intelligible speech or a difficulty understanding language.

**APPROACH:** The walk toward the end of a diving board before the hurdle.

**AQUATIC EXERCISE:** Water activity generally done in a vertical position with the face out of the water.

**ARTERIAL (ar TE re al) GAS EMBOLISM (AGE):** A condition in which an artery is blocked by expanding bubbles of gases. May rupture tissue and blood vessels, causing decompression sickness and death. (See "the bends.")

**ASTHMA: (AZ mah):** A respiratory disorder characterized by wheezing, tightness in the chest, and labored breathing.

**ATLANTOAXIAL (at LAN to AK se al) INSTABILITY:** A weakness in the ligaments between the first two vertebrae.

**AUTISM (AW tizm):** A mental disorder characterized by extreme withdrawal, absorption in fantasy, and inability to relate to people.

**AUTONOMIC (aw to NOM ik) NERVOUS SYSTEM:** The part of the nervous system that regulates involuntary functions, including the operation of the heart, smooth muscles, and glands.

**BACK GLIDE:** A technique for moving through the water in a supine position.

**BASAL METABOLIC (met ah BOL ik) RATE:** The amount of calories the body burns at rest.

**BEHAVIOR OR EMOTIONAL DISTURBANCES:** Any of a group of antisocial behavior patterns occurring primarily in children and adolescents, such as overaggressiveness, overactivity, destructiveness, cruelty, truancy, hostility, and poor judgment.

**"THE BENDS":** Common name for decompression sickness, a painful and sometimes fatal condition that occurs when nitrogen bubbles out of the blood too rapidly to be expelled from the body by breathing.

**BICEPS:** Long muscle on the front of the upper arm, used to flex the arm and forearm.

**BOBBING:** The skill of submerging and pushing off from the bottom to return to the surface.

**BODY ALIGNMENT:** The position of the body in preparation for an entry.

**BODY ROLL:** A rotating movement of the body around the midline.

**BREAKPOINT:** The area of the pool where the depth changes from shallow to deep.

**BUOYANCY:** The upward force a fluid exerts on bodies in it.

**BUTTOCKS:** The back of the hips that form the fleshy parts on which a person sits.

**CALF MUSCLE:** The muscles at the back of the lower leg, used to extend the ankle.

**Cardiovascular (KAR DE O VAS KU LAR) disease:** Disease of the heart and blood vessels; commonly known as heart disease.

**Cardiovascular endurance:** The ability of the heart, lungs, and circulatory system to sustain vigorous activity.

**Cardiovascular system:** The heart and blood vessels, which bring oxygen and nutrients to the body through the circulation of blood.

**Carotid (KAH ROT ID) artery:** A major artery located in the neck.

**Catch:** The stage in a stroke when the swimmer first engages the water in a way to start moving; the start of the power phase.

**Center of buoyancy:** The point around which the buoyant properties of the body are evenly distributed.

**Center of mass:** The point around which the weight of the body is evenly distributed.

**Cerebral (SER Ĕ BRAL) palsy (PAWL ZE):** A central nervous system dysfunction in which the person has limited or no control of the muscles.

**Cholesterol (ko LES ter ol):** A fatty substance made by the body and found in certain foods. Too much cholesterol in the blood can cause fatty deposits on artery walls that may restrict or block blood flow.

**Chronic (KRON ik):** (Of a disease or disorder) developing slowly and persisting for a long period of time. (Of a disease) recurring frequently.

**Circle swimming:** Swimming in a counterclockwise pattern around the line on the pool bottom in the lane's center.

**Cluster:** A group of YMCAs in a specified demographic area.

**Cognitive (KOG nĭ tiv) disability:** A disorder characterized by below-average ability to learn and to adapt socially. The most common form of intellectual impairment.

**Congenital (kon JEN ĭ tal):** Existing at or dating from birth.

**Connective tissue:** Tissue that supports and binds other body tissue and parts.

**Coronary (KOR o ner e) artery disease:** A condition that results from the narrowing and hardening of the coronary arteries, which carry needed oxygen-rich blood to the heart.

**Cystic (SIS tik) fibrosis (fi BRO sis):** An inherited disorder of the glands that causes abnormalities in respiration, perspiration, and digestion, as well as hyperactivity of the autonomic nervous system.

**Disability:** The loss, absence, or impairment of physical or mental fitness that is observable and measurable.

**Displacement:** The volume or weight of the fluid displaced by a floating or immersed body.

**Diving board:** A diving apparatus that consists of a flexible board secured at one end and a fulcrum below the board. Also called a springboard.

**Diving platform:** A stationary structure for diving.

**Diving tower:** A structure used for diving that includes diving platforms at several heights. Towers used for competitive diving often have platforms that are 1 meter, 3 meters, 5 meters, 7 1/2 meters, and 10 meters high.

**Down syndrome (SIN drōm):** A genetic condition that usually causes delays in physical and intellectual development.

**Drag:** The resistance of water on a body moving through it.

**Drift (side) current:** A current that moves parallel to the shore.

**Drowning:** Death by suffocation when submerged in water.

**Dynamic inertia ( ĭ NER shah):** The tendency of a body in motion to stay in motion.

**EMS Dispatcher:** A person who answers a 9-1-1 telephone call and may instruct the caller in first aid or CPR techniques while EMS is responding to the emergency.

**Emergency medical technicians (EMTs):** A person who has successfully completed a state-approved Emergency Medical Technician training program; paramedics are the highest level of EMTs.

**Entry:** The part of a dive in which the body passes through the surface of the water.

**Equilibrium (e kwĭ LIB re um):** A state of balance between opposing forces.

**External oblique (o BLEK):** One of a pair of muscles on the side of the abdomen that connect the lower eight ribs to the groin, used to bend the torso forward and from side to side.

**F.I.T. principle:** A fitness principle that states that workouts must be of sufficient frequency (F), intensity (I), and duration, or time (T), to be effective.

**Feet-first scull:** Sculling technique for moving the body feetfirst in a supine position on the surface of the water using only the arms and hands.

**Feet-first surface dive:** A technique for moving under water from the surface with the feet leading.

**Figures:** In synchronized swimming, movements in the water composed of basic positions and transitions from one position to another.

**Fitness swimming:** A swimming program in which the workouts have a specified level of intensity and are sustained for a set period of time.

**Flat scull:** A technique using basic sculling motions to stay floating supine on the surface.

**Flexibility:** The range of motion in a joint or group of joints.

**Flight:** The movement of the body through the air in a dive.

**Flip turn:** A fast and efficient turn done in a tuck position; used in lap swimming and in the freestyle and backstroke events in competition.

**Force of gravity:** The pull of the earth on a body.

**Form drag:** The resistance caused by an object's shape and profile as it moves through a fluid.

**Freestyle:** A competitive event in which any stroke is allowed. The term is frequently used for the front crawl, since that is the stroke most often used in this event.

**Freestyle relay:** A common competitive event in which each member of a four-member team swims any stroke one quarter of the total distance.

**Frictional drag:** The resistance caused by an object's surface texture as it moves through a fluid.

**Fulcrum (FUL krum):** The part of a diving apparatus under the center of a diving board that lets the board bend and spring.

**Glide:** The stage of a stroke after the power phase when the body keeps moving without any swimmer effort.

**Grab start:** A competitive start often used from starting blocks for the fastest takeoff.

**Groin:** Each of two areas where the abdomen joins the thighs.

**Hamstrings:** The three muscles at the back of the thigh that flex and rotate the leg and extend the thigh.

**Headfirst scull:** A technique for moving headfirst in a supine position on the surface of the water using only the arms and hands.

**Head splint:** A technique used to stabilize the head and neck of a person with a suspected spinal injury.

**Head-tilt/chin-lift:** A technique for opening the airway.

**Hearing impairment:** Partial or total loss of hearing.

**Heat:** In competition, a procedure followed when there are more entrants in a swimming event than there are lanes in the pool.

**Heat exhaustion:** A form of shock, often from strenuous work or exercise in a hot environment.

**Heat stroke:** A life-threatening condition that develops when the body's cooling mechanisms are overwhelmed and body systems start to fail.

**Heaving jug:** A home-made piece of rescue equipment for throwing to a victim, composed of a 1-gallon plastic container containing some water, with 50 to 75 feet of floating line attached.

**Heaving line:** Floating rope, white, yellow, or some other highly visible color, used for water rescue.

**Hemiplegia (hem i PLE jah):** Paralysis that affects one side of the body.

**Hip flexors:** A group of muscles in the hip and thigh area primarily used to lift the leg.

**Hip/shoulder support:** A technique used to stabilize the body of a person with a suspected spinal injury.

**Hopper bottom pool:** A pool with a bottom that angles sharply up on all four sides from the deepest point.

**Hurdle:** The jump to the end of a diving board after the approach.

**Hurdle leg:** The leg lifted in the hurdle.

**Hybrid strokes:** Strokes used in synchronized swimming, composed of parts of different strokes.

**Hydraulic (hi DRAW lik):** A whirlpool created as water flows over an object; they have a strong downward force that may trap an unwary swimmer.

**Hydrodynamics (hi dro dy NAM iks):** The science that studies the motion of fluids and forces on solid bodies in fluids.

**Hyperextend:** To extend a joint as far as it will go.

**Hypertension (hi per TEN shun):** High blood pressure.

**Hyperventilation:** A dangerous technique some swimmers use to stay under water longer by taking several deep breaths followed by forceful exhalations, then inhaling deeply before swimming under water.

**Hypothermia (hi po THER me ah):** A life-threatening condition in which the body's warming mechanisms cannot maintain normal body temperature and the entire body cools.

**In-line stabilization:** A technique used to minimize movement of a victim's head and neck while providing care.

**Individual medley:** An event in which the competitor swims one quarter of the total distance using a different competitive stroke in a prescribed order (butterfly, backstroke, breaststroke, freestyle).

**Insulin (IN su lin):** A hormone that enables the body to use sugar for energy; frequently used to treat diabetes.

**Intensity:** How hard you work out when you exercise.

**Isokinetic (I so kĕ NET ik):** A principle in resistance training that means that the resistance automatically adjusts to the force applied by a person's muscles, so that as your muscles tire, and your effort weakens, the resistance also decreases, lessening the chance of injury.

**Jumpboard:** A recreational mechanism with a spring beneath the board that is activated by jumping on the board.

**Kapok:** A fiber used to fill life jackets and other flotation devices.

**Kinesthetic (kin es THET ik) awareness:** The perception of what the body is doing at any given moment.

**Lactic acid:** A by-product of exercise that may cause muscle soreness and fatigue.

**Laminar (LAM in ar) Flow:** The principle by which the molecules of a fluid that is moving around an object speed up or slow down to stay parallel to each other.

**Law of acceleration:** The principle by which a body's speed depends on how much force is applied to it and the direction of that force.

**Law of action and reaction:** The principle that for every action there is an equal and opposite reaction.

**Law of inertia (ĭ NER shah):** The principle that a force must be applied to move a body from rest, to stop a moving body, or to change the direction of a moving body.

**Law of Levers:** The principle that movement of levers is related to the force applied, the resistance that occurs, the force arm (the distance from where the force is applied to the pivot point), and the resistance arm (the distance from where the resistance occurs to the pivot point).

**Leading arm:** The arm reaching beyond the head when in the glide position. In the sidestroke, this is also called the bottom arm.

**Learning disability:** A condition that often affects children of normal or above-average intelligence, characterized by difficulty in learning basic procedures such as reading, writing, and numeric calculation.

**Lift:** In hydrodynamics, a force created by a body's shape and motion through a fluid, acting perpendicular to the movement.

**Lift:** In diving, the force of a diving board propelling a diver into the air.

**Ligament (LIG ah ment):** Strong elastic tissue that holds bones together at joints.

**Long shallow dive:** A dive for entering the water headfirst at a shallow angle with great forward momentum.

**Mainstreaming:** The process of including people with disabilities in the same programs and activities as the nondisabled.

**Masters:** A classification in some organizations for swimmers 19 years old and older and divers 21 years old and older.

**Medley relay:** A competitive event in which each member of a four-member team swims one quarter of the total distance and then is relieved by a teammate. The first uses a backstroke start and swims the backstroke, the second swims the breaststroke, the third swims the butterfly, and the fourth swims freestyle.

**Metabolic (met ah BOL ik) rate:** The amount of energy produced by the body in a given period of time.

**Motor function:** The brain's ability to direct purposeful physical activities.

**Multiple sclerosis (sklě RO sis):** A progressive disease characterized by patches of hardened tissue in the brain or spinal cord.

**Muscular dystrophy:** A hereditary disease characterized by progressive deterioration of muscles, leading to loss of strength, disability, and deformity.

**Muscular endurance:** The ability of muscle to contract repeatedly with the same force over an extended period of time.

**Muscular strength:** The ability of muscle to exert force.

**Obese:** A condition in which body fat exceeds 20 percent of total body weight for males or 30 percent for females.

**Orthopedic Impairments:** Disorders of bones, joints, tendons, blood vessels, and nerves that impede locomotor function.

**Osteogenesis (os to o JEN ĕ sis) imperfecta (im per FEK tah):** A genetic disorder involving defective development of the connective tissue and characterized by abnormally brittle bones; also known as "fragile bones."

**Overfat:** A condition in which the percentage of fat in the body is higher than recommended.

**Overload:** A fitness principle based on working somewhat harder that normal so that the muscles and cardiovascular system must adapt.

**Overweight:** A condition in which body weight is more than the average based on sex, height, and frame size.

**Paralysis:** Loss of sensation, voluntary motion, or both.

**Paraplegia (pah rah PLE jah):** Paralysis that affects the legs.

**Pectoral (PEK tor al) muscles:** Muscles of the upper chest wall that connect the chest with the bones of the upper arm and shoulder.

**Perthes (PER tās) disease:** Degeneration of bone of the femur in children followed by regeneration or recalcification.

**Physics:** The science that studies matter and energy.

**Physiological (fiz e o LOJ ik al):** Relating to the processes and functions of the human body.

**Pike position:** A basic diving position with the body bent at the hips and the legs straight.

**Pike surface dive:** A technique for moving under water from the surface by bending at the hips and descending headfirst with legs kept straight.

**Plummet:** A line from the midpoint at the tip of a diving board to the bottom of the pool.

**Power phase:** The stage when the arm or leg stroke is moving the body in the desired direction.

**Predicted Maximum Heart Rate (MHR):** An estimate of the fastest pulse possible for a person, calculated by subtracting the person's age in years from 220.

**Press:** A diver's downward push on a diving board before the upward recoil.

**Progression:** In an exercise program, gradually increasing frequency, intensity, and/or time so that an overload is produced.

**Progression:** In learning theory, an ordered set of steps, from the simplest to the most complex, for learning a skill.

**Prone:** On the front, face down.

**Prone float:** A stationary and face-down position in the water.

**Prone Glide:** A technique for moving through the water in a prone position.

**Propulsive:** Causing motion.

**Psychological (si ko Loj ik al):** Referring to the way the mind works and the attitudes, behaviors, and beliefs reflecting a person's state of mind.

**Pulse:** The beat felt in arteries with each contraction of the heart.

**Push leg:** The leg that pushes into the hurdle.

**Quadriceps:** The muscles at the front of the thigh, used to extend the knee.

**Quadriplegia (kwah drĭ PLE jah):** Paralysis that affects both arms and legs.

**Radial artery:** An artery located in the wrist.

**Rate of perceived exertion (RPE):** A method for determining the intensity of a workout based on how hard an individual feels he or she is working.

**Recovery:** The stage of the stroke when the arms and/or legs relax and return to the starting position.

**Rehabilitation:** Restoring a person to normal or near normal physical, mental, and social capability.

**Rescue breathing:** The technique of breathing for a nonbreathing person.

**Rescue tube:** A vinyl, foam-filled, floating support used in making rescues.

**Ring buoy:** A rescue device made of buoyant cork,kapok, or plastic-covered material attached to a line with something at the end to keep the line from slipping out from under your foot when you throw it.

**Rip current:** A current that moves straight out to sea.

**Rotary kick:** A kicking technique used for treading water; sometimes called the eggbeater kick.

**Safe diving envelope:** The area of water in front of, below, and to the sides of a diving board that is deep enough that a diver will not strike the bottom, regardless of the depth of the water or the design of the pool.

**Scuba:** Self-Contained Underwater Breathing Apparatus.

**Sculling:** A technique for moving through the water or staying horizontal using only the arms and hands.

**Sensory functions:** Hearing, seeing, touching, tasting, and smelling.

**Set:** A group of similar exercises performed together.

**Shepherd's crook:** A long pole with a hook on the end that can be used to either pull a conscious drowning person to safety or to encircle a submerged drowning person and pull the person to safety.

**Spatial orientation:** The understanding of one's location in space and position with reference to other objects.

**Specific gravity:** The ratio of the weight of a body to the weight of the water it displaces.

**Specificity (spĕ sĭ FIS ĭ te):** The principle that different exercises lead to different specific benefits for the body.

**Spina (SPI nah) bifida (BIF id ah):** A birth defect of the vertebral column, including deformed laminae (bony arches), incomplete closure of the laminae, absence of laminae surrounding a large area, or an opening in the vertebral column that allows the spinal meninges, the spinal cord, or both to protrude.

**Splits:** Segments of a race.

**Spoon-shaped pool:** A pool with a bottom that is rounded upward from the deepest point to all the sides.

**Starting block:** A platform competitive swimmers dive from to start a race. A bar or handhold is usually attached for backstroke starts.

**Static inertia (ĭ NER shah):** The tendency of a body at rest to stay at rest.

**Static stretches:** Slow, relaxed, sustained stretches held for a number of seconds.

**Straight position:** A basic diving position of the body with the body straight or arched slightly backwards and the legs straight and together.

**Streamlined position:** A body position with hands interlocked, arms straight and stretched overhead, head centered between arms, legs together, body straight, and toes pointed.

**Stroke frequency:** The number of complete arm cycles in a set period of time.

**Stroke length:** Distance traveled in one complete cycle of the arms.

**Stroke mechanics:** The analysis of the hydrodynamic principles that affect how swimmers move in the water and can improve propulsion.

**Supine (SU pin):** On the back, face up.

**Supine float:** A stationary and face-up position in the water.

**Swim meet:** A competitive event in swimming; may be a contest between teams or between individuals who are not grouped into teams.

**Synchronized (SINK ro nizd) swimming:** Rhythmical water activity of one or more people performed in a pattern synchronized to music.

**Tactile impairment:** Partial or total loss of the sense of touch.

**Takeoff:** The propulsive part of a dive in which a diver's feet leave the deck or the end of a diving board.

**Taper phase:** The 1-week to 3-week period in a training season before a peak performance, in which the person in training decreases distances but raises the intensity almost to racing speed.

**Target heart rate range:** The ideal heart rate range for an individual to maintain during exercise for greatest cardiovascular benefit.

**Tendon (TEN don):** A fibrous band that attaches muscle to bone.

**Throw bag:** A nylon bag containing 50 to 75 feet of coiled floating line, used in water rescue.

**Trailing arm:** The arm that rests on the hip in the glide phase of the sidestroke; also called the top arm.

**Training effect:** An improvement in functional capacity of a system (cardiovascular, respiratory, muscular) that results from an overload of that system.

**Trajectory (trah JEK to re):** The curved path of the body through the air.

**Trauma:** A physical injury caused by a violent action.

**Treading water:** A skill using arm and leg movements to stay stationary and vertical with the head out of the water.

**Triathlon:** A sporting event made up of three different activities, usually swimming, biking, and running, in that order.

**TRICEPS:** Large muscles on the back of the upper arm, used to extend the forearm.

**TUCK POSITION:** A basic diving position with the body pulled into a tight ball with knees drawn up to the chest and heels drawn to the buttocks.

**TUCK SURFACE DIVE:** A technique for moving headfirst from the surface with the hips and knees flexed to under water with the hips and knees extending.

**UNDERTOW:** A current that moves down the slope of a beach.

**UNDULATE (UN DU LĀT):** To move in a wavy, sinuous, or flowing manner.

**VARIABLE:** A quantity that may be changed, usually in relation to other factors in a situation or equation.

**VISION IMPAIRMENT:** Partial or total loss of sight.

**VISUAL AWARENESS:** The ability to stay focused on a reference point to determine your body's position in space.

**WAVE DRAG:** The resistance caused by turbulence in a fluid.

# Sources


American Alliance for Health, Physical Education, Recreation and Dance. *Safety Aquatics.* Sports Safety Series, Monograph #5. American Alliance for Health, Physical Education, Recreation and Dance, 1977.

The American National Red Cross. *Adapted Aquatics: Swimming for Persons With Physical or Mental Impairments.* Washington, D.C.: The American National Red Cross, 1977.

———. *Basic Water Safety.* Washington, D.C.: The American National Red Cross, 1988.

———. *Emergency Water Safety.* Washington, D.C.: The American National Red Cross, 1988.

———. *Lifeguarding.* Washington, D.C.: The American National Red Cross, 1990.

———. *Swimming and Aquatics Safety.* Washington, D.C.: The American National Red Cross, 1981.

Anderson, B. *Stretching.* Bolinas, California: Shelter Publications, Inc., 1980.

Armbruster, D.A.; Allen, R.H.; and Billingsley, H.S. *Swimming and Diving.* St. Louis: The C.V. Mosby Company, 1968.

Auerbach, P.S. *A Medical Guide to Hazardous Marine Life.* Jacksonville, Florida: Progressive Printing Co., Inc., 1987.

Besford, P. *Encyclopedia of Swimming.* New York: St. Martins Press, 1971.

Bigelow, J., editor. *The Works of Benjamin Franklin,* Vol. 4. New York: G.P. Putnam's Sons, 1904.

Brems, M. *Swim for Fitness.* San Francisco: Chronicle Books, 1979.

———. *The Fit Swimmer: 120 Workouts & Training Tips.* Chicago, Illinois: Contemporary Books, 1984.

Clayton, R.D., and Thomas, D.G. *Professional Aquatic Management.* Champaign, Illinois: Human Kinetics, 1989.

Clayton, R.D., and Tourney, J.A. *Teaching Aquatics.* Minneapolis: Burgess Publishing Company, 1981.

Collis, M., and Kirchoff, B. *Swimming.* Boston: Allyn and Bacon, Inc., 1974.

Colwin, C.M. *Swimming Into the 21st Century.* Champaign, Illinois: Leisure Press, 1991.

Cooper, K.H. *The Aerobics Program For Total Well-Being.* New York: Bantam Books, 1982.

Counsilman, J.E. *Competitive Swimming Manual.* Bloomington, Indiana: Counsilman Co., Inc., 1977.

———. Report of the 16th Annual Meeting, Council For National Cooperation in Aquatics, 1966.

———. *The Science of Swimming.* Englewood Cliffs, New Jersey: Prentice-Hall, Inc., 1968.

Edwards, S. *Triathlon: A Triple Fitness Sport.* Chicago: Contemporary Books, Inc., 1983.

Firby, H. *Howard Firby on Swimming.* London: Pelham, 1975.

Flewwelling, H. "Sparging System," in Gabriel, J.L., editor. *U.S. Diving Safety Manual.* Indianapolis: U.S. Diving Publications, 1990.

Forbes, M.S. *Coaching Synchronized Swimming Effectively.* Champaign, Illinois: Human Kinetics Publishers, Inc., 1984.

Gabrielsen, M.A. "Diving Injuries: Prevention of the Most Catastrophic Sport Related Injuries." Presented to the Council for National Cooperation in Aquatics. Indianapolis, 1981.

———. *Swimming Pools: A Guide to Their Planning, Design, and Operation.* Champaign, Illinois: Human Kinetics Publishers, Inc., 1987.

Hay, J.G. *The Biomechanics of Sports Techniques.* Englewood Cliffs, New Jersey: Prentice-Hall, 1985.

Jonas, S. *Triathloning For Ordinary Mortals.* New York: W.W. Norton & Co. Inc., 1986.

Katz, J. *Swimming for Total Fitness: A Progressive Aerobic Program.* New York: Bantam Doubleday Dell Publishing Group, 1981.

———. *The W.E.T. Workout.* New York: Facts on File Publications, 1985.

Knopf, K.; Fleck, L.; and Martin, M.M. *Water Workouts.* Winston-Salem: Hunter Textbooks, Inc., 1988.

Krasevec, J.A., and Grimes, D.C. *HydroRobics.* New York: Leisure Press, 1984.

Leonard, J., editor. *Science of Coaching Swimming.* Champaign, Illinois: Leisure Press, 1992.

Maglischo, E.W. *Swimming Faster.* Palo Alto, California: Mayfield Publishing Company, 1982.

Maglischo, E.W., and Brennan, C.F. *Swim for the Health of It.* Palo Alto, California: Mayfield Publishing Co., 1985.

McEvoy, J.E. *Fitness Swimming: Lifetime Programs.* Princeton: Princeton Book Company Publishers, 1985.

Messner, Y.J., and Assmann, N.A. *Swimming Everyone.* Winston-Salem: Hunter Textbooks, Inc., 1989.

Montoye, H.J.; Christian, J.L.; Nagle, F.J.; and Levin, S.M. *Living Fit.* Menlo Park, California: The Benjamin/Cummings Publishing Company, Inc., 1988.

National Safety Council. *Accident Facts.* Chicago, Illinois: National Safety Council, 1991.

National Spa and Pool Institute. *American National Standard for Public Swimming Pools.* Alexandria, Virginia: National Spa and Pool Institute, 1991.

National Spinal Cord Injury Center. *Annual Report.* Birmingham, Alabama: A Spinal Cord Injury Data Base at the University of Alabama at Birmingham, 1990.

———. *Spinal Cord Injury: The Facts and Figures.* A Spinal Cord Injury Data Base at the University of Alabama at Birmingham, 1986.

O'Connor, J. "A U.S. Accidental Drowning Study, 1980-1984." Thesis, University of Oregon, 1986.

Scott, G.P., editor. *Triathlon Federation USA: 1991 Competition Guide.* Colorado Springs: Triathlon Federation/USA, 1991.

Smith, J.R. *Water Polo in the Olympic Games.* Foster City, California: Foster City Press, 1984.

Thomas, D.G. *Swimming Steps to Success.* Champaign, Illinois: Leisure Press, 1989.

Vaz, K., and Zemple, C. *Swim Swim: A Complete Handbook for Fitness Swimmers.* Chicago, Illinois, 1986.

Vickers, E.J., and Vincent, W.J. *Swimming.* Dubuque, Iowa: Wm.C. Brown Company Publishers, 1984.

Welch, P., and Lerch, H. *History of American Physical Education and Sport.* Springfield, Illinois: Charles C. Thomas, Co., 1981.

Wiener, H.S. *Total Swimming.* New York: Simon and Schuster, 1980.

# INDEX

## MISSION OF THE AMERICAN RED CROSS

The American Red Cross, a humanitarian organization led by volunteers and guided by its Congressional Charter and the Fundamental Principles of the International Red Cross Movement, will provide relief to victims of disaster and help people prevent, prepare for, and respond to emergencies.

## ABOUT THE AMERICAN RED CROSS

To support the mission of the American Red Cross, over 1.3 million paid and volunteer staff serve in some 1,600 chapters and blood centers throughout the United States and its territories and on military installations around the world. Supported by the resources of a national organization, they form the largest volunteer service and educational force in the nation. They serve families and communities through blood services, disaster relief and preparedness education, services to military family members in crisis, and health and safety education.

The American Red Cross provides consistent, reliable education and training in injury and illness prevention and emergency care, providing training to nearly 16 million people each year in first aid, CPR, swimming, water safety, and HIV/AIDS education.

All of these essential services are made possible by the voluntary services, blood and tissue donations, and financial support of the American people.

## FUNDAMENTAL PRINCIPLES OF THE INTERNATIONAL RED CROSS AND RED CRESCENT MOVEMENT

HUMANITY

IMPARTIALITY

NEUTRALITY

INDEPENDENCE

VOLUNTARY SERVICE

UNITY

UNIVERSALITY